SCHOOLS
TEACHERS &
TEACHING

SCHOOLS TEACHERS & TEACHING

*Edited
and Introduced by
Len Barton
and Stephen Walker*

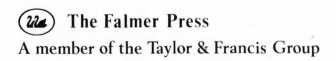 The Falmer Press

A member of the Taylor & Francis Group

First published 1981

ISBN limp   0 905273 22 2
      cased   0 905273 23 0

Jacket design by Leonard Williams

Printed and bound by Taylor and Francis (Printers) Ltd
Basingstoke
for
The Falmer Press
(A *member of the Taylor & Francis Group*)
Falmer House
Barcombe, Lewes
Sussex BN8 5DL
England

Contents

120743

Preface

Len Barton, Westhill College
Stephen Walker, Newman College

The papers collected in this book are all versions of presentations made at the 1981 Westhill Sociology of Education Conference. This annual conference is organized with the intention of providing an opportunity for those working in sociology of education to reflect upon developments in the discipline and, also, of stimulating further analysis and discussion. Each conference takes a specific area of debate in the sociology of education as a central theme. Whilst no hard criteria have been established for isolating which themes are given priority, an important principle that has been established at past conferences is that debate should reflect as wide a range as possible of different perspectives or analytical approaches. Given this principle, speakers invited to the 1981 conference were provided with a general brief in which they were asked to describe what they saw as the crucial sociological properties of the relationship between society, schools and teaching. Originally this theme was selected because it seemed to offer a basis upon which some contemporary issues like the opportunities for managing some synthesis of macro- and micro-sociological approaches in the sociology of education, or like the tension between structuralist and culturalist approaches to the social reproductive function of schooling, might be aired. However, as the conference proceeded the degree to which investigation of teachers and their work has moved from a fairly marginal position in the sociology of education to one in which it is regarded as having critical relevance was firmly established. For this reason we have made this relevance the area around which this book is organized. Not all the papers included in this volume directly address this crucial concern. Nevertheless, it is our contention that, at the very least, each paper raises issues which are inextricably related to what we take to be three important dimensions of this concern. These are the problems of conceptualizing teachers' ideologies and practices, the problems of investigating these ideologies and practices and the way in which future development of sociology of education is contingent on taking these twin concerns very seriously indeed.

Gifted with hindsight, perhaps we should not be too surprised that teachers and their activities should be given the prominence identified above. Notwithstanding the particular substantive concern, a great deal of inquiry in the past few years has either started or finished with an identification of the crucial location of teachers in educational processes. Be it as the 'gatekeepers' of educational and social resources, the actualizers of school values, as rule-makers, as the representatives of power élites in schools, the distributors of cultural capital, as the carriers of societal values or the mediators of societal contradictions, as reality definers and managers in classroom life – teachers occupy the point where the various paths taken in sociology of education converge. However, a good many of these teacher characterizations have emerged through research and analysis which have other educational concerns as a main focus. Indeed, though many pieces of research generate explanations of educational processes in which teachers' ideologies and practices are nominated as crucial

1

components, there are few studies which make these affairs the organizing topic of a sustained investigation. This is not to deny that important insights into teachers' understandings, experiences and motivations have been produced; see, for example, Woods (1980) and Grace (1978). What remains a problem, however, is that there is something of a noticeable lack of co-ordination of findings in which the connections between the results of rather disparate projects are clearly demonstrated and from which a cumulative body of knowledge is established which permits one to chart the ways in which the conditions of teacher action are articulated with other properties of the educational world with some surety. In short, it seems no real exaggeration to observe that apart from classic studies such as Waller's *The Sociology of Teaching* (1932) and Lortie's *Schoolteacher* (1975) we have no really developed study devoted to a sociology of teachers' work.

Given this observation, we are pleased, therefore, to be able to introduce a collection of readings that can be seen as identifying some of the problems and possibilities of such an extensive project. Whilst recognizing that it would be absurd to imagine that the discussions developed in the separate papers published in this volume satisfy the totality of demands which will have to be fulfilled if a sociology of teachers' work is to be established, we would still advance the claim that certain discernible themes emerge from the collection as a whole which provide some purchase on the problems involved in getting to grips with such an investigation. Clearly, the range of considerations these themes invite the sociologist to pursue is itself immense and no attempt is made in this introduction to describe all possible avenues of discussion sign-posted in the book. However, in our view, the importance of the need to develop a more systematic, sustained and substantial sociology of teachers' work lies in the contribution such a programme can make to our ability to attend to certain pressing contemporary concerns – contemporary concerns of the social scientist and contemporary concerns of the educator. These concerns can be distinguished as operating at three different levels – those relating to the historical development of both the discipline and the educational system, those which more closely relate to the structure and organization of schools and those directly linked with the everyday practices that constitute 'teaching' – and we have used these levels to provide a framework upon which the organization of the papers in the book is based. This should not be taken as meaning that we hold the levels to be exclusive or independent. In a significant number of the papers a key demand is for the precise *interrelation* between these levels to be demonstrated. Thus, for example, Lawn and Ozga argue that both the conditions teachers work in and their reactions to these have to be understood in terms of their structural location in the labour process and furthermore, that this location is essentially the outcome of a particular kind of historical development, the specifities of which require careful clarification if the end result is to be comprehended. Andy Hargreaves explores the thesis that the ideas teachers develop to cope with their *routine* affairs are importantly related to their involvement which is heavily conditioned by the way power is *institutionally* managed in these schools. This kind of emphasis serves to delineate what we take to be one of the many attractions associated with the development of a sociology of teachers' work. During the past few years the need to achieve a synthesis of macro- and micro-sociological approaches to the study of education have been voiced fairly persistently, although sometimes in a manner in which exactly how this can be achieved at the substantive level is underdeveloped. A variety of educational topics might be seen as areas which would permit this kind of development. One of the problems here, however, is of defining a field of study in which structural and interactional properties not only intersect but do so in a regular, analysable and significant fashion. The advantage of making the activity 'teaching' and the work teachers undertake to accomplish this activity a focus of research and analysis is that both have normative and creative features which persist over time, which are reportable and relatively easily available for analysis and which undoubtedly are strongly consequential for that form of institutional life known as schooling.

Although the general enterprise of achieving a form of synthesis in the sociology of education is important, we maintain, as noted earlier, that the discussion about the nature and conditions of teachers' work discernible in this collection contributes to the consideration of more local contemporary concerns. Exactly how this is so we argue in the introductions to each of the three separate sections into which this book is divided. However, we believe that one further general advantage of making teachers' work a main focus of attention is that this helps correct the unacceptable tendency in the sociology of education which Edwards (1980) identified in the last collection of conference papers – a tendency for theory to run in advance of evidence. One consequence of such trend, he notes, is the development of '. . . theories so general that it is impossible to define what confirming or refuting evidence would be like and theories which persistently present the 'real' story as taking place behind the backs of those whose actions give it life'. Throughout this book there is a conscious effort to bring 'people' back into analysis and investigation, an effort which is evidenced in the attempts made to document some of the ways educational processes are realized through the activities of one important group of social actors – teachers.

References

EDWARDS, T. (1980) 'Schooling for change: function, correspondence and cause' in BARTON, L., MEIGHAN, R. and WALKER, S. (Eds) *Schooling, Ideology and the Curriculum*. Lewes, The Falmer Press.

GRACE, G. (1978) *Teachers, Ideology and Control*. London, Routledge and Kegan Paul.

LORTIE, D.C. (1975) *Schoolteacher*. Chicago, University of Chicago Press.

WALLER, W. (1932) *The Sociology of Teaching*. New York/London, John Wiley and Sons Ltd.

WOODS, P. (1980) *Teacher Strategies,* London, Croom Helm.

1
Contemporary Concerns in their Historical Context

Introduction

The relationship between different levels of sociological explanation and the desirability of reaching some kind of synthesis has been, as was noted in the preface, a vital focus for debate in the sociology of education. However, discussion about synthesis in the discipline has not been restricted to questions of perspective differences. Two concerns which have an important place in the history of the discipline are, first, a concern with linking explanation at the theoretical level with the empirical conditions to which these explanations refer and, secondly, an enduring concern of all applied sciences, the question of linking research findings with policy formulation. Both of these 'linkage' issues are given detailed consideration in this section of the book. A key criticism established and defended in all six papers is that not only is theory so often separated from evidence but also that, frequently, such theorizing is presented in a form so abstract and inaccessible as to defy substantiation. The pressure exerted during the last decade for increased consistency and precision at the theoretical level in the sociology of education has led to the construction of more sophisticated and elaborate accounts in the discipline. But it has also meant that the language sociologists of education use, the issues they debate and the interpretation they offer have moved further and further away from the 'real' world of educational experience. This separation has unfortunate consequences, one of these being the creation of barriers between social scientists and policy makers. If the theories proposed in an academic context have little substantive support it is not surprising that practitioners and policy-makers either misunderstand them or treat them as irrelevant to their everyday interests.

If sociologists of education are to halt this rather dangerous drift into isolation then there would seem to be a need for careful inspection of current tendencies in the discipline in the practice of theorizing with a view to identifying causes. This need is given serious consideration in this section. Three particular trends in contemporary theorizing are isolated and the difficulties these create for any attempt to develop more grounded theory in the sociology of education (and, moreover, theory with a practical relevance) are pinpointed. These are the a-historical nature of a great deal of currently available explanations, the too ready use of untested conceptual and descriptive apparatus and, thirdly, the reluctance of theory-builders to undertake regular and detailed scrutiny of empirical conditions as part of a conscious struggle towards theoretical modification, elaboration or, even, falsification. There are, of course, many possible reasons which could be found to explain why these tendencies emerged. However, surely one of the most basic and common constraints has been the difficulty of establishing a distinguishable, definable and manageable sphere of educational activity which theory-builders, empiricists and practitioners alike recognize and accord significance. It is our belief that the development of a sociology of teachers' work – that is a sustained investigation of the peculiar interaction between those conditions, cultural relevances and creative responses which make up the activity 'teaching' – will provide such a unificatory framework. The temptation to be avoided however, is to imagine that in the development of such a sociology we have to jettison existing descriptions and explanations. This error is precisely the one which both Hargreaves and Whitty, albeit from different perspectives, identify as a major cause of the separations between explanation and evidence and theory and practice described above. To put it in a few words, the error involves a failure by sociologists of education to develop a strong sense of their own academic history. Although Hargreaves is concerned with one aspect of teachers' work, that of the relationship between teaching and social control, whilst Whitty is concerned with a broader discussion of the differences between various radical explanations of schooling and teachers, both writers regret the fact that the development of new or alternative theories or approaches is given priority in the discipline over the equally essential task of subjecting existing work to vigorous evaluation.

The writers of the other four papers in this section are similarly motivated by a desire to promote greater theoretical continuity and cohesion, by a wish to grant clarification of a historical context for sociological work a higher priority. They also share, however, a more specific concern. This is a determination to explore the relationship between changing historical circumstances and the ways in which teachers' work is to be conceptualized, on the one hand, and the consequences of these changes for teachers' work, on the other. Discussion ranges over historical changes and notions of teachers' professional identity and practices (Lawn and Ozga); the impact of government intervention and teachers' careers (Hunter); the forms social relationships in schools take within differing geographical environments (Williamson); and the ways in which aspects of schooling reflect dominant ideologies (Purvis). Nevertheless, we are reminded in each paper of the unique contribution a more developed understanding of the history of teachers' working conditions can make to a particular concern which many teachers are beginning to consider more frequently these days. Certain events in the world of education, such as redeployment and cut backs in expenditure, greater state interest and involvement in the curriculum and organization of schooling and moves aimed at making teachers more publically accountable, are serving to make the question of the extent of teachers' personal and professional autonomy rather more than a largely academic puzzle. The relevance the papers in this section have for teachers struggling with this concern is two-fold. First, by identifying those aspects of life in school which can be seen to persist over time and those which do not, they contribute to our capacity to specify just exactly what it is which constitutes certain situational and institutional constraints. Secondly, and relatedly, by illustrating how, throughout their historical development, the subtle and complex patterns and processes of schooling can be seen as both *serving* and *frustrating* particular interests and objectives and, by so doing, as establishing certain spaces for resistance, they provide support for that perspective of teachers which depicts them as possessing creative capabilities rather than as passive recipients of influences beyond their control.

Schooling for Delinquency

David H. Hargreaves, University of Oxford

The history of any substantive topic within any one of the many branches of the sociology of education is always, in part, also a history of the sociology of education as a whole. Every substantive topic has its own distinctive features, certainly, but no contributor to the field is ever wholly free from those wider forces and influences which shape the discipline as a whole. The fact is useful, for no speaker can assume that every member of his audience has a deep and genuine interest in his chosen theme. Since some of the audience may have but the most slender of commitments to the topic of schooling for delinquency – some of you may, in David Matza's terms, simply have 'drifted into delinquency' – my paper seeks to be not merely a modest contribution to that substantive area, but also an exemplification, within one selected area, of some much more general problems which affect many branches within the sociology of education in Britain today. That seems entirely proper at a Westhill conference, to which so many of us now turn as an annual opportunity to consider the wider horizons of our discipline. Although this is hardly an occasion in which to attempt a judicious appraisal of British sociology of education in general, I want to refer to four general issues which in recent times have come to give me cause for concern.

The first issue is the proliferation of theories within the sociology of education. In Britain we have come to see Basil Bernstein as our most significant theorist. More recently we have come to admire the writings of Pierre Bourdieu, and at present most of our theoretical interests are focused on various neo-Marxist theoretical positions, associated with the name of Althusser, Gramsci, Habermas, Bowles and Gintis, and so on. The majority of the most popular theoretical positions are notable for one feature: their extremely weak link to supportive empirical evidence. Most of them were initially propounded at a fairly high level of abstraction. Almost never are they stated in a testable form, so that any reader can specify quite clearly what would constitute a falsification or confirmation of the theory. When, on those relatively rare occasions, empirical evidence is brought against the theory, the theorist rarely responds directly to, or engages in, debate with the empirical critic. Rather, the theoretical position is elaborated, and usually in a form which renders the theory yet more abstract and thus less open to empirical test. There are two important consequences, both of which are especially serious at the level of the student who aims to achieve a basic mastery of our discipline. The first is that the theories tend to be treated as well-established, empirically grounded theories which are true; and the second is that the competent student is quite unable to perform the elementary task of specifying what would constitute an adequate test of the theory. As a result, most students in the sociology of education are provided with an exceptionally poor training as social scientists, for they become unable to distinguish between theory and evidence, and to learn the important skills of theory testing.

The second issue is the atheoretical nature of so much empirical work in the

9

sociology of education. Because the theorists are so reluctant to state their theories in a testable form, most empirical work is not directed to theory testing at all. Instead, the empirical work is conducted on a very crude theoretical base – and is then held to be 'exploratory' – and the theory is added on to the empirical work as a means of making sense of it and of locating it within the field as a whole. By this means a researcher legitimates his work and renders it attractive to professional colleagues. But this is no substitute for theory testing, which is one of the best methods by which a discipline can be advanced. In practice, the researcher is selective in two ways. First, he is carefully selective in the theories on which he draws. Usually more than one theory could be used to make sense of the data, but the researcher rarely treats the different theoretical positions as competitors which might be used to make conflicting predictions. Normally the researcher simply attaches to his work the most fashionable theoretical position with virtually no criticism or analysis of the theory. In so doing, of course, the researcher denies himself one of the greatest values of theory, that of sharpening and focusing the empirical questions he asks. Second, the researcher tends to be selective in the data he reports; a preference is shown for the data that 'fit' theory, and the rest is assigned to a peripheral position in, or even excluded from, the published work. It is thus that both theorists and researchers in the sociology of education conspire to sustain theories without subjecting them to adequately rigorous tests.

These first two issues might imply to the casual reader that I am pleading for a return by sociologists of education to a narrowly 'positivist' approach to the creation and testing of theory. That would, of course, be an entirely unwarranted inference. There is nothing that I have said so far which is incompatible with the views of some of the most influential figures in 'interpretive' sociology, such as Max Weber, Alfred Schutz and Glaser and Strauss (1967), as a careful reading of their works shows.[1] But it is beyond the scope of this paper to illustrate the failings with reference to recent interpretive – or neo-Marxist – writing by British sociologists of education. More to the point is the fact that during the 1970s British sociology of education was rich in conflict and polemic between different sociological perspectives. By the end of the decade – as was so well illustrated at the first Westhill conference in 1978[2] – our attention was moving towards reconciliation and the need to synthesize these different perspectives. It is at the crux of my argument that this synthesis will be superficial if it does not include, as part of its task, the careful formulation and testing of theories in the light of empirical evidence.

The third issue, which is a direct consequence of the first two issues, is the non-cumulative nature of both theory *and* research. As time goes by, theories do not become better, by which I mean broader in scope and more economical in content, either as a result of careful testing or as a result of subsuming earlier theories. Theories simply 'lie around' in the field, relatively vague and relatively untested. Empirical research fares no better. Very few studies actively seek to build on the work of earlier researchers, confirming or disconfirming earlier findings to put our knowledge on a sounder basis. Too often research evidence is inconsistent or incompatible. It is thus that many of the introductory text-books to the sociology of education inevitably end up as *catalogues* of theory and research, for there is no way that a reviewer can integrate the field into a coherent whole. There are very few areas in our discipline where we can confidently say that either theory or research is much better established than it was several years ago.

The fourth issue, again a product of previous issues, is that surprisingly little of our recent work is of any direct use to policy-makers in education. And this is true of both the dominant perspectives in contemporary British sociology of education, the ethnographic and the neo-Marxist. A reluctance to indulge in hasty or superficial policy relevance is surely to be applauded, but our distaste of policy relevance is not to be wholly explained by such proper caution. In the last year or two the most policy relevant research in education was *Fifteen Thousand Hours* (1979) by Michael Rutter (a psychologist) and his team. His work has rightly been heavily criticized for being insufficiently sociological.[3] However, sociologists of education are attacking Rutter from a position of weakness, for with few exceptions (most notably David Reynolds, who in any event works in a department of social administration) they have nothing positive of their own to contribute to the debate about Rutter's work. Without doubt, Rutter and Reynolds are working in an area which is of central concern to the sociology of education, but it is they, not sociologists of education, who have undertaken the work. Later in this paper I shall have much to say that is critical of Rutter and Reynolds, but I do so in a spirit which wholeheartedly commends the focus and policy relevance of their work. In singling out their work for criticism, I do so because of its general importance and because in many ways it provides an example of what more sociologists of education ought to be doing. In other words, if I may so put it with no suggestion of arrogance, my aim is to make good work better. If their work were truly inferior or misguided, it would not merit anyone's detailed critical attention.

The most exciting work that I have read by a British sociologist of education during the last year has been Frank Musgrove's *School and the Social Order*. This is an intemperate and ill-humoured attack on the work and achievements of sociologists of education. It is very easy to allow oneself to be so irritated by Musgrovian excesses that his criticisms, many of which are valuable and valid, are ignored. But much of what he says is consonant with the four issues I have raised and if we do not look at these soberly and honestly and vow to do better in future, then the whole future of our discipline is in jeopardy. The sociology of education is a young discipline but the licence given to youth is beginning to run out and there is much work to be done if we are to gain some maturity as a social science. Sadly, Musgrove entirely fails to build on his own critique. At the end of the book he treats his readers to his own personal preferences in a vision of a possible educational future, but this scenario has very little to do with the preceding critique of his sociological colleagues. This is no more than a clumsy attempt to throw dust in the eyes of his readers. It diverts our attention from the fact that Musgrove's own contribution to the sociology of education – which is certainly a substantial one – can be subjected to precisely the same criticisms that he flings at others. Perhaps Musgrove can do no better than the rest of us. Indeed, we must draw that inference, for in none of the areas he reviews does he show us with any clarity how we might be more accomplished architects of a finer sociology of education.[4]

The topic of schooling and delinquency is a ripe target for the criticisms that both Musgrove and I have made of the sociology of education. Much of the work on this topic in Britain over the last fifteen years is organized round one central question: 'Does schooling play an important causal role in the generation of delinquency?'. If it could be shown that some schools actively propel some of their pupils into delinquent careers, whilst other schools can actively insulate vulnerable pupils from delinquency, then that finding would have immense policy implications. If we could reduce juvenile delinquency by changing, at little or no expense, the internal operation of 'high delinquency' schools, then much human tragedy would be averted and scarce financial resources would be saved. But a review of the literature, both theoretical and empirical, of the last fifteen years shows that we cannot give a clear and confident answer to the question. There is more theory than research; the theories are manifold and stand in a very unclear relationship to one another; much of the recent research is very weakly articulated to the theory; none of the various theories has been adequately tested; very few of the research findings are cumulative.[5] The field is, in short, a typical representative of the sociology of education enterprise.

And it must be said at once that my own contribution to this field is as vulnerable as anyone else's. In 1967 I published my Lumley study which suggested that the school might be an important factor in the generation of delinquency. In the same year Michael Power published his study of inner-London schools from the outside suggesting that internal school factors might differentiate high-delinquency from low-delinquency schools. But my book displays a typical range of faults. With conventional modesty it proclaims itself an 'exploratory' study which provides no more than a provisional hypothesis that must be tested. Yet I failed to set out in detail the exact nature of that hypothesis and how it might be tested; and of course I, myself, never tested it. If anyone else tested it and found against my diffuse hypothesis, I could easily defend the hypothesis on the grounds that the testing procedures were inadequate or inappropriate or based on a misreading of my work. Moreover, I was highly selective in my use of theory. I could have used the existing theory and attempted to test it in the study. Instead I followed the more common procedure of reporting the data which are then nestled into my selection of some of the relevant theory (in particular the work of Albert Cohen). Had I used a different theory to authorize my work, I would doubtless have discarded some of the data presented in the book and introduced data which were never in fact published. Some of the data can be used in support of more than one theoretical position; but the book is written in such a way that it is very difficult for any reader to use the data to test competing theories.[6] These faults were not acknowledged at the time; this is the first occasion on which I have done so publicly. Even more to the point, no other sociologist has taken me to task for these faults. If I am a poor social scientist, I appear to be in good company.

The confession of defects and limitations is no more than a first step towards better sociological work. If we really want to know whether or not schooling contributes to delinquency and if we aim to uncover the precise causal mechanisms involved, then we must integrate theory and research in a much more systematic way than has been achieved in the past fifteen years. If we do not, then we shall be very little nearer to an answer after yet another fifteen years' work. So I here offer a programme of questions, whose purpose is to inform the design of future research and to act as a resource for the evaluation of future work.

1   What are the major theories of deviance and of crime/delinquency which are relevant to the theme of schooling and delinquency? Which of them explicitly assign a possible causal role to the school? Which of them are potentially applicable to the school as a causal agent? What predictions does each theoretical position make concerning schooling and delinquency? How precisely might each theory be tested?

2   How do the various theoretical positions and predictions relate to one another? Are different theories *congruent* with one another (i.e. do they make the same predictions)? Are the theories *competitive* (i.e. does one theory make the opposite prediction to another)? Are the different theories *complementary*

(i.e. do the theories make different but not incompatible predictions)? Does any theory make quite unique predictions (i.e. ones not covered by, contrary to or incompatible with, another theory)? Does such a process of sorting out the theories permit a theory of schooling and delinquency?

What is the nature of the research evidence on schooling and delinquency? How many of the findings are cumulative? How many are unique to one study? How many are contradicted between studies? How does the known evidence relate to the current state of theory? Are there any findings which are not covered by existing theory?

How do theory and known evidence relate to the various aspects of the school which may have causal significance – ideological, organizational, interpersonal; school life and classroom life; teachers and peer groups? How are the potential causal factors related to one another? Is the explanation multi-causal in that various factors must interact to have their effect? Or is the causal impact of school multi-causal in the sense that different factors may have common delinquency effects? How does the school's impact relate to other factors, especially those of the pupils' family background and community environment?

To attempt to answer these questions would be an important preliminary task for any sociologist who decided to work in this field, but it is too difficult and extensive for me to undertake in this short paper. Instead, I shall try to display some of the complexity of the theoretical and empirical issues involved and in so doing I hope to show how far we still are from being able to offer a clear answer to the fundamental questions of the topic of schooling for delinquency.

The contribution of sociologists, in both theory and research, to the study of crime and delinquency has a long and distinguished history. I shall select for discussion five analytically distinct theoretical positions.

First, cultural transmission theory (sometimes called cultural deviance and culture conflict theories), which is strongly associated with the names of Sutherland and W.B. Miller, and in this country J.B. Mays (1954, 1962). On this view the delinquent is socialized into delinquency because he is a member of a criminal, slum or lower class subculture. In such a setting, criminality is 'normal'; the delinquent is conformist to his own subculture. In the famous words of Sutherland and Cressey (1955), 'A person becomes delinquent because of an excess of definitions favourable to violation of law over definitions unfavourable to violations of law.' Miller (1958) believed that lower class youths were socialized into a set of values which were naturally orientated to crime and delinquency – trouble, toughness, smartness, excitement, fate and autonomy.

Second, control theory, grounded in the work of Durkheim, Thrasher and Hirschi.[7] The American origins of this theoretical position lie in the work on 'social disorganization' of Park and Thomas at the University of Chicago. The basic argument was that the social disorganization of the city, a product of migrations and industrialization, represented an erosion of community cultures and thus a collapse of social controls. Control theorists do not ask: 'What causes some people to become criminal?'. Instead, their initial question is: 'Why don't we all break the law more than we do?'. The answer is that most of us are socialized into attachments, commitments and beliefs which tie us to the social order and inhibit us from deviance. Where the controls are weak, a person is free to commit crime and delinquency.

Third, strain theory, most of which derives from the work of Merton (1957), and his reworking of Durkheim's concept of anomie. On this view the pressure towards deviance arises from a disjunction between cultural goals (economic success) and normative means, between aspiration and expectations. The criminal/delinquent is an innovator: he internalizes the goal but adopts illegitimate means to achieve the goal. The strain induced by an internalization of the goal accompanied by a lack of opportunity to realize the goal in socially approved ways is resolved by a criminal adaptation. Merton's general scheme is today thoroughly discredited, but it forms the background to Albert Cohen's (1955) re-conceptualization of the strain as status-frustration. In this view, the boy finds, especially in school, that he is evaluated by middle-class agents and standards. Some working-class boys internalize those standards, even though they fail by them, and so respond to this status frustration by inverting those standards in the creation of the delinquent subculture. Cohen does not entirely ignore cultural transmission theories of delinquency, for he posits two ideal types of delinquent. The first is the product of status-frustration, as described; the second is the 'stable corner boy' (a term taken from Whyte, 1943) who is less attached to middle-class standards and more in tune with lower class culture, and who commits delinquent acts as a product of such socialization not as a reaction against status-frustration.[8]

Fourth, subcultural theory, which is again linked with Cohen's work. Whilst for the cultural transmission theorists the delinquent subculture is a natural heir to slum culture and lower working-class values, for Cohen it is an active creation of status-frustrated youths who find a collective solution to their common problem. It is important to detach this notion of an emergent delinquent subculture from Cohen's thesis of motivating strain, since this approach to the subculture can be made compatible with control theory, which denies the concept of strain.

Fifth, there is labelling theory, which has been popularized in the work of Howard Becker (1963). This perspective is too well-known to require rehearsal here, even though it is still too often reduced to the naïve travesty that deviance is created because some people are labelled as deviant. The point I wish to make is that, in Becker's version, labelling theory attempts to subsume some earlier positions. Culture conflict theory is incorporated to a degree since the theory presumes that deviant labels arise when one group seeks to impose and enforce rules upon another group. Moreover, Becker ends his account with a discussion of the deviant subculture which is held to play an important part in the alleviation of strain, though in this view the strain is grounded in the fact of being labelled. On the other hand, labelling theory tends to ignore control theory and in some respects seems incompatible with it.

These five analytically distinct theoretical positions do not adequately represent all current theoretical work in the field of delinquency. Relative to the field of the sociology of education, delinquency theory has an impressive record of repeated attempts to produce 'mixed models' and to ensure that each new theoretical position incorporates its predecessors. The work of David Matza in *Delinquency and Drift* (1964) and in *Becoming Deviant* (1969) defies easy categorization in the terms of the above scheme, and Edwin Lemert's curiously neglected essay on 'The concept of secondary deviation' (1967) demonstrates how misleading it is to label him as no more than a labelling theorist.

Yet the scheme has some use in relation to the topic of schooling and delinquency. It can be seen at once that cultural transmission theory and control theory are the most natural allies of 'input theories' which would assign the major causal role in delinquency to the home and the community rather than to the school, whereas strain, subcultural and labelling theories are more consonant with 'process theories' which assign a causal role, perhaps even a major one, to the school. In fact, however, all the theoretical positions can be used to throw light on schooling for delinquency.

At the societal level, it is perhaps strain theories which, directly or indirectly, have most to offer. Cohen's reworking of Mertonian ideas suggest that schools are powerful evaluative agents of modern society which inevitably induce strain and failure among those who do not or cannot live up to the narrow academic and behavioural criteria imposed by teachers. Such a view would predict that delinquents would be found in disproportionate numbers in the low streams of secondary modern schools (McDonald, 1969) and, from Wadsworth's recent report (1979) from the national longitudinal study, that boys whose parents wanted them to go to grammar school and who did not succeed were significantly more likely to be delinquent than boys who were successful in gaining grammar school places. Strain theory would probably predict that in comprehensive schools, especially in an age of credentialism through public examinations and of growing youth unemployment, strain – and thus delinquency – are likely to increase.

At the family level, there is unquestionably evidence in support of both control and cultural transmission theories. Farrington (1972) has argued strongly against Power's inclination towards a process view of schooling and delinquency in favour of an input theory in which delinquency begins at home. The Cambridge study[9] shows the importance of family criminality among delinquents, which perhaps gives some support to a version of cultural transmission theory; and the demonstration that the parents of delinquent boys tend to show lack of affection, attention and consistent training is highly compatible with the substantial evidence in favour of control theory. In Wadsworth's study the most notable link to be found between schooling and delinquency was in parental interest in the boy's secondary education. He interprets this low parental interest as an index of low parental interest in other areas of the child's life and thus of generally weak controls. Not surprisingly low parental interest was indeed associated with a further index of weak controls – the broken family. All this, especially if taken in conjunction with the work of Harriet Wilson (see Wilson and Herbert, 1978) gives powerful support to control theory.

As far as I am aware, no-one wishes to deny the potential significance of 'input' approaches. There is no doubt, however, that some authorities greatly play down their significance. In my Lumley study I adduced evidence that the parents of boys in the 'delinquescent' subculture were less likely than the parents of 'academic' pupils to take their children with them for leisure purposes, to be severe in their response to low academic achievement, to be restrictive over smoking, and to expect help with household chores. But this finding was given very low salience in the general findings. West (1979), in one of the best recent reviews of the field given at the Westhill Conference two years ago, shows a strong preference for control theory which, strangely, is not matched by a balanced appraisal of input approaches, and Reynolds's contribution to the same conference is so taken up with linking micro and macro approaches to the school that he almost entirely ignores home background factors. Both Reynolds and Rutter rightly criticize the influential work of Coleman (1966) and Jencks (1972) in the United States for grounding their thesis in highly sensitive measures of pupils' individual and social characteristics but in crude measures of school and classroom factors. Rutter's work can be justly accused of an opposing imbalance: manifold and sensitive measures of the school, but weak indicators of social background. Reynolds is known to have better measures of social background, but they are not drawn upon in his influential 1976 article. It is, of course, important to demonstate that the school can and does have an independent effect on various educational outcomes (including delinquency) and the thesis of 'relative autonomy' is an important counter-balance to excessively deterministic neo-Marxist accounts of schooling. It is clear that ideological factors exercise a profound influence on how researchers shape, select and present their evidence. The current concern to demonstrate the independent effect of the school is in real danger of under-emphasizing earlier achievements in the sociology of education which showed the importance of home background. Amongst sociologists I detect a fear of being charged with adherence to an implicit deterministic model of social pathology, which at present is a path to heresy. Yet there is, nevertheless, substantial evidence in support of the theories (especially control theory) which stress the role of the home in the generation of delinquency.

To show that ideological positions can easily blind us to the existence of important continuities which we would rather not see and also deflect us from important research tasks, let us consider Paul Willis's widely read *Learning to Labour* (1977). In many respects the major significance of this book is its attempt to make an explicit link between micro and macro levels of analysis, to root ethnography in neo-Marxist theoretical positions. Although the book has very little to say explicitly about schooling for delinquency, its ethnographic descriptions of the counter-culture of 'the lads' is highly consonant with earlier work on the delinquescent subculture. The book demonstrates how the lads' counter-culture is grounded in fighting and the cult of machismo, in boredom and the search for excitement, in 'having a laugh', in sexism and racism. Willis then argues that

> though the achievements of counter-school culture are specific, they must
> be set against the larger pattern of working class culture in order for us to
> understand their true nature and significance.

In effect, Willis shows how 'the lads' draw upon the values of their fathers, who act as important role models. All this is massive evidence in support of a version of cultural transmission theory. Indeed, his account of the counter-culture is singularly reminiscent of one major delinquency theorist, W.B. Miller (1958), whose theory of cultural transmission drew particular attention to the values or 'focal concerns' of the lower working class – trouble, toughness, smartness, excitement, fate and autonomy. It is true that Willis emphasizes how these constitute a rational response to the situation, that the urge to autonomy represents, both in the boys and in their fathers, a massive attempt to gain informal control, symbolic and real, over their lives. Yet Willis's 'cultural resources' remain very little different from Miller's 'focal concerns'. Willis sets his analysis within neo-Marxist theory, but it is the cultural transmission theorist who is the more likely to see the research as a piece of empirical confirmation. I do not wish for one moment to underestimate the significance of Willis's contribution to the debate within neo-Marxist perspectives. He shows quite clearly that some of the macro theories have an inadequate grasp of the complexities of school processes. It is no mean achievement to offer a correction of the popular neo-Marxist theories, but we are being incredibly short-sighted if we fail to recognize that in so doing Willis is thereby reviving a version of the somewhat discredited cultural transmission theory. And in so doing, he is also, by implication, offering a corrective to the view that is currently being popularized by Rutter and Reynolds, that the school can and does make a contribution to the generation of delinquency that is independent of the input factor of pupil home background. That has not, in my view, been adequately demonstrated so far (though ultimately Reynolds may do so). But even such a demonstration would not take us far enough. I can make no sense of Willis's work except as an extremely complex *interaction* between certain pupils with a particular home background *and* a certain kind of school experience. I fear we are still a long way from unravelling the complexities of that interaction. It is one thing to show that schools can make a difference to delinquency, amongst other things; it is another to show exactly *how* that difference is made. Had recent work been more sensitive to earlier achievements, to home background factors and to control theory, then explicit predictions about the nature of the interaction could have been made and tested. And that would advance our knowledge much more effectively that the mere demonstration of an independent effect of the school.

In the field of schooling and delinquency, as in other areas of the sociology of education, the years pass by and more and more research evidence is collected. But the theoretical fashions are changing simultaneously and each fashion attracts its adherents. In consequence the same evidence can be marshalled in support of quite different theories. Let me give some examples. One of the better attested school process factors to be associated with delinquency is the enforcement by the school of certain rules (e.g. those against smoking and certain styles of dress and appearance) which are perceived by the pupils as illegitimate rules. But *why* should the school's, in David Reynolds's (1976) neat phrase, 'refusal to truce' in the matter of such rules help to generate high delinquency? The finding is highly consonant with labelling theory which would assert that, if some schools impose additional and alien rules on pupils, then rule-breaking and the labelling of deviants is actually being manufactured. Labelling theory can then go on to explain how, as a product of such labelling, the deviant pupils are being propelled towards delinquency. But a strain theory account is equally plausible. If some pupils see the imposition of these rules as a threat to their status and autonomy, to their aspirations for adult status, then the enforcement of the rules will act as a severe source of strain, and thus produce a problem of adjustment which can be solved by the creation of a delinquescent sub-culture. Another factor held to be associated with high delinquency is a high rate of staff turnover. To the labelling theorist there is an obvious explanation: if teachers remain in the school for but a short period, they will tend to rely to an unusual degree on the reputations of classes and of individual pupils which would serve to exacerbate the stigmatization of reputed deviants. On the other hand the control theorist can argue that a high staff turnover is likely to be associated with weak and inconsistent control, which would serve to release more pupils than usual from the bonds which tie them to conventional conduct. Again, it is generally acknowledged that delinquency is primarily a group phenomenon and that delinquency-prone groups (or subcultures, for some writers) develop within the school. In the Lumley study I showed a clear preference for a strain theory explanation. Clint and his friends were, I argued, subjected to various forms of status deprivation. The streaming system, and its associated mechanisms of regular promotion and demotion, ensured that those boys with a common problem of adjustment arising from the status deprivation found themselves in a common environment in which a delinquescent subculture could readily be generated. However it can be plausibly argued that the conception of strain is not strictly necessary. Cultural transmission theory can argue that if certain kinds of pupils with a similar background of criminally-orientated values and socialization patterns find themselves, for whatever reason, in a common environment, they will naturally become friends, according to the well-established social psychological principles of interpersonal attraction grounded in shared values and attitudes. Nor is control theory to be left out. Children from families that exercise weak control and supervision may well have a special need for a group of peers, since this is their most readily available source of security and companionship. Indeed, this is Thrasher's (1929) theory of gang formation. Various factors in school, which need not involve strain or cultural transmission, bring these pupils together and the gang experience may then further weaken the already weak controls and so further the slide into delinquency. (I shall note later how the school itself may directly help to weaken these controls.)

How do we choose between these different theoretical interpretations of the same facts? The answer is that we cannot unless we make more specific predictions from each different theory, and then test them as thoroughly as we can. Only then would it become clear that some theories may have greater scope than others, even though the total picture may require some sort of combination of theories. Only then would we be in a position to specify more precisely the causal mechanisms and their relative weights. And only then would we be able to make more confident policy prescriptions. The most important contemporary work in this field, that of Reynolds and Rutter, is overtly directed towards policy, yet both are weakly orientated to theory. In the work they have published so far, they are both eclectic and superficial in their use of theory and neither is seriously concerned with theory testing. I believe this approach to be unfortunate. The identification of factors which can be shown to be associated with high delinquency schools does not produce unambiguous policy implications. They may be identifying correlates of delinquency, not causes; they may be identifying minor rather than major causes. Only a comprehensive and thoroughly tested theory can form an adequate basis for policy, yet we seem to be little nearer to that than we were fifteen years ago.

The systematic search for a comprehensive theory of schooling for delinquency would have another great virtue. Any and every known or alleged factor which is associated with the generation of delinquency would be incorporated into one or more theoretical positions and then subjected to more detailed test. It is in this way that theory and research becomes more comprehensive and cumulative. In the Lumley study I noted the factor concerning the way in which the teachers were distributed among the streams, and noted the tendency for the teachers with lower qualifications and/or weaker discipline to be allocated to the lower streams. At the time I drew upon a version of status deprivation theory and interpreted this fact as but one of the contributory elements to the lower stream pupils' sense of deprivation – they knew and resented the fact that they were not given the 'best' teachers. The strain theory interpretation may be right, though today I have my doubts that the explanation is so simple. The finding is highly compatible with control theory. If the pupils who are most prone to delinquency on the grounds of weak family controls are also assigned to teachers with unusually weak controls, then we would expect the controls which bind the pupils to convention to weaken yet further. Control theory would seem to be supported by the finding; indeed, its position is greatly strengthened because it can now show how the delinquency-prone pupils are subjected to weak controls both in the home *and* in the school. The institution of the family and the institution of the school are jointly responsible for the generation of delinquency. Such a view opens the possibility that the school may insulate delinquency-prone pupils from delinquency if the school can provide controls that in some way act as a substitute for the weak controls provided at home. Significantly, one writer with a clear preference for control theory, Stephen Box (1971), has quoted the Lumley study as direct support for control rather than strain theory, and Wadsworth (1979) appears to take a similar line. Yet neither Rutter nor Reynolds takes this possibly significant variable of teacher distribution into account, either in general or in research terms. In fact, indirect support comes from the Rutter study, though the authors do not seem to recognize the significance of it. Some of the seven 'process variables' this study shows to be associated with high delinquency may well reflect a particular distribution of teachers and a control theory interpretation would be highly plausible. The first correlation is between high delinquency and the high autonomy of teachers in planning their own curriculum courses. At first sight this seems a most odd correlation which is difficult to interpret. Why should schools, where the planning and evaluation of the curriculum by individual teachers is not supervized or group-based, tend to be high delinquency schools? High autonomy in curriculum matters means that in this respect the teachers themselves are under weak controls. Now, if 'poorer' teachers are assigned to more difficult and delinquency-prone pupils, and if they have high curriculum autonomy, they may well adapt to that situation by reducing their academic demands on pupils, in line with the suggestion of earlier studies. The second association is that between high delinquency and high teacher autonomy in disciplinary matters. By the same arguments, delinquency-prone pupils may find themselves taught by teachers with weak disciplinary demands. This suggests, in short, that delinquency-prone pupils may find themselves in classrooms governed by weak controls, both academic and disciplinary. But the evidence is only indirect, for Rutter did not set out to test control theory or the teacher distribution variable directly. His measure may be tapping these variables, but we cannot be sure and so the advance in our knowledge of the causal factors is much smaller than it might have been.

It is also sad that even the basic organizational mechanism of a mobile, promotion-demotion system of streaming or setting, which earlier studies indicated might be an important causal factor in delinquency generation, is again only indirectly tapped, for one of the factors shown to be associated with high delinquency is the tendency of pupils *not* to remain in the same class or set during their school career; in other words, a mobile streaming or setting system, as opposed to a stable system in which pupils are allocated to streams or sets on a relatively permanent basis, is associated with high delinquency. The Lumley study noted both a mobile streaming system *and* teacher allocation to streams as factors in the generation of delinquency, but believed that the first was a more important causal mechanism than the second. Current research seems to be tapping this same group of variables but because it does not test the hypothesis in any explicit way, our knowledge has not improved as much as it might have. We still do not know the relative weights of mobile streaming and staff allocation in their contribution to delinquency. Is one more important than the other? Would a school with a mobile streaming system which ensured, through its staff allocation, relatively strong classroom controls, have a much lower delinquency rate than a similar school which allocates teachers with weak control to the lower streams? If the school has a non-mobile or stable streaming system, does it matter whether or not the low stream teachers have weak classroom control? How much more soundly based our policy prescriptions would be if we knew the answers to these questions.

On these matters Reynolds (1976) seems to be on unsure ground. He characterizes the high delinquency school as 'coercive' and seems to have in mind the kind of school described by Webb (1962). Reynolds notes:

In the absence of much normative commitment to the institution's demands that can ensure obedience, these unsuccessful schools appear subsequently forced to apply *a much higher level* of organizational control in the attempt to reach their goals and maintain commitment. (my emphasis.)

He then goes on to note that

'institutional control' which includes such factors as the degree to which silence rules are enforced in lessons, and the existence of various restrictions on movement and activity, is *higher* in the more problem prone schools . . . (my emphasis.)

Now it is not at all clear what Reynolds means by *high* control. It might be a quantitative judgement (a lot of control rather than a little) or a qualitative judgement (one type of control rather than another type). This ambiguity may be specially important for anyone seeking prescriptive implications from Reynolds at the classroom level. It would be easy to infer from Reynolds's account that the low delinquency school exercises relatively weak controls, which would be contrary to the predictions of control theory. But Rutter's work is supportive of control theory and against any suggestion that low delinquency schools are characterized by weak controls. Indeed, Rutter claims that the greater the inclusion of quiet periods when pupils are expected to work in silence, the lower the extent of the behaviour problems. Several measures which show a significant association between strong classroom control and low frequency of behaviour problems also fall just below the level of statistical significance in their association with low delinquency. Now the good classroom may have high control, but it is nevertheless a pleasant and rewarding place for pupils. Thus high delinquency schools display a low frequency of praise for pupil work and a high frequency in the setting of 'lines' and extra work as a punishment. This is, of course, consistent with Reynolds's (1979) description of the low delinquency school as 'incorporative'. My quarrel with Reynolds is the failure to clarify what is meant by 'high control' and its implications at the school and classroom levels – for it is here that we might be on the edge of unearthing some of the detailed causal mechanisms. As the evidence stands, it is clear that low delinquency schools are not marked by an absence of controls. It is more likely that they are characterized by strong controls which take particular forms (as yet difficult to specify) and are accompanied by a warm and friendly involvement in which pupils are accorded respect, responsibility and participation. But this, too, is also a form of control: control theory is about attachments and commitments. In the present sociological climate the concept of control is related to the more general concept of social control, and social control is usually seen as a coercive imposition of external controls (though the imposition may be masked into subtle forms). Social control has highly negative connotations in the sociological vocabulary; the less of it the better. This may explain the aversion of some contemporary sociologists' to control theory, and Reynolds' rather blunt use of the term 'highly control' to characterize the high delinquency school.

Because control theory is concerned with attachments and commitments rather than coercion, it is also about the generation of social order. Theories of delinquency, at least from the time of Thrasher (1929), have struggled with a tension between, on the one hand, the need of each individual person for a sense of meaning and order in a structured world and, on the other hand, the need of society (or more strictly of certain powerful groups within it) to achieve a kind of social order through coercive social control. And the two ideas are different, even though they are related. I suspect the evidence suggests that the high delinquency school espouses strong punitive controls (over rules perceived as illegitimate or through styles of enforcement that are perceived as illegitimate) which are alienating, and/or – I incline to the *and* rather than to the *or* – extremely weak controls which deny pupils a sense of order (i.e. an anomic disorder rather than alienating order) because they are not accompanied by the positive controls which generate commitments and attachment. The low delinquency school, a control theory approach would indicate, has neither 'high' nor 'low' control, but by a kind of 'optimum' control that balances imposed coercion with the inducement to commitment and attachment.[10] Control theory is strikingly apposite to the general findings of both Rutter and Reynolds and must surely be a prime theoretical candidate for testing in future research, provided, of course, sociologists can be persuaded to take the theory seriously, and recognize that control theory (unlike much of the current work on education and social control) is concerned with the beneficial effects of control on pupils.

And here is the twist. It may be that labelling theory can specify some of the basic mechanisms by which control theory operates. Normally labelling theory and control theory are seen as alternative, or at best complementary, theoretical positions. I want to suggest that though the theories may start from very different fundamental premises, they lead to common ground and so interpenetrate. If I had to nominate the central idea of labelling theory, it would not consist of the oft-quoted sections of Becker's *Outsiders* (1963). Rather, it would be Edwin Lemert's much earlier thesis that rather than deviance leading to social control it may be social control that leads to deviance. We can note at once that the concept of social control, which is at the heart of control theory, is also at the heart of labelling theory. Labelling theory does not deny the conventional wisdom, which is espoused by control theory, that control can lead to conformity and thus inhibit deviance. But it asserts that *under certain conditions* control attempts amplify rather than attenuate deviance. Lemert's concept of secondary deviation asserts that the social reaction to imputed deviance creates a problem for the person labelled as deviant. In some instances the best solution to this problem is the abandonment of the line of conduct which leads to the imputation of deviance, but in other cases the solution to the problem created by the labelling is the commission of yet further deviance. In this respect control theory is in no sense incompatible with labelling theory. It is simply that labelling theory deals with those cases where the controls are ineffective or have the opposite effect to that intended by the controllers *and* to that predicted by control theorists. It is apparent that this problem is central to clarifying the *kind* of control that should be operating in schools which seek to avoid generating high rates of delinquency. The control must be sufficient to induce the appropriate attachments, commitments and beliefs but at the same time not be of the kind that is likely to induce secondary deviation. This tension is central to the work of both Rutter and Reynolds. It may be that high and low delinquency schools can use essentially the *same* controls but that low delinquency schools reduce the negative consequences of the controls because the controls are balanced by other mechanisms which encourage pupils to feel that they are valued participants in school; or it may be that some controls (e.g. the enforcement of rules that pupils regard as illegitimate, or highly punitive reactions to deviance) are much more likely to induce secondary deviation and it is these controls to which high delinquency schools are addicted; or it may be – and the research is far less clear on this – that some schools operate controls which are generally too weak to induce commitment except among those who, by their own background, are already heavily constrained to commitment. This last possibility is the only one which requires control theory alone; the others all involve a combination of control and labelling theory.

There is also a further possibility, that the control characteristics I have just described should be ascribed, not to *schools,* but to *teachers.* David Reynolds quotes Michael Phillipson's (1971) insight that there is a tendency for sociologists to treat schools monolithically. Reynolds rightly pursues the line suggested by Phillipson, that we should be alert to *differences* between schools, even when superficially different schools look to be alike. Reynolds thus finds himself in a common position with Rutter; both address the question, 'Do schools make a difference?'. But both tend to treat *teachers* in a monolithic way; schools may be different and have different effects on various outcomes such as delinquency. But the difference is then neatly ascribed to differences in school 'ethos'. Both Rutter and Reynolds are favourably disposed to the concept of school ethos, because it is by this means that both can preserve intact their uncritically monolithic conception of teachers. The assumption allows both of them to ask the question, 'Do schools make a difference?' – and then to provide a resoundingly affirmative answer – without asking what is surely an inherent part of this question: 'Do different *teachers* make a difference?'.[11] In fact, of course, the evidence on this matter is tucked away in the findings. The scores on many of the Rutter indices are *averages* of many teachers involved in a particular school, thus masking what may be highly significant differences among teachers within the same school.

Now both Rutter and Reynolds may have important reasons for treating teachers in this monolithic way. After all, it is far less threatening to teachers if they think that the school, its ethos and effects are under research scrutiny rather than themselves as individuals in comparison not merely with other schools but with their own immediate colleagues. But ethnographic work and the earlier studies of schooling for delinquency point directly to the importance of teacher differences. That literature raises the possibility, which both Rutter and Reynolds side-step, that the high delinquency school may be a consequence of certain kinds of teacher being in charge of certain kinds of pupil. If we make two eminently reasonable assumptions, that some children enter school with a much greater predisposition to delinquency than others, and also that some teachers in their use of control may be much more likely to create the conditions favourable to the generation of delinquency than others, then a central research question becomes the identification and study of teacher-pupil interaction in those conditions specified in the assumptions. My own somewhat tentative work in this area (see Hargreaves, Hester and Mellor, 1975) suggests that there may well be some 'deviance-provocative' teachers who (following control theory) generally exercise weak, inconsistent, or confrontational controls, and who (following labelling theory) tend to condemn the actor rather than the act, which can help to induce secondary deviation. On such evidence one would predict that when deviance-provocative teachers are allocated to delinquency prone pupils, the school would have a high delinquency rate. If such a prediction were tested and confirmed, then there would be important policy implications, which might be directed, not at changes in the ethos or general operation of the school, as Reynolds and Rutter now contend, but at changes in the conduct of particular teachers and/or the way they are allocated to particular pupils. It is, of course, possible that both kinds of policy implication would be justified by the evidence. In any event, our policy prescriptions would be much more specific than they are now.

The history of theory and research in the field of schooling for delinquency has in Britain been a tortuous and disjointed one. We have made some progress,

certainly, but the advances we have made are partial and uneven. The failure to produce and then test a comprehensive theory of schooling for delinquency – which
would probably consist of a combination of the different theoretical positions – has
inhibited the design of definitive research, which alone can unravel the causal complexities. And as long as the causal nature of the variables shown to be associated with
schooling and delinquency remains as obscure as it still is today, then the policy implications of the work will continue to be tentative, partial and perhaps even
misleading. Over the years in this field theoretical preferences and combinations have
swung wildly from study to study, and such theoretical preferences have greatly influenced the variables which each study has taken into account and held to be important. The foundations of the study of schooling for delinquency are shaky, but those
foundations must be improved, if they are to be built upon. In view of the complex-
itites involved, it is impossible not to sympathize with Rutter and Reynolds in their
apparent impatience with theory. And, to be fair, it should be recognized that
schooling for delinquency was for them but one of several themes. But it also cannot
be denied that their refusal to attempt the difficult task of systematizing the theory
and of taking into account all the variables which past research has suggested might
be important, has the effect of reducing the ultimate strength and significance of
their contribution to the important question of schooling for delinquency. I do not
wish to be unduly harsh in my criticisms of them, for there is much in their work to
admire, and it must be said, to return to my opening theme, that their work is better
than most that is to be found in British sociology of education. A few areas have a
better than average record for a cumulative approach to theory and research – work
on education and social mobility is perhaps a case in point. As for the rest of us,
unless we put our theoretical and empirical house in order, and create a more
systematic social science of the sociology of education, then we shall disappoint those
who had faith in the promise of our discipline and give further fuel to those critics
who will rejoice in our discomfiture.

Notes

1   Whilst I am asserting that all theoretical perspectives are (or should be) concerned with the
testing of theories, I recognize that there are difficulties in testing more than one theory at the
same time because different theoretical perspectives sometimes take different stances on the
form such testing might take: what would constitute an adequate test, what the nature of the
relevant evidence should be, and so on? 'Interpretive sociologists' continue to wrestle with
Weber's tension between causal-adequacy and meaning-adequacy, but most have not totally
rejected the former in favour of the latter.
2   See BARTON, L. and MEIGHAN, R. (1978).
3   See, for example, the reviews by REYNOLDS, D., HARGREAVES, A. and BLACKSTONE, T.
(1980) in *British Journal for Sociology of Education* 1 (2); and by HEATH, A. and CLIFFORD, P.
(1980) 'The seventy thousand hours that Rutter left out' *Oxford Review of Education*, 6 (1),
pp. 3–20.
4   Musgrove's book contains a highly original and penetrating analysis which contradicts some
neo-Marxist accounts of the relationship between education and social control during the nineteenth century; but unfortunately he then fails to specify with any precision the relationship
between the two accounts. It is a great pity that Musgrove declined to make this more positive
contribution, for had he done so other sociologists of education would have paid more attention to his criticisms. As it is, Musgrove has broken the unspoken rules of the academic club,
which require that distinguished academics do not attack the foundations of the reputations of
distinguished colleagues. If one breaks the rules in this way, one takes the risk that other
members of the club close ranks and defeat the critic by ignoring his reproaches.

5 See HARGREAVES, D. (1980) for more detail on the problems of the cumulative nature of the present evidence.
6 Some of the material, for example, is highly compatible with labelling theory. Other writers used this study in support of control theory (see main text).
7 See HIRSCHI, T. (1969) as well as BOX, S. (1971) and KORNHAUSER, R.R. (1978) for interesting discussions.
8 The whole issue of different 'types' of delinquent has been badly neglected, even though it is very important, since if there are different types, different causal processes may be involved. Far too little attention has been paid, for example, to DOWNES, D. (1966) work here.
9 See WEST, D.J. and FARRINGTON, D.P. (1977).
10 In the field of schooling for delinquency nobody seems to have followed up the interesting suggestions made by BARAKAT, H. (1969). This is a potentially rich source of theory for both Rutter and Reynolds.
11 It could be argued that because delinquency is only one of the school variables in the work of Rutter and Reynolds their neglect of the earlier suggestions on teacher differences can be defended. This defence cannot be sustained. An unfortunate chasm has grown up between the primary and secondary school sectors, and had Reynolds and Rutter been more sensitive to the work at the primary school level on teacher differences, especially in the work of Neville Bennett at the University of Lancaster, and the more recent work of Maurice Galton and Paul Croll at the University of Leicester, they would have been bound to take the variable of teacher differences into account or make an explicit defence for not doing so.

References

BARAKAT, H. (1969) 'Alienation: a process of encounter between utopia and reality', *British Journal of Sociology* 20, pp. 1–10.
BARTON, L. and MEIGHAN, R. (Eds) (1978) *Sociological Interpretations of Schooling and Classrooms: A Reappraisal* Driffield, Nafferton Books.
BARTON, L. and MEIGHAN, R. (Eds) (1979) *Schools, Pupils and Deviance* Driffield, Nafferton Books.
BECKER, H. (1963) *Outsiders,* New York, The Free Press.
BENNETT, N. (1976) *Teaching styles and pupil progress* London, Open Books.
BOX, S. (1971) *Deviance, Reality and Society* Holt, Rinehart and Winston.
COHEN, A. (1955) *Delinquent Boys* New York, The Free Press.
COLEMAN, J.S. (1966) *Equality of educational opportunity,* Washington, US Government Printing Office.
DOWNES, D.M. (1966) *The Delinquent Solution* London, Routledge and Kegan Paul.
FARRINGTON, D. (1972) 'Delinquency begins at home' *New Society,* 21, pp. 495–7.
GALTON, M., SIMON, B. and CROLL, P. (1980) *Inside the primary classroom,* London, Routledge and Kegan Paul.
GLASER, B.G. and STRAUSS, A.L. (1967) *The Discovery of Grounded Theory* London, Weidenfeld and Nicholson.
HARGREAVES, D.H. (1967) *Social Relations in a Secondary School* London, Routledge and Kegan Paul.
HARGREAVES, D.H. (1980) 'Classrooms, schools and juvenile delinquency', *Educational Analysis* 2 (2) pp. 75–87.
HARGREAVES, D.H., HESTER, S.K. and MELLOR, F.J. (1975) *Deviance in Classrooms* London, Routledge and Kegan Paul.
HIRSHI, T. (1969) *Causes of Delinquency* Berkeley, University of California Press.
JENCKS, C., SMITH, M., ACLAND, H., BANE, M.J., COHEN, D., GINTIS, H., HEYNS, B. and MICHELSON, S. (1972) *Inequality,* New York, Basic Books.
LEMERT, E. (1967) *Human Deviance, Social Problems and Social Control* Prentice-Hall.
KORNHAUSER, R.R. (1978) *Social Sources of Delinquency* Chicago, University of Chicago Press.

McDONALD, L. (1969) *Social Class and Delinquency* London, Faber and Faber.

MATZA, D. (1964) *Delinquency and Drift* John Wiley.

MATZA, D. (1969) *Becoming Deviant* Prentice-Hall.

MAYS, J.B. (1954) *Growing up in the city,* Liverpool University Press.

MAYS, J.B. (1962) *Education and the urban child,* Liverpool University Press.

MERTON, R.K. (1957) *Social theory and social structure,* Chicago, Free Press.

MILLER, W.B. (1958) 'Lower class culture as a generating milieu of gang delinquency' *Journal of Social Issues* 14, pp. 5–19.

MUSGROVE, F. (1980) *School and the Social Order* London, John Wiley.

PHILLIPSON, M. (1971) 'Juvenile delinquency and the school' in CARSON, W. and WILES, P. (Eds) *Crime and Delinquency in Britain* Oxford, Martin Robertson.

POWER, M.J. *et al* (1967) 'Delinquent schools?' *New Society* pp. 542–3.

REYNOLDS, D. (1976) 'The delinquent school,' in HAMMERSLEY, M. and WOODS, P. (Eds) *The Process of Schooling* London, Routledge and Kegan Paul.

REYNOLDS, D. (1976) 'When pupils and teachers refuse a truce: The secondary school and the creation of delinquency' in MUNGHAM, C. and PEARSON, G. (Eds) *Working Class Youth Culture* London, Routledge and Kegan Paul.

REYNOLDS, D. (1979) 'Bringing schools back in' in BARTON, L. and MEIGHAN, R. (1979) *op. cit.*

RUTTER, M. *et al* (1979) *Fifteen Thousand Hours* London, Open Books.

SUTHERLAND, E.H. and CRESSEY, D.R. (1955) *Principles of Criminology* Lippincott.

THRASHER, F.M. (1929) *The Gang,* Chicago, University of Chicago Press.

WADSWORTH, M. (1979) *Roots of Delinquency,* Oxford, Martin Robertson.

WEBB, J. (1962) 'The sociology of a school' *British Journal of Sociology* 13, pp. 264–72.

WEST, D.J. and FARRINGTON, D.P. (1977) *The Delinquent Way of Life* London, Heinemann Educational.

WEST, G. (1979) 'Adolescent autonomy, education and pupil deviance' in BARTON, L. and MEIGHAN, R. (1979) *op. cit.*

WHYTE, W.F. (1943) *Street Corner Society,* Chicago, University of Chicago Press.

WILLIS, P. (1977) *Learning to Labour,* Farnborough, Saxon House.

WILSON, H. and HERBERT, G.W. (1978) *Parents and Children in the Inner City,* London, Routledge and Kegan Paul.

Left Policy and Practice and the Sociology of Education

Geoff Whitty
King's College, University of London

It has become something of an orthodoxy, from Williamson (1974) to Demaine (1980), that the so-called 'new sociology of education' of the early 1970s abandoned the Fabian policy-oriented tradition of the Halsey-Floud era and substituted for it a belief that the sociology of education could itself transform the world via its radical critique of the assumptions underlying the classroom and professional practice of teachers. It has become a further orthodoxy that, on finding the consciousness of teachers less than easy to transform and indeed not the root of the problem anyway, the new sociologists abandoned the world of educational practice in the mid-1970s and adopted a pseudo-revolutionary stance which refused to have any truck with the educational institutions of the capitalist state (Reynolds and Sullivan, 1980) or with reformist political parties such as the Labour party (Demaine, 1980). This has led, according to some of these commentators, to a misguided and dangerous theoretical dogmatism on the part of neo-Marxist sociologists of education, which has sanctioned political inaction by the left and led it to neglect real possibilities for practical and policy interventions in and around state education in contemporary Britain.

In this paper I want to reflect upon the validity of these observations, particularly in respect of their applicability to the sort of work in which Michael F.D. Young and I were heavily involved in the mid-1970s (Whitty and Young, 1976: Young and Whitty, 1977). In deciding to focus here on the relationship between *left* policy and practice and the sociology of education, I am reflecting not only my own tendency to select areas of work within the field on the basis of their potential relevance to left political and pedagogical practice, but also what I take to be the concerns of some of our major critics. I am not, therefore, wishing to claim that policy and practice in education are synonymous with left policy and practice, or that work in the sociology of education must necessarily be guided by such interests. I should also make it clear that the terms 'policy' and 'practice' are merely very approximate shorthand terms for the sorts of issues with which I am concerned. 'Policy' is thus intended to signal an area of political and ideological practice *around* education, while 'practice' in its more restricted sense is intended to refer to pedagogical and professional practice *within* education. Both terms then clearly entail 'practice' in its broader sense and my concern is thus with the relationship between the sociology of education and left political and ideological practice in *and* around education. My remarks are arranged in four sections. The first concerns the way in which British sociology of education developed during the 1970s. The second involves some rather more specific comments about the work undertaken by Michael Young and myself in the mid-1970s. The third section looks at some work currently being carried out in America and Australia, and leads into a final section that concludes that those in Britain who wish to build a relationship between the sociology of education and left policy and practice might learn some useful lessons from such work.

I

Firstly, then, there is a sense in which issues of policy and practice have become progressively marginalized during the 1970s. The radical 'possibilitarianism' of the new sociology of the early 1970s has been discussed and criticized too often to warrant lengthy consideration here (see Whitty, 1974: Sharp and Green, 1975). The recognition by many writers associated with this work that the transformation of lived reality was a more complex undertaking than they had initially envisaged provides part of the explanation for the subsequent attraction of, on the one hand, more sophisticated work on the nature of advanced capitalist societies and, on the other hand, more detailed investigations of the nature of life in classrooms. What is not clear is why so few writers have returned to questions about what *would* constitute significant interventions for change in ways consistent with the insights of new theory or the findings of empirical research. Thus, in the mid and late-1970s, few sociologists of education showed much interest at all in influencing policy and practice in and around education. Rather, they tended to retreat into a spurious academicist stance which eschewed not only the possibilitarian excesses of the 'new sociology of education', but also the policy-orientation of earlier traditions.

It also seems that the various strands associated with the 'new sociology of education' became separated out in a manner which has been neatly captured in a recent review of the state of the field by Caroline St John Brooks for *New Society* (Brooks, 1980). There she suggests that some of those involved in the 'new sociology of education' have subsequently taken what she termed a 'theoretical path' and others a 'less theoretical direction'. She argues that the former path was taken by those, such as Geoff Esland, whose main concern was with the ways in which 'the interests of dominant groups in society are translated into social values which inform schools, which in turn replicate the social structure'. The other direction, she suggests, attracted those, such as Martyn Hammersley, who are 'more interested in what goes on in schools'. Although there is probably no inherent reason why one of these directions should necessarily be more theoretically-inclined or empirically-oriented than the other, Brooks is correct to note the tendency for those concerned with the broader issues to spend much of their time in highly abstruse neo-Marxist theoretical debates, whilst the other group has often been more concerned to produce a succession of classroom and staffroom ethnographies than to develop theory from them.[1] However, what is interesting about *both* groups in the present context is that not only has any conception of sociology itself as a practical world-transforming enterprise largely disappeared from their work, they even exhibit a considerable reluctance to give any serious consideration to the practical *implications* of sociological work for teachers and policy-makers.

This lack of a practical orientation has thus been as true, if not more true, of those who have concentrated on classroom ethnography as it has been of those engaged in theoretical debate. In quoting Hammersley as favouring a research model based upon a supposedly disinterested anthropological style of fieldwork, Brooks suggests that he is untypical in this respect. Yet my own view is that his stance is, in fact, fairly typical of the position taken up by ethnographers working within the sociology of education. Their position was made very clear by Sara Delamont in her contribution to the first Westhill conference (Delamont, 1978) in which she explicitly distanced herself from classroom studies in the 'illuminative evaluation' tradition. She suggested that that sort of work, which clearly is committed to the improvement of classroom practice, was in danger of getting ethnography a bad name. Even those few sociologists, such as Vulliamy (1976, 1978) who do persist in trying to explore the practical implications of ethnographic studies for teachers are generally considered as falling somewhat outside the mainstream ethnographic tradition. Certainly, nowhere amongst sociologists of classrooms today do we find writers like Gorbutt (1972) and Bartholomew (1973) in the early 1970s who treated their work as a radical possibilitarian endeavour.

Some of those identified with a possibilitarian approach in the early 1970s have, of course, subsequently become aligned with the more macro-theoretical approach. This has produced a rather more ambiguous relationship between the neo-Marxist approaches to the sociology of education and questions of policy and practice. While the initial interest in neo-Marxist theories did spring from the relative neglect in the early 'new sociology' of the broader contexts of educational practice and was often part of a search for more adequate strategies of educational and social change than those implied in that work, questions of policy and practice have subsequently tended to be confronted only as issues within Marxist *theory*. Although deep excursions into Marxist theory may be an important prerequisite for assessing the significance of left interventions in and around education, it is noticeable how few of the more theoretically-inclined writers have ever returned from these excursions to the questions of practice with which many of them began. There have, of course, been many *critiques* of existing policy and practice, but there has been little consideration of the opportunities for alternative and oppositional practice (Williams, 1973). Indeed many of the critiques have been used to 'confirm' the sort of domination, correspondence and reproduction theories which seem to cast doubt on the possibility of alternative policies and practices let alone assigning to them any broader political significance. Even Paul Willis's work (Willis, 1977), which is in many ways one of the few exceptions to the trends outlined here, has often been treated in this 'pessimistic' vein rather than as a springboard for exploring the possibilities for left interventions in and around education.[2] This lack of interest by some of those most centrally involved in the field in elaborating political and pedagogical alternatives to existing practice is, however, perhaps hardly surprising when those who have made tentative attempts to do so have been so frequently misinterpreted or had their work condemned by others on the left as ritual sloganizing. This is an issue to which I shall return when discussing some of my own work, but for the moment I merely wish to reiterate the point that the principal orientation of both empirical and theoretical work in the sociology of education in the latter half of the 1970s was essentially an analytic rather than a practical one.

There are, of course, those on the left who see this as being an appropriate defensive tactic in the current political and ideological climate. Personally, I am not convinced that it is even that. Sociology has come under attack in recent years not only because of its 'radical' and 'subversive' image (Gould, 1977) but also for its lack of utility of any sort. Digby Anderson, a right-wing critic of 'radical' sociology, has scathingly written of its 'adolescent' approach to sociology, which treats the subject as more of a debunking exercise rather than a practical enterprise (Anderson, 1980). Left academics often try to sidestep such charges of uselessness with the rhetorical question 'useless for whom?'. I do not, however, believe that this is a sufficient response any more than is the argument that sociology is itself a form of 'practice', when it is used to avoid questions about its relationship to *other* forms of practice. For it is not only those on the right who question the utility of much that passes for left academic work in sociology, such charges also frequently come from the left. The lack of any significant practical or policy orientation in most sociology of education today, including that which is supposedly radical, is paralleled by a lack of any organic relationship between such work and those groups for whom one might have expected left theoretical work to have some political value. Such a separation has certainly had unfortunate political and educational effects and, for this reason, it is important not to dismiss the comments of writers such as Demaine (1980) however much they may exaggerate and misrepresent the nature of the problem.

The fragmentation which has occurred between empirical and theoretical approaches in the sociology of education during the 1970s, and between both approaches and questions about policy and practice, has tempted some people to dismiss the whole of the 1970s as an eccentric interlude in the subject's development. The publication in 1980 of an important new book by one of the founding fathers of British sociology of education (Halsey *et al*, 1980) has helped to make such an interpretation fashionable (Brooks, 1980). However, it can also be argued that the present conjuncture is one in which it may be feasible to begin to rework in a more sophisticated manner the links between theory, research and practice, which were naïvely glimpsed by the 'new sociology of education' at the start of that decade but subsequently obscured from sight in the fragmentation described above. Indeed, the possibilities for doing this certainly seem brighter now than they have done for some years. The reasons for this are various but, ironically, one reason is that neo-Marxist theoreticism seems to have run its course for the time being and some of its former advocates have begun both to re-assert the importance of empirical research and to re-emphasize the location of their work within a specific political project. Theory itself has thus begun to direct us back to the analysis of specific conjunctures rather than merely general systemic relationships and has encouraged us to conceive of wider possibilities for intervention than those prescribed by the more restrictive modes of neo-Marxist theory which reached their zenith of popularity in the mid-1970s. One does not have to go all the way with Hindess and Hirst and their colleagues (Cutler *et al*, 1977/78), since many other contemporary writers continue to believe that the basic tenets of contemporary Marxism can be recast in terms which do *not* result in theoretical incoherence and political inaction (see, for example, Barrett *et al*, 1979). Thus the increasingly complex theoretical armoury of relative autonomies, conditions of existence, specificities and specific effectivities which they have begun to develop is not of purely theoretical interest: for some writers, at least, it has re-sensitized them to the possibilities for, and significance of, left political and ideological practice within those institutions which Althusser characterized rather too simply as Ideological State Apparatuses.

Thus, even if Demaine (1980) is right to claim that one effect of the importation of over-simplified versions of neo-Marxist theory into the sociology of education in the mid-1970s was to minimize the possibilities for left policy and practice in and around state education, this should no longer be the case today. Interestingly, writers in other fields have been somewhat quicker to grasp the significance of recent developments in Marxist theory. Media studies, a field which arguably has suffered even more from theoretical excesses and theoretical dogmatism than the sociology of education, has begun (as a glance through recent issues of *Screen Education* will reveal) to overcome the separation between theory, empirical work and the development of left practices within and around the media. Similarly, we find that a new journal called *Critical Social Policy* is currently in the process of being launched, a venture which only a few years ago might have been considered by some to be a contradiction in terms. Again, in the sociology of race relations, writers such as Ben-Tovim and Gabriel (1979) have also argued that recent theoretical developments can be used to justify a reconsideration of the sorts of policy issues which Marxist analysis in the mid-1970s tended to regard as 'outside its scope, if not positively "diversionary"'. Indeed, many of Ben-Tovim and Gabriel's comments about the sociology of race relations would be almost equally appropriate as a commentary on the recent history of the sociology of education.[3] It may even be possible to discern some stirrings of a greater concern with issues of left policy within the sociology of education itself. Certainly, at a theoretical level, the latest Open University course in the sociology of education, E353 *Society, Education and the State* (Open University, 1981) pays far more attention than did E202 *Schooling and Society* (Open University, 1977) to the specificities of political and ideological practice in and around education. Consideration of the significance of such developments for future action remains harder to discern. However, very recently I have received invitations to contribute to a conference of sociologists on 'policy in education in a period of contraction',[4] intended to explore the 'possibility of a reformulation of policy which is realistic yet positive', and to a collection of original papers[5] designed to bring 'questions of educational policy formulation and implementation to the forefront of the sociology of education'.

Nevertheless, such initiatives are certainly not yet typical of the field, although my own view is clearly that they should be welcomed and encouraged. I am not, however, arguing that we should merely replace the classroom practice orientation of the early-1970s with a policy-orientation for the discipline in the early-1980s. What I am suggesting is that, if the sociology of education is to make a significant contribution to left policy and practice, it will have to explore the implications of recent theoretical work for our understanding of political *and* pedagogic practice in and around education. Neither context of intervention should be discounted by theoretical fiat, although political calculation may advise giving greater emphasis to one area than the other in any particular empirical situation. Unfortunately the divorce betwen empirical and theoretical work in the sociology of education, and the almost exclusive concentration of the former upon pedagogical rather than political contexts and of the latter on ungrounded macro-theory, has denied us much of a basis at all upon which to calculate the significance of particular modes of intervention in or around education.

II

The work in which I was engaged with Michael Young and other collaborators in the mid-1970s (Whitty and Young, 1976: Young and Whitty, 1977) – recently dubbed by Bates (1980) as 'new developments in the new sociology of education' – was, however, a conscious attempt to transcend the prevailing separation between theoretical and empirical work in the sociology of education and to relate both to questions of left pedagogical and political practice. The intended nature of our intervention was recognized by some of its earlier reviewers, with George Mardle describing *Explorations* as 'an important part of the radical left's attempt to respond to the Great Debate'[6] (*Times Educational Supplement*, 26 August 1977) and Raymond Williams claiming that *Society, State and Schooling* was the 'most *hopeful*, serious and vigorous book on English education (he had) read for many years' (my emphasis) (*New Society*, 5 May 1977). Yet both these assessments contrast sharply with recent claims that this sort of work is pessimistic, nihilistic and utterly irrelevant to contemporary educational concerns. Not only have mainstream educationists such as Taylor (1978) dismissed our work as of limited or even negative value to teachers and policy-makers, but other writers on the left – themselves apparently concerned with the relationship between sociology of education and socialist educational and political practice – have also suggested that our work is irrelevant or even damaging to their concerns. Thus our political stance has recently been represented as typical of an 'ultra-leftist ideology (which) invites abstentionism from political work and substitutes revolutionary slogans and despises all "reforms"' (Demaine, 1980), whilst our observations on educational practice have been seen as, at best, vacuous and, at worst, contributing to the educational deprivation of working class pupils (Demaine, 1980: Entwistle, 1979: Reynolds and Sullivan, 1980). Given the nature of our original objectives in producing the volumes, it is obviously quite alarming that the work is open to such interpretations. Thus, while it is also important to notice that the relevance of this same work has recently been far more positively evaluated elsewhere (Bates, 1981),[7] some response to the criticisms is now called for. This is particularly the case in an article such as this which shares the disquiet of some of these critics that the sociology of education should apparently have so little to say of relevance to left policy and practice in contemporary Britain.

Clearly our work is ambiguous insofar as it is open to the variety of interpretations described above. Nevertheless, it is not easy to see how either of our two volumes could have been read as typical of the sort of neo-Marxism that dismisses the viability of socialist struggles – within the Labour Party or within state education – by theoretical fiat and political dogma. Although, as Raymond Williams pointed out (*New Society,* 5 May 1977), this type of work 'is still labelled and caricatured by orthodox politicians and the press', one might have expected colleagues on the left to share his own view that it was typical of a more 'open, enquiring, but still deeply committed' form of Marxism. The work was, as some of the critics grudgingly admit, self-consciously exploratory and, hence, probably inevitably flawed with the sort of inconsistencies and confusions which the critics claim to have identified within it. Though some of these were more the product of our critics' proclivity for lifting sentences out of context than genuine internal inconsistencies, others were an understandable consequence of the attempt to explore what was, as we explicitly argued, largely uncharted territory. Nevertheless we were concerned to explore that territory and to suggest that the terrain, and the intervention strategies appropriate to it, had a far more complex and contradictory character than most available theories – whether liberal, social democratic or Marxist – seemed to attribute to it. Given the exploratory, tentative and, on occasions, contradictory nature of our writings, the charge of theoretical and political dogmatism is surely hard to sustain, whilst that of inconsistency is, in part at least, the result of our attempt to confront the complexity of an empirical world whose reality Demaine implies we ignored. A more appropriate target of criticism would perhaps be the failure of most of those involved in this venture – and, one must add, most of its critics – to undertake the sort of work necessary to refine and clarify some of the ambiguities and inconsistencies within these embryonic sketches of the nature of the terrain and possible ways of traversing it.

Let us, however, explore a little further some of the criticisms which have been made of this work, in the hope that this will help us to clarify the nature of the contribution which work in the sociology of education might or might not make to left policy and practice in the future. One frequent criticism is that our work has been merely sloganistic and essentially vacuous in its prescriptions for practice. Another has been that the sociologists of education of the 1970s have lacked the close links with policy-makers that were typical of their predecessors of the 1950s and 1960s.

Both these points have an element of truth in them, but both of them fail to grasp that the relative lack of *detailed* policy-prescriptions in the work is consistent with the critique of prevailing policy-making procedures which has been a central feature of the new sociology of education in all its various guises. Since part of the critique of provided schooling for the masses has been concerned with the political and professional processes that have traditionally defined its form and content, it is hardly surprising that – as both Williamson (1974) and Demaine (1980) point out – the sociologists of the 1970s did not share the same sort of relationship to leading Labour party politicians as that enjoyed by Halsey and Floud. The practical implications of our work for socialist political and educational practice are as much concerned with the ways in which policy is made as with specific substantive policies.

To this extent, it might even be argued that Bates (1980) is correct to defend Michael Young from those of us he sees as wanting to impose upon Young a more detailed prescriptive programme. However, over generalized injunctions *can* easily merge into vacuous rhetoric and work which claims to speak to a specifically socialist political constitutuency certainly needs to define its ultimate aims in rather more explicit terms than a catch-all phrase like 'human betterment'. Sharp (1980) is therefore right to demand a clearer political programme than has hitherto been offered, but that programme will almost certainly involve a search for new procedures for clarifying the nature of appropriate 'new forms of knowledge and pedagogy'. Bates' own suggestions about how tangible policies are to be arrived at are almost entirely ones of intra-professional process and, in this respect, the suggestions of Richard Johnson in a recent article (Johnson, 1981) are more consistent with the sort of analysis which Young and I were offering in *Society, State and Schooling*. In this article, Johnson argues that the Labour Party should break with its traditional approach to producing policy for education and approach its development in a manner more in keeping with its democratic and egalitarian socialist ideals. Policy, he suggests, should be developed from the grass-roots, growing out of popular experience, not merely handed down by professional politicians and the professional educationists who randomly emerge as advisers to its NEC sub-committee. Further, he argues that the Party itself should become a more important context of education, just as radicals in the past often established their own agencies of self-education. But that is not by any means the same thing as arguing that those committed to socialist conceptions of democracy and equality should leave capitalist schooling to its own devices and advocate a policy of de-schooling, a position which both Demaine (1980) and Reynolds and Sullivan (1980) suggest Young and I adhere to – or, at least, 'flirt outrageously' with! Rather, it is to suggest that socialists would be better placed to intervene in struggles over the form, content and control of state education and to remedy some of the crucial absences of traditional Labour Party policy on such issues (Bleiman and Burt, 1981) if they were also constantly struggling to develop new skills and forms of democratic practice within the Labour movement itself. A strategy of linked struggles was precisely what was being advocated in *Explorations* and *Society, State and Schooling*.

Although one might therefore expect the 'new sociologists' to be active in the grass roots of the labour movement rather than merely 'well-connected' (Williamson, 1974), a recognition of the long-term importance of grass roots struggles does not imply that the more conventional contexts of educational policy discourse should be spurned, since into these are inserted initiatives which demand an immediate response. Nor does an argument that it is politically essential for socialist educators to be involved in and build alliances with other elements of the labour movement constitute a retreat in 'workerism' (Donald, 1979). Nor is the left somehow faced, as Demaine seems to imply, with a straight choice between the new sociology of education and the Islington Labour Party as the authentic voice of socialist education. Rather, a basis for constructive dialogue between different sections of the left urgently needs to be constructed. One would not expect sociologists either to carry off-the-peg policies into the labour movement or to celebrate uncritically the conventional wisdom of that movement. Nevertheless, one might expect that those sociologists of education who were committed to that movement would have something valuable to contribute towards the clarification of its aims in the realm of education and to their translation into political and pedagogical strategies appropriate to the current conjuncture. Certainly the over-theoretical orientation of much neo-Marxist sociology of education has proved a barrier to this, but this is exactly what Young and I were suggesting in our writings. Far from being written off by theoretical fiat, as Demaine and Reynolds and Sullivan argue, the Labour party and its policies for state education were seen as a vital context of intervention.

Interestingly, at the same time as suggesting that our work has nothing of significance to say to educational practitioners, the same writers suggest that the work could have some very dangerous consequences for practice. Specifically, Entwistle (1979) and Reynolds and Sullivan (1980) argue that those few practical suggestions that do exist in our work are mischievous and anti-socialist. They suggest that we seek to trap working class pupils in a curriculum rooted in and restricted to a celebration of working class life as it is. This, I suggest, is a wilfully misleading – indeed mischievous – reading of our work. Thus, although the contemporary equivalent of the *'really* useful knowledge', which Johnson (1979) tells us early working class radicals sought 'in order to understand their condition in life . . . and how to get out of (their) present troubles', would clearly have to *relate* to the realities of working class life, it would hardly be uncritical of it. Although, in order to be meaningful to working class kids, it would almost certainly make use of the sorts of penetrations already present within working class culture, it would not celebrate that culture *per se*. Given the nature of that culture as described by writers such as Willis (1977, 1979) and the role which it clearly plays in the process of social reproduction, there would be little mileage for socialists in mere celebration and re-inforcement. What Denis Gleeson and I were explicitly arguing for in our work on the social studies curriculum was a meaningful *and* critical education (Gleeson and Whitty, 1976), a positive contribution to debates about the nature of a progressive curriculum that is conveniently ignored by most critics. Even so, we recognize that the nature of a genuinely progressive curriculum is highly dependent upon its articulation with other cultural phenomena; it is therefore by no means fixed for all time in a particular mould, as the defenders of the traditional curriculum as the only hope for a socialist future seem to believe.

The thrust of our work is, then, precisely against dogmatic solutions to both theoretical and practical questions. Certainly, neither the curriculum of state education nor the Labour Party as a context of educational policy-making is defined *a priori* as an inappropriate context of socialist intervention. Indeed, it is just because (as Demaine argues, apparently believing that we claim the opposite!) their character is not theoretically given but rather historically constructed and struggled over, that the position of Entwistle or Reynolds and Sullivan over what constitutes a definitive socialist strategy for education is the dogmatic and unhelpful one. I do not, therefore, find the argument that our own position is wrong – though well it may be – *because* it is different from either Lenin's or Gramsci's an especially convincing or compelling one. Indeed, I would find it odd if, for example, what was a progressive policy for working class education in Italy in the 1920s was adequate for the context of Britain in the 1970s or 1980s. Thus, when Entwistle says that our criticism of traditional education policies of the left in Britain for ignoring the issue of ideology would put Gramsci in error as well, it would not – even if it were true – be quite the damning criticism that Entwistle takes it to be. In fact, it can only result from his taking a position totally at odds with Gramsci's own highly developed sense of history and conjunctural politics. Hegemony takes different forms in different contexts and hence counter-hegemonic struggles must, if they are to contribute to the struggle for socialism, take forms appropriate to the specific historical context in which they take place. A sociology of education which can contribute to left policy and practice therefore needs, as Sharp (1980) has argued, to offer us a clearer understanding of the nature of that context, a project which requires the sort of articulation between a theoretical, empirical and political programme which has been largely absent from the British scene. Our own work certainly did not provide it, but neither was it as irrelevant to that project as its critics now suggest.

III

It is not, however, my intention to perpetuate needlessly the sectarian tradition of British sociological work in which charge is met with counter-charge in a thoroughly negative manner. Instead, I want to suggest that it can make a refreshing change to examine some of the work that has been going on in educational studies in America and Australia in recent years. The sort of work which I am referring to here has been heavily influenced by British and European theoretical perspectives in the sociology of education, but it has demonstrated more successfully than much of the British work the fruitfulness of relating theoretical and empirical studies of education and exploring their implications for left pedagogical and political practice. It recognizes that the detailed analysis of the inner dynamics of capitalist societies and the location of potential contradictions within them (Sharp, 1980) should not be conceived of as a purely theoretical exercise, even though it needs to be theoretically-informed. Although the reaction of some British observers has been to dismiss much of this work as theoretically crude and naïvely eclectic, closer inspection reveals that there may well be some important lessons to be learnt form it. Certainly, American writers on the curriculum, for example, have been more concerned than their contemporaries in Britain to interrogate macro theories with empirical research and *vice versa* in the manner advocated by David Hargreaves at the first Westhill Conference (Hargreaves, 1978). Although some of the earlier examples of empirical work by the more critical curriculum writers sometimes used excerpts from classroom talk merely to *confirm* rather crude pre-given domination and correspondence theories and thus perhaps obscured opportunities for intervention, some of the more recent work coming out of America shows promise of providing a better basis for the *development* of both theory and practice than most work being carried out in Britain at the present time.[8]

It seems that, although part of the attraction of British and European social theory for these writers[9] lay in its contrast to the prevailing atheoretical traditions of American sociological and educational research, some of them seem to have been able to separate their critique of empiricism from a continuing belief in the necessity of doing empirical work.[10] They also seem to have been more successful than their British counterparts – with the possible exception of Richard Johnson and his colleagues at Birmingham (e.g. Johnson, 1979) – in making constructive use of a variety of types of theory that are too often treated as mutually exclusive in the sectarian atmosphere of British sociology. The other refreshing aspect of at least some of the critical perspectives on schooling being developed in America is even more directly pertinent to my theme here today. This lies in the attempt to explore the implications of their theoretical and empirical work for left practice, particularly in the context of pedagogical practice (e.g. Giroux and Penna, 1979) but, very recently, also in the area of political policy around education (e.g. Apple, in press). One reason for this is, as I have suggested elsewhere (Whitty, 1981), that critical perspectives in the sociology of education made their initial impact in America within curriculum studies. The location of this work within departments of curriculum and instruction has brought critical sociological discourse into contexts centrally concerned with educational practice in a way which has all too rarely happened in Britain. Here such perspectives have generally been developed within sociology of education departments and sections that are often seen as quite separate from the curriculum and methods sections of the same institutions. Thus the institutional location of the American work, together with its greater empirical content, has helped to create a style of critical sociological theorizing about schooling which is more accessible to the concerns and experience of educational practitioners than has hitherto been the case in Britain. Very recently these perspectives have also begun to make an impact within departments of educational policy studies in the States. This is not to claim that even curriculum studies in the USA is dominated by this style of work, but it is to suggest that such perspectives are better placed to influence policy and practice than they are in Britain. This is particularly ironic given that there is almost certainly a stronger tradition of left policy and practice in and around education in Britain than there is in the USA, even though it has developed with very little reference to left theoretical work in the sociology of education.

I now want to explore some of these American developments in a little more detail. Michael Apple is probably the best-known of the American writers to utilize British and European critical social theory in his analysis of the curriculum. His book, *Ideology and Curriculum* (Apple, 1979a), was an important intervention within curriculum studies in America but, arguably, did suffer from some of the limitations of neo-Marxist sociology of education in Britain. His work immediately following the completion of that book, including parts of his paper at the 1979 Westhill conference (Apple, 1979b), was even more limiting in some respects since it was over-reliant upon the application to schooling of broader theories of the labour process. However, Apple's more recent work reveals some interesting shifts and is developing into a much more complex analysis of schooling in which the specificities and specific effectivities of political and ideological practice are more clearly recognized. Something of this double shift in Apple's work can be glimpsed in the internal tensions within the paper 'Curriculum form and the logic of technical control' (Apple, 1980), which was presented to the Westhill conference in January 1980. In the first part of that paper he argued that there was a clear, though mediated, relationship between the movement towards packaged curricula in schools and the changing modes of control within capitalist production relations. He claimed that the form which such teaching materials took made a particularly significant contribution to the formation of the type of 'possessive individual' appropriate to the current stage of the development of capitalism. Although he recognized that schools had had a certain amount of relative autonomy and that the development of capitalist social relations was an uneven one, the bulk of the paper seemed designed to illustrate an almost relentless march of the logic of capitalism through American schools in a quasi-Hegelian fashion. He suggested that curricular packages constrained teachers in ways which would make it extremely difficult for them to organize the social relations of the classroom in ways which would contest rather than affirm the hidden curriculum which he had detected in those packages.

Nevertheless, although he confessed to a considerable pessimism about the possibilities for more than token resistances to the process which he had charted, at the end of the paper he did recognise the existence of continuing opportunities for resistance to the dominant ideology on the part of both teachers and pupils and raised the possibility that resistances and contradictions within schools might provide a significant site of political education and intervention. There was then a considerable tension within the paper, with the early part seeming to illustrate an almost *a priori* claim about the necessary outcome of the dynamics of capitalist development, and the latter part recognizing quite explicitly that 'the creation of the kind of hegemony "caused" by the increasing introduction of technical control is not "naturally" pre-ordained . . . (but) something that is won or lost in particular conflicts and struggles'. Yet it remains somewhat unclear how far his self-confessed pessimism in this particular case is the product of the sort of self-fulfilling prophesy which Giroux (in press) and Wexler (in press) argue can be a real danger in reproduction theories and how far it derives from a realistic empirical assessment of American education and American politics in the current conjuncture. Certainly, insofar as the paper allows for at least elements of the latter reading, it constitutes not only a move beyond simple correspondence and reproduction theories but also an advance upon the sort of contested reproduction models in which resistances merely affirm, in ironic manner, the process of reproduction. In his very recent papers (e.g. Apple, in press), Apple pays even more attention to the ways in which the contradictions and resistances that he identifies might become significant sites of pedagogical and political intervention by the left.

A similar recognition that the precise relationship between schooling and the broader dynamics of capitalist societies, and the opportunities for left interventions in and around education, are not issues that can be treated as given has produced, in England, an increasing emphasis upon contradictions, relative autonomies, resistances, specificities, etc. But even this has been a largely theoretical exercise and the complexity which has been introduced into recent analyses has been at a level of generality that is of little positive value for calculating the possibilities for intervention in any particular conjuncture. It is here that the continuing empirical tradition within American educational studies is of particular importance. While, as yet, progress towards the sort of sociology of education that could be of relevance to left policy and practice has been limited, the sort of empirical work being carried out by American writers such as Jean Anyon is essential if sociological studies of education are to have any real significance for the development of explicit strategies of pedagogic and political intervention.

Some work by Anyon (1981) is indicative of the sort of theoretically-informed empirical research being carried out in the USA which is largely absent from the contemporary British scene.[11] In a paper entitled 'Social Class and School Knowledge', Anyon offers us an analysis of material gathered from a research project that looked at the different characteristics of five elementary schools in an East coast city. As in some of her earlier work (e.g. Anyon 1979, 1980), the paper is explicitly located within the theoretical traditions of a critical sociology of education but, whereas the earlier papers were largely illustrative of existing theory, in this paper she begins to use her data to interrogate and refine theories of reproduction and to identify possible points of transformative intervention. She considers in detail the curriculum, pedagogy and evaluation practices of the five schools and the response of pupils to them. Using data on the social composition of the intakes of the schools, she characterizes them as (in two cases) working class schools, a middle class school, an affluent professional school and an executive elite school. She identifies distinct differences between the schools, many of which could certainly be seen as supporting crucial elements of reproduction, and even correspondence, theories. However, she also identifies contradictions within *and* between educational and other contexts which offer support to the view that schools cannot be seen as contributing unproblematically towards social reproduction. The contradictions and the resistances that she points to are not treated as mere ironies in an overwhelming process of reproduction, but as possible sites of intervention. Thus she has tried in a much less abstract manner than the more purely theoretical writers to analyze which aspects of schooling may, in these particular contexts, be seen as reproductive in their effects and which as non-reproductive and potentially transformative. She argues, for instance, that a lack of successful ideological incorporation – as opposed to physical containment – of working class pupils, together with their spontaneous perspicacity[12] concerning the nature of what is being done to them, is a possible source of vulnerability. The emphasis in the middle class school on the possibility of individual success is seen as having only limited power to mystify class relations in the context of a contracting job market for these same pupils, while the emphasis on creativity and meaning-making in the affluent professional school is seen as coming into conflict with the new demands being made on these professional classes by the bureaucratic rationality of the corporate state. Even the rigorous understandings of the nature of the system being developed in the executive elite schools could, she contends, be turned to very different political purposes than the maintenance of class advantage.

That this sort of empirical study can provide a basis for thinking about the nature of a left pedagogy in more concrete terms than most British offerings on this theme is demonstrated in an even more recent article by Anyon where she outlines the sorts of pedagogic strategies that she herself would employ in working upon such contradictions and resistances (Anyon, in press). These examples, and others like them elsewhere in the literature, are certainly insufficiently developed as yet to sustain Anyon's strong claim that they are likely to 'facilitate *fundamental transformation* of ideologies and practices on the basis of which objects, services, ideas (and other cultural products) are produced, owned, distributed and publicly evaluated' (Anyon, 1981, my emphasis). Indeed, this particular claim is somewhat reminiscent of the excesses of the first phase of the 'new sociology of education' in the early 1970s. Nevertheless, there is a stronger empirical base to the American work which makes it less susceptible to the charge of 'vacuous rhetoric' and provides it with a better basis both for refining theory and for identifying specific contradictions towards which intervention strategies might usefully be directed. Another important strength of Anyon's work is that she seems to be moving towards a position that recognizes that whether contradictions, penetrations and resistances prove reproductive or non-reproductive in practice depends upon how they are worked on via concrete pedagogical interventions and how they are articulated with broader political strategies. Thus she is not content merely to chronicle the existence of resistances as a form of consolation for the left in a period of reaction (Hall, 1979) or to romanticize and applaud working class resistances *per se* in the way which it is sometimes suggested is encouraged by Willis's work (McRobbie, 1980: Giroux, in press). It is nevertheless important to recognise that Anyon's work points us in a fruitful direction rather than to see her work as providing a set of answers that can immediately be generalized. Other studies of the curriculum-in-use in American schools, such as McNeil (1977) and Popkewitz (1981), suggest that class differences in curricular provision, enactment and perception are not always so stark and it would seem important to explore gender, race and religious differences, as well as more immediate conjunctural, institutional and interactional factors. Yet the methodological conclusions that we should draw from these other studies are similar to those I have pointed to above. Thus, NcNeil argues that only the research strategy of 'going into schools, of taking time to feel and hear curriculum-in-use, brought to light many new insights which might otherwise have been unknown or underestimated'. Her own ethnographic research challenges, she tells us, some important aspects of the 'critical' paradigm in curriculum studies as well as the 'management' one. Further her insistence on combining elements of traditions that have largely remained separate in Britain allows her, like Anyon, to identify in relatively concrete terms the existence of contradictions, resistances and points of vulnerability in the process of reproduction.

I have concentrated here on research which gives empirical content to concepts such as contradiction and resistance. Other work might usefully throw light on the increasingly fashionable, but still largely abstract, concepts of the 'relative autonomy' and 'specific effectivity' of political and ideological practice. I am not suggesting that the American writers have progressed very far along this path but I am arguing that there are aspects of their work which we need to emulate if the sociology of education in Britain is to rediscover an orientation that is of significant value to left policy and practice. Australian writers also seem to be more aware of the limitations of non-empirical theoretical work and un-theorized empirical work in this respect. Although Dean Ashenden (1979) has pointed to a crisis in the relationship between Marxist writers on education and left teachers which is reminiscent of the situation over here, there is already, in some respects, a tendency for their work to be more empirically-based and more oriented towards the realms of policy and practice than most of our own. At the level of curriculum and pedagogical practice, Ozolins' (1979) embryonic work on what a working-class curriculum utilizing the 'penetrations' of the Australian equivalents of Willis's 'lads' might look like is one example. At the level of policy-interventions, the work of Freeland and Sharp (e.g. 1981) is particularly interesting, even though it reveals similar tensions to those which I suggested were implicit in Apple's contribution to the Westhill conference last year.

IV

In contrast with a lot of contemporary British work, these American and Australian developments reveal a willingness to interrogate theory with empirical research and *vice versa*, as a basis for identifying opportunities for left interventions in and around education. The empirical work has been directed towards various levels of analysis that have often tended to be confused or collapsed to produce a neat, but sometimes oversimplistic, model of the role of schooling in the reproduction of capitalist societies. For most of the writers involved, their empirical work has led them to qualify existing correspondence and reproduction models of education under capitalism, though some have raised very fundamental questions about the utility of the whole theoretical paradigm that was initially the stimulus for their research.

Wexler (in press) and Giroux (in press), in particular, have argued that the reproduction model which has dominated neo-Marxist theorizing about education in recent years may, in fact, serve to legitimate the very logic of domination which much of the early work in this tradition seemed to illustrate. It may thus have obscured the potential significance of contradictions, resistances and relative autonomies and the human capacity for transformative interventions. They therefore insist on drawing on the strengths of both humanistic and structuralist forms of analysis and avoid theoretical dogmatism in a way which has generally been theoretically unfashionable in Britain.

This combination of a continuing empirical tradition with a tendency towards a healthy form of eclecticism has produced a style of research that has been rare in British sociology of education in the 1970s, whilst the attempt to explore in concrete terms the implications of sociological analysis for left policy and practice has been even rarer. Young and I, and our collaborators, were advocating work of this nature in Britain in the mid-1970s but far too little of it has ever taken place. Interestingly, much of the American and Australian writing acknowledges an affinity with our work, though by no means an uncritical one (e.g. Sharp, 1980). Nevertheless, the initiative in terms of developing analyses relevant to left policy and practice is very clearly located elsewhere than in Britain at the present time, and is beginning to have a significant impact on publishers' lists over here. Forthcoming work by Henry Giroux and Michael Apple (Giroux, in press; Apple, in press) will, I suspect, be particularly important. Giroux has tried to develop a concept of radical pedagogy that seeks to challenge the prevailing social relations of the classroom and draws upon existing resistances and penetrations to create the sort of curriculum that could contribute towards transformative social action (Giroux, in press). In his very recent work, Apple has also shown an increasing concern to consider the practical implications of his work and, more explicitly, to explore the possibilities for the development of 'interesting and workable socialist models of pedagogical and curricular arrangements' (Apple, 1981). The American writers have, perhaps understandably given the nature of the political context in which they work, been rather less clear about broader policy interventions by the left, and here the Australian work is perhaps more instructive (e.g. Freeland and Sharp, 1981). Nevertheless, Apple has recently begun to consider in concrete terms the appropriate left response to current political and ideological developments around education in the States. The following passage from his paper on 'Class, culture and the state in educational interventions' is indicative of the way in which, even while retaining his basic belief in the significance of the dynamics of capital accumulation for the social relations of education, he moves away from any notion that theoretical dogma can simply provide answers to questions about appropriate practice in particular contexts. He states quite explicitly that:

> There are no general principles, no easy answers, to the question of when and where one should support (liberal) reforms. It is decidedly dependent on the balance of forces within a specific arena. Only by analyzing the specificity of each individual location can one make a decision on appropriate strategies . . . (Apple, in press)

Thus Apple shows a greater awareness than some of the other American writers of the need to analyze empirically the broader context of educational interventions by the left, since the success of such interventions is dependent on the disposition of political and ideological forces around education as well as within it. There is no hint here of a dogmatic abstentionism, but rather a recognition that sociological work could make an important contribution to the development of appropriate left interventions in political policy-making around education. It is certainly ironic that, in 1981, such issues should be confronted in the USA, whilst being relatively rarely considered in the sociology of education in Britain, a society with a long history of socialist politics. But the existence of such work elsewhere – growing as it does out of the very style of theorizing that Demaine (1980) dismisses as irrelevant to left policy and practice in Britain – suggests that there are other ways to proceed than by rejecting the sociology of education of the 1970s as an eccentric interlude in the history of the discipline, that can conveniently be forgotten as the sociologists of education of the 1940s and '50s join forces with the new generation of the 1980s (Brooks, 1980).

Notes

1   There have, of course, been various programmatic calls to overcome the dichotomy. See, for instance, HARGREAVES, A. (1980).
2   In a forthcoming article in *Interchange,* Paul Willis himself suggests that his work has been misinterpreted on this point.
3   Ben-Tovim and Gabriel suggest that unless the sociology of race does rediscover a policy-orientation 'it will continue to be dismissed as irrelevant in Whitehall and Town Hall, and likewise as academicist and elitist in less formal political contexts'. They say that 'the current crisis in the field of academic race relations arises in part from its reluctance to become involved *in* the political process' and that 'its abstention from this area is, of course, not without its political consequences' (BEN-TOVIM, G. and GABRIEL, J. 1979).
4   This seminar, organized by Henry Miller of Aston University and Jenny Shaw of Sussex University, subsequently took place at the University of London Institute of Education and further meetings are planned.
5   The proposed volume, edited by John Ahier and Michael Flude, will be published by Croom Helm, probably in 1982.
6   The articles in *Explorations* did, in fact, pre-date the Great Debate but were published while it was in progress.
7   It is interesting, in view of my later comments on the style of work being carried out in Australia and the USA, that our work has often been more favourably evaluated in those countries than it has in Britain.
8   Many of the ideas contained in this section were developed during discussions with Madeleine Arnot in the course of preparing a paper on 'Recent radical perspectives in American curriculum studies' for the SSRC Curriculum Studies Seminar at the University of Birmingham in January 1981.
9   The writers I am concerned with here do not form a 'school' in the traditional sense, but they have all been perceived as part of a growing 'critical' tradition in American curriculum studies. Amongst them are Jean Anyon, Michael Apple, Henry Giroux, Tom Popkewitz, Joel Taxel and Philip Wexler.
10   There is considerable variation amongst these writers in the amount of empirical work they have actually carried out. Jean Anyon's record is particularly impressive in this respect, but there are also many interesting empirical projects being carried out by graduate students in the various universities where these writers are based.
11   The exceptional nature of Paul Willis's *Learning to Labour* (WILLIS, P. 1977) in this respect is evidenced by the frequency with which it is cited as support for theoretical arguments that lack any other obvious empirical reference point.
12   This idea has similarities to Willis's concept of 'penetrations'.

References

ANDERSON, D. (1980) 'Have the supersaver sociologists asked for it?', *The Times Educational Supplement* (14 March).

ANYON, J. (1979) 'Ideology and United States history textbooks' *Harvard Educational Review* 49.3.

ANYON, J. (1980) 'Social class and the hidden curriculum of work' *Journal of Education* 162.1

ANYON, J. (1981) 'Social class and school knowledge' *Curriculum Inquiry*, 11.1

ANYON, J. (in press) 'Elementary schooling and distinctions of social class', *Interchange*.

APPLE, M. (1979a) *Ideology and Curriculum*, London, Routledge and Kegan Paul.

APPLE, M. (1979b) 'The production of knowledge and the production of deviance in schools' in BARTON, L. and MEIGHAN, R. (Eds) *Schools, Pupils and Deviance*, Driffield, Nafferton Books.

APPLE, M. (1980) 'Curricular form and the logic of technical control' in BARTON, L., MEIGHAN, R. and WALKER, S. (Eds) *Schooling, Ideology and the Curriculum*, Lewes, Falmer Press.

APPLE, M. (1981) 'Social structure, ideology and curriculum' in LAWN, M. and BARTON, L. (Eds) *Rethinking Curriculum Studies*, London, Croom Helm.

APPLE, M. (in press) 'Class, Culture and the state in educational interventions' in EVERHART, R. (Ed) *The Public School Monopoly* Boston, Ballinger Press.

APPLE, M. (in press) *Culture, Class and the State: Reproduction and Contradiction in Education*, London, Routledge and Kegan Paul.

ASHENDEN, D. (1979) 'Australian education: problems of a Marxist practice', *Arena* 54.

BARRETT, M., CORRIGAN, P., KUHN, A. and WOLFF, J. (Eds) (1979) *Ideology and Cultural Production*, London, Croom Helm.

BARTHOLOMEW, J. (1973) 'The teacher as researcher', *Hard Cheese* 1.

BATES, R. (1980) 'New developments on the new sociology of education', *British Journal of Sociology of Ecucation* 1.1.

BATES, R. (1981) 'What can the new sociology of education do for teachers?', *Discourse* 1.2.

BEN-TOVIM, G. and GABRIEL, J. (1979) 'The sociology of race – time to change course?' *The Social Science Teacher* 8.4.

BLEIMAN, B. and BURT, S. (1981) 'Beyond the comprehensive ideal', *Socialism and Education* 8.1.

BROOKS, C.ST.J. (1980) 'Sociologists and education', *New Society*, 4 September.

CUTLER, A., HINDESS, B., HIRST, P. and HUSSAIN, A. (1977/78) *Marx's Capital and Capitalism Today*, Vols. 1 & 2, London, Routledge and Kegan Paul.

DELAMONT, S. (1978) 'Sociology and the classroom' in BARTON, L. and MEIGHAN, R. (Eds) *Sociological Interpretations of Schooling and Classrooms: A Reappraisal*, Driffield, Nafferton Books.

DEMAINE, J. (1980) 'Sociology of education, politics and the left in Britain', *British Journal of Sociology of Education* 1.1.

DONALD, J. (1979) 'Green Paper: noise of crisis', *Screen Education* 30.

ENTWISTLE, H. (1979) *Antonio Gramsci: Conservative Schooling for Radical Politics*, London, Routledge and Kegan Paul.

FREELAND, J. and SHARP, R. (1981) 'The Williams Report on education, training and employment: The decline and fall of "Karmelot"' *Intervention* 14.

GIROUX, H. (in press) 'Hegemony, resistance and the paradox of educational reform', *Interchange*.

GIROUX, H. (in press) *Ideology, Culture and the Process of Schooling*, Lewes, The Falmer Press.

GIROUX, H. and PENNA, A. (1979) 'Social education in the classroom: The dynamics of the hidden curriculum', *Theory and Research in Social Education* 7.1.

GLEESON, D. and WHITTY, G. (1976) *Developments in Social Studies Teaching*, London, Open Books.

GORBUTT, D. (1972) 'The new sociology of education', *Education for Teaching* 89, Autumn, pp. 3–11.

GOULD, J. (1977) *The Attack on Higher Education – Marxist and Radical Penetration*, London, Institute for the Study of Conflict.

HALL, S. (1979) 'The great moving right show', *Marxism Today*, January.

HALSEY, A.H., HEATH, A.F. and RIDGE, J.M. (1980), *Origins and Destinations*, Oxford, Oxford University Press.

HARGREAVES, A. (1980) 'Synthesis and the study of strategies: A project for the sociological imagination' in WOODS, P. (Ed) *Pupils Strategies*, London, Croom Helm.

HARGREAVES, D. (1978) 'Whatever happened to symbolic interactionism?' in BARTON, L. and MEIGHAN, R. (Eds) *Sociological Interpretations of Schooling and Classrooms: A Reappraisal*, Driffield, Nafferton Books.

JOHNSON, R. (1979) 'Three problematics: Elements of a theory of working class culture' in CLARKE, J., CRITCHER, C. and JOHNSON, R. (Eds) *Working Class Culture – Studies in History and Theory*, London, Hutchinson.

JOHNSON, R. (1981) 'Socialism and popular education', *Socialism and Education* 8.1.

McNEIL, L. (1977) 'Economic dimensions of social studies curricula: Curricula as institutionalized knowledge', doctoral thesis, University of Wisconsin-Madison.

McROBBIE, A. (1980) 'Settling accounts with sub-cultures', *Screen Education* 34.

OPEN UNIVERSITY (1977) *Schooling and Society*, Milton Keynes, Open University Press.

OPEN UNIVERSITY (1981) *Society, Education and the State*, Milton Keynes, Open University Press.

OZOLINS, U. (1979) 'Lawton's "refutation" of a working class curriculum' *Melbourne Working Papers 1979.*

POPKEWITZ, T. (1981) 'The social contexts of schooling, change and educational research', *Journal of Curriculum Studies* 13.3.

REYNOLDS, D. and SULLIVAN, M. (1980) 'Towards a new socialist sociology of education' in BARTON, L., MEIGHAN, R. and WALKER, S. (Eds) *Schooling, Ideology and the Curriculum*, Lewes, Falmer Press.

SHARP, R. (1980) *Knowledge, Ideology and the Politics of Schooling*, London, Routledge and Kegan Paul.

SHARP, R. and GREEN, A. (1975) *Education and Social Control*, London, Routledge and Kegan Paul.

TAYLOR, W. (1978) 'Power and the curriculum' in RICHARDS, C. (Ed) *Power and the Curriculum*, Driffield, Nafferton Books.

VULLIAMY, G. (1976) 'What counts as school music?' in WHITTY, G. and YOUNG, M. (Eds) *Explorations in the Politics of School Knowledge*, Driffield, Nafferton Books.

VULLIAMY, G. (1978) 'Culture clash and school music: A sociological analysis' in BARTON, L. and MEIGHAN, R. (Eds) *Sociological Interpretations of Schooling and Classrooms: A Reappraisal*, Driffield, Nafferton Books.

WEXLER, P. (in press) 'Structure, text and subject: A critical sociology of school knowledge' in APPLE, M. (Ed) *Cultural and Economic Reproduction in Education: Essays on Class, Ideology and the State*, London, Routledge and Kegan Paul.

WHITTY, G. (1974) 'Sociology and the problem of radical educational change' in FLUDE, M. and AHIER, J. (Eds) *Educability, Schools and Ideology*, London, Croom Helm.

WHITTY, G. (1981) 'Curriculum studies: A critique of some recent British orthodoxies' in LAWN, M. and BARTON, L. (Eds) *Rethinking Curriculum Studies*, London, Croom Helm.

WHITTY, G. and YOUNG, M. (Eds) (1976) *Explorations in the Politics of School Knowledge*, Driffield, Nafferton Books.

WILLIAMS, R. (1973) 'Base and superstructure in Marxist cultural theory', *New Left Review* 82.

WILLIAMSON, B. (1974) 'Continuities and discontinuities in the sociology of education' in FLUDE, M. and AHIER, J. (Eds) *Educability, Schools and Ideology*, London, Croom Helm.

WILLIS, P. (1977) *Learning to Labour*, Farnborough, Saxon House.

WILLIS, P. (1979) 'Shop-floor culture, masculinity and the wage form' in CLARKE, J., CRITCHER, C. and JOHNSON, R. (Eds) *Working Class Culture – Studies in History and Theory,* London, Hutchinson.
YOUNG, M. and WHITTY, G. (Eds) (1977), *Society, State and Schooling,* Lewes, The Falmer Press.

The Educational Worker? A Re-assessment of Teachers

Martin Lawn, Westhill College
Jenny Ozga, Open University

This paper is an attempt to put together various strands of our work on teachers and our criticisms of existing work. Two principal directions have informed our work, a re-examination of teacher union history, and a re-examination of the concepts of professionalism and class as applied to teachers. In both cases we felt that the application of the concepts of professionalism and class analysis were inadequate, particularly where they categorized teachers as middle class professionals. The dominant sociological model had classified teachers as upwardly mobile, status seeking, new middle class members, and it seemed that more radical class analyses, to our dismay, echoed these conclusions, though using new approaches to professionalism derived from theories of the State and education, and neo-Marxist models of class. In both cases, the conclusion that teachers are middle class professionals had been reached by using the same historical evidence, the only differences were ideological, i.e. whether this was a *Good* or *Bad Thing*.

Our dissatisfaction with those conclusions stems from past experiences as teachers or education employees with people who did not, by their actions or beliefs, support their validity. Dissatisfaction was fed by the poor quality of much of the research on teachers and its lack of complexity, especially with regard to class and professionalism. The social reality of teaching, working and organizing with other teachers, seems to be a lost dimension of this literature. This feeling was exacerbated by further continued research on the past history of teachers, particularly the National Union of Teachers and the Teachers Labour League.

This paper tries to view teachers as being within a process of development as part of the Labour movement. It tries to redefine useful ways of seeing class and professionalism as part of this process. It tries to consider what evidence exists for understanding the labour process of teaching and looks at one aspect of this process, computerization in schools.

Professionalism

The quest for the signifying characteristics of professionalism is one on which researchers on teaching seem constantly engaged. Its dominance in the research on teachers seems at times to lie not just within the contributing disciplines or ideological viewpoints of the research, but in an overwhelming 'commonsense' view

The paper was written as a workshop paper at the Westhill Conference and was meant to provoke its audience. It was re-written with the help of comments received from Len Barton and Steve Walker, David Hargreaves and Roger Dale. Sometimes we were unable to act positively on these comments. During its re-writing the paper seemed to become more, not less, polemical. It should be treated as a position paper for a new approach to teachers and not as a well referenced model of scholarly argument.

that there is no other conceivable position. Professionalism and teaching seem synonymous.

As the critical researcher analyses this term in all its theoretical complexity or contradictory usage, it begins to lose shape and definition. This difficulty is nowhere more apparent than in the research of Ginsburg, Meyenn and Miller (1980)[1] which applied a number of theoretical perspectives to a fieldwork exercise on teachers, trying to understand their use of professionalism and trade unionism. This interesting study makes one relevant point (for our purposes), saying that:

> There is a considerable degree of uncertainty and oscillation in the expression of such views (on trade unionism and professionalism) at least to researchers.
>   (p. 180)[2]

Although they were talking here of their respondents, this statement could easily be applied to their theoretical input – a survey of the literature.

The dominant practice is the application, using varying criteria, of the trait theory of professionalism and its related variant, professionalization (trait theory as a process). One example, better than many, should suffice. Parry and Parry[3] in their analysis of teachers' failure to use the professionalization strategy successfully, define professionalism as –

> A strategy for controlling an occupation in which colleagues, who are in the formal sense equal, set up a system of self-government. This involves restriction of entry to the occupation through the control of education, training and the process of qualification. Another aspect is the exercise of formal and informal management of members' conduct in respects which are defined as relevant to the collective interests of the occupation. In addition, there is the use of occupational solidarity and closure to regulate the supply of services to the market and which serves also to provide a basis for the domination of institutions, organizations and other occupations associated with it. Finally, there is the reinforcement of this situation by the acquisition of state support in order to obtain, if possible, a legal monopoly backed by legal sanctions . . . in so far as an occupational group is able to practise all or most of these things it will be exercising the power of professionalism.[4]

Asher Tropp (in *The Schoolteachers*)[5] adopts a similar approach, also argued historically. He regards teachers as being generally successful on most counts (traits) in becoming a profession. Tropp holds the view that teachers, by their own efforts, within a consistent strategy followed by most of them for at least a hundred years, and with the eventual tacit or active support of the State, have become professionals. By professionals he means *de facto* controllers of the education service. There is no general agreement in most 'professionalism' theory on whether the State helped to license them as a group acting in its interests or whether teachers won the grudging support of the State by acting in mildly contrary ways.

Our opposition to or unease about this view of professionalism is probably generated by a disbelief in the hegemonic nature of the concept – the idea that a group of people with different locations and contradictions, during a long period, could hold to a consistent strategy or view of themselves which is divorced from the conditions in which they worked and the social movements in which they were involved. This is not to deny a value in understanding and applying the term professional to teachers, but to argue the need for an awareness of the complexity of the idea.

Our argument, expressed briefly, would be that the term 'professionalism', in its use by teachers and the central and local State, changes; includes variations of meaning and contains elements remarkably similar to the aims and actions of other (and not only white collar) workers.

We would suggest that at least one way in which the term was used by the State, from about 1918–20 onwards, was as a means of controlling the radical and extended actions of teachers as to their work conditions. It was also connected to the shift in attitude towards the education service by the State itself in this period (from the Fisher Act to its eventual, partial dismemberment). The role of the elementary teachers was to alter due to this new function, determined by working class demand, technological change, and their own unrest. Questions as to the 'right to strike', 'Labour affiliation' and Civil Service membership were all raised but it is the growth of the professional ideology which dominates the actions of central and local government and co-opts elements of the teachers' organizations.[6]

Yet there are also other ways in which professional demands may be viewed. In our view, it may represent commitment to a craft ethic similar to other skilled, craft unions. If we take away the theoretical perspective of the 'occupational strategy' and substitute a craft-related ethic and strategy, then the way in which teachers' actions may be viewed alters significantly. Can the demand for a qualified workforce and control over training be seen as part of a natural resistance to local and central State control (similar to the craft demands on apprenticeship control, and the rule book used in the Scottish 'ca-canny' disputes etc.)? Can the resistance to teacher ancillaries and low wages be seen as similar to the battles against dilution constantly waged by the skilled workers in defence of their knowledge and control over the work process? Can the defence of the public service of education be seen as the defence of the quality of work against the demands of the employer in maximizing profit? Well, if not, why not? Elements of industrial trade unionism, that is the unification of all workers, regardless of skill level in the single trade, can also be seen as part of a 'professionalism'; note the NUT decision, in 1917, to widen membership.

Professionalism is a complex concept, involving contradictions and group and historically specific meanings. The view that it is a personal and group responsibility may have coincided with the view of a section of teachers and/or even dominated an historical period. The view that it is a way of challenging the employer's control of the labour process merits examination.

At times, professionalism figures as a means of resistance or a means of control or both. At periods of crisis, even the elements of a rhetoric of control may lose their dominance over some teachers as there appears a recognizable gap between rhetoric and reality – the situation prevailing in the disabled education system today. In periods of relative 'calm', a rhetoric of State professionalism may exercise more 'commonsense' influence over larger sections of teachers.

What we are hinting at is a recognition that the term generates meanings according to the material bases and shared ideological views of different parties. The major contradiction is still between the meanings generated by the employers and employees but these are not always historically distinct nor are they always possible to separate.

The idea of 'service' appears, in variations, on both sides of the contradiction. Earlier this century the belief of teachers, municipal employees and civil servants in public service responsibility was not at odds with elements of the employers' views. That the rhetoric and the reality of that 'service' became separated is the lesson of the later part of the twentieth century. Service, whether described as professional or not, is a strong element of most work.[7] Each occupational group may express it differently. This service was often expressed within a struggle for better conditions of work. Consequently, the battle for improvements in one area was seen as part of the fight for the other – this has certainly been the case in education. The role of the State was revealed within the struggle (in certain periods) over conditions of work, pay or public provision.

Instead of asking 'are teachers really professionals or not?', let us ask 'what has been excluded from our understanding of teachers through the dominance of *a priori* assumptions about professionalism and its significance?' In asking the latter question, it may then be possible to return to professionalism and question its nature and its material base.

For us, there are two interesting areas which produce fruitful ideas on teachers and their work; first, the socialist and neo-Marxist class analyses of skilled and white collar workers which have created some insights into the problems involved in understanding class and teachers, if not the solutions; second, the growth of new historical research on teachers' own work experience, allegiances and organizations suggests new complexities in analyzing teachers' work.

Class and Teachers

Underlying most commonsense usage of the term professionalism is an association between professionalism and the middle class, and, indeed, this is also the connection made by theorists in this area whether ideologically of the Left or Right. For example, Asher Tropp saw a gradual move this century away from the working class social origins (and some political or educational sympathy) of teachers, by a process of partially successful professionalization (increased remuneration, higher qualifications and some policy making influence) towards a recognized middle classness. There is a general agreement with Tropp's thesis from the politically opposed perspective adopted by Finn, Grant and Johnson (1979):

> Professionalism can be understood as a petit bourgeois strategy for advancing and defending a relatively privileged position. (p. 170)[8]

Both views, though differently interpreted, are based on a simplistic view of professionalism and its relation to class. There is no recognition of the contradictions involved in the term as it is used by different groups over historical periods nor how it may have positive and negative aspects, from the point of view of a progressive standpoint.

Recent neo-Marxist or structural Marxist analysis of class position (threading through Althusser, Poulantzas and Erik Olin Wright[9]) in its attempt to throw over the lack of 'hard' explanation of social change and the role of the state that they felt was the major weakness of Marxist scholarship, have taken positions which seem to us to view class as a static entity. Class takes on an unacceptable degree of abstraction from concrete work situations, and ignores the dynamic role which people have in society in resisting and creating alternatives.

In education as a service, teachers are generally viewed as State functionaries with the main responsibility for ideological control and social and cultural reproduction of capitalism. This view accords with the economic analysis of Crompton[10] who sees teachers, amongst others, as paid for out of surplus value created by industrial workers, and garnered by the State to reproduce itself. The two general arguments – a group paid for out of surplus value to act as the State's agent, and for its ideological, cultural and economic reproduction and domination – set up teachers in ways which make them irretrievably lost to the progressive or labour movement. The only light on the horizon, apparently, is when control over their working lives becomes so oppressive that their resistance may be shaped by university professors and lecturers!

This proposition is simplistic in essence, if not in its explanation. Teachers may be State functionaries but this is not, nor could it ever be, a comprehensive explanation of their behaviour or analysis of their position.

All education does not serve the purposes of the State all the time. If it did it would leave the demands for a better, well-equipped education service demanded by teachers and the Labour movement since the 1870s looking very silly – an extreme case of historically consistent false consciousness! Instead we should be able to argue several possibilities from their actions – that they had a different view of education and wanted control of the system (locally or nationally) to enforce their views over the local or central State's view; that they had little respect for education and its purpose but were demanding a clear, fulfilled minimum agreement about those things valuable to them (reading and writing etc.); that some members of the working class wanted a better service to enable them to succeed within the rhetoric of the State (for equal opportunity etc.); that their demands, radical and practical, were absorbed by the State and, in periods of low militancy and pressure, its own demands substituted; that the State, in different periods, had no clear policy as to mass education except that it should be cheap and/or efficient and in other periods that it should serve other ideological or technological purposes – and so forth. The blanket use of the term 'State functionaries' hides too many historical, local and particular possibilities and, importantly, ignores teachers' attempts at working class alliances on education and their varied interpretation of their role as perceived by the State, and their resistances to it.

The question of payment from surplus value is a difficult area for all Marxists. The invisibility of the product is real enough. Yet (following Hunt)[11] isn't it necessary to recognize the increasing complexity and changing operations of capitalism in its drive to increase the accumulation of capital? The rigid distinction between the productive and non-productive worker ought to take on more analytical complexity when the latter increasingly outweighs the former, and they, in turn, seem about to be replaced by robots! As capitalism has become increasingly sophisticated so the growth of bureaucratic, service and distribution functions has grown. The production of value now needs a related body of work associated with its *realization*. A greater proportion of capital is devoted to the creation of invisible commodities generating the thesis of the 'collective labourer'. The generation of value is now undertaken outside as well as inside the factory and, since the 1920s, the State has taken a more direct role in this process – for instance, the creation of apprenticed skilled labour is now undertaken in universities, schools and the Manpower Services Commission. Aren't teachers part of this 'collective labourer', producing a labour force, a commodity improved in value?

The recognition that teachers are workers, by nature of their economic position as employees, and yet still acting as agents of the State introduces us, whatever its other faults, to the notion of contradiction in the teachers' position.[12] But let us take the notion of contradiction further. All workers suffer a contradiction between themselves and their work; this is based, at root, on the fact that they are cheated every day of some of the value of their labour and that, in continuing working, they are reproducing capitalism. There are further contradictions based on sexual, racial, hierarchical and geographical factors plus their historical memory of their position (within their family, factory or skill). Yet, with all these contradictions, the capitalist or the state cannot simply override and dominate the worker. There has always been conflict and resistance, and economic and ideological initiatives based on them, at different historical periods and, hence, an accumulation of experience paralleling the accumulation of capital. Why then should teachers be different – the main contradiction is between the employer and the employee. Other contradictions are secondary or even non-antagonistic.

Our position is that the exploration of these contradictions and the understanding of the major contradiction is underdeveloped and needs further work. We will refer to this later.

If class is an important concept in the understanding of teachers, it cannot be reduced to an economic relationship nor to a cultural or ideological function *alone*. The material base is essential for understanding the world but it is not its only creator. Class is also a relational concept involving several factors (economic, political or social) and a process (not static condition) taking place over historical time.

E.P. Thompson[13] takes a position on class which opposes the structural Marxist position and, we argue, would better serve the exploration of teachers, their class and labour process. In Thompson's words:

> . . . class is not, as some sociologists would have it, a static category – so many people standing in this or that relation to the means of production – which can be measured in positivist or quantitative terms. Class, in the Marxist tradition, is (or ought to be) *a historical category,* describing *people in relationship over time,* and the ways in which they become conscious of their relationships, separate, unite, enter into struggle, form institutions and transmit values in class ways.
>
> Hence class is an 'economic' and it is also a 'cultural' formation: it is impossible to give any theoretical priority to one aspect over the other . . . what changes, as the mode of production and productive relations change, is the *experience* of living men and women. And this experience is sorted out in class ways, in social life and in consciousness, in the assent, the resistance and the choices of men and women.
>
> (Thompson, 1979)[14]

To look at teachers in this way we need evidence about their actions, contradictions and labour processes – their consciousness and their condition.

Historical evidence has been limited and mainly confined to incidents related to 'professionalism', though Asher Tropp's book does provide interesting cases which are seen as aberrations by Tropp in the development of teachers as a professional group.

One particular period, from 1916–1920, was a watershed in the relation between teachers and the State. During this period the teachers were involved in an extensive series of guerilla strikes and disputes with over half the local education authorities in the country; were considering the affiliation of the major teachers' union to the

Labour Party and were also involved in a series of formal discussions on alliances with other white collar workers. To these events, footnotes in Tropp's book, may be added the researches of Brian Simon in this period – the swing to Labour was so strong in the country that Special Branch reports on leading radicals amongst the teachers were included in a special Board of Education file 'Drift of Teachers to the Labour Party', which also includes a report on a deputation to Baldwin, the Prime Minister, by prominent Conservatives concerned at the national drift to Labour and pleading for a positive Conservative educational policy.[15]

The significance of a period like this has been lost over the years. The bare bones of the relationship between teachers and the State are revealed in the issues raised in the national press at the time. Should teachers strike? Should they become professionals? Does the State have a new responsibility to workers' education? The degree of the conflict between teachers and their employers can now, in retrospect, seem both tentative and fundamental. For instance, to many rural teachers their immediate oppressor was the local vicar or parish council and was becoming their county council; yet for urban teachers, questions not just about the local authority but the nature of education under capitalism were being raised. The drift to the Labour party, and beyond to the Communist Party, was both a recognition of class interests and a recognition that education was a shared interest with the working class. The significance of this tentative, open alliance nationally was not lost, in this period, on Lloyd George, who allegedly pointed out to his Cabinet, when supporting Fisher's new, expensive education Bill, that at the head of each continental revolutionary movement were ex-teachers.

Progressive elements in the State produced a more sophisticated policy with regard to teachers than the previous use of local authority henchmen acting as fairly omnipotent cost-cutters, etc. The proposal to make teachers civil servants with a new 'status' was rejected, as it would have created a direct employment link between teachers and the central State – the Board of Education was unwilling to make that relationship open and said so.[16] The creation of a new 'professionalism', combined with the better financial conditions built into the Burnham Scales, was a policy which, if not the sole prerogative of the central State in the twenties and thirties, made it the beneficiary – it encouraged responsibility and autonomy of classroom decision-making in conjunction with a consistent policy of breaking the ideological and strategic alliance between the teachers and the Labour movement – by sacking militants etc.

The teachers' movement and strength through this period was part of, and cannot be isolated from, the resurgent working class militancy in the second decade of this century, which was in retreat by the early twenties. For the purpose of our argument, this was not an isolated, discrete event, but indicative of, and revealing about, the main antagonistic contradiction between the teachers as employees and the central and local State as employers. Their relationship has never been merely reducible to crude physical and economic exploitation. Different contending factions within capitalism can have quite different educational policies – the consecutive post war governments could move from the Fisher Act to the Geddes 'Axe' on spending. These policies were made strategically and tactically – Fisher's Act was not just far-sighted investment in 'human capital' (his phrase) but was a tactical response to the war, and the enormous working class demand for education. Teachers have also taken a number of different actions which have been used to construct a theory of consistent professionalism; at times in apparent harmony with central controls, at other times in open conflict. Each helps us to interpret the other.

There is a lost history of teachers, which people like Gerald Grace[17] have started to uncover, which should be revealed, involving individual experiences, local traditions, developing class consciousness, and antagonistic and non-antagonistic contradictions among teachers and between teachers and their employees.

Proletarianization

To our knowledge, there is little in the way of detailed, historical evidence of the changing nature of working conditions in schools and the roles and skills of teachers.

Our assumption is, in this tentative thesis, that there is a connection between the increased proletarianization of teachers' work, de-skilling and re-skilling, and 'class in itself' actions of teachers. These are all part of the same thing – the nature of work, degrees of autonomy over decision-making, political and social actions as individuals or in a group, and resistance to change and promotion of changes. If class is a relational concept, proletarianization of work is an economic and a social process – a process of change and resistance expressed in individual, school-based and national developments. In passing, we have referred to evidence of discontent about the nature of the education service and the working class/Labour movement alliance; what we will try and offer here is evidence that work processes and the quality of work are subject to similar forces in education as they are elsewhere, particularly in white collar work. Again, our difficulty lies in the fact that while this subject is developing in many work areas, education is still treated as an area apart, patrolled by professionals. Hence we are forced, at this stage, to make our case by inference, and by extrapolation from the experiences of other workers.

The changing nature of capital has led to a growth of white collar, service sector workers. These workers are, we believe, in the process of proletarianization earlier undergone by industrial workers. Proletarianization follows from the removal of skill from work, the exclusion of the worker from the conceptual functions of work. Worker autonomy is eroded, the relationship between employer and employee breaks down, management controls are strengthened and craft skills and the craft ethic decline.

The lack of clear outlines of a production process has allowed sociologists to see only reproductive or hidden functions of the State expressed in education and to continue to treat teachers as separate from other workers and public servants.

Today, most of the working class in Britain is in service industries, which may be treated as theoretically non-productive. Yet one has to recognize that without the specialized, fragmented processes that capitalism has created – such as personnel management, supervisory staff, warehousing staff, financial and administratve offices, distribution and sales – *value* could not be *realized*. In the production and realization of value, many different workers, in many places and often unconnected from each other, act, in total, as 'collective labourers'. Education is one of the more specialized parts of the means of production and the role of the State, since the 1920s, has been to take over some of the functions of private capital and integrate and reorganize them.

Proletarianization is a process which affects all work – directly at the point of production but of necessity, sooner or later, at the points of distribution or realization of value. If education is part of the creation of value, expressed as a trained work force, then this process will be analyzed and re-structured to increase its efficiency (productivity). This process will be constant; that is, it will always be occurring in some place at any time, but it will also occur in varying degrees as moments of crisis necessitate strategic re-structuring. This change will not only be a response to the crisis (production of new grades of trained workforce etc.) but will take into account the degree of resistance likely to result. Resistance will be at a higher ideological level during periods of general working class militancy and when there is full employment: the latter condition must surely be the explanation for the difference between the 1964 conflict over the Schools Council and the 1978–81 non-conflict over the Great Debate etc.

It is only relatively recently that the idea of proletarianization has come to be applied to white collar workers. Crompton, for example, has developed it in relation to insurance workers, where, she argues, proletarianization through the introduction of technology and the rationalization and centralization of control 'substantially transformed' the class situations of insurance employees in the 1960s.[18]

It is this argument that Bowles and Gintis[19] used in relation to the development of the United States education service. Although their arguments might not be directly used in relation to our own very different educational history, they tried to show, like Raymond Callahan (in *Education and the Cult of Efficiency*)[20] that the education service was influenced by the application of business methods generated in the pursuit of industrial efficiency by Taylor etc. The development of the scientific management movement, involving task allocation, detailed curriculum control and text selection, they argue, introduced the 'social relations of the production line'. This view of teachers places them, like other workers, firmly against the background of the constant transformation of the production process by capital in its drive to extract and accumulate – the education system is affected in the same way as other areas of work.

The use of a guided, limited 'professionalism' and the creation of a mock part-nership with central and local government is the British equivalent of this transfor-mation of the education service. Business efficiency methods have been slow to reconstruct British industry and their use in education, *viz* corporate management techniques, are a recent phenomenon. Instead, as Lord Eustace Percy (President of the Board of Education in the 1920s) made clear in his autobiography,[21] the extremism of some teachers could be controlled by a system of licensed autonomy. He borrowed from British colonial experience notions of 'indirect rule' – the eman-cipation of parts of local authority and teacher work was not intended to endanger 'real tactical control of (the) social service[22] but remove *unnecessary* central powers. The sophistication of Whitehall and the Board of Education in the twenties has been further explored by John White;[23] to his tentative conclusion that the centralized system was dismantled in anticipation of the first Labour victory at the polls should be added our own suggestion – that it was part of the development of a means of con-trolling teachers ideologically (with the generation of a limited 'professionalism') and by means of finely tuned tactical control in a system which now needed guiding not directing.

In what senses are teachers proletarianized? How have their conditions of work in teaching altered to illuminate the possibility of proletarianization? Further to this point – in what ways has the purchase of labour power from teachers been realized by increasing control of organization, by mechanization, and by growth of supervision?

Using the general process, as analyzed by Harry Braverman,[24] as our starting point, we suggest that in teaching, as in other kinds of work:

There is a long term tendency through fragmentation, rationalization and mechanization for workers and their job to become deskilled, both in an absolute sense (they lose craft and traditional abilities) and in a relative one (scientific knowledge progressively accumulates in the production process) . . . Thus the worker, regardless of his or her personal talents, may be more easily and cheaply substituted for in the production process.[25]

We recognize that there are problems in describing teachers as skilled workers, but argue that skill is not only a technical term, denoting control over a complex process and involving an understanding of that process – it is also a social term. Skill is a creation of labour control over the workplace and the job content.[26] Skill implies a relationship to the process of conception *and* execution, the strength – or weakness – of the relationship to these processes is demonstrated by the terms skilled, semi-skilled and unskilled. Today, even skilled work, whatever the length of the training period, is confined to execution, and excludes conception. Planning is divorced from execution and, in turn, is now (in the draughtsman's office, in engineering) able to be described as skilled, semi-skilled etc.

Earlier this century, teachers trained each other, mainly in the workplace (the school) but increasingly in pupil teacher centres and the new municipal colleges. Generally, experienced teachers, the senior or headteacher, taught the inexperienced the trade. The need for certification, the clear recognition of skill, was recognized by teachers. The role of the State, in its indirect control of local authority colleges (the intake and numbers in teaching) and its influence on the content of the courses was often seen by teachers as the opponent of a teacher-controlled skill. By the 1920s elementary teachers felt that they were in greater control of their workplace and job content, after the serious conflicts of the previous decade and the gradual weakening or dismantling of parts of the education code. Increasingly it appears as if the definition of skill has been created by the teacher but in response to interventionist financial investments or initiatives taken centrally. Skill is a contested concept. The relative autonomy is a recognition of this contestation and of teacher definition of work/education. Skill has been seen recently in terms of technical attributes, specialized tasks and career structures and scale posts, reflecting the increased intervention by the employer, consistent with the changing nature of the labour process elsewhere. It has been weakened in terms of teacher definition of the conception and execution of work (education).

This weakening has occurred during periods of teacher over-production and a decline of the ideology of working class guardianship over the education service (which was how it was increasingly seen by 1920 through the initiative of the Bradford Charter of 1917 and the education alliance with the TUC) and an acceptance of ideas of partnership. It resides in a rhetoric of autonomy. The fight against cheap teaching labour was a fight over the quality of education for the working class – resistance to the dilution of craft skill by the introduction in the First World War, and after, of unskilled, untrained teachers was a conscious act in defence of education and training, defined by the teachers or their allies themselves. De-skilling involved a political response similar to that created in the industrial working class in this period.

Teachers and the Labour Process

The proletarianization of work involves a number of different aspects. The major aspect is, obviously, the loss of skill or craft or traditional knowledge. This is a continuous process which may have sudden changes and swift movements, depending on technological change and its applications, the nature of the production process and the ideology and history of the workforce. There are also a number of contingent aspects; the loss of autonomy, the increase of supervision, creation of re-skilled specializations and increase in stress – all a recognized part of proletarianization. Proletarianization may move through a number of steps in relation to work. First, by treating the worker like a machine: the Taylor movement in production control, systems management, behavioural objectives, etc., all try to reduce the variability and creativity of the individual in relation to the work process, reducing the 'irrationality' of the worker. Second, the worker is tied directly to the machine – as an appendage – where the machine controls the pace and content of the work. Third, if possible, the machine may, if cheaper, be substituted for the worker.

Braverman, writing about white collar clerical work, describes it in its early days as a craft, with master craftsmen (the bookkeeper or chief clerk) maintaining total control of the record-keeping process and young apprentices or journeymen (clerks, ledger clerks, office boys) learning their trade in the office. As the accounting of value becomes more complex

> . . . The intimate associations, the atmosphere of mutual obligation, and the degree of loyalty which characterized the small office became transformed . . . The characteristic feature of this era was the ending of the reign of the bookkeeper and the rise of the office manager as the prime functionary and the representative of management.[27]

Work is now reduced from being an understanding of the whole process and becomes more and more, the steady, unvarying, part of the whole. Thought, or conception, is eliminated from the work, though not the worker, and the mind is used as 'the equivalent of the hand of the detail worker in production'.[28]

This description has parallels with the historical development of schools from being small enterprises, not created by but (in practical process) controlled by teachers with some whole view of their work, to the rise of the large school with the creation of administrative and supervisory tasks in which teaching is part of a production line process. Headteachers moved from being *'primus inter pares'* and the trainers of the inexperienced, to become managers of human and technical resources. Teaching in many schools is now the endless repetition of similar data in numerous, brief encounters. There is no sense of the whole enterprise at all, and the rise of administration is a response to the need to control the complexity of the process and the movement of the de-skilled unit worker.

Teaching has been intermittently altered and changed in its labour process by the steady rise of specialized or supervisory staff in the school. The slow rise through the wage scales, determined locally and then nationally, has gradually given way to 'career structures' and 'promotion ladders', all involving increased supervisory or managerial responsibility. By 1945, headteachers were paid on a separate salary scale and by 1956, the old allowances for assistants (given in large schools for advanced teaching work in or in lieu of rare headteacher promotion) were replaced by a series of graded posts, deputy headships and department heads. The comprehensive schools produced more specialist functions in the subject areas and in pastoral work. The general supervisory work of a deputy head or head of department has, over the last few years, increased in detail and specification. Deputy heads now act as public relations officers, as personnel managers, as curriculum co-ordinators or innovation leaders and with increased responsibility for timetabling – the last a new 're-skilled' job, understood by a few teachers in the schools. Heads of departments may now, through increased rationalization in schools, be organizers and integrators of complicated schemes of work they were not trained to undertake, yet they are being re-skilled on the job. Faculty meetings, heads of departments cross-school meetings and top management meetings are a feature of supervisory and management work in schools.

Pastoral work is a major area of school work, concentrated now into the hands of a few 're-skilled' teachers responsible for discipline, but also a major school link with social services. Pastoral heads (heads of school 'houses') may spend a lot of time each week meeting parents, the police, the educational welfare officers, the educational psychologists, social workers, the child guidance clinic and doctors, and visiting homes or attending case conferences. School Disruptive Units are fairly common, as are youth workers/teachers, school counsellors, careers teachers and liaison teachers (with Middle/Primary schools).

The specialized part of school teaching is one side of this equation but the other is the re-definition of jobs, once recognized as accorded responsibility by age or experience, as middle or top management. The graded and promotion posts are increasingly supervisory posts not just reflecting the proliferation and integration of school functions, and they are combined especially in the present cutbacks with a full teaching load. They are there to boost productivity. As Aronowitz notes:

> The working supervisor is merely a person who performs two jobs. She is responsible for actually producing the same amount of paper herself as the subordinate; in addition, she is held responsible for the production of the subordinate as well.[29]

The new H.M. Inspectors' report on Schools remarked that middle management in

> most schools had not been able to relate the allocations of non-teaching time to the special responsibilities which these teachers were expected to fulfil. Instead, it appears that schools could do no more than squeeze a little extra monitoring time and hope that any gaps would be filled.[30]

Responsibilities that they should be undertaking were described as, for department heads, the 'guidance, supervision and support' to department teams, and it was recognized for pastoral heads that many of their duties could only be performed 'when the pupils concerned are present'.

There is a diminishing of the quality if not the quantity of work. At the same time, it is commonly expected that many school teachers, in a period of contraction/falling rolls, should be versatile, general teachers. Redeployment within schools is often referred to as increased 'flexibility'.[31] With the rise of the re-skilled staff, there is also a tendency towards de-skilling staff. This is evident in maths and sciences, and was remarked upon by the H.M. Inspectors in relation to the increased use of worksheets (more in fact than they had anticipated).

> Worksheets may be developed through shared experience of members of the department and they can be a useful support, enabling inexperienced teachers and non-mathematicians to have suitable material available.[32]

Widespread redeployment, within or between schools, can only lead to a further weakening of skill as these teachers employed as general teachers, using worksheets, programmed course or in teamwork, became more common. Is there a connection between the rise of the flexible, general teacher and the new emphasis on reading, science and language *across* the curriculum?

One recent piece of research which brings together the ideas about de-skilling we have discussed above and some detailed empirical research is Buswell's study of the effect of curriculum packaging on one large school in the North of England.[33] Her concern was a broader one than ours, in that she was looking at the relationship between pedagogic change and social change, but she does argue that the curriculum packaging systems used in this school de-skilled teachers. It is interesting to note that her examples come from across the curriculum, from the mathematics teacher who ran a Mathematics club in the lunch break in order to compensate for the deficiencies of the programmed approach, to the Humanities teacher who condemned the packages as containing not only prepared materials but a predetermined method of transmission – 'we're just glorified clerks now' was his verdict on their effect. A further point worth developing is the evidence gathered by Buswell that the introduction of packages reinforced the tendency towards the separation of content, pedagogy and assessment as specialist tasks, thereby removing the curriculum as an area of knowledge from the teachers and placing it in the hands of the local curriculum adviser. Yet another area worthy of further investigation is Buswell's categorization of teacher response to the pressures for proletarianization inherent in the learning packages. These ranged from acquiescence, through ambivalence to modification and resistance. Significantly members of the group resisting these learning packages – by delaying the process of writing modifications of an externally produced system, by sabotaging the systems in various ways – were found to be leaving teaching altogether.

Curriculum specialists, known as curriculum co-ordinators, teacher leaders or even plain Faculty Heads, are the new specialists, the planners, in this divorce of conception from the execution of work. The qualitative aspects of teaching decline as the quantitative rate increases. This view of de-skilling is similar to the recent ideas of Michael Apple[34] but it is only a part of a wider view of labour control over the workplace, not just a relationship to knowledge or techniques. What passes as 'skill' depends on the strength of the employees in the labour process. It is not de-skilling if the workers control its implementation and daily operation, combining an eclectic or pragmatic use of the materials with the creation of alternative practices. It is not the programme itself which de-skills but the acts of teachers who implement the programme recognizing their loss of physical and ideological control over the work process. Teachers may in fact deliberately choose to use programmes because of the insidious position they are now in with regard to class sizes, poor capitation allowances, lack of class cover and the rise of assessment procedures: in the H.M.I. Report maths teachers used worksheets because of the demands made on them. But, in a changed educational climate, these programmes will be used or rejected by teacher control of the work process. The costs of retraining teachers have been, in the main, borne by teachers. It is they who spend out of school time on curriculum meetings, on teacher centre conferences, on in-service training.[35] The Open University provided a readily accessible opportunity for teachers to pay for their own retraining.

There has been an association between stress at work and the nature of the modern labour process; this is also related to absenteeism and high personnel turnover rates. Stress is a subjective concept and many teachers refer to stress as an element in their work. Absence from work is generally regarded as being connected to stress. As Kyriacou has noted,[36] the Department of Education and Science made special payments, since 1975, to teachers in schools designated as stressful in order to reduce high turnover. Teachers mention poor working conditions, time pressures, poor school ethos as well as 'pupil misbehaviour' as factors in stress production. Hodge (quoted in Kyriacou) notes the recent doubling of male teachers dying towards the end of their career and that the number qualifying for a breakdown pension trebled; headteachers generally seem to be retiring earlier. Stress, in a period of contraction, education cuts and redeployment, will increase: Kyriacou notes the strong correlation between a poor career structure and lower job satisfaction in causing stress. Work absenteeism, he notes, was caused by poor career structure, by too much work to do and lack of time for individual pupils, by demands for:

> Efficiency of production and increased workloads, emphasising the quantitative at the expense of the qualitative aspects of work. The rise of solutions based on counselling or 'somatic' therapy are already being suggested. Work won't change but the teacher will have to.[37]

Technology and the Labour Process

The process of re-skilling and de-skilling may be given a significant boost by the introduction of computer, microprocessor and microelectronic applications in education. Apple has argued that it involves a qualitative change in work control from simple to technical control of teachers' work.[38]

We are not discussing here the intrinsic value of microprocessors nor the creative uses to which they may be put, but the way in which they accelerate labour processes which we have described.

Computers are increasingly used in school administration, in repetitive data collection and retrieval on school rolls, details of individual pupils, their subject options, etc. Computers are a qualitative shift in the nature of work, however, and relationships alter and change. Local education authorities may now 'plug in' to this information directly and school performance may be more easily monitored. As computerization may soon be used in classroom administration (pupil records and marksheets), monitoring of pupil *and* teacher performance is easier. It has also been suggested that information may be gathered on the attendance at in-service training courses, amongst other uses.[39]

An increasing use of computers is in computer-assisted learning packages (CAL). These are usually based on American work, and are mainly in the essential, shortage subjects – maths, physics, chemistry, economics and geography. CAL enthusiasts refer to the higher order skills, improving teaching standards and the new subjects which may be taught in this way. There is another side, related to our argument. CAL 'packages' have to be written by somebody. That person is in an increasingly specialized job. At the moment, it is suggested that to reduce costs, groups of teachers create their own 'packages'. Yet this is a complicated business, requiring time, skill and theoretical understanding – for instance, Ron Jones describes qualities needed in the CAL 'packages':

> Such skills as problem-solving, decision-making . . . divergent as well as convergent thinking skills, such as flexibility, fluency, originality, preference for the complex.[40]

The writing of the CAL packages is a problem – at the moment they are generally agreed to lack quality or be inapplicable to the United Kingdom because of their cultural specificity (made in the USA etc.). The skills that are needed in the 'packages' can only come from experienced teachers as will the recognized capability to alter and improve the 'packages' in the school.[41]

This process appears to be an accumulation of the workers' knowledge, absorbed into the memory of the machine; it is also more than just factual knowledge – it is the experience and thought, the creative aspects of teaching which are so absorbed. The experience of teaching over many years may be built into the machine memory which can then reproduce that experience at will in many situations where the 'package' is used. The problem though is that in education, and particularly the computing education lobby, this process is not recognized – a process which could lead to the replacement of the teacher. The lack of forethought, the naïvety of statements is exemplified by the passing reference to the fact that computers may be programmed to have:

> the human attitudes of humour, warmth, criticism . . . patience and praise.[42]

Given that this high-flown enthusiasm has echoes of past, now-deceased developments in education (like programmed learning), it is still taken increasingly seriously in the way it will re-skill some teachers and possibly even replace others. As the NAS/UWT recently noted:

> The time and expertise involved in writing a major educational proramme for a computerized system are equivalent to the time and expertise involved in writing a textbook.[43]

In other words, most teachers will not be involved in this conception process. They will be plugging into CAL modules or perhaps fiddling new learning sequences from 'sub-routines' devised elsewhere. Their relationship to the new technology is clear:

> no teacher is expected to have a detailed knowledge of computer technology, maintenance, operation or telecommunications systems. They and their students are expected to use the computer as a natural extension to their daily work.[44]

But as computer application in industry demonstrates, the technology appropriates skill from the worker and even worker consciousness; as Mike Cooley shows in computer-assisted design, thought on the part of the worker (in this case, the draughtsman or architect) is a positive disadvantage:

> it is a tool for silencing the common sense and creativity of the skilled worker.[45]

The machine controls the pace, content and form of the work. The worker is an appendage. Job evaluation, for instance the time necessary to complete operations, is known to the computer. The worker does not know what else the computer knows – whether or not there is a reliability of performance check, etc. It is difficult to retain those qualitative aspects of work, as Cooley notes, when faced with a controlled, quantitative output. For the re-skilled, some work will be initially created in programme-making or certain specialized school applications (timetabling). Birmingham has, since 1974, had a team of computer specialist teachers who, on a peripatetic basis, train teachers in schools to operate the large investment in computerization now under way in the LEA: they attend to faults in the computer but also offer 'advice' to teachers on CAL packages or related software (books or courses). Their status to the class teacher, even the new re-skilled computer teachers, is that of a specialist – knowing the system, its alternatives and functions – and controlling access to learning materials.

Within the school, the increased use of microprocessors will lead to the creation of a new management or supervisory position – providing special assistance to the teachers, scheduling equipment and giving teachers an on-the-job training.

As falling rolls and secondary reorganization continues, with the demand for shortage subjects, the claims for computer applications, especially the new microprocessors, increase – Harry MacMahon explains this clearly:

> The greater the number of students, the wider the range of curricular materials, the more intensive the progress monitoring, the more widely dispersed the students, the smaller the staff/student ratio, the more heterogenous the student population, the greater the management problems and correspondingly, the greater gains to be made through computer assisted management of the learning system.[46]

Computer applications, are ideally suited to the split-site school (with mixed ability, overcrowded classes, few teachers and in-built assessment procedures) and so is the de-skilled teacher. Quality control, as an LEA Inspector explained to us recently, is the job of the Inspectorate.

Incidentally there is one other familiar aspect of computer application; it is undertaken in intensive shiftwork. Mike Cooley has noted the trend to shiftwork and the consequent social and personal disruption it causes. Shiftwork is necessary to justify the investment in the technology and also because it is capable of continuous operation. A recent article in *Computers in Schools* mentions this possibility:

> The whole role of the school may have to be redefined in future curriculum development. One possibility is a much stronger link between schools and the outside world whereby subjects are offered to shift workers with free time, housewives or the elderly, on a drop-in-and-learn basis. The traditional classroom approach would obviously be of no use here as groups would vary in size, ability, motivation and subject interest. But using a microcomputer with multiple terminal access would enable each user to select one of a group of subjects of specific difficulty whilst the teacher would act in a tutorial capacity.[47]

The school could extend its hours and reorganize itself to cope with shiftwork. Computer appreciation courses for the local community, for instance, would need evening shiftwork – an American High School computer project found it

> feasible to offer night courses in programming to community members (to) small business operators and others, such as (the) county engineer and the business manager of the local hospital . . .[48]

As the NAS/UWT makes clear, in the not too distant future, tuition in some shortage departments will be undertaken by computers, and as computerized instruction costs drop so

> it would be foolhardy to assume that . . . an evaluation (comparing the effectiveness of teachers versus machines) would result in the continued employment of large numbers of teachers.[49]

Our argument then is that the labour process in schools will increasingly resemble, as part of a continuous, historical process, work in factories and offices. Workforce flexibility, quality control, de-skilling and re-skilling are now, in effect, in schools.

Alongside the technological change in work, there has been a consequent reaffirmation of employer control over the labour process. Self-evaluation documents are now common in local education authority schools; job definition, from head-teachers to class teachers, is becoming clearer as are supervisory duties and hierarchies. Appointment with a specified job contract, necessary for evaluation and dismissal purposes, is common.

The particular crisis and restructuring of the education service should not be studied to the exclusion of deeper, long term processes affecting teachers. The present policies of recent governments seem to be aiming for increased teacher productivity, increased control over the work content of teaching and a tentative movement to fixed term contracts and job specification.

Conclusion

Our arguments centre around ways of seeing teachers' work in common with other kinds of work – as a means of survival (paid employment) and as a service. Value is created by work but only the employer sees value in entirely financial terms.

Professionalism among teachers could be seen as an expression of service to the community, common to other kinds of work; as an expression of skill or craft or expertise; as an expression of the defence of either or both of these elements. It may also be seen as an externally created force, binding the teachers into a particular view of their work. We have suggested that each view may have a different base amongst teachers and may have had dominance in their work at different historical periods. It may indeed be losing its grip on some teachers altogether. It is neither a reactionary nor a progressive force in all its elements; different versions of it may oppose each other.

The education service has not been seen merely in terms of the imposition of employer or State demands, either implicitly or explicitly, even though these have often prevailed. It has also been seen by teachers as of value for their own purposes, expressed in terms of provision, quality or access; purposes which were often not just theirs, but an expression of a service commitment. Professionalism is, in part, an attempt socially to construct 'skill'; autonomy was, in part, the creation of a defensive space around that 'skill' by teachers.

Class we have proposed as a relational concept, involving ideological, historical and social factors, and as an historical process. We have also tried to discuss the labour process, the economic or material base of this historical process. It is obvious from our discussion that the main contradiction, for us, must always be the one between the employer and employee. During this paper, we have not referred to other contradictions in detail, but no complete historical examination of teachers could exclude the changing relations between the male/female, secondary/elementary and rural/urban teachers, amongst others.

We have tried as part of the explanation of teacher development to bring together disparate information on the changing nature of the labour process, and to draw attention to the effects of computerization. It may be that teachers really cannot be treated in this way and we must start with Althusserian arguments or develop notions of the bureaucratic state but our *feeling* would be that enough attention has gone into dividing teachers from others in the Labour movement. We must begin by seeing congruencies as well as looking at contradictions – and the latter must always be sensitively assessed in order not to *create* new divisions.

There are many questions this short paper did not treat directly, through lack of space. One of these would be the interesting notion of autonomy and, obviously, we would not see it as entirely state-given nor as a middle class responsibility – we would have to include the notion of defensible space in the social construction of skill which is created in the school and in political or educational alliance. The first real attempt to reduce autonomy might not be from within the Green Paper debate, but may come from necessary standardization of some teacher work which will precede its mechanization.

The implications of this tentative analysis in areas associated with teaching have not been stressed despite their immediacy in the particular crisis in education today, which does not need describing here.

The fields of curriculum studies and educational administration, both involved in response to the crisis, depend in the main on the simplistic notions of professionalism, class and work which we have criticized. The recent national curriculum debate was held without any explanation as to where teacher autonomy *originated,* but assumed that it was a *bad thing* – again this could easily fit in with the views of the radical sociologists and the radical Tories! If teachers were viewed in other ways, we have suggested, new explanations for their behaviour might be sought and more complex analyses generated in the disciplines mentioned, and though this is obviously not our principal objective in putting forward this argument, it might offer a beneficial side-effect!

In this paper we have not, perhaps, countered the points made by neo-Marxist and other analyses; what we have done is suggest that there are other questions which should at least be raised and their implications explored. In stating our case we have taken on complex issues and condensed a great deal of complex material. We recognize these deficiencies in the paper, but emphasise that it is a position paper produced with the intention of provoking discussion and at least raising an alternative to what has become an orthodoxy of the right and the left. Much further careful empirical and theoretical work needs to be done.

During this paper we have taken issue with dominant ideas about professionalism as applied to teachers. We have argued for complexity and contradiction in applying this term and for one way of interpreting it – as a means of control and defence over the labour process. It was not our purpose here to argue that the term 'professionalism' however interpreted is sufficient explanation for all teacher ideas and actions. Sometimes the term is itself rejected as being insular or irrelevant by teachers – this is not just a recent phenomenon. This we see as not in contradiction to our argument, but a further extension of it.

References

1 GINSBURG, M., MEYENN, R. and MILLER, H. (1980) 'Teachers' conceptions of professionalism and trades unionism: An ideological analysis' in WOODS, P. (Ed) *Teacher Strategies: Explorations in the Sociology of the School* Croom Helm.
2 *ibid* p. 80
3 PARRY, N. and PARRY, J. (1974) 'The teachers and professionalism: The failure of an occupational strategy' in FLUDE, M. and AHIER, J. (Eds) *Educability, Schools and Ideology* Croom Helm.
4 *ibid*
5 TROPP, A. (1957) *The Schoolteachers* Heinemann.
6 OZGA, J. and LAWN, M. (1981) *Teachers, Professionalism and Class* Falmer Press.
7 Introduction – 'People's Autobiography of Hackney', 1976, *Working Lives, Volume 1, 1905-1945* Centreprise.
8 FINN, D., GRANT, N. and JOHNSON, R. (1977) 'Social democracy, education and the crisis' *Working Papers on Cultural Studies* 10, *'On Ideology'*, Centre for Contemporary Cultural Studies.
9 For example, ALTHUSSER, L. (1972) 'Ideology and ideological state apparatuses' in COSIN, B. (Ed) *Education: Structure and Society* Penguin; POULANTZAS, N. (1975) *Classes in Contemporary Capitalism* New Left Books; WRIGHT, E.O. (1978) *Class, Crisis and the State* New Left Books.
10 See CROMPTON, R. and GUBBAY, J. (1977) *Economy and Class Structure* Macmillan.
11 HUNT, A. (1977) 'Theory and politics in the identification of the working class', in HUNT, A. (Ed) *Class and Class Structure* Lawrence and Wishart.
12 APPLE, M. (1981) 'Curricular form and the logic of technical control: Building the possessive individual' in BARTON, L., MEIGHAN, R. and WALKER, S. (Eds) *Schooling, Ideology and Curriculum* Falmer Press.
13 THOMPSON, E.P. (1978) 'Folklore, anthropology and social history', *Indian Historical Review* Volume III, Number 2.
14 *ibid* pp. 20–21.
15 SIMON, B. (1974) *The Politics of Educational Reform 1920-1940* Lawrence and Wishart, pp. 72–74.
16 Part of continuing Ph.D research project (Lawn), on teachers and the Labour movement.
17 GRACE, G. (1978) *Teachers, Ideology and Control* Routledge and Kegan Paul.
18 CROMPTON, R. (1976) 'Approaches to the study of white collar unionism' *Sociology, Volume 10, Number 3.*
19 BOWLES, S. and GINTIS, H. (1976) *Schooling in Capitalist America* Routledge and Kegan Paul.
20 CALLAHAN, R. (1976) *Education and the Cult of Efficiency* New York, Free Press.
21 PERCY, LORD E. (1958) *Some Memoires* London, Eyre and Spottiswoode.
22 *ibid* p. 123.
23 WHITE, J. (1975) 'The end of the compulsory curriculum' in 'The Curriculum – The Doris Lee Lectures' 1975, University of London, *Studies in Education* 2.
24 BRAVERMAN, H. (1974) *Labour and Monopoly Capital* Monthly Review Press.
25 A summary of part of Braverman's work in ZIMBALIST, A. (Ed) (1979) *Case Studies in the Labour Process* Monthly Review Press, pp. xv, xvi.
26 An interesting discussion of this approach is in MORE, C. (1980) *Skill and the English Working Class 1870-1914* Croom Helm.
27 BRAVERMAN, H. (1974) *op. cit.*, p. 305.
28 *ibid* p. 319.
29 ARONOWITZ, S. (1973) *False Promises – the Shaping of the American Working Class Consciousness* McGraw Hill, p. 301.
30 H.M. INSPECTORATE/DES (1980) *Aspects of Secondary Education in England* HMSO, p. 61.

31 Evidence for 'flexibility' of teaching staff is growing especially in literature related to 'falling rolls', i.e. BRIAULT, E. (1980) *Falling Rolls in Secondary Schools* Slough, NFER; SHAW, K. (1977) 'Managing the curriculum in contraction' and LIGHTFOOT, M. (1977) 'The educational consequences of falling rolls' both in RICHARDS, C. *Power and the Curriculum* Nafferton.

32 HM INSPECTORATE/DES (1980) *op. cit.*, p. 133.

33 BUSWELL, C. (1980) 'Social change and pedagogic change' in *British Journal of Sociology of Education,* 2 (3).

34 APPLE, M. (1981) *op. cit.*

35 CASEY, T. (1980) Secretary of the NAS/UWT, quoted in *Times Educational Supplement* December.

36 KYRIACOU, C. (1980) 'Occupational stress among schoolteachers: a research report', CORE.

37 *ibid.*

38 APPLE, M. (1981) *op. cit.*

39 BROOKSBANK, K. (1980) (Ed) (Society of Education Officers), *Educational Administration,* Councils and Education Press, p. 107.

40 JONES, R. (1980) 'Microcomputers; their uses in primary schools', *Cambridge Journal of Education,* Volume 10, Number 3.

41 *ibid,* and JOINER, L.M., SILVERSTEIN, B.J. and ROSS, J.D. (1980) 'Insights from a Microcomputer Centre in a Rural School District' in *Educational Technology* Volume XX, Number 5, May.

42 JONES, R. (1980) *op. cit.*

43 NAS/UWT (1980) 'Micro-electronics: Is there a future for teachers?' NAS/UWT, December.

44 TINSLEY, D. (1978) 'Educational computing facilities in Birmingham' *Trends in Education* Volume number 2, HMSO.

45 COOLEY, M. (1980) *Architect or Bee? The Human/Technology Relationship* Hand and Brain Publishing.

46 MACMAHON, H. (1978) 'Computer managed learning – the newly accessible educational technology', *Trends in Education* Volume 2.

47 COOKE, B. (1980) 'The microcomputer in the classroom', *Computers in Schools* Volume 2, Number 7.

48 JOINER, L.M., SILVERSTEIN, B.J. and ROSS, J.D. *op. cit.*

49 NAS/UWT (1980) *op. cit.*

Politicians Rule O.K.? Implications for Teacher Careers and School Management

Colin Hunter, Leeds Polytechnic

The year 1974 is a suitable date to identify as marking the commencement of a significant shift in the definition of the career of teaching and the place of the education system in our society. It was the year of local government reorganization; of two fiercely fought general elections in the aftermath of the miners and power workers strikes and the three day week; and it was the time of a growing awareness of the economic consequences of the oil price rises. From that year the economic crisis was mirrored in the changes of available resources for education by the decreasing ability of teachers and educationalists to define the use of these resources, and in their declining status *vis-à-vis* the economic and political structure of society. The most significant variable in this change, I suggest, has been the increasing overt politicization of education. This paper seeks to sketch the logic inherent in the development of the current situation of teachers and schools first by identifying the larger political context in which the education crisis is manifest; second, by relating some of the consequences for and strategies of teachers in coping with their changing position; third in identifying some unintended consequences and possible space for alternative developments which the contradictions of the present government policy are generating; and lastly to place the tensions identified in the educational field within a wider and crucially important political debate.

The Political Context

The present government policies can be viewed as a radical solution for capitalist survival. Their relative extremism has helped to clarify the often opaque connections between the economic, political and educational systems. It needs to be stressed, however, that these policies, especially with regard to education, are a more rigorous extension of the policy directions of the previous Labour Party administration. They are a logical outcome of upholding the dominant interests within monopoly or corporate capitalism.

Two of the main aspects of corporate capitalism are the centralization of capital and the increasing bureaucratization of its organization, serviced by an increasingly elaborate financial superstructure. These developments took place in the industrial sector as the state widened the scope of its functions in order to maintain the conditions for capital accumulation. There is then an interesting connection between the politician and the capitalist in that the holders of state offices must, in their own interest, maintain and support the accumulation process because the State's revenue, and hence the very power of the State's officers, depends on it. The government must therefore not only stay within the limits imposed by the requirements of the accumulation process, but, as the society becomes more complex, take on a new range of functions in promoting the accumulation process itself.

There is therefore less potential and actual tension in the policy formulation of capitalist parties of the Right than there is for those parties which attempt, in part at least, to present non-capitalist or Socialist alternatives within a capitalist framework. For the latter to compromise is to accept the definitions of reality of the Right, but not to compromise is to declare a revolutionary intent which would almost certainly be a recipe for electoral self-destruction. Perhaps this is the core of the explanation of the lack of greater success of egalitarian socialism through the efforts of the Labour Party in Britain. Its social democratic ideology has concentrated, not on changing the reward structure based on a market mechanism, but on alleviating the effects of the market on those who suffer most – through welfare provisions – and in trying to give a fairer distribution of opportunities for gaining the well rewarded positions. So Barbara Castle in 1975 maintains that:

> The most important part of the standard of living of most of us depends on the great complex of services we call 'public expenditure'. They are not only the key to the quality of life, they are the key to equality . . . the great advances . . . have come from better education, better health services, better housing and the better care of the old, the disabled and the handi-capped in life.[1]

The total social wage rose as a proportion of consumption (not to be confused with total wealth) from a third in the mid-fifties (33% in 1955) to three fifths in the early 1970s (59% in 1973).[2] This growth was not based on the premise of funda-mentally redistributing wealth, but of allocating a larger slice to the 'underclass' by increasing the size of the national cake. It involves a substantiating of the process of capital accumulation (mostly private accumulation) and is the basis of the deep con-tradiction in social democratic ideology of the twin goals of efficiency and social justice. It means that on the one hand there is a commitment to rules governing un-equal distribution while, on the other hand, it is ideologically committed to im-proving the material levels of those who stand to lose by the application of those very rules.

But what happens when the national cake stops growing quickly enough to fulfill the expectations already generated? In 1974 this situation was triggered off by the raising of oil prices and the effects of the three day week. Initially there is an economic crisis, but because of the increasing government involvement in the economy, the struggles over wages and profits are translated from the economic to the political sphere. This unmasks the crisis avoidance strategies of deflating class conflict by keeping increases in wages higher than the level of prices; that is, by allowing wage negotiations relatively to improve the standard of living for the disen-franchised classes at the cost of 'civic privatization'.[3] This involves, for the underclasses, the acceptance of the system as a whole within which they pursue private based goals. The strain of these strategies in an economic crisis is made manifest in wage disputes, high inflation and a crisis in government finances and balance of trade figures. This produces, in the political field, a rationality crisis in coping with these economic problems. Since 1974, this has involved social spending cuts, higher unemployment, stricter social control and calls for a more efficient reproduction of the workforce. All of these aspects have had a considerable effect on the education system and are the basis of the increasingly overt politicization of education. However, as Habermas, O'Connor, Adams and Daniel Bell[4] have pointed out (from differing viewpoints), the effects of the rationality crisis and the consequent policy decisions can intensify a legitimation crisis in the political system which relates in a dialectical fashion to a motivational crisis in the socio-cultural system. I argue here that it is the workings of the latter crisis which produces potential space for alternative answers to those of government in response to the rationality crisis, and in part are actually generated by the contradictions within the present governments severely instrumental ideology.

Effects in Education

Before 1974, and especially in the 1960s, the education system was characterized by expansion, and such reforms as comprehensive reorganization, ROSLA, enhancement of teacher training facilities, and other aspects of higher education, stemmed from policies based on the firm goals of greater equality and efficiency. Since then the post economic crisis period has been dominated by the need for politically directed education to service industry more efficiently, but at the same time with less resources at their disposal. An early warning of this emphasis was given by Shirley Williams when Minister of Education and Science, at the North of England Conference in January 1977:

> We must find the most effective ways of using a budget, which, though large, is no longer increasing in real terms; and we must redeploy the resources of teachers and buildings released as a result of the declining birthrate.
>
> All this would be a big enough programme of work for the next five years. But it will not suffice. For, perhaps partly as a reaction to the speed of change in education, many voices of criticism have been raised, about standards of achievement in schools, about discipline, about the quality of teaching . . .
>
> I am convinced we have resources enough to make our next priority an improvement in the quality of our education parallel to the remarkable improvement in its quantity that I have already outlined . . .
>
> The juxtaposition in our country of one of the longest periods of compulsory education in the world with a poor record of low productivity, low growth, low investment, and indifferent design and marketing skills must make us all reflect.

The major thrust of the Great Debate of 1976 and 1977 was a systematic attempt by the Labour Government to wrest the populist mantle from the Conservatives in answering the critics that the previous spending on education had failed to deliver the goods. It also capitalized on the legitimation crisis which had been affecting education as exampled in the William Tyndale Case; the Bennett study on teaching methods; the quandary teachers found themselves in regarding whether or not to act as trade unionists or professional associations; and conflicts in expectations and values which were being made evident within the large school staffs of the comprehensives, as, for instance, exampled in some of David Hargreaves' work.[5]

The consensus between politicians, teachers and educationalists of the 1960s had, by this period, evaporated and this gave the opportunity for politicians to legitimize their intervention in the educational process to a far greater extent than they had been able to do previously. This they did with alacrity under the umbrella of 'accountability' and with supporting slogans such as 'declining standards', 'insufficient attention to the basic subjects', 'ineffective discipline' and 'questionable teaching methods'. The underlying rationale of all this was efficiency, as exemplified in the significant Green Paper 'Education in Schools' of 1977:

> Underlying all this (criticism of schools) was the feeling that the educational system was out of touch with the fundamental need for Britain to survive economically in a highly competitive world through the efficiency of its industry and commerce. (p. 2)

and later

> It is vital to Britain's economic recovery and standard of living that the performance of manufacturing industry is improved and that the whole range of Government policies, including education, contribute as much as possible to improving industrial performance and thereby increasing the national wealth. (p. 6)

So trends are perceived in the Labour Party policies which focused on 'efficiency' rather than 'social justice'. It was these same trends which were later intensified considerably by the Conservative government of 1979. These included cuts in real terms of spending over the whole range of educational activity and often legitimized by reference to falling rolls; a growing governmental influence in curriculum and public examination policy; and government administered testing or monitoring of specified subjects at various ages. More recently, the severe strain placed upon the schools meal service; the potential loss of many teachers' jobs by compulsory redundancy; the fall in the availability of discretionary awards; the growing number of potential school closures; and the initial small 1981 teachers' wage offer are some of the immediate results of the reduction of resources available through the more standardized Block Grant System, the new Capital Expenditure control system and the capping of the Higher Education Pool. Perhaps the clearest example of the changing status and potency of teachers is the current negotiations for a conditions of service agreement. Teacher Unions and Association have shown themselves split in their approach to management and, because of the contraction of the service, they have less sanctions to bargain with than they had when previous discussions on this topic took place in 1970–71.

But even what constitutes management is shifting and becoming more centralized. The new Block Grant System involves the government in needing and receiving greater information of what the authority is doing before it decides what level of rates should be given for the next year. As John Cretton (1980) remarks, 'the more central government looks in detail at what each Authority is doing, the greater its capacity for control, and the direr the threat to local independence'. There is, therefore, a changing relationship of power with regard to central and local government which is restricting the ability of manoeuvre of the latter. A consequence of this is that as the availability of funds becomes tighter, their redistribution by local authorities to educational local services becomes increasingly based on political rather than educational criteria, and has had the effect of undermining to a great extent the broad political consensus in educational management at Town and City Hall that has been evident since the second world war.[6] This growing antagonism is fanned by the overt ideological actions of the present government with the introduction of such policies as the Assisted Places Schemes; by their attacks on mixed ability teaching and Mode 3 examinations; and the support for more standardized curricula examinations, for different (and defined) ability groups. Increasingly therefore there is much evidence to suggest a greater tension between the political, bureaucratic elements in education (dominated by coping with economic constraints) and the professional requirements and standards of teachers within schools. Increasing demands are being made on the outcome of teaching in schools with regard to accountability and aspects relating to industrial efficiency, while the resources offered to fulfil the increasingly specified goals are systematically being pared back.

Effects on Teachers

Teachers are therefore under external pressure. However, this pressure is made all the more acute in that it is imposed directly within the terms of reference which they had already identified as being basic to maintaining and enlarging their professional competence. These can be classified in the three main areas of general status, teacher/pupil ratios and career structure.

A particular aspect of post war teacher rhetoric (though not only exclusive to this period) has been their repeated request that they require public esteem in order to be able to fulfil their all important educative task. Their prestige has usually been linked to the status of education as a whole within the community and society.[7] The recent frontal attacks on their efficiency, particularly regarding 'standards', by government, industry and media; and the lowering of resources and salaries in real terms has made most problematic the existence of the required status. For example, Boyson (1975 p. 28) confidently equates low salaries with 'the low esteem in which teachers are held by the rest of society'. This cannot be dismissed merely as a persuasive ideological definition for, whatever its veracity, it has to be viewed as an authoritative ideological definition as its proponent holds a significant position in education in a Government which has the ability and intention to act as if it were true.

The second area involves the lowering of the teacher/pupil ratio which teachers have consistently campaigned for to improve both the context for learning and their working conditions. They have done this at the same time as negotiating for more pay. Both strategies are in direct contradiction of the present ruling definition of educational management which is rationalized in terms of 'savings' and 'efficiency'. The greatest proportion of educational spending is teacher salaries so that those areas which have campaigned most successfully in the past for smaller teacher/pupil ratios now face the greatest threat of both compulsory redundancies and the raising of present teacher/pupil ratios.

In the third area, the Burnham teacher career structure, which was painstakingly constructed to gain as much advantage as possible from an expanding service, is now experienced as a demotivating factor in a contracting situation. Falling rolls decrease the possible posts for promotion, particularly for the newer entrants to the profession both within and between schools, and this is exacerbated by the trend of a smaller proportion of teachers leaving the profession.[8] The main bottleneck is between Scales 2 and 3[9] but in a contracting situation this will become even more problematic in the future.

This was supported in a recent study of West Yorkshire schools affected by falling rolls (Hunter and Heighway 1980) where much of the evidence could be related to Becker's ideas of career (Becker 1976 and 1977). In this he links the notion of 'situational adjustment', in which individuals take on the characteristics defined by their situational constraints, with that of 'commitment'. If the actor has developed a secure and non threatening situational adjustment, the commitment will be directed to preserving the *status quo*. The many illustrations of this strategy in the study, which reflected the effect of adaptation to the overt politicized control mentioned above were highlighted in three main forms.

First, there was much evidence of teachers ensconced in their positions with few opportunities of moving either between schools or within their present school, complaining of becoming 'stale' or 'falling into a rut'. Heads talked of much of the curriculum becoming 'fossilized' and long term aims being lost in the *ad hoc* solving of immediate contingencies.

Second, many teachers who had positions of seniority defined within the terms of the prevailing structure were antagonistic towards suggestions for any change to that structure if it entailed a questionning of their prestige or a threat to their authority. Indeed it was argued that the relatively greater resources and opportunities at the disposal of higher scale staff were used towards maintaining their own motivation often at the expense of those below them.[10] In some schools, on the other hand, there had emerged a clear division between the younger and older staff. The former were involved with the children organizing field studies, trips, camping, drama, music activities and so on, while the latter, with higher responsibility allowances for administrative duties involving a lower timetable commitment, were seemingly able to fulfil their obligations without much effort. This was an obvious source of frustration for the younger staff concerned, particularly as the contraction of the service lessens the promotion currency of involvement in extra curricula activities.

Third, there was clear evidence that a number of teachers, reacting to the constraints confronting them, opted out to a greater or lesser extent by focusing their search for personal fulfilment elsewhere than in the school or classroom. The 'moonlighting' jobs undertaken, the non-education courses enrolled in, and the involvement with other outside school interests were often complemented by a growing instrumental attitude to the teaching jobs. These are some examples in which the effects of authority and decision making at the macro level are seen to affect the teacher at the chalk face. They are examples of how, in part, the education system is adapting to the political, economic and demographic contingencies and constraints which lie outside the control of the school and educationalists.

Contradictions and Possible Space for Manoeuvre?

The picture presented is only a partial one, however. It is argued by Gramsci, for example, that every dominant culture, or hegemony, has within itself its own contradictions which often present space for emergent alternative or oppositional characteristics and movements. (See Williams 1976). Some contradictions in the implementation of the present government's policy are already becoming identifiable.

The options open to the Tories on making schools accountable was either through a nationally enforced curriculum or parental choice or a combination of both. The 1979 Education Bill shows that they are going for the 'combination' option, but first priority was given to parental involvement. As Carlisle wrote, 'our parents' charter will place a clear obligation on central government and on local authorities to take account of parents' wishes when allocating children to schools, and requiring all schools to publish prospectuses giving details of their examinations and other results'.

The idea is to force schools – in the context of falling rolls and potential closures and a more active Assessment of Performance Unit – to compete for parental favour and thereby, it is thought, subject them to a popular demand for 'basic' education and 'higher' academic standards. Although on the statute books, the process of implementation is already slowing down because the expense of producing the prospectuses in time and money is much greater than the resources that other departments and policies of the government are willing to give local authorities. Indeed, the Block Grant awards of December 1980 for the 1981–82 local authority budgets require Councils to spend less in real terms than previous years, and the scheme has a built-in mechanism which gives the opportunity to 'claw back' grant from those authorities who spend more than these lower levels calculated by the government. This aspect of the Bill has therefore been deferred at present by the DES. Their curriculum plans and their recommendations for the schooling of handicapped children face similar difficulties. The 'Framework for the Curriculum' is unprecedented in that it challenges the position of local authorities which are given clear responsibility for the curriculum in the present system. However, the plans for a common core curriculum involving substantial changes will be nullified if not complemented by extra resources and, because of the government's economic policy, these are not forthcoming.[11] Similarly the August 1980 White Paper 'Special Needs in Education', while close to the educational ethos of the Warnock Report, requires large resource imputs. It has been estimated in one northern Metropolitan District that £773,900 was required per year for administration and support service costs in setting up and maintaining the specified registers and activities. However, in Section 38 of the White Paper it states:

> The development of the education service will need to take place within the financial limits set by the public expenditure plans which the Government has announced.

The most optimistic it can be is that the present 'modest' levels of spending in this area will not fall.

> The Government's plans for a reduced total level of public expenditure on education assume that the level of expenditure on special education under existing arrangements will not be reduced in real terms up to 1983–84.
> (Section 20).

The educational aims of the Report are thus negated by the contradictory economic policies.

There are other aspects of policy which have negative connotations for the government. After the cuts of December 1980, the Secretary of State for Education and Science, Mark Carlisle, implicitly admitted that they would detrimentally affect standards.[12] It could be argued that this is directly contradictory to the manifesto pledge twenty months previously which stated that 'we will give each child the chance to progress as far as his or her abilities allow'. The enlarged HMI Report in February 1981 which looked specifically at the effects of cuts on schools, also proved to be an embarrassment to the government. (See *Education* 20.2.81, p. 160 'Mr Carlisle alone finds solace in the cuts findings').

The 1981 teachers' pay award of 7% in the light of the 6% cash limit policy could add fuel for potential teacher intransigence, especially as teachers still possess the sanction of refusal to do dinner duty which is still not part of any conditions of service agreement.

On a broader scale, by cutting the social wage and shifting the emphasis from direct to indirect taxation, the government are overtly penalizing those less able to afford the rising cost of services. In education, parents are being asked to contribute much more to school meals, visits, books, raw materials for practical work and so forth. This could conceivably accentuate social class differences and the heightening of consciousness of differentials could detrimentally affect the government's future election prospects.

A positive possible educational unintended consequence of government policies concerns an outcome of the existence of the large number of young unemployed. It has given local authorities a significant impetus in producing more comprehensive 16–19 tertiary systems. Although this was not a high priority in the Conservative Party programme, the government is providing substantial resources indirectly through the Manpower Services Commission, making it one of the few growth areas in education today. Although on the surface such initiatives could be seen as only alleviating and hiding the full extent of the unemployed situation, they could also act as important initiatives in disseminating the consciousness and structure for recurrent education which may be necessary in beginning to come to terms with structural unemployment – a concomitant of the increasing introduction of micro-technology. It needs to be stressed that the latter effect would be an unintended consequence of government policy and that contradictions are at work in the present situation which may have positive connotations for future development.

Besides this necessarily conjectural analysis of contradictions at a macro level, there are signs of more positive, alternative interpretations to schooling and teaching emerging as a consequence of the effects of cuts and falling rolls at the school level, as evidenced in the West Yorkshire study. Some schools met the challenge of less resources by emphasizing greater resourcefulness which often involved tremendous improvization from staff members. In this approach power is not regarded in zero-sum terms whereby there is only a certain 'amount' available for distribution in a hierarchical and mechanistic structure. Power is regarded as expandable and, if not shared explicity through appointments to hierarchical positions, it is generated in a more open organic structure whereby involvement and opportunities for initiative are given to the whole staff regardless of organizational status – in short, there is less situational adjustment but situations are adjusted. One example found was the 'negotiated' timetable in which participation is inbuilt into the organizational structure. In this, the year heads are in charge of a year group's timetable and they have to consult with heads of departments and/or individual staff for their time; or departments and/or individual teachers offer 'packages' to negotiate with year-heads their preferred timetable. The necessary co-operative spirit between teachers to make this open form of organization viable is constantly alluded to by most of the staff interviewed, usually in a positive manner. It is acknowledged here that there are potential weaknesses that such 'creative turbulence' could engender. For example too much turbulence can be demotivating; and the line between genuine and pseudo-participation is often difficult to identify. (See Hunter 1979 a). However, such a fundamentally based change in attitudes as described could be a basis for opening up quite different questions about the management of schools and to cause a rethinking of previously taken for granted assumptions.

Is the position of Head too central and dominating in the running of schools? Why are ongoing training schemes for Heads not part of their contract? Might short term contracts for Heads and teachers be a possibility? Might it be possible to move a proportion of teachers and Heads around different schools to try to engender turbulence and alleviate the possible silting up effects of static staffs? Might school-based or school-focused in-service training become an integral part of the ongoing organization of the school? Might the whole concept of 'career' in the teaching profession be reviewed? Instead of the Burnham system, which is basically geared to expansion, might a more flexible arrangement be formulated which could simplify the often elaborate structures of school management and give greater recognition to those who retain a full teaching timetable? Dudley Fiske (1979) suggests that a possible way is to give teachers a basic career grade which is adequately remunerated, and then the posts of responsibility could be recognized instead by a reduction of timetable and teaching loads instead of extra payments. Might such a system offer greater possibilities for posts of responsibility to be rotated round the staff thereby offering greater involvement and participation for a greater number of teachers? To what extent should Local Authorities help: by making available staff developmental tutors; by encouraging developmental curriculum teams from a number of schools; by motivating schools in the planning to meet the needs of falling schools? What should the role of the local advisors, or HMIs be? What should their relation be to elected members? What should be the relationship of local to central governments?

The important point is not these particular questions, but that teachers and educationalists in experiencing the tensions of the present situation, could question and challenge the *status quo* which in turn could offer alternative and oppositional directions to the dominant policy thrusts, and indeed could be facilitated by the effects of the contradictions inherent in the present ruling policies. Above all it needs to be understood that edicts of central or local government are necessarily a one way process and that there are limits to the efficiency of administrative policy implementation. They may highlight, or at best suppress, but not resolve the belief and motivation crises. Truancy, maladjustment, lack of motivation, radical alternatives, non-economic instrumental goals will not disappear because governments enforce a core curriculum and monitor national standards in the interests of British industry, or because local authorities pass on government cuts in a disingenuous manner.

The Main Political Issue

But this tension is reflected at a higher level in the changes manifested in our life styles by accelerating technological developments which will potentially alter the level at which people are able to control their own lives. The crucial issue revolves around the accepted interpretation of democracy – whether it is to remain representative or become more participative. A fuller discussion of the consequences of each type appears elsewhere (see Hunter 1979 b) but, briefly, the former encourages the dominance of hierarchical systems, civic privatization, and an accent on specialists which could conceivably lead to a benevolent totalitarianism or more probably to a welfare-state authoritarian conservatism if the vast communication and information processing facilities are controlled by a small élite – a combination of 1984 and Brave New World.

Alternatively there is evidence of movements towards participative democracy in such activities as community politics, industrial democracy and the feminist, anti-racialist, conservationist, and anti-nuclear lobbies. In education this latter emphasis is seen in the emphasis in teaching pupils how to think rather than what to think; in seeking to confront rather than adapt to the present *status quo* as outlined in this paper.

Ultimately it now means that we as educationaists have to become politicized, to seek to define and work for alternative interpretations of the aims and goals of education. To remain neutral is positively to accept the *status quo* and to adapt to the present dominant policy structure. Perhaps an understanding of the present political situation should not merely be an academic exercise but part of a foundation for committed action.

Notes

1 Cited by Paul Adams.
2 See Hansard July 15th 1975.
3 The term is from HABERMAS, J. (see 1976 p. 75) as is the identification of the connections between the economic, rationality, legitimation and motivation crises (see p. 49) See also PATEMAN, T. (1978).
4 HABERMAS, J. *op. cit;* O'CONNOR, J. (1976) *The Fiscal Crisis of the State* St. Martins Press; ADAMS, P. *op. cit.;* BELL, D. (1974) 'The Public Interest' Fall.
5 This was also the period when Jencks (in *Inequality*) and the plethora of social and cultural reproduction theorists on the sociology of education were emphasizing the irrelevancy and inability of the educational system in promoting directed change in society, thereby reflecting and adding to the legitimation crisis.
6 Note for example that many Labour-held Authorities in the 1950s and early 1960s preferred to keep their grammar schools as the best route for social mobility of the bright working class pupils. Also later in 1960s comprehensivization was introduced by many Conservative controlled Authorities.
7 See for example BURKE, V. (1971) *Teachers in Turmoil* particularly Part 3 Chapter 1 p. 127.
8 In 1972 9.5% of teachers left teaching and a further 11% changed schools. In 1976, wastage was 6.5% and the turnover rates had halved. See DES (1977) *Education in Schools* Page 16.
9 Numbers of teachers in Primary and Secondary Schools 1977: Scale 1. 135,800; Scale 2. 149,400; Scale 3. 60,200; Scale 4. 25,900; Senior Teachers. 5,300.
10 One example of this was the Scale 2 teacher who said: 'We are supposed to be mixed ability, but the year leader keeps the bright children for himself. I know what he's doing. I suppose that keeps him motivated.'
11 Mr. Gordon Cunningham Education Officer for the Association of County Councils said the proposals 'would be neither appropriate for all pupils nor practicable because schools could not achieve the targets set without more specialist teachers and equipment'. *Times Educational Supplement* 23.1.81.
12 Though his wording was ambivalent. The planned £65 to £70 million cut on school spending 'would have some impact on educational provision and the numbers employed in the service'.

Bibliography

ADAMS, P. (1981) 'Social control or social wage: on the political economy of the "Welfare State"' in DALE, R., ESLAND, G. and MCDONALD, M. (Eds) *Education and the State. II Policy, Patriarchy and Practice.*

BECKER, H (1976) 'The career of the Chicago public school teacher' in HAMMERSLEY, M. and WOODS, P. (Eds) *The Process of Schooling,* London, Routledge and Kegan Paul.

BECKER, H. (1977) 'Personal change in adult life' in COSIN, B., DALE, I.R., ESLAND, G., and SWIFT, D. *School and Society,* London, Routledge and Kegan Paul.

BOYSON, R. (1975) *The Crisis in Education,* London, *Woburn Press.*

BURKE, V. (1971) *Teachers in Turmoil,* Harmondsworth, Penguin.

CRETTON, J. (1980) 'Quantifying the dire threat to local independence' *Education,* Nov. 11. p. 441.

DEPARTMENT OF EDUCATION AND SCIENCE, (1977) *Education in Schools, A Consultative Document,* London, HMSO.

DEPARTMENT OF EDUCATION AND SCIENCE, (1980) *Special Needs in Education,* London, HMSO.

FISKE, D. (1979) 'Falling Numbers in Secondary Schools – Problems and Possibilities' Paper presented at North of England Conference.

HABERMAS, J. (1976) *Legitimation Crisis,* London, Heinemann.

HARGREAVES, D., HESTER, S., and MELLOR, F., (1975) *Deviance in Classrooms,* London, Routledge and Kegan Paul

HUNTER, C. (1979a) 'Control in the comprehensive system' in EGGLESTON, J. (Ed) *Decision Making in the Classroom,* London, Routledge and Kegan Paul.

HUNTER, C. (1979b) 'The politics of participation, with specific reference to teacher-pupil relationships' in WOODS, P. (Ed) *Teacher Strategies,* London, Croom Helm.

HUNTER, C. and HEIGHWAY, P., (1980) 'Morale, motivation and management in middle schools' in BUSH, T., GLATTER, R., GOODEY, J. and RICHES, C. (Eds) *Approaches to School Management,* London, Harper and Row/Open University Press.

JENCKS, C. *et al* (1972) *Inequality: A Re-assessment of the Effect of Family and Schooling in America,* New York, Basic Books.

PATEMAN, T. (1978) 'Accountability, values and schooling' in BECKER, T. and MACLURE, S. *Accountability in Education,* Slough, NFER.

WILLIAMS, R. (1976) 'Base and superstructure in Marxist cultural theory' in DALE, R. *et. al. Schooling and Capitalism,* London, Routledge and Kegan Paul.

Contradictions of Control: Elementary Education in a Mining District 1870-1900

Bill Williamson, University of Durham

The aim of this paper is to examine the form of elementary educational provision in two mining villages in the Northumberland coalfield in the late Victorian period. It is intended as a contribution to an explicitly historical sociology of education, seeking to trace in a very local study of two schools the much larger moments of social change in society itself, expressed as the rise of industrial paternalism and the formation of an urban working class. The aim of the paper here is to clarify the structural linkages between schooling and society in this period.

Elementary education in the late Victorian period massively embodied the social and political dominance of an industrial and commercial bourgeoisie. This paper seeks to show how that dominance was both institutionalized in the practice of schooling and how it was resisted and challenged by working people themselves. Through the Board of Education, the School Boards and, at a local level, through the management committees of single schools, a system of resource allocation, curriculum setting and pupil evaluation was set up which reflected directly the class relations of Victorian society.

So far as the historical record allows, it is the aim of the paper to reveal something of the social relationships of the two schools although it is not possible to set out a full historical ethnography. The paper is offered, therefore, as a mere footnote to the larger study of elementary education in Victorian Britain, a very minor contribution to a growing area of study. (See Johnson 1979).

The assumption from which I begin is that many of the theoretical themes of the sociology of education can be illuminated and refined in the context of very specific local studies and that, indeed, there has to be a creative dialogue between theorizing and empirical research from which both necessarily benefit. Careful historical research sets firm limits on theoretical generalizations and empirical research itself can only make sense when it is guided by theory. The value of local studies is that the role of schools in the process of social reproduction and cultural transmission can be inspected in the context of a much wider institutional mosaic to help understand how schooling related, for example, to patterns of employment in an area or to religion and structures of political authority. In this way the relative importance of the school in the process of social reproduction can be assessed against the role of other institutions in this process. For the period in question there are strong grounds for believing that the school had a limited role in this respect.

Historical studies also serve necessarily to emphasize the importance of taking time seriously in any account of the social relations of schooling. For relations in classrooms reflect historically specific relations between schools and society. At the end of the paper the importance of this is illustrated in a brief discussion of counter-school culture.

The main points I seek to press, however, are these. First, while the evidence of the two schools shows clearly the dominance of local bourgeois groups over the civic affairs of the villages and symbolizing, therefore, the social relations of British society as a whole during this period, there are many contradictory aspects to that domination. The power of the landowners and mineowners in these villages reveals itself clearly in the *form, funding, content* and *control* of the schools themselves. Nevertheless, despite their enormous power the elementary school was an underpowered institution with a severely circumscribed potentiality for controlling and moulding the children who passed through it. The powerlessness of the school is revealed not just in its limited resources but also in the behaviour of the children themselves resisting the controls of the school.

Secondly, the local bourgeois groups who supported education in the two villages may have done so in the belief that education was a potent force of social control. This belief, certainly, was a strong one in the coalfields of Northumberland and Durham in the 1840s (Colls 1976). But that is only one aspect of their involvement with education. On the basis of limited materials, this paper suggests that the provision of schooling was an aspect of the way they staged their own class position, clothing wealth with a civic dignity without which their claims to respect would have been groundless. The provision of schooling, therefore, says just as much about how local bourgeois groups perceived themselves as it did the way in which they perceived the working classes.

Thirdly, while local studies of particular schools and their communities can generate a rich seam of data which is the stuff of history itself, there is a sense in which studies can never be simply local. The changes which can be traced in the schools over the thirty year period discussed can only be explained by reference to changes in British society as a whole.

While it is possible to connect aspects of the curriculum of the elementary school to the way in which the Victorian bourgeoisie viewed the working classes – and out of which came the well-known stress on the virtues of thrift, temperance and the strengthening of family life – it is also important to grasp that there were conflicts within that bourgeoisie and that the form of capitalist society itself was rapidly changing in this period. A subtle shift was taking place in the form of industrial paternalism. In the part of the Northumberland coalfield examined in this paper the shift was from what I wish to call 'squirearchal paternalism' to 'industrial paternalism'. This shift can be traced directly in conflicts over the importance of schooling.

One group, landowners, felt it was sufficient to rely on the traditional controls of work and community. The industrialists, dealing with generalized labour free of the traditional controls of locality were interested in schools. Underlying this shift, quite apart from changes in the structure of markets for coal and the scale of industrial production itself, were changes in the character of the labour force itself both in terms of its geographical mobility and political consciousness.

The provision of schooling by mining companies in the latter part of the nineteenth century was less the result of the need to control a labour force or pre-empt the independent growth of working class education as had, arguably, been the case earlier in the century. Rather it was to attract labour to the mines or, to be more precise, to attract a particular form of labour, namely, sober family men eager to better themselves and their children.

None of these points are, of course, novel but they do have implications for the way in which sociologists should develop a theoretical understanding of the relationship between education and society.

The villages discussed in this paper lie approximately seven miles west of

Newcastle upon Tyne up the Tyne valley. Heddon-on-the Wall is an ancient village with historical traces in Saxon history. During the period under discussion the people of Heddon found employment on farms, in the pit and in the quarry. Throckley, although with a recorded history going back to mediaeval times, was an industrial village constructed almost entirely by the Throckley Coal Company from the late 1860s onwards.

Elementary Education: The Patrons

In order to begin properly my account of the schools of these two villages I want to quote from the Catechism from *The Book of Common Prayer* of the Church of England.

> My duty towards my neighbour, is to love him as myself, and to do to all men, as I would they should do unto me. To order myself lowly and reverently to all my betters: To hurt nobody by word nor deed: To keep my hands from picking and stealing, and my tongue from evil speaking, lying, and slandering: To keep my body in temperance, soberness, and chastity: Not to covet or desire other men's goods: but to learn and labour truly to get mine own living, and to do my duty in that state of life, unto which it shall please God to call me.

The children of Heddon school were required to learn the whole thing and if they were unlucky they might have been asked to repeat it, in front of the whole class, to either the visiting School Board inspectors or the Ecclesiastical inspectors. Such recitation was part of the examination which all nineteenth century Board Schools were given under the Elementary Code and as a result of which were (or, as the case may be, were not) allocated central government funds. I quote it fully, however, for it would be difficult to find a more concise and eloquent account of the principles which guided the educational practice of Heddon School and, simultaneously, the tedium of studying there.

Education was one of the major forces shaping the class position of working people: it embodied massively dominant assumptions about their role and status, conceiving no other role for them than that of manual work as subordinates. And what it reflected, as recent historical work has made clear, was a long standing attempt to so control the learning of working class people that they would fit in without protest to dominant structures of work and political authority. (See Johnson, 1976, Laquer 1977, Colls, 1976, Flynn 1967).

No one can say how well the public educators of the late nineteenth century achieved their purpose. But that purpose was a clear one with a coherent rationale. Religion and Catechism had a big part to play in it, as did poetry and the three R's. The Victorians had well-worked-out justifications for the curriculum of their schools and it is easy to detect, in the unique history of particular schools, the subtle but direct effects of a much more central and powerful impulse which showed itself in the way schools were staffed, financed, run and controlled entering directly the daily experience of thousands of children. Heddon school was no exception; indeed it was all too typical of schools in the colliery districts of the North.

The early history of Heddon school is unrecorded though it stems from the period of the 1820s, being set up by Mrs. Bewicke, the major landlord of the area.

The main building of the present school was built by the National Society in 1851. The later development of the school from 1886 onwards is recorded in the school log books and it is these upon which I mainly base my account of the school.

From the 1870s onwards to 1903 the school was under the jurisdiction of the Newcastle School Board and the rural Dean of Corbridge. The local vicar was always the correspondent of the school, or school secretary and the Board of managers included the vicar, Major Calverly Bewicke and Mr. J.C. Bates, landowner, mine-owner and Justice of the Peace. The regular voluntary subscribers to the school, their subscriptions amounting to more than the annual government grant or the sum collected in the so-called 'school pence' from the children, were local landowners, including a rich vicar, and the owners of Heddon colliery. The management and control of the school was, therefore, in the hands of the most powerful men in the village. Those who symbolized authority and respectability were thus closely associated with education and it was an association reinforced by regular visits to the school and regular contact with the children. The log book for November 6th 1886 reads: 'Rev. C. Walker and C. Bewicke Esq. visited the school. They looked at copy books and registers and questioned infants in Arithmetic'. Mr. Bewicke gave the children an annual treat in the grounds of Close House. Mr. Bates lent his field for school sports. Miss Bates often came to the school to help with the needlework. The vicar, of course, was a daily visitor and helped a great deal in teaching. When the Reverend Bowlker's wife died the children attended her funeral.

Such contact has a particular sociological importance in legitimating the dominant position of the village rich. Howard Newby has argued, for instance, that through close involvement with the village such people were able, through 'an ideological alchemy' focused on the idea of community, to 'convert the exercise of power into "service" to those over whom they ruled'. (Newby, 1977, p. 55).

Apart from such formal contact between children and managers there was extensive informal contact. Casual work on local farms was always available for the children, particularly during the harvest, and, despite the fact, as I shall show, that the school had chronic problems of attendance, even the school managers were not averse to employing children. The log book of August 15th 1886 notes: 'Several children are working in the gardens of Close House. I sent word to the gardener that school had commenced again and asked him to dismiss the boys'. And in a small parish of no more than nine hundred people the local gentry were known personally to many; they were not distant figures of an anonymous authority but were closely involved in the lives of the children and their parents.

There are no records which document the reasons for their involvement in the school. In the vicar's case it was clear; it was part of his job and flowed from a long-standing preoccupation of the church with the education of the poor. For the others it might have seemed a clear case of *noblesse oblige* or a natural extension of their other roles as Poor Law Guardians or Justices of the Peace, tempering their awesome authority in this respect with the charity their Church required of them as gentlemen.

In the case of the Throckley Coal Company the situation is different. Their reasons for providing schools are a little clearer and could not possibly be understood simply in terms of a theory of social control.

The school was opened shortly after the pit. It was founded in 1871 and opened in the Easter of 1873. The school was built well before the colliery was fully developed and well before the house building programme was complete. The school, therefore, played a key role in the recruitment of labour. The issue of controlling labour may have entered their calculations, just as it had influenced the provision of schools elsewhere in the coalfield. (See Colls, 1976). Again, the Throckley coal company was typical of other companies in this respect. The provision of schooling was seen by the coalowners from the 1844 strike onwards as a way of suppressing discontent. (Moore, 1974, p. 80). Later, however, the companies were more concerned with a more generalized form of control made necessary by the break-up of local ties as the coalfield expanded and labour mobility increased.

Some support for this idea comes from some comments by Sir William Stephenson, leading Methodist and the principal coal owner in Throckley. He was a founder member of the Newcastle School Board. At the opening of Westgate Road School in 1899, he had the following to say, stressing the need for schools to have the co-operation of parents:

> It is palpable to every observer who walked the streets of Newcastle that there was a want of restraint and observance of the social amenities on the part of the children of the city. He did not like to see such wanton destruction of trees and flowers, and so much gambling among the boys . . . There was much rudeness observable, especially to ladies.
> (Press cutting: Stephenson Family Scrap Book).

Schooling was in part, a corrective to such aberrant behaviour. In the first instance, however, Throckley Coal Company provided a school to attract a respectable labour force.

But the provision of schooling, as with the provision of other civic amenities, tells us something, perhaps, of the personal aims of men on the fringes of knighthoods and enoblement. Building schools was evidence of their civic position, a way for men of industry to claim a legitimacy and political authority which did not depend solely on their possession of great wealth.

The Stephensons were very prominent in local politics, religion and commerce. The Spencer family, joint shareholders in the pit and local steelmakers, were equally prominent in the civic, religious and commercial life not just of the immediate area but of Tyneside as a whole. They were trustees of a workingmen's club in Newburn which provided evening classes in science, mechanics and steam. They organized concerts and general lectures and they, too, were pillars of the local religious establishment being the principal benefactors of Newburn Church. (Newburn Church Magazine 1885). And J.B. Simpson, mining engineer and a director of the company, was a major supporter of Armstrong's College (later Newcastle University) in Newcastle. Sir William Stephenson also founded public libraries in Elswick and Heaton, two suburbs of Newcastle. They were all prominent members of the local ruling class and the provision of education was an important part of the way they sought to define their own class position. Their rise to prominence in the area is symbolic of the shift from the paternalism of squirarchy to the industrial paternalism of an ascendent bourgeoisie extending its hegemony. (Benwell Community Project).

The Coal Company constituted themselves as the Board of Managers of the School and Mr. Stephenson himself appointed the first headmaster. The company took a direct role in the daily running of the school with the pit manager being a regular visitor to the headmaster and having general supervisory responsibilities over the school. School matters came up regularly at the monthly meetings of shareholders and it is clear from the school log books that the recurring problems of the school were the same as those at Heddon school; how to establish the authority of the school and the routines of regular attendance on parents and children for whom the school was often experienced as punishment and which led to nowhere in particular.

The Meaning of Education

This leads to the theme of the meaning of education to working class people in this period and this can be usefully discussed under the general theme of attendance.

For the children school attendance was a duty and their parents faced prosecution for not ensuring their attendance at school. Successive Education Acts from 1870 onwards during the decade leading to Mundella's Act in 1880 built up the legal framework of compulsory attendance but the obligation on children to attend predates the legislation. Although there is no surviving documentary evidence to prove this definitively in the Heddon case, there are good reasons for believing that the parents at Heddon did make an effort to send their children to school. There had been a school there for a long time before the 1870 Act. It was closely connected to the church. Two of the principal landowners were keen supporters of elementary education. Finally, from the early 1880s onwards where evidence does exist, it is clear that most children stayed on at school to complete the course. The idea of schooling was therefore not a new one to the people of Heddon or to working people of the mining districts of the north east more generally.

It was a qualified idea, however, and, like many other parents of elementary school children at the time, their attitude to school was influenced by the cost of it and the availability of other ways of keeping their children busy, either in work or at home. This is reflected in the almost despairing report of J.R. Blakiston to the Board of Education in 1886:

> There is a strong reason to believe that there are still many thousands of children over the age of five and some over six, and even older, who have never been inside a schoolroom. There is an innate dislike in the people of the north-eastern Division to do anything upon compulsion. Even when sufficient visitors are employed to go regularly from house to house, some parents contrive, by frequent migrations and otherwise, to elude their vigilance, others to defy their action. The 'law's delays', the smallness of the fines imposed on offenders, and the unwillingness of many Benches to convict, continue to paralyse the action of compelling bodies wherever money can be earned by children. (Blakiston 1886, p. 263)

It did not occur to Mr. Blakiston that regular attendance at school is best secured, not with the stick, but with the carrot, and that his inspectors' observations, from which he compiled his report, reflect the poor quality of education the schools offered and not the wilful neglect of parents. The parents of Heddon could have no reason to expect much from education, their own experience of it having been so slight and unrewarding. Twenty years previous to the Blakiston report, Mr. J.L. Hammond reported to the Schools Inquiry Commission on the state of schools in Northumberland and, referring to schools for working men, had this to say:

> Practically in these schools nothing is taught beyond reading, spelling, cyphering and writing. There is little pretence of attempting even geography or grammar . . . Intellectually considered, the instruction given at these schools is extremely meagre. In fact, no mental faculty of the pupils

is exercised or even interfered with by the teacher.

(Hammond 1867, p. 276)

He did praise, however, the 'neatness, method and regularity imperceptibly instilled by the system' and claimed:

> They have one merit; except in the higher rules of arithmetic they do not pretend to teach more than they do teach; and even an illiterate parent can test pretty carefully the progress his son makes at such a school.
>
> (Hammond 1867–1868, p. 275)

Heddon school fits well into these general descriptions. The assumptions about the education of workers which were common in late Victorian England and which stressed, within a more general ideology of *laissez-faire,* the importance of school as an agent of social control penetrated Heddon school directly, affecting its resources, staffing, curriculum and results.

Resources

In 1882 the cost of education per pupil was 35s. 3½d. This was for the country as a whole. In London it was 53s. 5d. and in the country outside London 41s. 4¼d. These figures come from Matthew Arnold's General Report for 1882 and he was emphatic that the cost was too high. (Arnold 1883, p. 196). His view was that the parental contribution to the cost of education should be higher on the grounds that:

> It has so often been said that people value more highly and use more respectfully what they pay a price for, that one is almost ashamed to repeat it.
>
> (Arnold 1883, p. 320)

At this time Arnold was probably the most influential government spokesman on education, being the Chief Inspector of Schools. His figures, however, are slightly misleading since they do not break down the overall figures into their separate components.

Under the Revised Code regulations from 1861 onwards, education was paid for from three main sources: central government grants; fees ('school pence'); and voluntary donations. In the case of Heddon school, as can be ascertained from the school Cash Book, each source contributed about one third of the total cost and that, naturally, the biggest single cost was teachers' salaries. Parents in Heddon were relieved from paying fees from September 1891 when the school became entirely free, an event which prompted the Head to note: 'The attendance has been very good since free education was adopted in our school'. (School Log Book, September 18th, 1891). Without quite a high level of voluntary contribution, the school would not have been financially viable; a fact, which under the Elementary Code regulations, reflected both meagre central government funding and the academic performances of the school itself since the grant was paid dependent on the children passing tests in the three R's and on the level of their attendance. Arnold's views about paying for a service thus neglects a vital element of the calculation, the ability of people to pay. It is clear that for some parents in Heddon the 'school pence' were a priority they just could not afford; a real deterrent to sending their children to school.

Table 1 shows that it was not until the turn of the century that the annual grant per pupil reached more than £1.00 per annum.

Table 1   Cost per pupil: Heddon School 1885–1903

	No. of scholars for whom accommodation is provided	Pupils Registered	Average Attendance	Annual Grant £	s	d	Grant per pupil (New pence)
1885	136	124	108	65	6	0	52
1890	136	136	135	85	10	11	62
1895	172	177	161	132	16	0	75
1900	172	—	142	147	18	0	52
1903	172	—	151	154	8	0	102

Source: Board of Education Parliamentary Grants and School Cash Book.

When a parent could not meet the school fees, the Attendance Officer of the School Board could make an application to the Board of Guardians for the fees to be paid by them. The Log Book notes, on December 22nd 1886, 'Attendance Officer to apply to guardians for payments of Robert Napier's fees'. And in 1889, in an entry which suggests that school fees were for some children a deterrent to their attendance and a financial strain, the Head notes: 'I sent Geo Hepple home for his school-fees and he never returned for the rest of the week'. School fees could not be met at times of industrial trouble. A log book entry in March 1887 notes: 'Several children absent this week on account of the school pence, the strike affecting several families'. The figures above, however, simply emphasize that, consistent with the explicit aims of the Revised Code, education in Heddon was cheap.

School pence also presented problems in Throckley. The Throckley school suffered, too, from lack of resources. In a reference to the parents the Head noted on. November 29th, 1876, 'The children are attentive to their lessons but we cannot get the parents to provide them with books'. School fees were something of a deterrent to attendance, just as they were at Heddon. Nor was it simply a question of wrong priorities among careless parents. A log book entry for November 16th, 1877 notes:

Made out a list of absentees today. A good many sent word that their children were in want of books and clothes. Some had not their school money. Not a few of those who have respectable parents are anxious for their children to get on with their learning but cannot afford to send them. Consequently many of the best scholars are kept at home.

The Company's response to this was to deduct school fees direct from paypackets. In June 1880 they resolved that:

It having been reported that the School fees are in arrears a considerable sum: it was resolved that arrangements be made for all men to pay a fixed amount every fortnight, the same to be deducted from wages.

(Throckley Colliery Records, 1880)

There is no evidence that this device worked for the problem of attendance, particularly that of girls who frequently stayed home to help their mothers, remained a constant worry for the Head and his managers.

The problem of scarce resources leads on to the question of the staffing of elementary schools.

Staff

Teachers' salaries represent the single largest charge to the income of the school. In 1878/9, the total income of the school at Heddon was £205 10s. 10d. Total expenditure for that year was just over £150 and, of this sum, £138 17s. 6d. went on teachers' salaries. Three grades of teacher existed in the school, Headteacher, assistant teacher and pupil teacher, the latter receiving her own education and training for the profession. Between 1886 and 1900 there were four headmasters in the school, thirteen assistant mistresses and seven pupil teachers and monitors. One head teacher, Mr. Grocock remained for just over one year. These figures suggest, in contrast to the cosy myth of the close knit village school, that Heddon school experienced quite a high level of teacher turnover in the period before the 1902 Education Act. There is no obvious explanation for this except that, relying mainly on young women teachers, marriage and child rearing would take its toll on the staff. Here, of course, is one of the nicer ironies of Victorian education. The full moral force of it was felt by the children through the work of their young lady teachers, hesitant, poorly trained and, in the case of pupil teachers, not much older than the pupils themselves. One tetchy comment in the log book for December 1st 1889 emphasizes this point: 'I had to speak seriously to F. Stephenson (Candidate) about bringing her lessons very imperfectly done'. Earlier that year the Head had to warn the pupil teachers about their own poor attendance! These young girls were the front line troops of Victorian education. It was via them that the children experienced the formal curriculum of elementary education.

Curriculum

The staff of the school were not in control of what they should teach. The Elementary Code dictated what they should do although they did have some freedom in the selection of teaching materials. What they taught, however, reflected directly the dominant values of the time. In their songs and poetry, their history and geography, the values of patriotism and deference were heavily underlined. The object lessons of the pupil teachers emphasized such virtues as honesty and kindness and the whole emphasis of the school was on the development of standards of appropriate behaviour. The April 1886 entry to the log book illustrates this quite well. Singing lessons for the coming school year were set out as follows:

Division 1   (Infants and Standard 1)
The Rainy Day
Hold the Right Hand up
The Robin

Division 2

        Welcome to Spring Birds
        The Robin
        The Squirrel
        Blue Bells
        Evening

Division 3

        Patriotic Song
        Who is a Patriot?
        Before all Lands
        Rule Britannia
        God Save the Queen

The poetry to be learned is listed as follows:

Class 1	Goldsmith's Traveller
Class 2	Wreck of the Hesperus
Class 3	After Blenheim (Changed to Lucy Gray)
Class 4	Village Blacksmith
Class 5	The Two Little Kittens

And the texts which the school would use are listed as:

Readers:	*Geographical*	– Nelson's 'World at Home'
	Historical	– Nelson's 'Royal'
	Literary	– 1, 2, 3, Nelson's 'New Royal'
		– 4 'Masterman Ready'
		– 5, 6, 7 'Settlers in Canada'

    Singing for the younger children was an indulgence in a mild and mainly innocent rural nostalgia. For the older children songs were an induction to the values of Victorian imperialism. This was the period of the expansion of the colonial Empire, a period of confidence tarnished only by the awareness that Britain's world leadership in industry and technology was being overtaken by other nations, particularly Germany. But the themes in the poetry stressed traditional virtues of the home and the hearth and where it did extend the range of children's emotions it reached no further than a shallow sense of pity for the misfortune of others – 'Lucy Gray' is a good example, as is 'The Wreck of the Hesperus' – in both cases the object of pity being most unlikely ever to be encountered in the daily lives of these children. 'The Traveller' by Goldsmith and 'The Village Blacksmith' by Longfellow both emphasize a sentimental attitude to the village and to home and the timelessness and inevitability of the social order itself. In 'The Village Blacksmith' we find the following verse, celebrating the virtues of hard work and toil:

        Toiling, – rejoicing, – sorrowing
        Onward through life he goes
        Each morning sees some task begin
        Each evening sees it close;
        Something attempted, something done
        Has earned a night's repose

The poetry fare of the school should not be thought of as an idiosyncratic selection on the part of the head. He was drawing on opinions which were quite firmly held by the Board of Education itself. Even the inclusion of poetry in the school curriculum had a very explicit rationale. Once again, Matthew Arnold tells us what it was. In his General Report for 1878 he insists that 'good poetry is formative'. It has, he says, 'the precious power of acting by itself and in a way managed by nature, not through the instrumentality of that somewhat terrible character, the scientific educator . . . We enlarge their vocabulary, and with their vocabulary their circle of ideas. At the same time we bring them under the formative influence of really good literature, really good poetry'. (Arnold 1878, pp. 187–188). And in his 1880 report he takes up the same theme again: 'Good poetry does undoubtedly tend to form the soul and character; it tends to beget a love of beauty and of truth in alliance together, it suggests, however indirectly, high and noble principles of action, and it inspires the emotions so helpful in making principles operative'. (pp. 22–201). He goes on to regret the influence of Lord Lyndhurst in recommending Goldsmith to schools, preferring instead the popular Mrs. Hemans (The Wreck of the Hesperus) and such poems as 'The Graves of a Household', 'The Homes of England' and 'The Better Land'.

Patriotic values were also reinforced at key points in the royal calendar and when events in the Empire overseas gave grounds for special celebration. During the jubilee celebrations of sixty years of Victoria's reign, a Union Jack and Royal Standard were placed above the Queen's picture and flags were given out, together with instructions about processions. The log book of June 30th 1897 reads: 'This afternoon, in school 500 Jubilee Mugs were distributed by Miss Violet Margaret Bewicke to all the children in the parish up to fourteen years of age'. Miss Bewicke was given a 'beautiful casket' and the whole room was decorated with flags. Less important royal occasions were also marked with day-holidays. In 1893, July 6th, the log book notes. 'Holiday all day on account of marriage of the Duke of York with Princess May of Teck'.

The Diamond Jubilee was a very important event in the village and so, too, were military successes overseas. The log book for May 21st, 1899 reads: 'Half holiday this afternoon in honour of the relief of Mafeking'. The June 6th entry; 'Closed this afternoon in honour of the British occupation of Pretoria'. And, in what must have seemed a truly idyllic month, on June 20th the children were given another half day on account of a visit to Newcastle by the Prince and Princess of Wales. That the South African war was exposing British military weakness and the Government was greatly concerned with the health of army recruits was not something which the parents of Heddon would have been aware of. The history and geography taught in the school were clearly not very well developed. Geography was taught from 1888 onwards, most likely in response to Board of Trade prompting. In the Board's Report for 1886-7 it was noted that:

> It is beginning to be widely felt that, in schools where geography is not presented for a grant, it is a subject of which the future citizens of so wide an empire should not be wholly ignorant and that the wives, sisters and daughters of soldiers, sailors and settlers should read books that treat the subject in an interesting and intelligent style.
>
> (Board of Education 1886, p. 273)

It is interesting that the rationale for geography teaching was aimed particularly at the women, those who would be left behind, encouraging them to see in their husbands' colonial exploits the unfolding of an historic mission which they themselves could not properly oppose. The theme of empire was often reinforced by guests to the school such as the Church Missionary Society when magic lantern shows would be given. On July 10th 1902, the Rev. Stenson from South Africa gave the children a lecture on that part of the British Empire.

The women were a target, too, of another Victorian preoccupation, savings and self-help. In 1891 a savings bank was opened in the school to encourage the children to save. There is no specific record of the reasons given. A Board of Education report for 1895 sets out the rationale for encouraging those schemes. The Heddon case could hardly have been unaffected by thinking of the following kind:

> Experience has shown that many of the evils which weigh most seriously on the industrial classes in this country are the results of improvidence and waste. But some of these evils admit at least of partial remedy. To learn how to economise slender resources, how to resist temptation, needless expense, and how to make reasonable provision for future contingencies is an important part of education. Such knowledge is calculated to protect its possessor from much trouble and humiliation, and to help him greatly in leading an honourable and independent life.
>
> (Board of Education 1895, p. 483)

This instruction points out that the lesson learned will be passed on to the whole household; and it went on to raise the prospect that, through thrift, working men might lift themselves up into self employment. And finally, the connection with drink is made:

> Thrift and temperance are very nearly allied; each is helpful to the other, and having regard to the enormous waste caused by intemperance, there can be little doubt that if the people of these islands were more temperate and thrifty our home trade and the profitable employment of our people therein would be very greatly increased.
>
> (Board of Education, 1895 p. 484)

The curriculum of the school is not simply the formal subjects which are taught; it includes everything that constitutes the formal life of the school as a comunity. It includes the way in which knowledge and learning are tested and the way in which children are punished. (Bernstein 1971).

Under the Elementary Code there was an incredible amount of testing in schools. The children of Heddon were treated to regular examinations. In the case of the upper standards, examinations were run on a fortnightly basis. The pupil teachers, of course, were under constant examination, often having to give formal object lessons in preparation for both the diocesan and state inspection. And the reason for all this was a clear economic one. Inadequate performance in basic subjects could lead to the withdrawal of the grant. The Inspector's report for May 26th, 1890, underlines the pecariousness and urgency of the situation for the school: 'The Merit Grant is recommended solely on account of the epidemic, since elementary subjects were not up to the mark. Much better results of instruction will be expected next year (Article 115 (i))'. The children of Heddon must have experienced school as a series of hurdles to be jumped or ambushes to be avoided, for failure meant additional work or punishment.

Punishment at Heddon was frequent. Between February and the end of March 1886, punishments are recorded for playing among the shrubs on the Church hill, running and playing in the school, truancy, stopping younger children on their way to school, throwing stones, climbing trees in the playground and unruliness in lessons. And the log book has frequent entries of the following type: 'Gilbert Tailford sent home for insubordination. Returned next day with message that he had to be caned'. (October 21st, 1886); 'Punished J. Wright and M. Charlton for being in girls' yard' (June 4th 1887); 'I punished Harry Brown and John Laws for climbing the playground walls' (October 30th, 1888); 'I punished Wm. and Ed. Scott for using bad language', 'Punished Harry Brown for insubordination' (June 10th, 1890).

Most of the time the punishments are the trivia of a petty tyranny but occasionally they are serious. Harry Brown was actually expelled and had to find alternative schooling in Horsley. The log reads: 'I punished Harry Brown for stone throwing. He retaliated by wounding me in the leg, and on being brought before the magistrates his father was bound over to answer for his good conduct and he was ordered to be taken away from the place and pay the costs'. (Feb. 12th, 1894). That the children often retaliated is seen in the following entry: 'Punished Geo. Swallow for playing away from school yesterday afternoon and gave him a second dose for kicking me after he had been punished'.

The underlying problem was, however, attendance. Like many schools of its type the problem of actually keeping the children in regular atendance was a constant source of worry, not least because the grant depended on good atttendance levels. The attendance figures for the school for the years 1885 to 1900 are shown in Table 2.

Table 2   Attendance Levels, 1885-1900 – Heddon School

Year	Pupils Registered	Average attendance	Percentage attendance
1885	124	108	87.0
86	120	113	94.1
87	145	111	76.5
88	152	112	73.6
89	142	132	92.9
1890	136	135	99.2
91	133	131	98.4
92	181	136	75.1
93	172	154	89.5
94	193	165	85.4
95	177	161	90.9
96	169	151	89.3
97	172	155	90.1
98	152	153	100.0
99	139	137	98.5
1900	145	142	97.9

Source: Board of Education Parliamentary Grants and calculation from school records.

The figures taken overall, indicate that in the closing decades of the nineteenth century average attendance figures gradually improved. This was no small achievement

---

since during this same period the school experienced a very high level of pupil turnover, as well as of staff. Table 3 shows this very clearly. Geographical mobility on the part of farm workers no doubt explains these figures, for what they show is that the average length of stay of children at the school dropped sharply near the end of the century. These figures undermine totally, at least in the case of Heddon and perhaps, too, of other rural schools throughout the country, the image of a stable small community where everyone is known to everyone else. Friendships among the children of Heddon were being constantly broken up by the regular movement of agricultural labour.

Table 3   Average No. of years Attendance at School

Years	1876–1879	1880–1884	1885–1890
Boys	9.4	9.7	3.1
Girls	9.0	8.0	3.4
Total enrolments	18	42	187

Source: Calculated from school log books and attendance registers.

The official figures conceal, however, two features of the attendance problem. The first is its seasonal character and the second is its age-specific form. Younger children seem to have been much more regular attenders than older ones, presumably being less affected by the pulls of work, and girls attended for a longer period than boys. Figures given in the school log book (see Table 4) for February 28th, 1896 indicates something of the sex difference.

Table 4   Numbers of Children in Different Standards – 1896

Standards		All	1	2	3	4	5	6
Boys	No.	55	15	11	11	8	8	6
	%	44	27.2	20.0	20.0	14.5	14.5	3.6
Girls	No.	70	12	10	17	18	8	5
	%	56	17.1	14.2	24.4	25.7	11.4	7.1

Sources: Calculated from school log figures.

The sex differences are not large. There were more girls at school than boys and they seem to have stayed the course slightly better, a fact no doubt reflecting differences in opportunities for work. For the boys work on the farms or in the pit were easily available; there were few opportunities outside domestic help for the girls and, not being a large parish, the opportunities for domestic work were, in any case, quite small.

The seasonal problems of attendance come out vividly in the school log. The entries speak for themselves. 'Several pupils reported to the Attendance officer. All were under fourteen years of age and working without a certificate' (June 8th, 1886). 'Vicar called and "looked up" some absentees as the attendance is falling on account of harvest' (Sept. 8th, 1886). 'Attendance very low on account of hinds leaving the neighbourhood' (April 16th, 1886). 'The attendance in the upper standards is very bad today as many of the boys are potato gathering' (Oct. 11th, 1889).

These are the systematic distortions of gathering in the harvest. But there were many other factors which would reduce attendance. The weather was a big factor. The entry for May 5th, 1896 reads: 'Rain very much desired has fallen all this morning, but while it will be very beneficial to the crops it has a most disastrous effect on the average. The attendance is less than 50 this morning'. Such entries are very common. The children were not averse to run with the hunt either. The entry for March 1st, 1897: 'Fox hounds met in village this morning. Eight boys are absent this afternoon having gone after them. They will come up for judgement in the morning'. And if the school work had been strenuous, say through having another examination, children would often take time off to recover. The entry for May 21st, 1886 reads: 'Attendance gradually rising though some have not returned yet since the examination – six weeks ago, notably A. Hepple'. On occasions the school even took pre-emptive action. On May 5th, 1886 the school was deliberately closed in anticipation of high levels of absence: 'School closed all day as I ascertained that many children would be absent with parents leave on account of Auction Sale at neighbouring farm'. But it was not always possible to anticipate events in this way. The entry for December 1st, 1886 makes this clear: 'Many children absent on account of a fire in the neighbourhood'.

The award of attendance tickets in 1887 seems to have had some effect but this was not as important as the adoption of free education in September 1891. Prizes for good attendance were given out on prize days and despite the official figure which I have quoted it is clear that this attendance problem was seen by managers and teachers alike as the most intractable one the school had to deal with. Perhaps the clue to why this was so lies, in the end, in what the school could really do for its pupils and for most of them school must have seemed an irksome interlude between being really a child and having a job and the idea of a job had clearly much more appeal than the dreary routines of school.

Performance

Elementary education was both intended and experienced as a terminal education; it carried no promise of better things to come although, through the trades union movement, skilled workers were demanding better opportunities from the early 1870s onwards. Nor was it an education keyed into the experience of the children. The staff were poorly trained and the schools had few resources. The grant system imposed a heavy emphasis on the acquisition of pretty basic skills and encouraged stylized, repetitive and highly formal teaching. The results are catalogued in the Inspectors' annual reports, all of them carefully recorded in the school log book, constant reminders to the Head of the need to improve his performance. On May 12th, 1886 the Inspector wrote:

> The children passed a fair examination in the Elementary subjects, but the staff is not quite strong enough for efficient teaching. More intelligence should be shown when questioned on the Reading and prompting should be checked. The Grammar was bad in the second standard and below fair in the sixth standard; on the whole a failure. Pieces of short poems should not be learned as to destroy the sense. Copy books need more attention. The needlework was pretty fair; the work in the second standard must not be fixed. The old admissions register and the Report of last year were

missing. The first standard had no desks and were taught in the small infant classroom. In singing the ear test should be more practised.

This is the full report of the Inspector and it testifies well to the limited objectives and expectations of the Board. The report for the following year indicates little improvement. 'The Elementary subjects were decidedly below fair, nearly all points requiring much improvement. English was a failure, as the Repetition was neither accurate nor intelligent and the Grammar generally weak.' Complaints about spelling, monotonous reading, teacher shortage and inability on the part of the children to understand what they read litter these reports. One rather enigmatic comment even suggests that school children were expected to deteriorate as a consequence of their education. 'The upper part of the school passed better than the lower *which is unusual*' (my emphasis). It is clear that the scholastic achievements of the children, at least insofar as these were measured at the time, were very low. Here, perhaps is the mechanism which Pierre Bourdieu identified to explain the way working class people devalue schooling, through which the real lack of opportunities in education became 'intuitively perceived and gradually internalized' (Bourdieu 1974, p. 34). In short, since it offered little to working class people, the school was something which they themselves devalued.

The Inspector's reports should not be taken at their face value, however. They indicate that a very narrow range of qualities were being measured and they reflect, too, something of the class system within which the school functioned and the position of the school Inspector in that system. The great gulf which separated the children from their educated superiors comes out clearly, as most other class-related differences do, in the Inspector's attitudes to English and Grammar and Reading. In Heddon these were invariably bad. But what is being measured? An earlier inspection of schools in 1861, admittedly in County Durham, gives us a clue. In his famous report to the Education Commission of that year A.F. Foster notes, writing about Sunday Schools: '. . . the teachers conducted their earnest catechizing, and the pupils their earnest and intelligent answering, in one of the most uncouth dialects it was ever my lot to hear' (quoted in Seeley 1973, p. 328). The Northumberland dialect of the children of Heddon must have sounded strange to the school Inspector's ears and I hazard a guess that, like many educators of today, he confused the form of speech with its meaning, attributing ignorance to children whose main fault, if indeed it is a fault at all, was the unselfconscious and authentic use of their own dialect with those little deviations from standard English grammar which rendered their speech unique. Presented with such ignorance on the part of their superiors, what response other than hopeless resignation to failure was it more appropriate to make?

In history and geography the story is much the same. For children intended for the pits or work on the farm, what appeal could there have been in the far flung exploits of colonial adventures or the details of dynastic history? And what pleasure was there in the dull repetition of both poetry and prose when its relationship to their own experience or even the language which they used was so remote that learning became a punishment? It is hardly surprising that the harvest and the hunt were much more attractive alternatives to school.

Finally, if they devalued school, then it was hardly surprising for, quite apart from the school's limited achievements and the doubtful pleasures of attendance, it was a commonly held view, particularly among employers, that school was not worth it anyway. In his report to the Royal Commission on Agriculture, Mr. Coleman noted the attitude towards education of several Northumberland landowners, including those of Mr. Clayton, a landowner in the Heddon district and the man who held the mining royalties for the Heddon pit. Mr. Henry Bacon Grey Esq., farming 265 acres, noted for the Commission: 'Effects of the Education Acts: increased expenses to the farmer in summertime. It is a loss to the labourers, and the children of from 12 to 14 years are not so rosy and healthy as when they worked in summer and went to school in winter. They do not learn so cleverly, for the younger ones used to remain half workers for a longer time, and so they did not need to slur their work to keep forward and hereby were trained more perfectly' (Royal Comission on Agriculture, 1882, p. 25). And Messrs Joicey, in their returns said: 'The Education Acts have increased the farmers' expenses and deprived the labourer of a little help in bringing up his family'. Mr. John Cookson was emphatic: 'Children are not employed, the Education Acts are a perfect nuisance to the farmer and a great hardship to the labourer: he ought to have the summer months for his children from 11 yrs old. The children prefer the 3 Rs to the new code'. With such attitudes tenaciously held by their employers what possible value could the parents of Heddon, particularly the itinerant ones, place on keeping their children at school?

One final point, which bears on the point made at the beginning of this paper, namely, that it is vital to frame the social relations of schooling in time. It has become something of an orthodoxy in modern sociology that the development among some groups of children of a 'counter-school culture' is a reaction to the fact of failure arising from a recognition, however inarticulate, that school is a race in which they cannot succeed (See e.g. Willis 1978, Hargreaves 1969). The evidence of rejection of school given here, slight though it is, could not properly be explained in these terms. Ther was no expectation in Heddon and Throckley that anyone should succeed at school; the success of schooling was measured by how well the children were prepared for their social position. Given this, it was hardly likely that these children possessed any sense of failure. J.P. Robson, a Tyneside song writer sums my argument up nicely in his song, 'The Pitman's Happy Times' which evokes the period I am writing about: his verse can stand as my conclusion:

> We didn't heed much lairnin' then,
> We had ne time for skyul;
> Pit laddies work'd for spendin's sake
> An' nyen was thowt a fyul.

Conclusion

In the course of this century, but particularly since the end of the Second World War, the villages discussed in this paper have been utterly transformed. Both have been absorbed into the sprawling conurbation of Tyneside and the pits have gone.

The society sketched out here, with its firm imprint of paternalism which showed directly in its schools, has gone. It has given way to the rise of local authorities and much higher levels of central state funding of education. Organized labour has found a key role in the state itself and one aspect of this is the growth of the idea of a ladder of educational opportunity with its attendant anxieties about success and failure. Nervous pupil teachers have been replaced by well trained and well organized professionals and education has lost all its connection with local sponsorship. The people who live in the villages now do not necessarily work in them and for those who do work it is likely that their employer is a government agency or large company with headquarters far away from the Tyne.

Corporate capitalism and the Welfare State have replaced the small employer and forms both of paternalism and self help. How this society can best be described is not my concern here. What is important is that Heddon and Throckley symbolize an earlier phase in the development of a capitalist society. To explore fully the educational experience of working people during that phase would require many more local studies of the sort attempted here. For this much is certain; the experience of schooling varied considerably according to whether the area in question was rural or urban, whether the industrial base lay in mining or in manufacture and whether towns were new or old. It is well known, too, that attitudes to education varied, even among working people themselves, according to religious outlook and social status. (See e.g. Middleton and Weitzman 1976). The experience of education for working class people, even during this period, was as variegated as the working class itself. To point this out is not to render sociological generalizations about, say, education and social control, invalid; it renders them complex. The underlying order of that complexity is, however, something which an historically orientated sociology of education could profitably explore.

References

ARNOLD, M. (1852–1882) *Reports on Elementary Schools 1852–1882* London, Wyman and Sons Ltd. (1908).

BENWELL COMMUNITY PROJECT (1978) *The Making of a Ruling Class: Two Centuries of Capital Development on Tyneside* Newcastle upon Tyne, Benwell.

BERNSTEIN, B. (1971) 'On the classification and framing of educational knowledge' in YOUNG, M.F.D. (Ed) *Knowledge and Control: New Directions for the Sociology of Education* London, Collier-Macmillan.

BLAKISTON, J.R. (1886) 'General report of the year', *Board of Education Reports*.

BOARD OF EDUCATION (1886 and 1895) *Annual Reports* London, HMSO.

BOURDIEU, P. (1974) 'School as a conservative force' in EGGLESTON, J. (Ed) *Contemporary Research in the Sociology of Education* London, Methuen.

COLLS, R. (1976) 'Oh happy English children. Coal, class and education in the North East'. *Past and Present* No. 75. November.

FLYNN, M.W. (1967) 'Social theory and the industrial revolution' in BURNS, T. and SAUL, S.B. (Eds) *Social Theory and Economic Change* London, Tavistock.

HARGREAVES, D. (1969) *Social Relations in a Secondary School* London, Routledge and Kegan Paul.

HAMMOND, J.L. (1867–68) 'Northumberland. Reports from Commission'. *Schools Inquiry Commission 1867-8* vol xxviii Part vii.

HEDDON-ON-THE-WALL SCHOOL (1867–68) *Log Books,* Heddon-on-the-Wall School, Northumberland.

JOHNSON, R. (1976) 'Notes on the schooling of the English working class 1780-1850' in DALE, R., ESLAND, G. and MACDONALD, M. (Eds) *Schooling and Capitalism: A Sociological Reader* Milton Keynes, The Open University Press.

JOHNSON, R. (1979) 'Really useful knowledge;. Radical education and working class culture 1790-1848' in CLARKE, J., CRITCHER, C. and JOHNSON, R. (Eds) *Working Class Culture: Studies in History and Theory* London, Hutchinson and Co. Ltd.

LAQUER, T.W. (1977) 'Working class demand and the growth of English elementary education 1750-1850 in STONE, L. (Ed) *Schooling and Society: Studies in the History of Education* Baltimore, The John Hopkins University Press.

MIDDLETON, N. and WEITZMAN, S. (1976) *A Place for Everyone: A History of State Education from the Eighteenth Century to the 1970s* London, Victor Gollanz.

MOORE, R. (1974) *Pitmen, Preachers and Politics* London, Cambridge University Press.

NEWBURN CHURCH MAGAZINE (1885) Newburn Church, Vicarage, Newburn Road, Newcastle upon Tyne.

NEWBY, H. (1977) *The Deferential Worker* London, Penguin.

ROYAL COMMISSION ON AGRICULTURE (1882) 'Report on Northumberland' (Mr. Coleman) Reports of the Assistant Commissioners, London, HMSO.

SEELEY, J.Y.R. (1973) 'Coal Mining Villages in Northumberland and Durham: A Survey of Sanitary Conditions and Social Facilities' M.A. Thesis, University of Newcastle upon Tyne.

STEPHENSON, SIR W. (1899) Press cutting in Stephenson Family Scrapbook, Extracts in Newburn Library (Reference Section), West Denton, Newcastle upon Tyne.

THROCKLEY COLLIERY RECORDS (1880) Northumberland Record Office NRO/407.

THROCKLEY SCHOOL (1876–1921) *Log Books,* Northumberland Record Office.

WILLIS, P. (1978) *Learning to Labour* London, Saxon House.

The Double Burden of Class and Gender in the Schooling of Working-Class Girls in Nineteenth Century England, 1800–1870

June Purvis, The Open University

Introduction

In *The Sociological Imagination,* C. Wright Mills (1959) claimed that 'all sociology worthy of the name is "historical sociology"'.[1] Yet within one of the main sub-disciplines of sociology, the sociology of education, there have been few historical studies.[2] Since the Second World War, the sociology of education has been primarily concerned with issues such as social class inequalities in education, the social construction of educational knowledge, classroom interaction and the problematic relationship between the macro and micro levels of analysis.[3] Most of these studies have been ahistorical or, at best, offered what Mills has called 'the dull little padding known as "sketching in the historical background"'.[4] The ahistorical nature of much sociology of education plus the emphasis upon social class inequalities has obscured other fundamental issues such as gender divisions:[5] after all, it was in the century prior to the twentieth that the origins of some of the greatest structural inequalities in access to education between girls and boys, men and women, are to be found. In this paper I wish to concentrate upon the schooling of working-class girls in England from 1800–1870 and, through such an exercise, I hope I might be able to show how historical study can be a part of the sociological imagination within sociology of education.

Much of the recent discussion on the education of working-class girls in the nineteenth century has concentrated upon the post- rather than pre-1870 situation. In particular, writers such as Carol Dyhouse and Anna Davin have illustrated the way that ideas regarding the social nature of women in society influenced the education of working-class girls after 1870 by making curricula content sex specific.[6] A common assumption about working-class education before 1870, however, is that there was a homogeneity in educational provision for boys and girls. Sara Delamont, for example, in a recent statement claims as 'an historical fact' that in the middle of the nineteenth century, the content of working-class education in both Britain and America was hardly differentiated by sex though by 1920 the content was sex-specific.[7] Delamont, however, offers no historical evidence to support this wide generalization. Though such a statement may apply to those forms of schooling organized by the working class, such as dame schools and Sunday schools, much more research is needed before we can accept such a generalization.

Sunday schools, for example, were an important means of teaching working-class children to read, though the teaching of writing was a controversial issue, often confined to a weekday class.[8] By 1850, some two million working-class children were enrolled in Sunday school and there appears to have been an almost even division between the number of male and female scholars.[9] This does not mean, however, that curricula content for boys and girls was undifferentiated, especially if classes were segregated by sex. In particular, the use of Biblical texts as teaching material undoubtedly stressed hidden gender messages. Marianne Farningham, for example, born in 1834 in Eynsford, Kent, the daughter of a village postmaster, remembers that the reading material published by the Sunday School Union contained no references to 'great women':[10]

> My father gave us two monthly magazines published by the Sunday School Union, the *Teacher's Offering,* and the *Child's Companion.* In one of these was a series of descriptive articles on men who had been poor boys, and risen to be rich and great. Every month I hoped to find the story of some poor ignorant 'girl', who, beginning life as handicapped as I, had yet been able by her own efforts and the blessing of God upon them to live a life of usefulness, if not of greatness. But I believe that there was not a woman in the whole series.[11]

Similarly, though in some dame schools working-class boys and girls might share a common curriculum, in other dame schools this was not so. Thomas Cooper, for example, the auto-didactic, working-class radical, recollects how 'Old Gatty' who ran a dame school taught reading and spelling to both boys and girls but knitting to girls only.[12] In other words, we cannot ignore gender as a structuring variable in those forms of educational provision organized by the working class for working-class boys and girls *before* 1870.

However, I would like to claim that, in the period 1800–1870, it is particularly in those forms of schooling offered by the middle classes for working-class children that gender is a major structuring variable. To concentrate, as Richard Johnson has done, upon the way that such middle class provision has acted as a form of class-cultural control,[13] is to ignore the way that gender could operate as a means of control too. And I would like to stress that we can only begin to understand how gender acted in this way by referring to wider issues outside the context of such schooling, issues such as gender ideologies – especially the gender ideologies relating to girls and women that were held by the middle classes[14] – and the sexual division of labour both within the family and within paid employment. Within this paper though, I shall particularly concentrate upon gender ideologies.

My aims in this paper are threefold. First, I shall discuss gender ideologies relating to women and girls, especially the gender ideology that became a part of dominant bourgeois culture. Secondly, I shall attempt to trace the ways in which bourgeois gender ideology helped to shape the curricula and content of schooling for working-class girls, a shaping which helped to influence both the structural conditions which teachers confronted within the classroom and the future participation of their female pupils in waged labour and in family life. Thirdly, I hope to illustrate that through the provision of such gender-specific schooling, working-class girls suffered a double handicap: as members of the working class, they were offered an education that was sharply differentiated, segregated and inferior to that offered to middle class children, since secondary education was possible for the latter but only elementary education for the former[15] and, as working-class girls rather than working-class boys, they were offered a schooling that was unequal and inferior in comparison with that of their brothers. I will now explore these issues in further detail.

Gender Ideologies for Women and Girls in Nineteenth Century England

In nineteenth century England, gender ideologies were part of social class ideologies and like class ideologies were subject to change over the course of the century. It is important for the social historian of education to remember, however, that, though masculinity and femininity are historically specific social constructions which vary both within and between social classes, within nineteenth-century society masculinity was the superior gender form. Nineteenth-century England was both a capitalist and patriarchal society within which inequalities in economic, political and cultural power gave men many advantages.[16] The dominance of men and subordination of women was evident within a range of social structures, social relations and activities but perhaps the one area within which a gender hierarchy was most evident was the nineteenth-century household. Women and girls in both working class and middle class households would learn that femininity involved creating a context within which boys and men could live.[17] Generally, femininity was defined in relation to masculinity and, above all else, this meant serving men.

Within the context of a highly stratified class society, it is hardly surprising that by the middle of the century, the gender ideology of the bourgeoisie had become the dominant gender ideology. As Catherine Hall (1979) has suggested, the period 1780–1832 was a time in which an industrial, capitalist society with a large and influential bourgeoisie was created and also a time in which the ideas of the Evangelical sect about women becoming the 'moral regenerators of the nation' if they looked after home, husband and family became an integral part of the dominant bourgeois culture.[18] Bourgeois gender ideology took the form of stressing women's domestic role as household managers, wives and mothers, rather than stressing any part that women might play in economic production. A specific form of sexual division of labour was advocated within the household: while the ideal location for women was within the private sphere of the family, with prime responsibility for the care of her husband, children and the home, the ideal location for men was within the public sphere of work, earning sufficient to support those who were economically dependent. Thus historians and sociologists have called this ideology the 'domestic ideology'.

Elsewhere,[19] I have suggested that bourgeois domestic ideology embodied three major assumptions. First, that the notion of separate spheres was frequently couched in biological terms as a 'natural' division between the sexes. Secondly, that since women were primarily wives and mothers, they were essentially 'relative' rather than autonomous beings, defined in relation to men and children. Thirdly, that women were inferior and subordinate to men. Within the dominant bourgeois culture, therefore, femininity became synonymous with domesticity or extensions of domesticity such as domestic service, and masculinity with the world of waged labour outside the home. The emphasis upon the assumed moral and religious power of women as wives and mothers created, however, a basic contradiction for them in a society where economic production was given primary status and men held economic, political and ideological power.

Bourgeois gender ideology developed within a specific economic and political climate which provided the conditions for its success. First of all, there was the considerable influence of various religious groups such as the Evangelicals, Unitarians and Quakers who, by the mid-nineteenth century, accepted the notion of separate spheres for men and women and the importance of women within the 'charmed circle of the home'.[20] Secondly, important changes in the economic structure of society, in particular the development of an industrial, commercial and factory system, physically separated homeplace and workplace. This helped to create a division between production and consumption, between public and private spheres. The home based feminine role assumed a new ideological and cultural importance as it provided a stable environment that would offer support to men for their tasks in the public sphere. As one writer was to claim in 1865:

> We feel that man's character never attains its full development save when he was engaged heart and soul in the great battle of life. We feel that women's character has never attained to its perfection save when we see her as the loving wife and tender mother. Man is formed for the turmoil and the labours of the outer world, woman for the peace and quiet of home.[21]

Investigating gender ideologies within the working class during the period 1800–1870 is much more problematic since it is difficult to judge the relationship between a possible domestic ideology for women and its practice. One of the main problems relates to historical sources. The sources describing working-class lives are of three main kinds. First, there are the numerous accounts written by middle class commentators and observers, accounts that contain their own value judgments and suppositions about working-class life. Secondly, there are the autobiographies written by working class people themselves. Most of these are written by men, not women, and a large number seem to exclude any detailed account of family life and the sexual division of labour within the home.[22] In a number of autobiogaphies, wives in particular are often conspicuous by their absence.[23] Thirdly, there is the oral evidence given by working-class people to the various government commissions and reports, evidence that is gathered and collected within particular ideological frameworks. Overall, the available sources would seem to indicate that, in the first half of the nineteenth century in particular, it was commonly assumed that women within the working class had two roles – that of waged worker and that of wife and mother. In practice, when home and workplace shared the same location, many married working-class women were engaged in various 'cottage industries' such as weaving, lace-making, straw-plaiting, glovemaking. In rural areas too, where the wages of the husband were low, women had 'little choice'[24] but to engage in waged labour. But even when women did work in this way, they were also expected to do various domestic tasks such as cooking, housework and child care. Many accounts recording this are to be found in the government reports of the 1840s. For example, the Rev. Peter Benson of Devonshire, in evidence presented in 1843, claimed that the woman working in the fields:

> does not go out till after her husband in the morning; he takes his dinner (a crust of bread, and sometimes, though rarely, a slice of cheese or cold bacon) by the hedge-side, or in his employer's outhouse, and she is always back in time to get his supper ready. The husband, therefore, does not suffer in any way. Where there is a family probably the children are not so well attended to as if the mother were at home. The eldest daughter, perhaps, is kept at home (who might be at school), to look after the younger children.[25]

Similarly, a Somerset farmer claimed that women with a family must have one day at home each week to see to family matters.[26] Examples like this illustrate only too well the dual demands of home and waged labour in the life of women in rural areas and the way that daughters, especially the eldest daughter, was socialized into her feminine role. In the domestic industries, on the other hand, it may have been somewhat easier for women to meet the dual demands of wife/mother and waged worker since the home was the place where both sets of tasks were performed. About the middle of the century, however, mechanical inventions began to revolutionize various cottage industries, especially the weaving of textiles,[27] and the transfer of waged labour from the home to the factory made it much more problematic for working class women with children to engage in full time industrial employment. As Ivy Pinchbeck (1930) has pointed out in her classic study, the majority of female factory workers were not married women but single women and girls who could not be supported at home.[28]

About this point in time, many working-class men and women began to articulate their own fears about the effect on family life, and on wage levels for men, of women's employment in factories. In 1841, for example, some male operatives demanded the gradual withdrawal of all females from the factories, claiming that the 'home, its care and its employments, is woman's true sphere'. They further complained that women brought up in factories could not 'make a shirt, darn a stocking, cook a dinner or clean a house'.[29] Such a viewpoint was increasingly taken up during the second half of the century by the working class, especially the predominantly male trade union movement. Though women's trade unionism was especially strong in the textile unions founded in the 1850's,[30] the attitude of bodies such as the TUC to women's waged labour outside the home was often hostile, especially if women sought to enter jobs that had previously been the province of men. The lower levels of pay traditionally earned by women, together with their lower level of technical skills, could lead not only to male unemployment but also depress the status of an occupation. At one TUC Conference, for example, held in Nottingham in 1883:

> when one of the women delegates complained, 'If women were not allowed
> to earn a livelihood what must they do', the male delegates shouted with
> derisive laughter, 'Get married!'.[31]

And of course some working class women themselves, accepting the view that the place of married women was in the home, supported the withdrawal of married women from waged labour. In one report of 1859, women stressed that it was the duty of employers to pay the menfolk an adequate family wage to enable them 'to keep their wives in comfort at home', without the necessity of sending them to work in the mills.[32]

The separation of home and workplace that occurred in a number of forms of waged labour around the mid-nineteenth century, helped to establish the conditions for a working-class family form which might approximate the bourgeois ideal of a wage earning husband and an economically dependent, caring, emotionally supportive wife and mother. The dual demands of waged labour and domestic work which had been made upon working-class women in the early part of the century could possibly be tipped much more on the side of domestic work with participation in those home based, part-time, poorly paid, casual forms of waged labour that were an extension of domestic skills, e.g. sewing, taking in washing, cleaning.[33]

Bourgeois gender ideology, however, as we have seen, stressed woman's domestic role of household manager, wife and mother: to engage in waged labour of any kind was to be unladylike, for both daughters and married women, though unpaid philanthropic work was acceptable.[34] The daughters of the bourgeoisie were brought up to expect economic dependency upon some male and, generally, marriage, with economic dependency upon a husband, was regarded as the end state for the middle class girl.[35]

Now the bourgeoisie attempted to impose certain aspects of their own gender ideology upon working-class females through the kinds of educational provision they offered – before 1870 most of the formalized educational provision for the working classes was the result of middle class voluntary effort. In particular, they attempted to impose the ideal of full time domesticity for married working-class women: this was articulated as the ideal state to which working-class girls should aspire in the educational programmes provided for them.[36] To use education as a vehicle for imparting bourgeois class and gender ideologies was, therefore, an attempt to impose a specific family form on working-class life, a form, it was hoped, that would bring stability to society. The moral power of the working-class wife and mother was seen as critical in a newly emerging industrial society: social problems such as poverty, crime, political unrest and drunkenness were often attributed to her failure rather than to the wider social, economic and cultural changes that were taking place. However, the attack upon working-class wifehood and motherhood did not mean that the bourgeoisie wished to impose a new cultural form of family life that was the same as their own. The differences between their conceptions of femininity for middle-class and working-class women must be maintained, and thus the bourgeoisie emphasized the *practical* rather than managerial skills of the working-class housekeeper, wife and mother. The class differences in the conceptions of femininity that the bourgeoisie supported are even more pronounced in the case of working-class girls than working-class women. The bourgeoisie did not believe that working-class girls should be 'provided for', like their middle-class sisters: instead, working-class girls were expected to provide for themselves through engaging in waged labour. Within the educational context, therefore, we find an emphasis upon 'useful' knowledge as opposed to the 'useless' knowledge, such as the accomplishments curriculum, that many middle-class girls were taught.[37] In ways such as this, therefore, the educational provision offered by the middle classes maintained and legitimated the social distance between middle-class and working-class girls. Education for working-class girls was not to be a vehicle for social mobility but a means of maintaining the *status quo*.

In the institutional forms of education for working-class girls that I shall consider, we shall find that 'useful' knowledge was often narrowly interpreted as teaching domestic skills that would prepare girls for employment as domestic servants. This emphasis upon teaching domestic skills had, of course, two main advantages from the point of view of the bourgeoisie. First of all, it would offer a supply of well-trained domestic servants who were suitable for employment in the middle-class household. Secondly, it would help to prepare working-class girls for the future ideal state of the competent, practically skilled wife and mother. And it is of interest to note that after 1870, when a national system of state education became possible, it would appear that schooling for motherhood became a major concern[38], especially around the turn of the century. By this time, the distinction between the public sphere of work and the private sphere of the home had become much more separated, and females came to be increasingly identified with the latter. The influence of the 'domestic ideology' upon the schooling of working-class girls may, therefore have involved different emphases in the pre- and post-1870 situations. In this paper, though, I am only concerned with the pre-1870 situation which I shall now examine in greater detail.

Schooling for Useful Women's Work in Waged Labour and in Unpaid, Domestic Services Within the Home

Despite the heterogeneity of educational institutions provided by the middle classes for working-class girls,[39] we find a similarity in overall emphasis upon preparing girls for useful work in typically feminine occupations such as domestic service[40] and also for those unpaid, practical, routine household chores that might be performed in a home, especially in a future state of wifehood and motherhood. In this paper, I shall concentrate upon charity schools, schools of industry and the day schools of the two main religious Societies – the British and Foreign School Society (largely supported by religious dissenters) and the National Society for Promoting the Education of the Poor in the Principles of the Established Church (the Church of England).

As McCann (1977) has noted, charity schools were rooted in eighteenth century concepts of patronage and servitude.[41] The intentions of the founders were to provide a moral, religious and useful training for poor children through a curriculum of religion, literacy and some practical skill that had vocational value.[42] Busyness and usefulness were regarded as good in themselves for the lower orders. By a combination of 'useful labour' and 'mental stimulation'[43] it was hoped that poor children would be brought up to habits of 'early industry' that would prepare them for those 'subordinate situations in society to which they may be called'.[44] Charity schools were expected, therefore, not only to socialize poor children into industrious habits and skills by which they could earn a living but also to preserve, rather than change, the existing social class hierarchy. For girls, however, the articulation of such aims was set in a different context to that for boys in that the aims usually related to the sphere of the home. The curriculum for girls stressed, therefore, the teaching of domestic skills, especially useful plain sewing such as the making of shifts and petticoats.[45] Such sewing skills could be utilized in domestic service, in the parental home of the girl and in any future family of her own. The extent of gender differentiation in the curriculum may be portrayed in the following report from one charity school:

> The girls are taught to read, knit, spin, sew, and mend their own clothes, so as to fit them to be useful daughters, and good wives: the boys (besides being improved in their reading) are instructed in writing and arithmetic.[46]

Examples such as this illustrate how girls were not offered the range of curricula open to boys. Gordon (1950)[47] in fact claims that, generally in charity schools, writing was rare and arithmetic rarer still for girls. The concern with training in religious and moral principles and with conduct was expected to sustain the young girls once they had left the schools and were engaged in waged labour. Some schools, such as those organized by Hannah and Martha More in the Mendip Hills, offered certain rewards or inducements to past pupils in order to encourage behaviour that was seen as desirable conduct:

> In order to encourage chastity and good morals in the single woman, the patronesses present every young woman 'of good character', who has been educated in their schools, and continues to attend religious instruction there, with five shillings, a new Bible, and a pair of white stockings on the day of marriage.[48]

How many young women passed the test, in any one year, we do not know! It is also difficult to estimate the number of charity schools that were established and the number of girls who were educated within them.

Some of the charity schools were also called schools of industry, a term which appears to apply to a broad range of institutions which emphasized schooling for useful employment. And it is in these schools, directly preparing working-class boys and girls for waged labour, that gender differentiation is most pronounced – a statement that appears to be valid for both single sex and mixed sex institutions. Girls were trained especially for domestic service while boys were prepared for a wider range of occupations. For example, in the 1820s, at Cheltenham School of Industry for Girls, the pupils were trained to be under-servants since it was felt that this 'useful class' of servants who would 'quietly and properly' do 'all sorts' of household business, was much needed.[49] Thus the girls were taught baking, milling, washing, ironing and every 'other kind of household work' – how to spin wool, flax and hemp; how to knit; to sew; to plait whole straw for baskets; and how to cut out and make clothing, which was afterwards sold at reduced prices to the poor. Such a curriculum would, it was hoped, prepare girls for the sphere within which they would hereafter move as 'servants, wives, or daughters'. Socialization into an appropriate form of conduct and behaviour is, therefore, considered an important aim of the school – attention to religious duties, to order, to neatness, to cleanliness and to earning an honest living are stressed.[50]

Preparing girls for an honest living in domestic service meant a prohibition upon teaching one of the basic literacy skills – writing. Writing was considered a dangerous skill since 'ignorant parents' attach to it the idea of 'scholarship' and 'capability', ideas which might encourage the seeking of forms of waged labour that involved less manual work and higher levels of income than domestic service.[51] In other words, the acquisition of the skill of writing was seen as a potential lever for occupational mobility and hence a threat to the clearly stratified, social class hierarchy. However, while the evils of writing and even of reading are mentioned in relation to girls, no such reference is made in the case of boys. Thus the sketch of a plan for a school of industry for boys at Cheltenham involves a curriculum of reading, writing, spelling and cypher, and though the boys are to be trained for 'farmers' or other servants',[52] they are to learn an entirely different range of skills to those domestic skills taught to working-class girls: in particular, boys were to be taught skills that could be performed both within and outside the private sphere of the home, e.g. weaving, basket-making, the making and mending of shoes, the making of ropes, twines and sacking, gardening, assisting in making hedges and ditches, the occasional mending of roads.[53] Examples such as this illustrate vividly how even within one occupation, i.e. domestic service, a sexual division of labour may be upheld and reinforced by the differential educational experiences offered to working-class boys and girls within a school of industry. We find a similar gender differentiation in curricula in mixed sex schools of industry.[54]

Certain aspects of bourgeois class and gender ideologies then, influenced curriculum content in both charity schools and schools of industry. In particular, the idea of separate spheres for the sexes, especially the idea that the female sex should be primarily located within the private sphere of the home while males engaged primarily in activities outside the home, meant that girls and boys were offered a gender-specific curriculum that reflected their respective spheres. However, the main middle-class providers of elementary schooling for working-class children before 1870 were the National Society and the much smaller British and Foreign Schools

Society since, between them, they offered over 90% of the voluntary school places.[55] And it is particularly in these forms of schooling that bourgeois class and gender ideologies are most evident. This is not surprising. The patrons of both Societies were largely drawn from that strata of society that possessed both the time and level of income to support such philanthropic activity, i.e. the middle and upper classes. The Evangelicals, for example, whom we have already mentioned as important proponents of bourgeois domestic ideology in the early part of the century, were an influential reforming group who had an active interest in educating the lower orders.[56] Let us first of all, therefore, look at the provision offered by the National Society.

The aims of the National Society are stated in its first annual report of 1812:

> to communicate to the Poor generally, by the means of a summary mode of education, lately brought into practice, such knowledge and habits, as are sufficient to guide them through life, in their proper stations, especially to teach the doctrines of Religion, according to the principles of the Established Church and to train them to the performance of their Religious duties by early discipline.[57]

The National Society was concerned, therefore, with offering working-class children that basic knowledge and conduct considered appropriate for their social class. The latter was taken so seriously that rules were drawn up for both parents and children. Parents were expected to impose certain standards of appearance and certain standards of conduct upon their children in that pupils were to be clean, washed, hair combed, attend school and church regularly[58] – even though parents paid for their child's school. Similarly, pupils were expected to work hard at their lessons, to be respectful and obedient to their teachers, to be kind to each other and never to tell lies, cheat, steal or swear.[59] The National Society sought, through such a system of rules, to exercise organizational control over both parents and pupils: in particular, it would appear that parents had little client control in terms of participating in those decision-making processes that determined what was taught in the schools. As Elizabeth Merson (1979) has recently observed of Bramshaw National School, Hampshire, such schools were established not as a result of popular demand but as institutions conferred by those who 'knew best'.[60] The National Society therefore, upheld an ideal world[61] for its schools through the system of rules, since the working-class child would be taught not only his/her social station in life but also how to become an honest, clean, kind, reliable, trustworthy person – the ideal future citizen. We find references in the log books kept by national schools to occasions when the rules have been broken. For example, at Northam Girls' School, Hampshire, Mrs. Elizabeth A. Davies, the schoolmistress, records in the log book entry for 27th April 1864 that the two Aldridge girls, Alma and Agnes, have left the school because after 'frequent warnings' she had sent one of them home to 'wash her hands & face & comb her hair'.[62]

The National Society offered both mixed and separate educational provision (either in separate schools, separate departments or separate rooms) for boys and girls. At the Central Schools of the Society, at Baldwin's Gardens, for example, we find both a girls' and a boys' room.[63] The Rev. Tregarthen claimed, in 1867, that schools for girls were found mainly in the towns rather than the villages.[64] This is not surprising: the catchment area of village schools might not have been large enough to support the expense of single sex schools and, in addition, there may have been great prejudice against schooling working-class girls in the more traditional, rural areas. What we do find is that, within any one county, a variety of educational forms was possible. In Yorkshire, for example, in the 1860s, the Church of England schools inspected by the Rev. Charles Routledge included 39 boys' schools, 35 girls' schools, 123 mixed schools, 35 infant schools and 80 evening schools. The total number of scholars reveals another common feature of National schooling, namely that there were more male than female pupils – in this particular case 17,834 of the former as opposed to 14,356 of the latter.[65] Sometimes a girls' school would be mixed with an infants' school. This was so at Whitby, in the 1860s,[66] and at Bramshaw School, Hampshire, from 1819.[67] Where this occurred, girls usually suffered an educational disadvantage in comparison with boys. Infants and girls would often be in one room, taught simultaneously by a female teacher and her assistants. As late as 1870, the Rev. W.J. Kennedy, Inspector for Church of England schools in Lancashire, Cheshire and the Isle of Man, pointed out the handicaps of such a system:

> The chief defect I have to regret in the organization of schools is, that schools for boys and girls are too much crowded with infants. This is especially the case in some girls' schools, and the evil is rather on the increase I fear, because in my district some managers are attempting to reduce the expense of the schools by having one certificated mistress for both girls and infants . . . It is not only that infants in the same room with girls are noisy and interfere with good order and discipline, but the infants themselves require the care and teaching of a trained and experienced mistress, and ought neither to be neglected nor regarded as little more than a means of bringing a certain amount of grant to a school by swelling the average attendance.[68]

It is highly probable that more girls than boys were in mixed schools with infants since femininity, not masculinity, was linked with child care. Female pupils might help in the care and teaching of younger children.

Not surprisingly, the educational standard attained by girls was often inferior in comparison with that attained by boys, especially boys educated in a single sex school managed by a master. The Rev. Allington, for example, claimed that in those Church of England schools inspected by him in Suffolk, the girls failed much more frequently than the boys in 'all subjects' and in 'all standards' though the differences in educational attainment between boys and girls was less noticeable in mixed schools.[69] The whole issue of the importance of separate versus mixed schooling for the educational standard of working-class girls in the nineteenth century needs careful, thorough investigation. My own research tends to suggest that, on balance, girls tended to attain a higher educational standard in mixed schools taught by a master. The Rev. Barry, for example, Inspector for the Counties of Gloucester and Somerset, observed that the mixing of some boys' and girls' schools under a master resulted in a 'great improvement' in the arithmetic of the girls.[70] Where girls could be taught by the male teacher who taught the boys, there was always the possibility that they could attain that higher standard in the 3Rs, especially in arithmetic, that the boys had traditionally attained. There is evidence, too, to suggest that parents preferred a mixed school that was taught by a male rather than female teacher[71] and that the master of a mixed school could discipline the boys more successfully than a mistress.[72] As Matthew Arnold was to state in 1852:

the education of girls, when they learn with boys and from a master, appears to me to gain that very correctness and stringency which female education generally wants.[73]

The issue of mixed or single sex schooling for working-class girls plus the question of the sex of the teacher appears, therefore, to hold crucial consequences for educational standards and educational attainment. Despite the importance of such organization issues, however, one thing is certain – in any form of schooling organized by the National Society, girls were offered a gender-specific curriculum.

The pattern of gender differentiation in the curriculum was established by the Central Schools in Baldwin's Gardens: here, in two rooms, one to hold 600 boys and the other to hold 400 girls,[74] both boys and girls participated in prayers, ciphering, religious exercises, writing and reading in the morning but, in the afternoon, the boys continued with ciphering, writing, reading and arithmetical tables while the girls were taught knitting and needlework till half past four and then arithmetical tables till 5 o'clock.[75] Such a gender-specific curriculum for girls was justified in terms of preparation for a future life in domestic service and in marriage:[76] in particular, the teaching of domestic economy served both these aims. In a list of school materials and books sold by the Society we find the titles of two books that are likely to have been used in teaching girls – *Household Matters* and *Lessons on Housewifery*.[77]

Though the quality of education varied greatly within the National schools, we do find a number of complaints that such a schooling only prepared working-class girls for the superior kinds of domestic work. Mr. Booth of Lincolnshire, for example, complained in 1843:

> Dairy-maids are very difficult to get because of the National schools; they all want to be housemaids, or mantua-makers, or something of that sort. They object to such work as the dairy; they are too delicate for that. I think education makes the boys rather better; you can reason with them; they understand you easier: they generally get out at 10, so that they are not so much taught as the girls.[78]

Statements such as this do reveal that the National schools may have prepared working-class girls for entry into a higher range of occupations than would have been possible without such a schooling. Other sources indicate, too, that in other parts of the country working-class girls may have been kept at a National school longer than their brothers,[79] though this should not blind us to the fact that fewer girls than boys attended anyway and that their attendance was much more intermittent than that of the boys.[80] Despite the limited kind of occupational mobility that National schooling may have offered, working-class girls were still prepared for useful women's work – either in low-paid, waged laour or in unpaid domestic services in the home.

The aims of the British schools, like those of the National schools, were to offer poor children the 'rudiments' of education and to provide a training in 'morals and good conduct'.[81] A basic curriculum of reading, writing, arithmetic and needle-work was recommended for the girls, the lessons for reading to include extracts from the Holy Scriptures.[82] It was generally thought by this Society, which was largely supported by dissenting religious groups such as the Quakers, that a small payment helped to encourage attendance and remove any stigma attached to charity.

The main reason that was constantly stated for educating girls in British schools was that such education would help them to become competent future wives and mothers. Such a justification was frequently reiterated by the Ladies Committee of the Society whose main task was to superintend female education. For example, in 1833, this Committee warned that too many friends of the poor were willing to train girls as servants and to forget that they will one day be mothers:

> Needlework and household duties are too important to be neglected or despised; but they must not be allowed to interfer with moral and intellectual cultivation. If girls are to be trained with a view to becoming the wives and mothers of industrous and intelligent mechanics, their education must be less of the lip, and more of the heart.[83]

Statements like this reveal that the education of poor girls was often defined in terms of their future relation to men and children, especially male children, rather than in terms of any individual needs of any one girl. The relative nature of girls was, of course, an essential ingredient of the domestic ideology, and educating girls for a future state of wifehood and motherhood was seen as one way to alleviate social problems. Through emphasizing the importance of full time motherhood, such middle-class ladies were attempting to impose a specific bourgeois form of family life since, as we have previously noted, most working-class mothers, in the first half of the nineteenth-century at least, engaged in some form of waged labour. The realities of working-class life, especially the continual struggle to avoid starvation, a struggle in which the waged labour of a wife and mother would be necessary, were conveniently ignored.

We find, however, a curious paradox within the British Society in that, despite the number of statements stressing the importance of education for poor girls, the actual provision of schools was such that there were far fewer places for girls than for boys. In 1833, the Ladies Committee complained:

> Prejudices which, so far as boys are concerned, have long since passed away, still hang around the instruction of girls, and, it is to be feared, will not easily be dissipated.[84]

Throughout the period I am considering, the bulk of the resources financed education for working-class boys. In a patriarchal society where masculinity was the dominant gender form, priority was given to boys and boys were the target clientele. Though the necessary statistics do not exist whereby we may calculate the number of boys and girls who had been educated in British schools by the 1860s, we may obtain some idea of the scale of the issue by looking at the figures for the total number of pupils who had passed through the two central schools at Borough Road. Thus by 1864, 66,204 pupils had passed through the Boys' School but only 25,221 through the Girl's School.[85] For working-class girls, therefore, part of the burden of their gender was the fact that their education was considered less important than that of their brothers and thus fewer school places were provided for them.

We find in the British, as in the National schools, that though boys and girls were both taught the 3Rs and religious instruction, girls only were taught the skill of plain sewing. The following list of clothes, made in the 1820s, by girls at the Portsea school, Hampshire, vividly illustrates how working-class girls were taught to make practical clothes for persons of all ages:

HALF-PRICE CLOTHING PLAN
Articles made and sold from October 1823 to October 1824. – 207
pincloths; 156 shifts; 11 aprons; 6 boys' shirts; 3 women's caps; 217 girls'
caps; 30 infants' bed-gowns; 54 infants' caps; 24 infants' shirts; and 5
women's bed-gowns.[86]

Similarly, at Worcester Girls' School in 1824, 42 frocks and various other 'useful
articles of clothing' had been made and were distributed as 'rewards' according to the
'merit' of the children.[87] Sometimes too, the girls were involved in cleaning duties
within the school: this was so at Tottenham where the elder girls were employed 'to
keep the schoolroom clean and assist the mistress a little in her apartment.[88] The
British schools then, like the other forms of schooling provided by the middle classes
that we have considered, helped to prepare working class girls for both domestic service and women's work within the family. And the following statement from the
Ladies Committee in 1821 makes it quite clear that the Society was well aware of this
dual aim:

> those persons ought to be well instructed in the first principles of Religion
> and Morals, to whom the early care of the infant mind is committed, and
> from whom first impressions are derived. It cannot be expected that
> mothers, who are destitute of every moral principle, can be the means of
> instructing their offspring in the duties they owe to God, their parents, or
> to society. To accomplish these great purposes, the cultivation of those who
> are to occupy the station of servants is highly necessary; they are constantly
> with the children of the rich and the poor: by their example, their care,
> their reproofs, and their disposition, much of the future conduct of the
> rising generation must be directed.[89]

Whether prepared for domestic service or family life, working-class girls would learn
that a major part of their activities would involve creating a context for the lives of
other people.

Both the National and British schools shared certain features in common, and
some discussion of these features is necessary when considering the educational
experiences these schools offered to working-class girls. First, both kinds of schools
employed not only schoolteachers but also utilized a monitorial method of teaching
(especially up to the 1840s) whereby pupils were engaged in instructing their peers in
a mechanistic, repetitive, chanting manner. The Rev. Cook, for example, in a report
on his inspection of schools in the Eastern district of England in 1843–4 notes that the
monitor was often a child of 8 or 9 years of age who was directed to repeat answers of
the Catechism in sentences and then to make the class repeat them in turn.[90] The implications of such a method of rote learning for the quality of education for working-
class girls is, of course, profound. Memorization of dates, verses from the Bible and
other books, poetry, lists of sovereigns etc. became a key feature of the learning process rather than an understanding of the meaning of what was being taught. And the
emphasis upon public rather than private individual reading and learning would undoubtedly help to create confusion. Consequently, we find many critical comments
made on the monitorial method of teaching by the various inspectors. The same Rev.
Cook, for example, commented on the long list of gross mistakes, omissions and
mispronunciations of principal words: he complained that even in the recital of the
Lord's Prayer it was common to hear children say, 'Our Father charter heaven'.[91]

Secondly, both National and British schools, during the first half of the century, began to employ inspectors and to widen the curriculum to include subjects such as political economy, history and geography.[92] However, though the curriculum was widened by 1850, girls did not participate in these new subjects to the same extent as boys did. In particular, needlework was still retained as a gender-specific subject for girls which meant there was less time devoted to other less practical areas. Evidence presented to the Newcastle Commission on Popular Education (1861) claimed that in girls' schools the greater part of the afternoon was given up to needlework.[93] This is not to deny that changes had occurred in access to a broader curriculum for some girls. By 1854, for example, at the Girls' Model School of the British Society, the curriculum included modern geography, practical arithmetic, object lessons, English history, reading, spelling, dictation, English grammar, Scripture reading and interrogation, domestic economy every Friday morning from 9.15 to 9.45 and needlework every afternoon from 3.15 to 4 o'clock.[94]

Thirdly, another feature that both the British and National Societies shared was that both provided facilities for the training of teachers, the former at Borough Road and the latter at its Central Schools.[95] The whole issue of teacher training was greatly aided by the introduction, in 1848, of a state aided, five year, pupil-teacher apprenticeship which could be offered to pupils who had completed elementary education up to the age of 13. Applicants for such apprenticeships had to possess certain modest educational standards in the 3Rs, geography and scripture, as well as certain practical skills in the classroom.[96] However, in addition to this, female applicants were also expected to be able 'to sew neatly and to knit'.[97] As I have argued elsewhere,[98] in this way, female pupil teachers became a resource for teaching working-class girls specific domestic skills. They thus helped to maintain those sexual divisions that were already evident in the educational provision offered by the two Societies and to promote those gender expectations that were regarded as an aspect of femininity.

Fourthly, both National and British schools responded to various educational codes and restrictions imposed by the state in order to receive financial aid. In particular, the Revised Code of 1862 introduced a 'payment by results' scheme whereby a grant of twelve shillings per child per annum could only be earned under certain conditions. Thus four shillings of the grant could be given if a child attended schools regularly (under a qualified head teacher), while the remaining eight shillings could only be awarded if a pupil attained a satisfactory standard in an annual examination conducted by an HMI in the 3R's. If a child failed in any one of the 3Rs, two shillings and eightpence was deducted from that child's grant. The examinations were arranged in a hierarchy of standards and each child was expected to progress to the next level at the end of each school year.[99] As Frith (1977) has pointed out, the Revised Code, with its rules of attendance, reduction of education to standards and reliance on measurements and examinations, marked a new state in the rationalization of education for the working class.[100] The effect of such changes upon the process of schooling for working-class girls was profound: schooling became even more of a daily grind in the 3Rs, religious instruction and sewing. The widening of the curriculum that was at least possible for some working-class girls by the mid-century, was whittled away. It was not until 1867 that schools could attract a higher grant if they taught extra subjects, known in 1875 as specific subjects, but since these extra subjects could only be taught in Standards IV, V and VI, few working-class girls or boys experienced such a broadening of the curriculum. Hurt (1980) has suggested that the proportion of working-class children benefiting from such changes in the second half of the century never rose beyond the 4.4% of 1883.[101]

Fifthly, both of the Societies shared in common the fact that the attendance of working-class girls in their schools was irregular and intermittent. Throughout the period under discussion, the working classes were generally involved in what Henry Mayhew (1851) called 'the struggle to live'[102] or what Joseph Lawson (1887) later called the struggle for the 'necessaries of life'.[103] This did not encourage favourable attitudes towards education, especially when the choice lay between starvation and literacy. The pull of the necessity of child waged labour is evident throughout the century. Even in areas where girls stayed at school longer than boys – as in many agricultural districts where the opportunities for waged labour was often restricted to domestic service – their schooling was much more intermittent than that of boys since they were frequently kept at home to engage in unpaid, domestic duties. These issues are well illustrated in a statement made by the Rev. W.W. Howard in 1866–67. Thus when speaking about the irregular attendance of children in the schools in the West of England he suggests that this is due to the:

indifference of the parents to education; having little or none themselves, and not having learnt that it has a money value, while they are pinched to obtain food and clothing for themselves and family, they grudge the money spent on what they cannot appreciate, as well as the money, which the children might be earning towards their own support . . . Little fellows of 8 years old are made useful in farm work. They sometimes turn up again in a night school, knowing nothing, and finding it very hard to learn . . . The girls in agricultural districts are better off, though kept at home too often, when it is necessary to 'help mother', or 'to nurse the baby'. But where lace making or gloving are rife, many girls never go to school at all, and live their lives and pass away to a hereafter in a state of ignorance, which is a disgrace to humanity.[104]

Other evidence does suggest that it may have been particularly the eldest girl in a family who was kept at home to mind the children or sent into waged labour.[105]

With the passing of the 1870 Education Act, a state system of national elementary schooling became possible, bringing together the previously fragmented system of educational provision. Even so, the social class divisions in educational provision for girls were stoutly maintained. Most middle class girls were still educated outside the newly-emerging state sector since they were mainly educated by governesses within the private sphere of their parents' home. It was the working-class girl who might attend the emerging board schools. As H.G. Wells (1934) was to comment in his autobiography, the 1870 Education Act was not an Act to provide a common universal schooling for all social classes but an Act to educate lower class children for employment in lower class occupations.[106] For working-class girls, however, the provision of a state system of national education meant a renewed emphasis on education for motherhood rather than education for employment, a renewed emphasis that was especially pronounced in the latter decades of the century when grants were made for the teaching of cookery and laundry work.[107] But not all working-class girls experienced such a state system of schooling since school attendance was not made compulsory until 1880 and not made free until 1891.

Conclusion

In conclusion, I would like to make three points. First, I have tried to show how certain aspects of bourgeois gender ideology, which became a part of the dominant class ideology, pervaded the curriculum and content of certain forms of schooling provided by the middle classes for working-class girls. The dominant gender ideology helped to establish a pattern of sexual divisions within such schooling, a pattern that was incorporated within the state system of education that developed after 1870. Secondly, I have tried to illustrate, in those forms of schooling I have considered, how working-class girls experienced the double burden of class and gender. The burden of class is particularly evident in both the poor material conditions of working class existence and in the often unfavourable attitudes towards the schooling of children. But in addition to such handicaps, working-class girls also suffered the burden of their gender. Their education was considered less important than that of their brothers by both their parents and the middle-class providers. Consequently, fewer girls were sent to school anyway, and fewer places provided for them than for boys. Once within the school, the gender-specific curriculum taught to working-class girls held important implications for their social placement within the economic structure and within the family. As girls, rather than boys, they were prepared for low-paid, women's work in waged labour and unpaid, woman's work within the family. The schooling of working-class girls from 1800–1870 helped, therefore, the social reproduction of sexual divisions within the labour market as well as the cultural reproduction of the sexual division of labour within the family. Finally, I would like to end with a plea for more detailed historical work within the sociology of education. Such studies can extend the sociological imagination, provide fruitful data for grounded sociological theory, illuminate the relationship between education and social structure in different historical epochs, help us to understand the origins of the English educational system and reveal some of the continuities and differences between past and present educational practices. A word of caution is, however, necessary. As a number of points within this paper illustrate, we cannot assume glibly that the intension of the providers of education for working-class children always corresponded to the reality in practice. What is needed is much greater use of working-class autobiographical sources and, where possible, the use of oral history. Only in this way can we further elaborate upon the fundamental issue of linking the micro level of a child's experience of education with the macro level of voluntary or state provision.

Acknowledgements

The research upon which this paper is based is part of a much larger, continuing project which was initially financed by the SSRC and is now financed by the Open University. I would like to express my grateful thanks for this financial support. I would also like to thank Madeleine Arnot (previously MacDonald), Lecturer in Educational Studies at the Open University for her constant support, encouragement and constructive criticisms of my work. Any inadequacies in this paper are, however, my own.

Notes and References

1   MILLS, C.W. (1959) *The Sociological Imagination* Oxford, Oxford University Press, p. 146.
2   See, for example, BANKS, O. (1955) *Parity and Prestige in English Secondary Education,* London, Routledge and Kegan Paul; MUSGRAVE, P.W. (1968) *Society and Education in England Since 1800,* London, Methuen; MUSGRAVE, P.W. (Ed) (1970) *Sociology History and Education,* London, Methuen; VAUGHAN, M. and ARCHER, M. (1971) *Social Conflict and Educational Change in England and France 1789-1848,* Cambridge, Cambridge University Press; SHIPMAN, M.D. (1971) *Education and Modernization,* London, Faber and Faber; and the article by WILLIAMSON, B. in this volume.
3   The literature is extensive here. For recent discussion of some of these issues see BARTON, L. and MEIGHAN, R. (Eds) (1978) *Sociological Interpretations of Schooling and Classrooms: A Reappraisal,* Driffield, Nafferton Books.
4   MILLS, C.W. (1959) *op. cit.* p. 154.
5   OAKLEY, A. (1972) *Sex, Gender and Society,* London, Temple and Smith pp. 159-160, suggests that 'gender' refers to the socially constructed categories of masculinity and femininity while 'sex' refers to biological divisions that determine whether one is of the male or female sex.
6   DYHOUSE, C. (1976) 'Social Darwinistic ideas and the development of women's education in England, 1880–1920' in *History of Education,* 5 (1); DYHOUSE, C. (1977) 'Good wives and little mothers: Social anxieties and the schoolgirl's curriculum, 1890–1920' *Oxford Review of Education,* 3 (1); DYHOUSE, C. (1978) 'Towards a "feminine" curriculum for English schoolgirls: The demands of ideology, 1870–1963' *Women's Studies International Quarterly,* 1; DAVIN, A. (1978) 'Imperialism and motherhood' *History Workshop,* Spring; DAVIN, A. (1979) '"Mind that you do as you are told": reading books for Board School girls' *Feminist Review,* 3.
7   DELAMONT, S. (1978) 'The domestic ideology and women's education' in DELAMONT, S. and DUFFIN, L. (Eds) *The Nineteenth Century Woman: Her Cultural and Physical World,* London, Croom Helm, p. 164. I should say, however, that Delamont offers an insightful and illuminating sociological analysis of women's education. It is distressing to find that a recent review essay by WARWICK, D. and WILLIAMS, J. (1980) 'History and the sociology of education' *British Journal of Sociology of Education,* 1 (3), excludes any reference whatsoever to the literature on the education of women and girls in nineteenth century Britain.
8   LAQUER, T.W. (1976) *Religion and Respectability: Sunday Schools and Working Class Culture,* Yale University Press, chap. 5.
9   *ibid* p. 147 and pp. 90–91.
10   FARNINGHAM, M. (1907) *A Working Woman's Life,* London, James Clarke, p. 46.
11   *ibid* p. 44.
12   COOPER, T. (1873) *The Life of Thomas Cooper, Written by Himself,* p. 7. The page number here refers to the reprint by Leicester University Press 1971.
13   JOHNSON, R. (1976) 'Notes on the schooling of the English working class 1780–1850' in DALE, R., ESLAND, G., MACDONALD, M. (Eds) *Schooling and Capitalism,* London, Routledge and Kegan Paul.
14   Ideology is a problematic term. APPLE, M.W. (1979) *Ideology and Curriculum,* London, Routledge and Kegan Paul, p. 20, notes 'Most people seem to agree that one can talk about ideology as referring to some sort of "system" of ideas, beliefs, fundamental commitments, or values about social reality, but here the agreement ends'. I am using the term 'ideologies' in this broad, general sense. Any comprehensive coverage of gender ideologies in the nineteenth century would obviously also have to consider those ideas relating to men and boys.
15   BANKS, O. (1955) *Parity and Prestige in English Secondary Education,* London, Routledge and Kegan Paul, p. 2. I do not have the space, within this paper, to give adequate coverage to the topic of the education of middle-class girls.
16   Patriarchy is another problematic concept. BEECHEY, V. (1979) 'On patriarchy' *Feminist Review,* 3, p. 66 notes that patriarchy is not a single or simple concept but has a whole variety of different meanings. At the most general level, she claims, it has been used to refer to male

domination and to the power relationships by which men dominate women. ROWBOTHAM, S. (1981) 'The trouble with patriarchy' reprinted in SAMUEL, R. (Ed) *People's History and Socialist Theory* argues for an historically grounded and dynamic approach when trying to define the concept.

17 DYHOUSE, C. (in press) *Girls Growing Up: The Socialization of Girls in Late Nineteenth and Early Twentieth Century England,* London, Routledge and Kegan Paul. I am very grateful to Carol for allowing me to read her manuscript and for the many references she has given me.

18 HALL, C. (1979) 'The early formation of Victorian domestic ideology', in BURMAN, S. (Ed) *Fit Work for Women,* London, Croom Helm, pp. 18–19, 25, 31.

19 PURVIS, J. (1981) 'Towards a History of Women's Education in Nineteenth-century Britain: A Sociological Analysis', Paper presented at the International Sociological Association Conference 'The Origins and Operations of Educational Systems' Paris, August 7–8 1980. (Forthcoming) *Westminster Studies in Education.*

20 HALL, C. (1980) 'Domestic Ideologies and the Middle Class: The Charmed Circle of the Home', A talk given at the University of London Institute of Education on 5th December.

21 Oxoniensis (1863) 'The education of women', a review of F. Power Cobbe: 'Essays on the Pursuits of Women' in the *Christian Observer,* July 1865 pp. 546–7,

22 See, for example, VINCENT, D. (1980) 'Love and death and the nineteenth-century working class' *Social History,* May, where this issue is discussed.

23 This statement is certainly valid for Thomas Cooper's autobiography (1873) *op. cit.*

24 PINCHBECK, I. (1930) *Women Workers and the Industrial Revolution 1750–1850,* London, George Routledge and Sons, p. 106.

25 *Reports of Special Assistant Poor Law Commissioners on the Employment of Women and Children in Agriculture,* (1843) reprinted by August Kelley, New York (1968) p. 101.

26 *ibid* p. 119.

27 PINCHBECK, I. (1930) *op. cit.* p. 111.

28 *ibid* p. 197.

29 quoted in *ibid* p. 200.

30 SOLDON, N.C. (1978) *Women in British Trade Unions 1874–1976,* Dublin, Gill and Macmillan, p. 10.

31 quoted in *ibid* p. 21.

32 quoted in LEWENHAK, S. (1977) *Women and Trade Unions,* London, Ernest Benn, p. 51.

33 Such waged labour was, of course, often hidden and rarely reached official statistics.

34 See, for example, SUMMERS, A. (1979) 'A home from home – women's philanthropic work in the nineteenth century' in BURMAN, S. (Ed) *op. cit.* and PURVIS, J. (1981) 'Women and teaching in the nineteenth century' in DALE, R., ESLAND, G., FERGUSSON, R. and MAC-DONALD, M. (Eds) *Education and the State,* Vol. 2 Lewes, Falmer Press, p. 361.

35 As Lady Howard said to her niece in Catherine Sinclair's novel *Modern Society* (1838) Edinburgh, William Whyte and Co., p. 27, 'Marriage is a woman's profession'.

36 In those forms of adult education provided by the middle classes for working-class women, the importance of domestic work within the home was continually reiterated too. See PURVIS, J. (1980) 'Working-class women and adult education in nineteenth-century Britain' *History of Education,* 9 (3).

37 The Schools Inquiry Commission in 1867–68 claimed that the education of middle-class girls lacked 'Want of thoroughness and foundation; want of system; slovenliness and showy superficiality; inattention to rudiments; undue time given to accomplishments, and those not taught intelligently or in any scientific manner; want of organisation' *Reports from Commissioners: Schools Inquiry Vol. 1.* (1867–68) pp. 548–9.

38 See especially DAVIN, A. (1978) *op. cit.* and DYHOUSE, C. (1976 and 1977) *op. cit.*

39 For example, charity schools, schools of industry, ragged schools, Sunday schools, day and evening schools.

40 HORN, P. (1975) *The Rise and Fall of the Victorian Servant,* Dublin, Gill and Macmillan, p. 71 notes that throughout the nineteenth century, domestic service was predominantly the preserve of women workers. In 1851, for example, there were three quarters of a million female domestics but only 74,000 men-servants.

41   McCann, P. (1977) 'Popular education, socialization and social control: Spitalfields' in McCann, P. (Ed) *Popular Education and Socialization in the Nineteenth Century,* London, Methuen, p. 9.

42   *The Reports of the Society for Bettering the Condition and Increasing the Comforts of the Poor,* (1800) Vol. II, London, W. Bulmer and Co., pp. 9–10 states, 'It is the endeavour of the society . . . to search for and disseminate "useful and practical knowledge with regard to the poor"'.

43   Davis, W. (1821) *Hints to Philanthropists,* Bath, Wood, Cunningham and Smith, p. 152.

44   *ibid* p. 152.

45   *The Reports of the Society for Bettering the Condition and Increasing the Comforts of the Poor,* (1808) Vol. V, London, Bulmer and Co. Extract from an Account of the School at Campsall by the Hon. Mrs. Childers p. 64.

46   *The Fifth Report of the Society for Bettering the Condition and Increasing the Comforts of the Poor,* (1798) London, W. Bulmer and Co., p. 275.

47   Gordon, S.C. (1950) 'Demands for the Education of Girls, 1790–1865', Unpublished M.A. Thesis University of London, p. 111.

48   *The Reports of the Society for Bettering the Condition and Increasing the Comforts of the Poor* (1800) London, W. Bulmer and Co. Extract from an Account of the Mendip Schools by T. Bernard, p. 308.

49   Davis, W. (1821) *op. cit.* p. 11.

50   *ibid* p. 11.

51   *ibid* pp. 11–12.

52   *ibid* p. 16.

53   *ibid* p. 16.

54   At Quatt Industrial School where there were 32 boys and 19 girls, the girls were occupied in household work, dairy work, washing, ironing, baking, making and mending their own clothes while 15 of the boys, with the assistance of the master, cultivated the land and looked after the cows, pigs and pony – PP 1850 XLII *Minutes of the Committee of Council on Education 1848-49-50,* Vol. II, Reports on Elementary Schools, p. 10.

55   Hurt, J.S. (1980) *Elementary Schooling and the Working Classes 1860–1918* London, Routledge and Kegan Paul, p. 4.

56   Hall, C. (1980) *op. cit.*

57   *First Annual Report of the National Society for Promoting the Education of the Poor in the Principles of the Established Church* (1812) London p. 18.

58   *ibid* p. 36.

59   *ibid* p. 37.

60   Merson, E. (1979) *Once There Was . . . The Village School* Southampton, Paul Cave, p. 9.

61   One is reminded of that statement, some 120 years later, by Waller, W. (1932) *The Sociology of Teaching,* repr. First Science Edition, USA, (1965) p. 34, 'The school must serve as a museum of virtue'.

62   quoted in Gadd, E.W. (1979) *Victorian Logs* KAF Warwickshire, Brewin Books, p. 127.

63   *Second Annual Report of the National Society for Promoting the Education of the Poor in the Principles of the Established Church* (1814) London, p. 194.

64   PP 1867 XXII: *Report of the Committee of Council on Education 1866-67,* Appendix no. 1 p. 234.

65   *ibid* p. 178.

66   *ibid* p. 65.

67   Merson, E. (1979) *op. cit.* p. 7.

68   PP 1870 XXII: *Report of the Committee of Council of Education 1869-70,* Appendix no. 1 Elementary Schools pp. 153–154.

69   *ibid* pp. 28–29.

70   *ibid* p. 67.

71   PP 1867 XXII: *Report of the Committee of Council on Education 1866-67,* Appendix no. 1 p. 233.

72 *ibid* p. 86.
73 ARNOLD, M. (1889) *Reports on Elementary Schools 1852–1882* (ed. by Right Hon. Sir Francis Sandford) London, Macmillan and Co., p. 17.
74 *Second Annual Report of the National Society for Promoting the Education of the Poor in the Principles of the Established Church,* (1814) *op. cit.* p. 194.
75 *ibid* p. 195.
76 GORDON, S.C. (1950) *op. cit.* p. 108.
77 *A Catalogue of School Materials and Books sold by the National Society's Depository,* Sanctuary, Westminster (n.d.) p. 18.
78 *Report of Special Assistant Poor Law Commissioners on the Employment of Women and Children in Agriculture* (1843) *op. cit.* p. 203.
79 See, for example, MADOC-JONES, B. (1977) 'Patterns of attendance and their social significance: Mitcham National School 1830–1839' in MCCANN, P. (Ed) *op. cit.* p. 46.
80 *ibid* p. 52; PINCHBECK, I. (1930) *op. cit.* p. 108.
81 *Report of the British and Foreign School Society,* (1819) London, Bensley and Son, p. 101.
82 *Fifty-Ninth Report of the British and Foreign School Society,* (1864) London, Rider, J. and W., p. vii.
83 *Twenty-Eighth Report of the British and Foreign School Society* (1833) London, Bagester S. Jun., p. 8.
84 *ibid* p. 7.
85 *Fifty-Ninth Report of the British and Foreign School Society* (1864) *op. cit.* p. 5.
86 *20th Report of the British and Foreign School Society* (1825) London, Taylor, R. and A., p. 58.
87 *Report of the British and Foreign Society* (1824), London, Taylor, R. and A., p. 76.
88 *22nd Report of the British and Foreign School Society* (1827) London, Vogel, J.B.G., p. 57.
89 *Report of the British and Foreign School Society* (1821) *op. cit.* pp. 25–26.
90 PP 1845 XXXV: *Minutes of the Committee of Council on Education with Appendices* p. 69.
91 *ibid* p. 69.
92 GOLDSTROM, J.M. (1977) 'The content of education and the socialization of the working-class child 1830–1860' in MCCANN, P. (Ed) *op. cit.* pp. 100–103.
93 PP 1861 XXI: Part IV: *Popular Education: Appendix: Minutes of Evidence taken before the Commissioners,* p. 127.
94 *The Normal Schools of the British and Foreign School Society (Female Department),* 1854: printed by the Society p. 17.
95 See, for example, BARTLE, G.F. (1976) *A History of Borough Road College,* Northamptonshire, Dalkeith Press, and for the National Society, HORN, P. (1978) *Education in Rural England 1800–1914,* New York, St. Martin's Press, pp. 276–278.
96 PP 1847 XLV: *Minutes of the Committee of Council on Education in August and December,* 1846 p. 2.
97 *ibid* p. 2.
98 PURVIS, J. (1981) *Women and Teaching in the Nineteenth Century, op. cit.* p. 366.
99 HORN, P. (1974) *The Victorian Country Child,* Kineton, The Roundwood Press, p. 41.
100 FRITH, S. (1977) 'Socialization and rational schooling: Elementary education in Leeds before 1870' in MCCANN, P. (Ed) *op. cit.* p. 85.
101 HURT, J. (1980) *op. cit.* p. 180.
102 MAYHEW, H. (1851) *London Labour and the London Poor,* Vol. 1 London, George Goodfall, p. 43.
103 LAWSON, J. (1887) *Progress in Pudsey,* reprinted by Caliban Books (1978) p. 41.
104 PP 1867 XXII *Report of the Committee of Council on Education, op. cit.* p. 114.
105 PP 1861 XXI Part II: *Popular Education, op. cit.* p. 65.
106 WELLS, H.G. (1934) *Experiment in Autobiography,* Vol. 1 London, p. 93.
107 DYHOUSE, C. (1977) *op. cit.* p. 21.

2
Contemporary Concerns
and the
School System

Introduction

Much work in the sociology of education in the last few years has been characterized by an interest in the various ways in which different facets of social structure *constrain* educational affairs. Thus, for example, social relations in school, the ideologies of both the official and the hidden curriculum, the very definitions of 'educating', 'teaching' and 'learning' have all been variously portrayed as fundamentally shaped and controlled by social forces located at a higher structural level than that of the institution. However, one criticism this work has attracted is that the extent to which schooling is either a relatively autonomous or a relatively determined domain is an empirical question yet to be properly addressed or substantiated. The great difficulty for those wishing to make such demonstration is, of course, the problem of showing precisely where and how structural properties penetrate institutional and individual educational lives. It is not surprising that teachers and their activities have become of crucial interest to those seeking to establish such a form of analysis and, indeed, much recent work in the discipline has been directed toward charting different aspects of the constraints which seem to act upon teachers as they accomplish their everyday interactions. Teachers, as we noted in the preface, can be represented as crucial mediators of structural forces and attention to how their activities might be explained through reference to pressures originating in, say, ideological or political formations has obvious attractions. Nevertheless, it has to be admitted that we know very little about the forms particular constraining influences take, the impact such influences have upon lived experience and, critically, the way these constraints are perceived, interpreted and acted upon by teachers themselves. This last point is important if we are to avoid portraying the influence of structural forces upon educational affairs in a crude and over-deterministic fashion – or using what Olson calls 'an imprinting model' of this penetration. Exploration and illustration of ways in which we might avoid this pit-fall by deliberately striving to explore the reaction and responses of teachers to external constraints identified by either sociologists or themselves is the common thread which runs through the various papers in this section.

The theoretical justification for concentrating upon 'how structure related to lived experience' is defended by Olson whilst the other writers explore the practical manifestation of this relationship through the work teachers undertake within specific educational contexts or programmes. Various aspects of the system of schooling which seem responsive to the influence of constraints emanating from outside the system are selected for investigation. Thus, discussion covers such apparently diverse concerns as the inter-relation between ideology, comprehensive re-organization and the ethos of individual schools (Reynolds and Sullivan); the question of innovation in education as exemplified in the story of the rise and fall of a community school (Fletcher); the question of innovation in education as exemplified in a case-study of the development and impact of a mixed-ability teaching project (Ball); the ways in which patterns of school organization frame and restrict the interpretation of curricular packages (Corbishley *et al*); and the social determinants and determining consequences of assessment practices in schools (Broadfoot). What each writer is at pains to demonstrate, however, is that, although the particular systematic features of schooling which they are concerned with are the real results of powerful external constraints, these outcomes are neither inevitable nor automatic. These features are portrayed as involving some form of flexibility, a flexibility which to a large extent is a direct consequence of how teachers perceive and react to the manifestations of these external controls. If we are to demonstrate, then, the extent to which schools can achieve a relative autonomy we need to be able to ascertain exactly where flexibility *is* achievable and exactly where it is *not*.

The Comprehensive Experience

David Reynolds, University College, Cardiff
Michael Sullivan, University College, Cardiff

At former Westhill conferences, we have presented papers on two quite disparate and separate themes. In *Bringing Schools Back In* (1979), we argued for a relative autonomy model of the relationship between the educational system and broader societal structures.[1] Using evidence showing the independent effects of school environments in South Wales in the generation of different levels of pupil deviance, academic attainment and truancy, we argued for schools to be seen as having quite clearly specified goals but as having substantial freedom to determine their means and their ultimate pedagogical strategies. Given that the use of these different strategies generates different kinds of pupil output, the school, as well as reflecting the needs of the capitalist economic and social systems, actually moulds in turn that wider society in an interlocking and interactive process. Schools – and the educational system in general – could be seen as in part determined and in part free from constraint. They were in part determined but also in part free in the determination of those factors and those forces that moulded them.

In 1980, we argued in *Towards A New Socialist Sociology of Education* for what we labelled a 'socialist' approach to the description, analysis and prescription that we undertake as sociologists of education.[2] Taking classical Marxist formulations as our guide, we argued that our description should be positivistic, concerned to objectify knowledge. Our analysis should not be over-deterministic or materialistic, as that of many of the vulgar neo-Marxist attempts of the last decade, and should be idealistic enough to preserve room for the independent influence of men, ideas and human purpose upon the general ordering of societal affairs. Most important of all, we argued that the 'new radicalism' that has been and still is in evidence in some quarters of the sociology of education was not necessarily socialistic in its orientation. Cultural relativism, the cult of individualism and a growing enthusiasm for forms of de-schooling we regarded as having profoundly unsocialist consequences. Classical Marxist formulations, as we understood them, argued that the bourgeois rationality of the school curriculum, and even some of the knowledge base of that curriculum, might be functional for working class social advance. A working class denied access to that knowledge base and that rationality would, in our view, have become partially disabled from forming its own future.

The aim of the present exercise is to take our two earlier themes, link them together and develop them further by examining the case study of the British comprehensive experience, which is defined as the movement towards and the effects of the introduction of unified schooling for children of all abilities.[3] Our 'relative autonomy' thesis and our hypothesis that 'new radicalist' practices in education may have profoundly unsocialist consequences will be further explicated and developed in this manner.

The History of Comprehensive Education

The chronology of the move towards unified secondary schooling for children of all abilities has been well documented[4] and need not concern us here, save only to note that a variety of factors in the 1950s and 1960s can be seen as providing an impetus for the adoption of comprehensive schooling as official Labour party policy at the 1964 General Election. Much sociological literature showed the selective system as inefficient in its operation by revealing inequalities of opportunity between social classes, a wastage of high ability children, the high margin of error that was involved in the 11 + selection procedure and by increasing doubt as to the stability (and therefore the predictive value) of intelligence test scores through life. By increasingly discrediting the selective system, these factors were predisposing of change.[5]

Furthermore, there was, by 1964, what can only be labelled as coincidental support for comprehensive reorganization from many groups.[6] For the working class, reorganization offered the prospects of upward social mobility. For the 'new' middle class, caught vulnerably between the capitalist class and the working class, the expansion of education was a kind of insurance policy that could preserve them and their children as employed in the burgeoning empire of Welfare State provision. Social engineering through education was clearly the ideology of the diploma holding class! For the traditional middle classes denied grammar school places by the population bulge, for the capitalist class seeking to maximize profit potential by utilization of the new technologies – for all these groups, comprehensive education had much to offer and much to promise. The interests of capital and of labour – often contradictory – were in this case coincidentally identical.

Proposals for comprehensive reorganization also suited both the short term political interests and fitted with the longer held social democratic ideology of the Labour party.[7] In the short term, it was clear that the secondary modern schools were unpopular with parents and the methods of eleven plus selection much distrusted. Since the grammar schools retained substantial status and popularity, there was substantial electoral gain to be obtained from the portrayal of comprehensive schooling as representing grammar school chances for all children, with new within-one-school selection procedures that were more 'fair' than the discredited eleven plus.[8]

Educational reform, furthermore, could sit easily with the broader social democratic or Fabian political ideology of the party leadership of the 1960s.[9] Since its inception in the early days of the twentieth century, the party had represented a loose alliance between the left wing socialists such as Keir Hardie and the other members of the socialist societies on the one hand; and the more liberal and socially conservative Trades Unions on the other. The Fabian manifestos that were adopted from 1918 were – just as that originally written by Sidney Webb – gradualist, pragmatic and designed to appeal to the mass of a British working class who were presumed to be cautious and conservative in outlook. Fabianism was not concerned to bring about the transformation of capitalism *to* socialism but it was concerned with the achievement of socialism *under* capitalism, by means of utilizing the Welfare State to compensate for the inequalities generated by free market capitalism. Fabianism was hostile to collectivism because it was – ever since the Webbs – hostile to communism and it was hostile to communism because of the restrictions upon individual freedom that communism was perceived to involve. Fabians believed in using the Parliamentary system to control the State, believing that the stone of capitalism could be worn away by Government action. Not for nothing was the title of the Fabian Society derived from that of the Roman General Fabius Cunctator, since he had been a man who never lost a battle but was a man who had never won a battle either.

The resulting liberal, social engineering type of educational reforms had – for the Labour Government of 1964 – three linked goals.[10] First, they were to accomplish a *greater development of talent* which would, in turn, generate more wealth both for the talented and for the collectivity, a goal which owed much to the revival in influence of the human capital school of economic theorists. Although this theory can be seen as dating from the writings of Adam Smith, the popularity of these ideas in the 1960s owes much to Theodore W. Shultz, an American economist who argued that education should be seen as a form of investment rather than a form of personal consumption, since 'by investing in themselves people can enlarge the range of choices open to them'.[11] Both the Robbins Report on higher education[12] and the Newsom Report[13] on the education of the child of less than average ability reflected this philosophy, with the latter arguing that '. . . there is much unrealized talent especially amongst boys and girls whose potential is marred by indequate powers of speech and the limitations of home background . . . the country cannot afford this wastage, humanly or economically speaking'.[14]

The second aim of educational reform – the amelioration and long term removal of *inequalities of opportunity* as between different social class groups – had been a consistent theme in the policy of the Labour Party of the early 1960s. Anthony Crosland spoke for many social democrats in the party when he argued that there was 'an irresistible pressure in British society to extend rights of citizenship'.[15] The research evidence showing consistent inequalities between social classes and racial groups in their educational opportunity[16] was interpreted as showing the influence of factors in the pupils' homes (such as material disadvantage or social deprivation) but also as reflecting on the nature of the bipartite system of grammar and secondary modern schools, which 're-inforced' or 'intensified' pre-existing differences between different pupil groups.

As well as ensuring the promotion of social justice and of equality of opportunity (with a hoped-for consequential reduction in social class antagonism), educational reform was hoped by many in the early 1960s to be capable of ensuring a *reduction in adolescent deviance,* both within and without the schools. In a strikingly similar way to the influence exerted by the 'blocked goal attainment' hypotheses of Cohen,[17] Cloward and Ohlin[18] upon the American Democratic government's War on Poverty that was launched in 1963, British research evidence of the same period consistently linked failure at school with the generation of delinquency outside. Whilst 'home factors' were usually held to be in part responsible for such deviance, many radicals and liberals argued, like the Longford Study Group Report of 1966,[19] that 'Anti-social behaviour in the child may arise from difficulties at home, *from unhappiness at school* (our emphasis), from physical or mental handicap or maladjustment, or from a variety of other causes, for which the child has no personal responsibility'.[20] School reform was, it was hoped, a factor that would succeed in curbing the tendencies of potentially troublesome adolescent youth, since many in the Labour Government were of the opinion – like liberals of old – that it was only the educational system that could stem the rise in adolescent deviance that was much in evidence at the time. The church had apparently lost its potency as a mechanism of control and the working class extended family had been fragmented by social changes such as slum clearance and increased levels of geographical mobility. Traditional curative measures such as approved schools, borstals and remand centres were known to have high levels of recidivism. The school, for liberals, was to become a solution to social problems both by unblocking opportunity for adolescents but also by the more successful initiation of potentially troublesome youth into mainstream society and its 'core' societal values.[21]

A substantial number of liberal educational reforms followed, then, in the mid and late 1960s. Expenditure on education was almost doubled as a proportion of Gross National product. The school leaving age was to be raised to 16. A rapid expansion of nursery education began and was linked with forms of compensatory education and positive discrimination that aimed to generate equality of opportunity for those groups regarded as socially deprived. A veritable plethora of innovations in the field of curriculum design and curriculum evaluation were also launched together with, of course, the Circular 10/65 which was issued 'requesting' local authorities to submit plans for the reorganization of their schools upon comprehensive and non-selective lines.

From Incorporation to Coercion

It is important at this point in our argument to note what had been happening in the 1960s to the secondary modern schools.[22] They catered for between 65% (in some parts of Wales) and 90% (in Essex and Surrey) of the cohort of secondary age pupils. Much of the evidence suggests that, for a variety of reasons both concerned with internal pressures from their teachers and partly external pressures from parents, they were developing what many comprehensive school advocates *could* have regarded as an authentic working class education, but an education that was, of course, an education in schools shorn of the talents of those of higher ability. Faced with cohorts of pupils more unprepared than before to put up with the neo-grammar school ethos that characterized many of the schools in the 1950s, with demands from parents for examination success, with the internally perceived need to generate sixth forms to enhance salary and career prospects for teachers and with the arrival of career teachers and headteachers who were committed to what they saw as the possibility of achieving working class cultural education through the means of the secondary moderns, the schools began to change themselves. Crucially, many accounts[23] locate the most important factors causing change as the internal pressures from teachers and headteachers.

What sort of changes were introduced in these schools?[24] Many modified their streaming system (moving to banding or to complete unstreaming) hoping to develop more positive attitudes to learning amongst those in lower streams. Many moved towards a 'truce' on issues like length of hair, uniforms, chewing gum and smoking, thus permitting greater autonomy. Many began to incorporate parents by means of parents' evenings, the encouraging of parental visits and the like. Many tolerated a more relaxed atmosphere and flattened status hierarchies between age groups, ability groups and between staff and pupils. They entered more pupils for external exams (up to 50% were entered for CSE or 'O' level in some schools) and many introduced 'progressive' teaching methods such as group work and pupil involvement in lessons of various kinds. Although the number of secondary modern schools attempting all these innovations would have been small, the great majority of secondary moderns would have been attempting some of them.

In essence, the schools were attempting to fulfil their allotted role of attaining goals concerned with social control/instrumental development of talent/expressive development of qualities of humanity and citizenship by attempting to tie their pupils into an acceptance of adult society and adult standards by means of developing relationships with the teachers who represented the adult society.

Control, akin to that of the therapeutic community, was often by relationship or by denial of relationship. Pupils and parents were incorporated, not coerced, into acceptance of school and therefore of adult standards. Crucially, the schools were collectivistic in orientation, since pupils were treated as members of classes and given a school experience common to all in the group and since the pupil's place as a member of the wider collectivity was frequently stressed, with a substantial emphasis upon the need to 'get on with' others in that collectivity.

However, it is important to note that the knowledge base of the curriculum was not substantially changed. The mixture of bourgeois academic subjects (history and English), of 'new' middle class rationalism (maths) and ultilitarian practical subjects (metalwork, woodwork) remained much the same over the twenty years between 1950 and 1970, with CSE increasingly used to measure progress in these 'conventional' subjects. CSE Mode Three – which is a form of internally set and marked but externally moderated exam – became utilized in many schools but was rarely used to permit pupils to develop their knowledge in areas conventionally regarded as outside the scope of the academic curriculum. New forms of assessment were therefore not really used to permit the discovery of 'new' knowledge but merely to discover the pre-existing corpus of socially-approved school knowledge by different means.

These secondary moderns were therefore emphasizing the 'expressive' goals of relationships using incorporative control strategies, were collectivistic in orientation and had a conventional view of the knowledge to be inculcated. The great majority of the evidence that exists upon the sociology of the school[25] suggests that such strategies of 'incorporative collectivism' should have been highly successful in generating outputs that were tied to the present social system, that were moderately successful at fulfilling future occupational roles and that were protected against future deviance by relationships that would have tied them to adults who were conformist in the role models they offered. Whilst these strategies may have generated a degree of instrumental academic success, it is with the more 'social outputs' of the educational process that their success would have been most marked.

The comprehensive schools that have emerged since the late 1960s are clearly very different kinds of organizations from the secondary moderns.[26] Whilst the early comprehensives (such as some in London, the West Riding and Leicestershire) were very similar to the collectivistic, incorporative, culturally and academically traditional secondary modern schools and were in fact often headed by former secondary modern headteachers, by 1970 only about 20% of the secondary school population was in such schools. Between 1970 and 1978, a further 50% of the school population went into the comprehensives, including a large number of the Labour authorities with a high proportion of grammar school places and a great respect amongst their populations for the instrumental and 'character moulding' expressive success of these schools: and also including a large proportion of the more middle class, Conservative controlled shire counties.

From consisting, apart from the Welsh rural counties where the comprehensives had replaced grammars *and* secondary moderns, almost completely of re-named secondary moderns and sometimes low status grammar schools that were often highly 'creamed' by direct grant schools, the comprehensive sector had added a large number of the grammar schools, their high ability children, their often middle class parents, and the latters' commitment to forms of character moulding *and* exam attainment as goals.

Whilst the goals of comprehensive education had been made explicit by the Labour Government – an instrumental development of talent, a reduction of adolescent deviance – and whilst there was substantial agreement upon their desirability from representatives of capital, from representatives of labour, from the new State employed middle class and probably even from the liberal wing of the Conservative party, the means and organizational forms suitable for the system were clearly left unspecified, apart from the Labour government's bland elucidation of six general organizational forms of comprehensive school and their general injunction to be 'non-selective' as in the 1965 Circular.[27] No statement of means appeared from the Department of Education and Science, from HMIs or from the polity in general; neither were there clear statements from the pre-comprehensive pressure groups like CASE or the Comprehensive Schools Committee, both of whose membership was split between liberal meritocrats and socialist egalitarians. Since the executive committee of the CSC, for example, had both Brian Simon and Rhodes Boyson as members, clear statements of neither goals nor means could be expected. Only skeletal formulations of means came from academic and intellectual sponsors of comprehensivization – Robin Pedley's[28] rhetoric about the purposes of comprehensives which 'must not let the kingdoms of Oxford, Cambridge and Sussex divert them from their true purpose of forging a communal culture' was distinctly short upon any clear formulation of the enabling means to attain his lofty goals.

In the absence of clearly spelt out guidance as to means, a variety of factors have conspired to generate comprehensives that are in many ways an extension of the old grammar school organizational structure, together with adaptations to the curriculum to cope with the consequences of such 'pattern maintenance'. This reflects both the influence of extra-system factors and intra-system factors.

Many extra system factors imposed constraints upon the school's choice of means in a way unknown to the teachers and headteachers of the former secondary schools. Parental pressure to maintain the 'ethos' and traditions of the grammar schools (especially in Labour authorities providing a high proportion of places), the discrediting of some of the more radical comprehensive heads such as Duane and Mackenzie,[29] the backlash against progressivism reflected in the Black Paper's[30] virulently expressed concern about growing permissiveness, the economic failure that suggested to many that the values necessary for industrial survival (punctuality, respect for authority) were being eroded in some of the incorporative secondary moderns and early comprehensives – all these factors were external pressures upon the new comprehensives of the early 1970s. Most important of all was middle class pressure to maintain the emphasis of the educational system upon the transmission of 'the grammar school character'. Secondary schools in the 1920s/1930s, and grammar schools subsequently, had often been pressured by their local middle class into aping the 'character-moulding' emphasis of the public schools, whose fees the middle class parents could not afford but whose outputs they coveted. The weakening of conventional morality in the early 1970s led to renewed middle class pressure upon the schools to 'pattern maintain' both their traditions of collective morality and their organizational form and ethos.

However, all these external constraints – upon means as well as goals – probably would not have been a determining set of factors upon the nature of the comprehensives had it not been for the nature of the headteacher and staff culture of the new fledgling comprehensives. In the schools going comprehensive in the early or mid 1970s, headteachers of grammar schools became heads of comprehensive schools in the great majority of cases. The academic organization of the schools (heads of departments, deputy/assistant headteachers) was also in most cases heavily dominated by grammar school staff. The organizational form of the comprehensives was therefore determined by those used to the form of the grammar school. What was, in terms of ethos, functional for the middle class outside the school was 'normal' for the members of the teaching staff that controlled the new comprehensives.

Under external pressure to preserve grammar school traditions *and* to develop more talent, the schools fundamentally chose pattern maintenance as their strategy. The grammar school organizational structure (with its high levels of coercive institutional control, low pupil autonomy and commitment to character moulding) was imposed upon all parts of the school, since it was clearly impossible to have one school ethos for the top streams and another for the bottom streams, except in authorities that had a differentiation at age 13 into 'schools for those sitting examinations' (i.e. the old grammars). The schools became – in their organizational form – grammar schools for all.

For lower ability children, the majority of whom would have been attending in the past the incorporative secondary moderns, the new comprehensives have, clearly, been a different experience. Except for some of those in the middle third of the ability range that may have been enticed into acquiescence and acceptance of the comprehensives through the schools' promise of examination success, these lower ability pupils would have been experiencing an atmosphere more alienating than in the secondary moderns. This atmosphere may also be more anomic, as we shall see subsequently. They are likely to be experiencing higher levels of coercive strategies, such as physical punishment, and are also likely to experience strict rule enforcement. They are likely to be controlled by bureaucratic, rather than charismatic, means and are also unlikely to be incorporated into the school organizations – prefectships, games captainships and house and society positions that would have been distributed widely in the old secondary moderns would now be increasingly taken by former grammar pupils who form the top streams of the comprehensives.

The Costs of Pattern Maintenance

Faced with external constraints to develop more talent and yet hold on to the conventional forms that for middle class parents promised the security of conventional character moulding for their children, the comprehensives were clearly constrained in their choice of means as well as choice of goals. The nature of the teachers in authority positions within the schools and the size of the organizations themselves all made the adoption of a grammar school organizational structure highly likely.

The adoption of such structure consequently left the schools in a difficult position. Many of them were worried by their inability to control their lower streams who were, in the early 1970s, exhibiting a variety of what were, for the schools, major problems. Although these problems were likely to be reflective of the nature of the schools' control strategies, change in those strategies would have been ruled out by external constraints. Nevertheless, the school staffs would have had considerable freedom to develop alternative strategies to orientate lower stream pupils towards acceptance of school goals. The schools could have permitted new pedagogical strategies such as the encouragement of group forms of learning within and without the classroom. Schools might have encouraged a more informal teaching ethos within the classroom or might have tried to experiment with new methods of teaching the conventional school curriculum. Schools might have changed, then, in a number of ways to meet the demands made upon them by the consequences of the 'pattern maintenance' of certain organizational structures.

What the schools chose to do was something very different from such possible modifications of within lesson ethos and within lesson methods. Put simply, the schools permitted a degree of collective and individual redefinition of the knowledge base that children acquired at school.[31] The pre-existing CSE Mode Three was eagerly seized upon as a way of generating a more 'relevant' curriculum for the child of below average ability and thereby as a means of motivating children in the lower streams. Sometimes the 'cultural relativism' of the new sociology of education, or the views of some neo-Marxists that the conventional 'bourgeois' curriculum was a no more valid way of seeing the world than the view of the child, was used to support this shift of strategy[32] and one does not need to be Julius Gould or the education correspondent of the Daily Express to detect this influence of sociological thinking upon teachers within certain schools and within certain geographical areas such as London. However, it seems much more likely that the decision to open curricular content for redefinition was taken in most schools because of the operation of pragmatic situational factors rather than because of any ideological conversion to the doctrines of the new radicalism. The (for teachers) 'problems' that the educational system was faced with necessitated changes in areas where change was practicable, and changes in pedagogical strategies also followed.

The revival in the influence of 'progressivism' which was reflected in the child-centred views espoused by the Plowden Report[33] created the possibility of a shift in strategy towards the use of more individually determined means of study such as project work. Further use of optional courses and the use of individualized timetables where pupils could perhaps select up to 70% of their total school time from a range of options was also encouraged. An increasingly individually determined curriculum, in both range of subjects and in their content, became the solution to their 'problems' for many schools.

It is likely that the two changes generate, simply, a lack of experience amongst pupils that they have in common and, assuming that there is variation in the actual knowledge that pupils discover or receive by the utilization of such methods as CSE Mode Three, a lack of curricular knowledge that is shared. Together with the increasing variation and heterogeneity in the hidden curriculum of teacher values, biases and prejudices which has resulted from the increasing differentiation of staff groups in larger schools and from the development of systems of management that locate teachers' primary responsibility towards small sub-units of staff such as departments or years, the effect is likely to be an increasingly sharply differentiated school experience for different children. A lack of collectively shared values, experience and knowledge amongst pupils because of this increasingly individualized and differentiated school experience, seems a reasonable description of low stream life in the modern British comprehensive.

For the former secondary modern pupils – instead of an emphasis upon control by relationships and by incorporation, an emphasis upon being given collective experience and stressing the interdependence between themselves, other individuals and the collectivity as a whole, instead of incorporative collectivism – the comprehensives represent increasingly coercive individualism, together with an attempt to cope with the consequences of the coercion by the encouragement of individualism in methods and increasing self-determination of curriculum content and range.

What have been the effects upon the pupils of this changed comprehensive experience? It seems likely that the comprehensives may well have held the academic attainments of those at the top end of the ability range and to have managed to inculcate for those children also many of those grammar school qualities of 'character' that middle class parents wanted preserved.[34] But the allocation of within school resources, the psychological concentration upon extending the grammar traditions to a further part of the ability range and the coercive, individualistic enterprise that represents the initiation into adult society for the bottom third or quarter of the ability range – all these factors may have led to the comprehensive schools becoming considerably less successful than the former secondary moderns had been in the social control and socialization into core societal values of their lower ability pupils.[35] Some possible academic gains for the middle third of the ability range – and probably gains for the system as a whole compared to its predecessor – may have been bought at the cost of a less successful initiation into acceptance of adult social values. The rapidly rising levels of delinquency, non-attendance and behavioural problems that are shown by official statistics may well reflect some real changes in adolescent behaviour, and particularly real changes in the behaviour of what must increasingly resemble an under class that emerges from their experience at the bottom of the comprehensives' streaming structures.

As well as perhaps changing the overall level of deviance and its distribution between ability ranges, comprehensives may have changed the *nature* of that adolescent deviance and delinquency in socially significant ways. Comprehensive schools are, of course, still likely to be generating deviance because of blocked opportunity, since adolescents may not be obtaining the means in their schools to attain the goals that they wish for, which may include such things as status, money, power, self-esteem, or esteem in the eyes of the wider society. Because the schools may not give their pupils the legitimate means of obtaining these goals, the pupils may (if we utilize the classical formulations of Cohen and Cloward and Ohlin) turn to illegitimate means to obtain them. These rebels are likely to be similar to those of past generations. Such delinquents might well be ambivalent about 'society', might be on the edge of the social system, may be marginal men and women or 'insiders turned sour' but they are likely to be firmly insiders and *intra*-system, since they at least share the same goals as the rest of a capitalist society. Most are likely still to be gang members and therefore clearly partially collectivistic, since they would recognize in their gangs the importance and salience of interests other than their own. They probably would in the past have seen the rules of the adult community as in many ways hypocritical and restraining their individuality but would probably have stayed within these rules or codes because they were incorporated by relationships with the adult society into acceptance of them. Similarly, they might have been critical of the value attached to marriage, yet still have been dragged into acceptance of it by their relationships with women.

They are likely to have shared many values of the wider working class culture – Paul Willis' bike boys[36] had an 'impudence before authority, liked domination of women, humiliation of the weaker, aggression towards the different'. They had 'a clear attachment to the conventional ideology of working and paying one's way'. Thus '. . . they largely accepted the values of those who locked them up. They certainly tried to outrage but their offence was basically at a surface level; it was cheek, shock, surprise, disgust, insubordination, insult. Never a basic challenge to institutional belief'. Willis's lads in *Learning to Labour*[37] and Cohen's East End boys[38] may also have been within-system enough to be engaged in an attempt to recreate the working class community. If delinquents, they were clearly social democratic delinquents!

After the comprehensive experience, though, the rebellious adolescents of this type probably form a considerably smaller proportion of an expanded total number of delinquents, and an increasingly larger proportion of the disaffected may be represented by those who are much more extra-system in their values, attitudes and behaviour.[39] This group can be characterized as showing the disaffection of the detached – the deviance of those who have not been successfully socialized into collective and socially approved values and norms. Not tied by relationships to adults, not inculcated with a collectivist orientation, allowed to follow individually determined ranges of curricular knowledge and increasingly encouraged by their schools to follow a curriculum which reflects their own experience, interests and feelings and which therefore increasingly concentrates less on the experience of other groups and of the remainder of society, these adolescents have become more detached from social life and now more frequently allow their own goals to be preponderant over those of the community. Disagreeing as to the nature of their own and societal goals as well as to the nature of approved means, they remain a group who have not been controlled enough to share collective standards.

Evidence to support this interpretation can be found in the growth in the proportion of total delinquence that is committed by individuals rather than by groups, the substantial growth in forms of crime that are negativistic rather than utilitarian (such as criminal damage offences) and the growth of forms of youth culture that are more extra system, such as punk culture.[40] Punk culture, for example, evidences extreme hostility to a wide range of forms of authority from the Royal Family to the school teaching profession, yet does not seem to be hostile to authority only because those who possess authority alter the rules of the social game to maximize their chances of winning. Punks appear nihilistic in the sense of disliking authority *per se* and join groups such as the hippies of the 1960s as potentially or actually anarchistic in belief and in orientation. Such anarchism and associated nihilism is clearly the desert of those who have rejected over-socialization in the public schools *or* those who have not been adequately socialized elsewhere. The punks, to use Laurie Taylor's analogy, would rather smash the fruit machine than play it rigged.

It is possible also that punk culture may be Fascistic in orientation in that it may be hostile to authority only because that authority has failed to provide the necessary desired guidance on what are acceptable standards. Many punks are violently against decadence in general moral standards and in sexual standards. Some punk groups use 'moral' as a term of approbation and give status to those who behave in accordance with conventional morality, although of course still giving status to those who shock the conventional world in their choice of dress, make-up, and the like. A hatred of that form of authority which has failed to provide moral guidance in a confusing, complex and rapidly differentiating world together with a nascent desire for the personal certainty that the extreme use of authority can bring is, at a cultural level, one of those factors associated historically with the rise of Fascism.[41]

What are our conclusions from this brief and somewhat speculative venture into judging the effects of comprehensive schools upon their pupils and ultimately upon wider societal structures? We understand now the reasons for the nature of the schools – they reflect the influence of outside definitions of goals and some constraints upon means. These constraints are mediated by the nature of the cultural, historical and class background of those teachers who control the comprehensives. We can see that these teachers' precise organizational resolutions of their 'problems' (resolutions which were not inevitable) posed, in consequence, problems for certain of their pupils. An extension of former grammar school structure to encompass the former secondary modern children and the results of the consequential denial of autonomy in former 'truce' areas that led to pupil disaffection, led in turn, to attempts to cope with this problem by individualizing instruction and allowing the inclusion of 'new' knowledge discovered by individual pupils as, in theory at least, of equal status to that of the conventional secondary school curriculum.

The results of this particular exercise of the schools' freedom to choose means may be the creation of a more anomic school environment for lower ability children, in which individuals consume, and therefore reflect, the influence of an increasingly differentiated body of knowledge. The coercion (as against the former incorporation) of the lower stream pupils is likely, combined with the individualism of the curriculum, to generate not just an oppositional output of children but an output whose opposition may be expressed in highly individualistic fashion.

Most important of all, the growth in the number of oppositional societal rebels may generate forms of youth culture that are opposed to conventional societal goals as well as approved means.

Conclusion

For those of us still engaged in wrestling with the continuing paradigmatic crisis within the British sociology of education, the comprehensive experience has much useful explanatory variance which can be utilized to advance our thinking. In particular, the experience can be related back to the two debates that we have attempted to contribute to over the last few years – the debate as to the relationship of the educational system and the wider society; and the debate as to which policy prescriptions are valid for the purposes of advancing social change of a socialist variety. It is with these two themes – and informed by our comprehensive experience – that we conclude.

Turning to look at the first of these issues, it is clear that much effort has been expended over the past decade in attempting to elucidate the nature of the relationship between the educational system and the wider societal structure. Theorists of class reproduction such as Althusser[42] or Bowles and Gintis[43] have attempted to demonstrate that the educational system directly reproduces the existing structure of societal relations. For Althusser, schooling is the means whereby existing relations between dominant and subordinate classes are perpetuated, since it inculcates the ruling ideology. After a period of subjection in school, the mass of pupils are 'ejected into production'. Although Althusser holds that there may be some relative autonomy within a capitalist society, it is clear that this autonomy is regarded as that of the 'cultural', 'the world of beliefs' or that of the 'ideological superstructure' from the economic base, rather than that of the State or the educational *system* from the needs of capitalism. The relationship between the educational system and the society is largely one of determination of the former by the requirements of the latter. Bowles and Gintis also have asserted a direct correspondence between the social relations of production and those of schooling. Relations between participants in the educational system 'replicate' the hierarchical division of labour characteristic of the economic sphere.

More recently, however, one can detect a growing assertion that the educational system may be relatively autonomous from the sphere of production, although in most recent formulations it is still regarded as highly likely that the system meets the needs of capitalism in an *indirect* rather than *direct* fashion. Bernstein,[44] for example, argues that there is no direct economic determination of education by the needs of production since the two spheres are relatively autonomous. Willis[45] also grants the 'educational paradigm' (i.e. the social relationships of schooling) a relative autonomy from the social relations of production or from what he labels the 'class paradigm'. Class factors alone, for Willis, do not detemine the nature of teacher/pupil interaction or the nature of the pupil output from the schools, since these latter outputs are determined by within system factors. Crucially, the reaction of certain groups (the 'lads') to their within school experience has class or wider societal ramifications, since both their rebellion and their subsequent celebration of working class culture confines them to membership of the working class after their school experience ends. Schools for Willis, therefore, in spite of their *apparent* autonomy from the needs of capitalism and from the 'needs' to reproduce the existing social relations of production, actually *indirectly* accomplish precisely that social reproduction. How this happens remains – for Willis and, I suspect, for most of those who are beginning to adhere to a relative autonomy thesis – somewhat unclear.

Our own past work in the secondary moderns[46] and our existing work into the comprehensives already discussed in this paper may possibly provide us with some clues to explain this puzzling paradox – that relative autonomy of the school from direct imposition of wider societal 'needs' or constraints does not lead to system change of any kind but, instead, to the perpetuation of the existing social relations of production.

In the secondary modern schools, the individual groups of staff had little independence in their choice of goals, which were a mixture of those concerned with expressive character moulding, utilitarian child minding and instrumental goals concerned with the acquisition of practical skills to make the children suitable for working class employment. These goals that the schools were designed to inculcate were to provide working class children with an education that suited them for employment as working class operatives. The goals for the schools would, if met, have ensured the reproduction of existing class relationships and of the existing social relations of production. The lack of specificity as to which means to adopt, though, left individual schools with a wide latitude as to which means to employ, the choice of which had implications for the nature of their output. Some schools utilized their freedom to adopt coercive collectivistic strategies and generated a somewhat rebellious, unqualified delinquescent output. Others chose incorporation and generated a successfully socialized conventional output destined for the skilled working class. Importantly, neither type of output represented a fundamental change in the nature of the society; neither represented a change in, or threat to, the existing social relations of production. The 'lumpen' element from some schools simply evoked control strategies from the local State and the children of the skilled working class were simply successfully incorporated. Capitalist local social structures could, by varying their control strategies, cope with the consequences of the individual school's choice of means. The school that they attended may of course have had considerable implications for the pupils as *individuals,* since it would have partly determined their level of skill and their wider social values, but none of the schools' outputs would have represented a threat to the continuance of wider capitalist social structures. Schools might make a difference to individuals, may even affect the nature of some of the values of the wider society but were unlikely to affect the mode of production of that society and its general *economic* organization.

The comprehensive schools also have had clearly specified goals and – unlike the secondary moderns – increasing constraints upon their means. They utilized their more restricted freedom to introduce coercive strategies with the bottom of their ability ranges and for that, and the numerous other reasons mentioned above, probably generate a substantial 'lumpen' element or under class of increasingly individualistic and anarchistic rebels. Capitalism nationally, though, can adopt coercive control strategies of the kind we see around us presently to deal with these children and, again, the system's partial independence in choice of means and the social consequences of that choice are of little importance in altering the nature of the existing social relations of production. Teachers have again not used their freedom to utilize strategies that will generate an erosion of capitalist structures.

Why is it that, with our studies as with those of many others, apparent substantial autonomy in choice of means has little effect in changing the existing societal structure? It seems likely that the answer is to be found in the constraints on action imposed by the *phenomenological* world of the teachers and in the ways in which capitalism partially controls the structure of schooling (and to an extent, therefore, the structure of the wider society) by its substantial control over the ideological world view of its teachers. The relative autonomy of the school is not utilized to generate system change because of the constraints of the *phenomenological* world, not of the *material* world.

The most salient constraints upon teachers may well not be of a material variety. The educational system has, in the past, enjoyed a form of 'licensed autonomy' from direct State control that is even now merely 'loosely regulated autonomy',[47] leaving it a considerable freedom of action in its choice of organizational structures. The children themselves are probably constrained only quite marginally by their material worlds and home environments – more and more reviews of the literature[48] upon the determinants of educability are now emphasizing the independence of children from environmental factors and the small size of the relationship between childrens' material environments in their early years of life and their intellectual or social status at adolescence. The recent results of the Oxford social mobility study, for example, argue that '. . . those circumstances of birth which we can measure do not exert a very powerful constraint on later achievements. The variations in the fates of men from similar social origins, even brothers, are impressive. This variability seems to extend to the "deprived" and we have been unable to discover a group who are "Born to fail" (except educationally)'.[49] The constraints that set limits to the freedom of the educational system are therefore unlikely to be found in the material world of the children or in the *direct* control of the system by capitalism or bureaucracies representative of capitalist interests.

The constraints in our view are likely to be of a phenomenological variety[50] and are likely to be deeply engraved. They can relate to every area of within school practice – to what is appropriate for different social classes, to what are appropriate methods, to what are appropriate relationships with parents and to what are appropriate relationships between teachers and headteachers, for example. It is, of course, important to be aware of the fact that these phenomenological constraints may be in part *structurally* determined. Many of the constraints may reflect on the class background of teachers – they have been, in general, first generation middle class, unsure of their new found status and therefore likely to over-display and to require an over-display in others of a middle classness that established bourgeois groups would find unnecessary. Many phenomenological constraints may reflect upon a work situation that atomizes teachers, individualizes instruction and splits teachers from other colleagues. Other constraints may reflect the influence of historical factors and the all too potent influence of the past upon the present.

But most importantly for our purposes here, many of the phenomenological constraints that may have the greatest salience, and the greatest effect in ensuring that the system's apparent relative autonomy is not used to generate social change in practice, may emanate from bourgeois ideological dominance of teacher world views[51] about the nature of the constraints imposed on them by the influence of extra-school environments. Bourgeois social science explanations of the working classes' cultural deficits and hypotheses as to the existence of cycles of deprivation or a 'culture of poverty' have been extensively propagated both through the mass media and teacher training. Continued State funding of educational research that attempts to individualize the explanation of educational failure, such as the great majority of the research that has emanated from the National Children's Bureau,[52] ensures that a vulgar environmental determinism becomes a key component of teacher ideology. Teachers are encouraged to view themselves as passive, responding to character deficient or deprived children who, because of their environments, require certain forms of educational process.

This environmental determinism was what was in the minds of the teachers at our past, coercive secondary modern schools, who responded to what they perceived as less educable, character-deficient pupils from council estates by tightening organizational controls. In the comprehensives also, perceptions of the ineducability of many working class children amongst the formerly grammar school headteachers and senior staff would have led to many of the problems we noted earlier and to the flirtation with a curriculum for the less able that shows a growing emphasis upon experiential rather than intellectual knowledge.

The ideological belief that certain types of children 'require' certain types of educational form and content because of the nature of their class background is what, given the organizational forms and strategies that such beliefs generate, ensures that the educational system does not utilize its independence from the material world in ways that are dysfunctional for capitalism. The resulting strategies which produce the rebellious 'lumpen proletariat' of the old secondary moderns or the rebellious detached 'lumpen proletariat' that are now generated, ensure the reproduction of the existing social relations of production, since neither of these above groups is likely to be a force for socialist revolutionary change. They lack skills, probably lack understanding of the nature of the world round them, probably lack self esteem and can be used, as the conventionally unskilled can always be used, against the skilled and 'respectable' working class. They are likely to be used by the capitalist class and/or *petit bourgeois* classes at times of instability in the social formation and may therefore be a force for social change of a fascistic nature. Such change, of course, merely assures the maintenance of capitalism by different political means.

Our explication of this puzzle (why the relative autonomy of the system from direct control is still resulting in the perpetuation of the existing social relations of production) leads conveniently to our second major area of within discipline controversy – the nature of what constitutes 'radical' pedagogy and school experience. Many within the discipline[53] have argued for 'new radicalist' policies to be practised, policies that are believed to generate social change of a 'socialist' variety. Much sociology of education has portrayed the 'bourgeois' curriculum as a structured misrepresentation of reality, designed to shield pupils from discovering the true nature of the capitalist society around them. Such a perspective has been encouraged by two groups – by those of the phenomenological persuasion such as Michael Young and by a large number of the neo-Marxists. For Young,[54] the curriculum is not necessarily a more adequate explanation of the nature of the social world than the large number of alternative bodies of knowledge that exist in any society. It is simply a body of knowledge that is purely ideological and functional for certain material interests. School knowledge for Young is not to be judged in terms of its accuracy in depicting an external reality but only in relation to the interests and power of those who create the knowledge. The neo-Marxists[55] have also been concerned to relativize the curriculum and to portray it as serving material interests. Poulantzas, for example, argues that 'The role of the bourgeois educational apparatus largely depends upon the operation of the myth of the neutrality and the objective nature of knowledge. This myth is the favoured form of ideological indoctrination, disguising its class function'. The recent self styled materialist Marxist framework of Kevin Harris also proposes that '. . . in capitalist liberal democracies formal education functions essentially not to reveal reality but rather to transmit to each generation a structured misrepresentation of reality'.[56] Similar enthusiasm within the last decade of the sociology of education has been shown for other varieties of new radical beliefs, such as deschooling (which even self styled 'socialist' writers appear increasingly to support) and also more individually determined curriculum goals and means.

Our new radicalism has, therefore, been increasingly opposed to compulsory schooling, advocates more individualistic forms of pupil experience and often comes close to a view which sees the school curriculum as reflecting a middle class body of knowledge that is not a superior account of reality to any other extra-school knowledge. Whether the practical effects of such policy recommendations make any substantial change in the existing social relations of production more likely is, however, highly debatable. The lower streams in the comprehensive schools have an increasingly differentiated and individualized school experience but this merely generates increasingly individualized opposition to the wider social structure. The lower streams in many cases almost 'de-school', yet this merely means these children are increasingly less likely to have the formal academic qualifications that purchase within-system advancement for other children. The lower streams may have a more 'culturally relevant' curriculum yet this may mean these children are increasingly encouraged to study in depth aspects of their own culture. Unless such 'culture' is treated critically and unless further exploration of the culture that one is a member of develops cognitive ability to the same extent as exploration of a variety of cultures, the intellectual experience of such curricular innovations concerned with the reflection of experiential knowledge may be less than that of the conventional school curriculum.

It is now clear that our comprehensive experience suggests that an output of pupils who have undergone in their schools a radical educational experience close to that advocated by the new radicalism is unlikely to be a socialist output. They will tend to be an individualistic, possibly anti-intellectual under class whose lack of formal education makes them more likely to be a fascistic, rather than a socialistic force, given that fascism can be accurately portrayed as the dictatorship of the 'lumpen proletariat' and of the uneducated. In the anti-intellectualism of the young, in their elevation of experience above the still small voice of reason, in their rampant individualism and lack of concern for other members of the collectivity, in their proneness to irrational cults such as astrology and palm reading – in all these factors one can detect the partial influence of a changing school experience. Of course, other factors than the nature of within-school experience are likely to be important determinants of these new varieties of youth culture – such as rapidly rising rates of youth unemployment, increased levels of relative material deprivation between regions and between social classes, and continuing social and economic problems for ethnic minorities. It is important to realise however, that the changing nature of youth culture was clearly visible from as early as 1975 onwards, whilst only fom 1976 or

1977 can one detect the influence of any of the macro societal changes of the kind just mentioned.[57] Certainly schools can reflect social influences but, given their relative autonomy, it is likely that they mould those influences also. The doctrines of the new radicalism that have been so popular within certain sections of the discipline may well – if we judge by our comprehensive experience – be functional for the growth of socialist advance of a conventional kind.

Notes and References

1 REYNOLDS, D. and SULLIVAN, M. (1979) 'Bringing schools back in', in BARTON, L. and MEIGHAN, R. *Schools, Pupils and Deviance,* Driffield, Nafferton.
2 REYNOLDS, D. and SULLIVAN, M. (1980) 'Towards a new socialist sociology of education', in BARTON, L., MEIGHAN, R. and WALKER, S. (Eds) *Schooling, Ideology and Curriculum,* Lewes, Falmer Press.
3 This article is based upon material in REYNOLDS, D. and SULLIVAN, M. *The Comprehensive Experience,* Open Books Publishing, (in press).
4 See for example RUBENSTEIN, D. and SIMON, B. (1973) *The Evolution of the Comprehensive School,* London, Routledge and Kegan Paul; and PARKINSON, M. (1970) *The Labour Party and the Organization of Secondary Education 1918-1965,* London, Routledge and Kegan Paul.
5 Major studies of this *genre* include FLOUD, J. and HALSEY, A.H. (1956) *Social Class and Educational Opportunity,* London, Heinemann; and VERNON, P.E. (Ed) (1957) *Secondary School Selection,* London, Methuen.
6 A useful summary of this thesis is contained in FINN, D., GRANT, N. and JOHNSON, R. (1977) 'Social democracy, education and the crisis', in CENTRE FOR CONTEMPORARY CULTURAL STUDIES, *Working Papers in Cultural Studies No. 10 – On Ideology,* Birmingham, CCCS.
7 See FENWICK, I.G.K. (1976) *The Comprehensive School 1944-1970,* London, Methuen, for further elaboration of this point.
8 Hugh Gaitskell, Anthony Crosland and Harold Wilson all portrayed in the 1950s and early 1960s the fledgling comprehensives as 'grammar schools for all'. See WILLIAMS, P. (1979) *Hugh Gaitskell,* London, Cape; CROSLAND, C.A.R. (1974) *Socialism Now,* London, Cape; WILSON, H. (1964) *The New Britain,* Harmondsworth, Penguin and (1965) *The Relevance of Socialism,* London, Weidenfeld and Nicholson.
9 See REYNOLDS, D. and SULLIVAN, M. (1980) *op. cit.* for further elaboration of this point.
10 See BERNBAUM, G. (1979) *Schooling in Decline,* London, Macmillan, especially pp. 1–16.
11 Schultz, quoted in BERNBAUM, G. (1979) *op. cit.* p. 8.
12 *Committee on Higher Education,* (Robbins Report) (1963), London, HMSO.
13 Report of the Control Advisory Council for Education (Newsom Report) (1963) *Half our Future,* London, HMSO.
14 *ibid.,* para. 3.
15 CROSLAND, A. (1974) *Socialism Now,* London, Cape, p. 193.
16 For example, FLOUD, J. and HALSEY, J. (1956), and DOUGLAS, J.W.B. (1967) *The Home and the School,* London, Panther.
17 COHEN, A.K. (1955) *Delinquent Boys,* Chicago, Free Press.
18 CLOWARD, R. and OHLIN, L.A. (1961) *Delinquency and Opportunity,* London, Routledge and Kegan Paul.
19 LONGFORD STUDY GROUP (1966) *Crime: A Challenge To Us All,* London, Labour Party.
20 *ibid.,* p. 21.
21 Further elaboration of this thesis is to be found in REYNOLDS, D. and JONES, D. (1978) 'Education and the prevention of juvenile delinquency', in TUTT, N.S. (Ed) *Alternative Strategies for Coping With Crime,* London, Martin Robertson.
22 Detailed information on this thesis is to be found in REYNOLDS, D. and SULLIVAN, M. (in press) *The Comprehensive Experience,* London, Open Books.

23   See for example RUBENSTEIN, D. and SIMON, B. *op. cit.*; and GRIFFITHS, A. (1971) *Secondary School Reorganization in England and Wales,* London, Routledge and Kegan Paul.
24   See for a general over-view TAYLOR, W. (1963) *The Secondary Modern School,* London, Faber.
25   See REYNOLDS, D. (1976) 'The delinquent school' in WOODS, P. and HAMMERSLEY, M. (Eds) *The Process of Schooling,* London, Routledge and Kegan Paul; REYNOLDS, D. and SULLIVAN, M. (1979) *op. cit.*; HARGREAVES, D., HESTER, S. and MELLOR, F. (1975) *Deviance in Classrooms,* London, Routledge and Kegan Paul.
26   See the evidence in BENN, C. and SIMON, B. (1970) *Half Way There,* Harmondsworth, Penguin; ROSS, J.M., BURTON, W.J., EVISON, P. and ROBERTSON, T.S. (1972) *A Critical Appraisal of Comprehensive Education,* Slough, NFER; STEEDMAN, J. and FOGELMAN, K. (1980) *Progress in Secondary Schools,* London, National Children's Bureau.
27   DEPARTMENT OF EDUCATION AND SCIENCE (1965) *The Organization of Secondary Education, (Circular 10/65),* London, HMSO.
28   PEDLEY, R. (1969) *The Comprehensive School (Second Edition),* Harmondsworth, Penguin.
29   See BERG, L. (1968) *Risinghill – Death Of A Comprehensive School,* Harmondsworth, Penguin; and MACKENZIE, R.F. (1970) *State School,* Harmondsworth, Penguin.
30   COX, C.B. and DYSON, A.E. (1975) *Black Paper 1975,* London, Dent.
31   See the evidence in DEPARTMENT OF EDUCATION AND SCIENCE, (1980) *Secondary Education in England,* London, HMSO.
32   See CLARK, M. and DAVIES, D. (1981) 'Radical education: The pedagogical subtext', in LAWN, M. and BARTON, L. (Eds) *Rethinking Curriculum Studies,* London, Croom Helm.
33   *Children and Their Primary Schools* (The Plowden Report) (1967) London, HMSO.
34   For an account of how middle class pressure operated in one area see MARSDEN, D. (1970) 'Politicians, equality and comprehensives' in TOWNSEND, P. *Labour and Inequality,* London, Fabian Society.
35   See the evidence in STEEDMAN, J. and FOGELMAN, K. *op. cit.*
36   WILLIS, P. (1978) *Profane Culture,* London, Routledge and Kegan Paul.
37   WILLIS, P. (1977) *Learning To Labour,* London, Saxon House.
38   COHEN, P. (1976) 'Subcultural conflict and working class community' in WOODS, P. and HAMMERSLEY, M. (Eds) *The Process of Schooling,* London, Routledge and Kegan Paul.
39   See HARGREAVES, D. (1979) 'Durkheim, deviance and education' in BARTON, L. and MEIGHAN, R. (1979) *op. cit.*
40   For an impressionistic account of punk 'culture' see YORK, P. (1980) *Style Wars,* London, Sidgwick and Jackson.
41   See SKIDELSKY, R. (1975) *Oswald Mosley,* London, Macmillan.
42   ALTHUSSER, L. (1971) 'Ideology and ideological state apparatuses', in *Lenin and Philosophy and Other Essays,* London, New Left Books.
43   BOWLES, S. and GINTIS, H. (1976) *Schooling in Capitalist America,* London, Routledge and Kegan Paul.
44   BERNSTEIN, B. (1977) 'Aspects of the relations between education and production', in *Class, Codes and Control, Volume 3,* London, Routledge and Kegan Paul.
45   WILLIS, P. (1977) *op. cit.*
46   See REYNOLDS, D. (1976) *op. cit.*; REYNOLDS, D. and SULLIVAN, M. (1979) *op. cit.*; REYNOLDS, D. and JONES, D. (1978) *op. cit.*; and REYNOLDS, D. (1975) 'When pupils and teachers refuse a truce', in MUNGHAM, G. and PEARSON, G. (Eds) *Working Class Youth Culture,* London, Routledge and Kegan Paul. Full details are available in REYNOLDS, D. *Bringing Schools Back In,* (in press).
47   As used in the formulations of DALE, R. (1979) 'The politicization of school deviance: Reactions to William Tyndale', in BARTON, L. and MEIGHAN, R. (1979) *op. cit.*
48   See for example RUTTER, M. (1980) *Changing Youth in A Changing Society,* London, Nuffield Provincial Hospital Trust; and also RUTTER, M. and MADGE, N. (1976) *Cycles of Disadvantage,* London, Heinemann.
49   HEATH, A. (1981) *Social Mobility,* London, Fontana, p. 165.

50 Whereas contemporary phenomenologists have often emphasized how individuals have a degree of *freedom* in how they construct their everyday worlds and a degree of freedom to change that construction of reality if they desire, classical phenomenologists such as Schutz were often at pains to point out that the phenomenological world of a society acted as a collective *constraint* upon individual freedom of action.

For Schutz the common-sense knowledge that exists for individuals could best be seen as a body of knowledge that reflects not so much the total sum of *individual* subjectivities as the accumulated typifications that are represented in a *societal* stock of 'taken-for-granted' realities. Our hypothesis is that occupational groups such as teachers may have a stock of knowledge – derived from their general social class position and their specific occupational location – that acts as a constraint upon their behaviour and therefore as a constraint upon the school careers and attainments of certain categories of children.

51 For suggestions of how this dominance may come about and for hints as to how this may affect teacher practice see WOODS, P. (1980) *Teacher Strategies – Exploitations in the Sociology of the School,* London, Croom Helm, especially the contributions of Hargreaves and Hartnett and Naish.

52 Examples are WEDGE, P. and PROSSER, H. (1972) *Born to Fail,* London, Arrow; and DAVIE, R., BUTLER, N. and GOLDSTEIN, H. (1972) *From Birth to Seven,* London, Longmans.

53 See REYNOLDS, D. and SULLIVAN, M. (1980) *op. cit.*

54 YOUNG, M.F.D. (Ed) (1971) *Knowledge and Control,* London, Collier-Macmillan.

55 See REYNOLDS, D. and SULLIVAN, M. (1980) *op. cit.*

56 HARRIS, K. (1980) *Education and Knowledge,* London, Routledge and Kegan Paul.

57 See the evidence on changing youth cultural styles in YORK, P. (1980) *op. cit.*

A Community School

Colin Fletcher, Sutton Centre Research Project

This paper is about one unusual school during the brief period 1973–77, which was probably when the very last rays of the 'golden age'[1] could still be seen. The teachers in this school had most of the initiative. Their new comprehensive offered the chance to change secondary education. The head had declared himself for community education and this could capitalize on the gains of progressive education. He and his staff avoided all they disliked in secondary schools, adopted progressive practices and moved on towards lifelong learning and community development. Generally speaking, school is the imposition of order, an order in which a few succeed, most are dispirited and many react with hostility. But in this school most felt some solidarity and some of those who could have reacted with hostility did not. All too late I realized that the issue was the relation between educational experience and class experience, but the question was deferred because there was so much experience in the school to account for. This accounting has taken the form of nearly five years of full-time participant observation.

There are two themes to the story. First the anthropological term 'tribe' is used to organize evidence. The term emphasizes the quality of experience and allows the significance of small events to be sensed. But the paper's claim is not to have minted a fresh coin for the coffers of educational sociology. The paper is the author's latest attempt to give an existential account;[2] to engage *in* field work rather than do research. A vital part of this commitment is to write a story which people to whom it belongs can then criticize. An existential method is not a species of the holy family of empiricism though. The claim here is that those who made the choices have criticized this text; to them it is true even if shallow. As for me 'when I tell any truth it is not for the sake of convincing those who do not know it, but for the sake of defending those who do'.[3]

This story is about the making of a small piece of educational history. These teachers certainly realized they had a chance and they took it. What they did manage to achieve matters here. What matters is that the mechanisms and myths of a non-alienating school are given due importance. So much time has been devoted to what makes a school alienating. So little energy has gone into beginning from the premise that a happy school is probably very different from an unhappy school and they cannot be usefully compared in the same terms.

All kinds of theoretical points are raised too. The head, for example, is clearly charismatic, a leader who speaks of staff democracy. Quite probably this paper could have looked at leadership and reform specifically or wrestled with the question of ideology. But an existential account does not accept the independence of theory. Some readers may, therefore, be unhappy with the cavalier use of special words. Other readers, I hope, will appreciate the enormous effort that was being made at Sutton Centre; the energy that went into committing the school to social change.

The Making of a School

Sutton Centre was built in the heart of the mining and hosiery town of Sutton-in-Ashfield. Up the M1 motorway, four miles towards Mansfield from Junction 28, £2 million had been spent to give this distinct township a new lease of life. At the time nearly half the town's 20,000 jobs depended upon mining and hosiery. In the not too distant future the mines would be exhausted and closed and fewer women would be needed to make clothing. The 25% share working in manufacturing would not expand – it would be fortunate not to decrease. New industry would have to be attracted for the population of 48,000 to remain the same size by the year 2,000 AD. Sutton Centre was a kind of flagship for a fleet of local authority spending. It was launched with the highest of high hopes.

The Centre was to be built as a full-sized secondary comprehensive school, physically integrated with other services (youth and community; adult education; day centre for the aged and physically handicapped); a lavish recreation block, co-owned by County and District Councils and, eventually, the area offices of probation, social services and registrar. The Deputy Director of Education spoke of 'bringing education back into the market place', and building 'a secular cathedral'. He continued 'no part of the building will have labels. If we can identify which is a school and which is social we have, to some extent, failed'. Added to this, the Centre was in the middle of the town without the sterilizing boundaries of fields or fences. The County Architect said that 'two sacred cows had to be slaughtered. The first was that schools must be surrounded by playing fields and the second is that town centres are commercial and so devoid of life at night'. The Deputy Director of Education and a senior architect spelled out the intended innovation in a Feasibility Study in 1971. 'The pattern of the town's life has been described as a wheel without a hub.' The Centre was designed to be just this hub and the axle upon which it would turn was to be a school.

In January 1973 Stewart Wilson became headmaster; he would not have overall control; he was to be responsible for the largest part, namely the only designated community school in Nottinghamshire. In November 1972 he had given a talk at a teachers' conference in Hartlepool and urged them to look beyond comprehensivization to community education. He listed barriers; those around buildings, teachers' roles, the curriculum; young people in schools; between head and staff and between school departments. His Hartlepool speech pounded away from the position that 'the sooner we take them (these barriers) down the better'.[4] Stewart Wilson was notable even then for his courage and his convictions. He was not going to embark on demolition alone. He expected to lead an entire staff against barriers which he regarded as demoralizing, divisive and destructive.

By January one deputy head had been recruited; by May 1st, the staff increased by a second deputy and five course directors. Stewart Wilson was continuously corresponding on matters of principle and practice. He sent extensive questionnaires at regular intervals and expected rapid replies. It became increasingly difficult to discuss philosophy by post. And so during one weekend in March 1973 decisions were 'thrashed out' at Stewart Wilson's previous school's field centre in Yorkshire. The result was a staff policy document which contained new ideas and new terms with which to describe them. Reasons were given for each choice so that details and implications could be worked out later. The prospect was that two full years of pupils would begin that September and be taught by twenty-four staff. The policy document set out the combination of progressive education and community education which they would develop together.

Aspects of Policy in 1973

All pupils were to be mixed by sex, ability, friendship group and according to feeder primary schools. The whole group would have the same tutor and the same curriculum throughout their five years together. By staff dispensing with non teaching time the group size would be reduced to twenty-four pupils. The group size would make a block timetable of five morning and five afternoon sessions possible. The two block sessions would be the same length because the first half-an-hour of each day would be spent with the tutor (who would also be the group's teacher in his or her subject). Breaks in the block of time would be taken by mutual agreement in the coffee bar which served the whole department. Here they would meet tutor groups of different years if, by virtue of open plan, they had not already done so. School would finish at 3.45 p.m. and the working day at 4.45 p.m. School would then reopen again and tutors would teach at least one evening or weekend session. For the pupils these 'eleventh sessions' would be voluntary, for tutors they would be compulsory by being part of a verbal agreement at interview. Voluntary too, would be first name terms between staff and pupils.

The course directors were responsible for twelve areas of study and activity: Basic Skills; Communications and Resources; Creative Arts (Fine Arts and Music); Environmental Studies; European Studies; Home Management; Literature and Drama; Mathematics; Personal Relationships and Community Service; Science; Sports and Leisure; and Technical Studies. The directors and tutors were to design courses which would integrate subjects as much as possible;[5] refer to the locality for materials and problems; encourage independent learning and be appropriate to adults (be they parents or not) who could attend any session – day or evening – without prior notice. Courses were also to encourage pupils to work out in the community either collecting information, helping others or using local venues. The pupils would work for CSE Mode III until the end of their fifth year and could begin 'A' level work as soon as they were ready.

Tutors would be responsible for the pastoral care of their group and make home visits at least twice a year to meet with all parents. There would be an equal balance between departments, all course directors held Scale 4 posts and other scale points were equally distributed. Each tutor group would have one representative on the 'school council' which would discuss and agree the code of conduct in consultation with the head. School council was actually also an unusual use of the word 'school'. As Stewart Wilson recalls:

> One of our first tasks at Sutton Centre – before it opened in fact – was to establish the name Sutton Centre and remove any vestige of the word 'school' from the title.[6]

This brief summary sets the scene and shows that from the beginning there were responsibilities which went with the 'bill of rights' drawn up for staff, parents/adults and pupils. Those joining the founding and formative staff were to find themselves stimulated into taking up obligations which the rights conferred.

In September 1973 there was the first intake from the five 'feeder primaries' in the fixed catchment area of the southern half of the town. There were anomalies too. One batch of entrants were from a neighbouring village who had 'passed' their eleven plus. Another batch were the older children of staff members; a further group was volunteered by nearby secondary schoools as children who had problems but who might 'fit in' at Sutton Centre. Those 'opting in' doubled the second, third and fourth year tutor groups in 1973–4. Each subsequent year the pattern was repeated, feeder primaries 'sent' their children of 11 and over, secondary schools outside the area and some parents tried 'to get pupils in' and were never refused. Sutton Centre, for its part, between 1973 and 1977 did not expel or seek to transfer a single pupil. By September 1976 the school had four full years, a staff of fifty-six and 11% of its pupils from outside the catchment area. The school's case was being accepted by the Director of Education as the staffing-ratio decision made in 1974 indicates:

> We only achieve the staffing necessary to give people time off in lieu by all working an eleventh session during the Centre's first year – five mornings, five afternoons and one evening or weekend session to prove that pupils and parents and the wider community could, and did, come back in the evenings for a proper two hour session in the activity of their choice.
> Having proved our case we were able to persuade the Director that we should have an extra injection of staff to allow for staff-time off in lieu.[7]

Strengthened with a 11% staffing allowance tutors were working the equivalent of five full days; developing Mode III CSE courses; teaching mixed-ability, mixed-sex groups with a common curriculum and making home visits at least twice a year. There were other functions too, particularly those associated with literature and drama, music, communications and resources and the tutor group. There had been problems, with the building though, and there still were. The school was not finished. As Stewart Wilson put it:

> . . . we had no workshop facilities when we opened and no indoor sports facilities for two years.[8]

1976 and In Search of a Framework

By 1976 Sutton Centre was attracting a lot of attention both nationally and internationally. Visitors came to see either the architecture or the educational activity. Ken Coates and Bill Silburn at Nottingham University thought wider than most and decided that the whole Centre ought to be understood. Coates and Silburn designed a five year research project to evaluate the Centre and its relation to the town. The Department of Education and Science funded most of the proposed work and Nottinghamshire County Council agreed to a fixed contribution. I was lucky enough to get the job of Senior Research Officer. In view of the length of time involved and the very nature of the Centre's purposes I asked at interview for an office on the premises. There was so much to learn.

First there was the absence of so many of the expected props; there were no uniforms, no 'O' levels, no bells, no houses, no prefects, no assembly, no corporal punishment and no staff room. Secondly there was very little written about community schools and verbal opinions could be found at either end of a teacher-academic spectrum. The staff spoke of meeting the challenge, the goal was for school and community to be inseparable. In their 'calls for change' organic analogies were often used – seeds, growth and the climate in which a community school could flourish. The impression though, was that teachers were too close to the action to move beyond their metaphors and their telling anecdotes. They were poles apart from those who set out to study them.

Academics were sceptical to say the least; by and large they wanted to test teachers' goals by means of mechanical analogies. If community schools were different, went the reasoning, then it would show in their structures and roles, channels of communication and decision-making procedures. Tests were invented and then dropped like lead down on to the school.[9]

Five years' research, though, gave the chance of an understanding closer than that of activists *and* the chance to collect evidence by methods more akin to an academic approach. It was possible to work alongside staff, share their aims, study the terrain and sight the obstacles. Conversations made a deep impression. The truly impressive aspect of Sutton Centre was not the school-community relations but the community *within* the school and its magnetism for some townspeople. The atmosphere was lively and enthusiastic. People looked forward to going into work; they were so slow to leave each day. The staff had the following kinds of things to say:

—everything is expected of you;
—you have to give so much energy to the place;
—we rely on talking with everybody;
—everything depends on everything else;
—the system is so delicate;
—we are developing a democracy.

These statements reflect qualities of mutuality and express the organic analogy in different ways. The choice was either to challenge what staff said or think it through. As their words were to be accepted, the question seemed to be how the 'community within' worked. What was needed was a more basic term than community; one which asked about the significance of the processes for the people concerned. Then one day a drama tutor was following behind a group on their way past the Research Office to the theatre. 'Behold, the braves of our tribe', he said. And so they were. This chance remark suggested referring to the community within as a tribe; of reasoning the way in which the ethos of community education had made Sutton Centre tribal. The term would help to show how different processes gelled. The following decisions were made about the word tribe:

A tribe: initiates members,
           incorporates members in seasonal and special ceremonies,
           idealizes membership.

The term, therefore, helped to collect together the many developments which had taken place since 1973; the human face of the Centre's philosophy. In the process the term would be developed further; the details of incorporation, for example, would be better understood by both participants and observer alike. What was required was to make the first step and work upon the axiom so casually suggested.

After a further year's fieldwork I felt that it could be claimed that three sets of processes; initiation, incorporation and idealization were at work at Sutton Centre.

Stewart Wilson's views had marked the stand from which the processes could develop:

> I believe absolutely in comprehensive education as a principle but I am saddened at what I see happening in practice in the name of comprehensive education.[10]

There was much that he and his staff were not going to let happen at Sutton Centre. And in addition to their aversions they were attracted to what else was possible. The label 'community school' allowed them to make a big push forward.

Initiation Processes

Not all of the research methods used have been confessed. It is also true that the flow of circulating papers was intercepted and copies filed. A diary was kept and there was 'lurking' too. When *lurking* a researcher eavesdrops. Early in May 1977 the following telephone conversation was overheard;

> Is that . . . Primary School? Hello, I'm a first year tutor. Two of my group would like to come back and tell your fourth years what it's like here. You know, assure them that they won't be beaten up in the toilets and how exciting it all is . . .

Later that term parents were being visited before their children had started at Sutton Centre. Their child was given a booklet and so were they; the child's was called 'Welcome: Come and Enter Sutton Centre', whilst that given to the parents was called 'How to Use Your Centre'. The child's booklet was not a list of do's and dont's: there was warm and positive phrasing and a cartoon on most pages. For example the page on The Code of Conduct read . . .

> We have a code of conduct for all users of the Centre, both young and old. We would like to think that you might wish to set yourselves the following standards when you join the Centre:
> * Attend regularly.
> * Arrive on time, morning and afternoon.
> * Take a pride in the way you dress and in your personal appearance.
> * Work to the best of your ability, and in all subjects.
> * Make full use of the facilities and opportunities the Centre offers you.
> * Do the best you can for the Centre, your tutor group, your parents, and yourself.
> * SHOW CONSIDERATION FOR OTHERS.

The pupils' booklet had been prepared as a communications and resources project. The parents' booklet, which applied equally to adults at large, was the work of the Sutton Centre Users' Association as their communications and resources project. Both the booklets and the prior visit were a 'sales pitch' with a difference – there was little or no cost to be met by the pupil or parent.

The family was invited to tour the school together before the end of the summer term to see for themselves. The new teachers, for their part, had a large file of documents and an in-service training day. The training day was intended to familiarize them with the community's characteristics as well as the Centre's practices. If the sessions began with school matters then there they stayed, so the morning was devoted to learning about the town.

A Foundation week had been developed for pupils. For their first week, apart from tours of the Centre, talks in the theatre, films and the 'Sensorium', the group stayed in their area and christened it with decorations and identities like 'Ian's Horrors', 'Rutter's Nutters' or 'Pete's People'. Initiates were adding phrases to the Centre's language. The 'Sensorium' was one of the fun parts of the week. Each pupil was led blind-folded through sounds and rooms full of 'things' to touch. They were being 'videoed' by pupils who had recently been through the experience themselves. The latter then showed their film to the new initiate and explained how to use the camera.

Initiations were the ways in which parents, staff and pupils separately and together were confronted so that they would understand the Centre. No new member was forced to rely on 'touch and feel' methods of discovery. People in each group participated. Roles were extended, for it was the responsibility of teaching staff and pupils to reach outward. Thus, although not immediately obvious, an element of broadly based initiation has its implication for the role of the head.

As Harry Rée has neatly observed:

> The one individual who needs to be convinced of the necessity of flattening the hierarchy is the one who it might seem will be the first to be flattened – namely the head.[11]

If the Head were to be the sole 'initiator', then the message is likely to be a mass formal communication – an official letter or meeting. Less actual information would be communicated and so 'learning the ropes' would depend more upon gossip and chance observation. When, in contrast, staff and pupils put together a welcome booklet, that which is communicated combines both what is expected of the reader and what the readers themselves might expect. In stepping aside and down the Head lets more realism into the content and less nervous distance in the exchange.

Harry Rée teazled more than one implication out of flattening the hierarchy. A little later he observes:

> . . . in shedding his power he has increased his influence.[12]

A Head who listens, it seems, is a head who is listened to. Rather than solely work through senior staff, the Head can talk with, and exchange influences with, anybody.

However important the consequences of shared initiations may be for the role of the Head, what matters here is that those variously responsible for first contacts have some cause to take an interest in what happens next to the new members. For in telling others what to expect, day-to-day involvements proved to be basic in the accounts. Whereas initiation 'rites' take place infrequently, incorporation is going on all the time.

Processes of Incorporation

Incorporation literally means being made part of a body; in this case being drawn into the school. Each person is asked to take two or more 'roles'. Incorporation is the opposite of a mutual rejection which can be traced to each person only having one role. It can feel like a trap if one wishes to be *just* a teacher or pupil in the school or *only* a parent outside the doors.

The basic philosophy on staffing structure was;

> Each Department has a Course Director and all Course Directors are equal in status and grade. Apart from the Head and three deputies there are no special administration or pastoral posts. All points which the Burnham system allows have been allocated to teaching posts.

The notes for the guidance of tutors on home visits had the following as the sixth point to cover:

> Find out which parents would like to help in the Centre. Would they help in coffee bars, listen to slow readers, use some skill they have to help children (craftsmen, photographers, local historians, etc.). Would they help with fund-raising – jumble sales, dances, fêtes, etc. Would they go on C and R's roll of people as resources if they have special knowledge or interests?
>
> Now is, of course, an ideal time to plug opportunities for adults in the Centre.

Communications and Resources (C and R) had developed in three directions since 1973. It was a teaching department in which pupils would spend part or the whole of a week on a project involving understanding, making and criticizing media.[13] Secondly, its graphics and reprographics served school departments and the Centre as a whole. C and R staff spent periods with other courses to develop their visual aids. Thirdly, C and R was a community resource open to all adults in the daytime and during three evening sessions to produce their own media with help if they wanted it. Projects brought adults into Communications and Resources, particularly if they wanted to develop films or print tickets and posters for some voluntary group they belonged to. They could work on 'Centre News' as well as expect to receive it every term. Adults and children were in about equal proportions on each of the evenings. There was usually also a sprinkling of tutors preparing coursework as well. There was a greater spread of ages and activities in Communication and Resources than anywhere else.

At the beginning there was no charge for adults attending evening sessions because the staff were not being paid. When the staffing allowance was made adults coming to daytime or evening classes were asked to pay 35p each time. There was no membership card, course fee or enrolment night, just 35p to Pay as you Learn. For adults there were special eleventh sessions like Coffee Pot; family sessions like Family German or taking a chance in the mainly children's 'classes'. Coffee Pot's members were largely separated or divorced women. It began as an eleventh session which invited speakers and organized trips. Gradually it came to run itself, just like the Rambling Club. Family sessions were offered in music, languages and technical subjects. Most parents preferred to work alongside other people's children.

Grandparents, aunties and uncles joined in classes with their young relatives whilst parents rarely did. They were in the same building doing something different and comparing other people's children with their own. The session registers showed a tapestry of attendance which varied with shift-work and the approach to learning. Adults tended to do something intensively, give it a rest and then do something else. The courses which ran like clubs, family Spanish for example, or those which led to 'A' levels had more regular attendances.

Those adults working for a voluntary group's needs soon learned that they could 'rent-a-room' at 5p per hour per head in which to rehearse, practice, play and have meetings. Two lecture theatres and three rooms were given the priority of 'outside' groups; from chess to football referees, from rock bands to drama groups. This facility was still available during school holidays.

Signs in each teaching space read: 'The cleaning lady in this area is . . .'. Stewart Wilson drove the 'bus for the cleaners' outing and the caretaker, cleaners, technicians and office staff all came to staff meetings and the end of term party. There had to be an agreement to keep spaces resonably clear of activity so that cleaning could take place in the 'buffer time' of 4.00 p.m. – 6.30 p.m. Even so, there was the vibrating rhythm of banter and chat as those tutors staying to eleventh sessions sorted themselves out, relaxed and tuned into the tensions of news and plans.

Some plans were plainly lighthearted. The Pancake Race was open to all tutor groups competing in years. Supermarkets, offices and factories sent teams in fancy dress. The Bionic Babies, the ladies from Woolworths, pounded round the town centre with a 'pancake that was not more than ½ cm thick and had no rubber reinforcements'. They won the fancy dress but not the race as the Police and DHSS's 'Export Models' had obviously been in training. The DHSS personnel were almost bound to win something as they had entered five teams. The prizes were mugs made at the Day Centre. Adult groups were asked to join in the summer fête and raise money for themselves in the process. Whilst firms and shops gave prizes and donations, groups like Skegby Old People's Home raised money specifically for their summer outing.

Some adults became seriously involved in the Centre by having at least three different commitments. First they staffed the coffee bars; some, like Uncle Jim's, even taking their name (Jim is a retired miner whose nephew did not want to come to school so he came with him for a while and then settled into a place where his nephew could find him easily. He likes smartness and clean jokes and has never joined a class as such). Other helpers joined classes as learner-helper-tutors. They liked to get there a little after the class was underway and stay behind briefly at the end for a chat. They liked to work and see that they had done something during their two or more hours. 'Adult literacy' came into being in 1974 when a helper in Basic Skills branched out on her own and recruited her own volunteer staff and 'pupils'.

The really dedicated adults got involved in the Sutton Centre Users' Association. Stewart Wilson wanted a broader group than a PTA. His deputy head 'community' set about forming an Association which had rights in relation to the Centre. The Associations applied pressure to have the first chaplain replaced and organized a petition to get the Sports Centre open to the public. The Association formed an Education Group which was concerned with opportunities to learn throughout the Centre.

By 1976 there were strains showing on those adults who were parents, helpers, class attenders and SCUA activists. Some were now over-stretched. Others had resisted having a career in the Centre and rested in a cul-de-sac on the way; they had limited their liability to allow themselves some free time. Many parents had been incorporated in their own right, that is as adults rather than as levers of control upon their children.

The pupils were experiencing incorporation as elaborate rights too. Each week, in tutor group time, pupils added more to their profiles.[14] Profiles include a record of activities so that a diary of life inside and outside school is kept. Pupils often drew pictures in their early years. Slowly these hardbacked books became thicker as subject tutors wrote comments, the pupils replied and the profiles were taken home for parents to read and then write their comments upon. Profiles belonged to the pupil. The tutor's comments tended to be encouraging and hopeful. Some may have resorted to a report writing code where, for example, 'A pleasant and constructive member of his group' may have concealed the opinion 'thick but harmless'. But most tutors wrote a close study of the term's work. Pupils' parents, in contrast, were more direct and prone to sharp criticism. One, for instance, read 'I know you are not trying hard so stop pretending'. For the first three years all the pupils had the same curriculum. Then the fourth and fifth years had two choices within the common core curriculum. Each week one session – called the tenth session – could be devoted to further work in any course they wished.

'Eleventh sessions' offered a further kind of curriculum choice. Every evening there were at least ten sessions to choose from including the library. Attendances at eleventh sessions were roughly one per child per week with 15,000 per year in all. One quarter of the total were adults, one fifth were pupils from other schools (primary and secondary) and a pattern was clearly established. Mathematics was the most popular with three evening sessions and never less than sixty attenders. More third and fourth year pupils attended; they were older and working on their CSEs. Home circumstances played a part too. In contrast to many of the pupils' homes the Centre was spacious, warm and quiet. Pupils began congregating at about 5 o'clock; many still yet to make up their mind which eleventh session to attend. At eleventh sessions they were out of their tutor group, but probably with relatives or friends, mixed in with all years and some adults. During the summer term there were many more outdoor eleventh sessions such as sailing on the reservoir. Through their tutor group representatives, and school council,[15] pupils asked for new eleventh sessions.

By 1977 tutor group time had become organized somewhat and the group notice boards usually showed that the weekly Bulletin was attended to on Mondays and Profiles on Fridays. The Bulletin was everybody's means of communicating with everybody else on matters ranging from the week's events to items for sale, from 'lost and found' to French vocabulary. The Bulletin also gave the attendance 'results' for the tutor groups, those with 95% and over; a special commendation for the '100%ers' and a 'buck up column' for those close to the generally accepted minimum of 90%. Once a fortnight the group redecorated its area and was inspected by the Head for the KSCT (Keep Sutton Centre Tidy) awards. Every six weeks or so the group would become a TUG (Tidy Up Gang) and clear up around their area – both inside and outside the building.

The 'bus was a big thing; a symbol of the curriculum. All staff were expected to take whole groups out and so tutor group's coursework experience was a matter of 'widening out'. The Profile card on the first year of Environmental Studies read:

> Starting with a survey of our Town and its life, we extend our study to our City, Nottingham, which we shall visit. We shall then go to take a look at our National Park, the Peak District, and our famous Forest of Sherwood.

Incorporation is practically experienced by having to become involved in the definition of problems as well as the determination of solutions. The Science profile card made this apparent:

> In the first two years pupils work very freely, first at acquiring basic techniques needed in laboratories and secondly at investigating topics suggested sometimes by staff and sometimes by the pupils themselves. They are encouraged to keep careful written records of their work and discoveries. Whether they are investigating electric fires, the composition of rocks or the way their own heart beats, we hope that they will be gaining scientific techniques which will benefit them later in life.

The curriculum was not everything though. One development had been that of 'suspended week' when the whole curriculum was literally suspended and the staff chose what to offer all the pupils. Suspended weeks were twice a year, adults came in for the whole project and generally the ages of pupils in each option were as mixed as in eleventh sessions. Some tutors went off camping with their group, others got together to dream up a joint offering. Option 28 in a list of 30 for summer 1977 read:

> Drama and the Theatre – Isabel and Sue.
> John Forrester of Sutton gets caught up with events one day in Nottingham. Come and join the fun, fighting, gun-smoke, cannon! Lights and sounds, the show of the century and you could be in it.

Option 29 was:

> Community Service – Gill Pike.
> Will consist of group activities taking over a playgroup, an infants' class, day centre, OAP's home.

Mathematics during suspended week took a light-hearted approach with curve stitching and origami. In December 1976 28% of pupils chose to do mathematics all week.

Whether or not pupils will benefit later in life remains to be seen. Whatever the outcome they were being of benefit to the Centre whilst being pupils. For the decoration of their areas was one of many contributions to the fabric. In Communications and Resources the tutor group made media and displays for the neutral areas of dining hall, corridors and exhibition space. Pupils were visitors' guides (not members of staff) for it was their place and tours were part of their social education.

Tutors were getting a large measure of their social education from home visits. Stewart Wilson had put this principle forcibly . . .

> I believe that as teachers we must undertake a far wider pastoral role than we have done hitherto. The community school teacher must be prepared to get in amongst the community – on their home ground as well as in the community school itself – and I mean getting inside the homes to meet the mums and dads so we can start to understand the housing and economic conditions under which our pupils and the wider community are living. This pastoral role isn't just concerned with dealing with a child's behavioural or emotional problems. It is concerned with his or her personal

development as an individual and as a member of the community. I would like to add a further extension to this principle, namely that the staff of the community school should live in the community they serve – but that is one I am hesitant about even though I and many of my colleagues do live in Sutton.[16]

Whether or not they lived in the town, tutors needed to know about its people and living conditions in order to develop their courses. Creative Art and Design, for example, covered areas of work in Art, Home Management and Technical Studies. The fourth year pupils were faced with the choice of nine modules from a list of thirty-three. Eleven of these choices were as follows:

Science preserves Food; Camping Cookery; Christmas Cookery; Quick Meals; Eating in AD 2000; Cheap Meals; Entertaining; Slimming; Making Clothes; Toy Making; Soft Furnishing.

Tutors soon found that fourth year boys chose camping, cookery and making clothes – particularly because the latter included making tee-shirts and printing slogans of the day upon them.

No tutor was exempt from being incorporated in the town and reciprocating through coursework. No tutor was forced to be marginal to the tribe's ceremonies. No tutor was more important than another when it came to pastoral care. One sentence on the notes for guidance of the tutors on home visits read:

Emphasize to parents that you are their first point of contact at school on any matter concerning their children.

The leaflet 'Approximately Twenty Eight Language Activities for Tutor Time' began:

Tutor time is, and must be, for the tutor and his/her group to come together and grow together, i.e. it is not teaching time.

Many tutors held meetings to discuss their group with those who taught them. Working parties of this kind were *ad hoc* according to need. There were no self-perpetuating groups apart from the agenda sub-committee which had the power to be frank and fearless and fix the tone of weekly staff meetings.

The agenda sub-committee (ASC) had been formed in 1975 to ease Stewart Wilson into some of the details of democracy. ASC had a representative from each department and it decided what would be discussed and how long would be allocated to discussion. The chairmanship of the staff meeting would rotate through the whole staff. The topic would be spoken to, groups would form to discuss further and return to vote on action. Major changes required a two-thirds majority vote. At least three times a term the emerging stresses were examined. Reviews of progress, 'battery-charging sessions', took the form of a one-day Conference on the optional day off – the annual governors' day. Small groups were again preferred to big sessions in order to give more junior members of staff a better chance of speaking.

The end of term events had become uproarious if not outright cathartic. 'Cock-Up of the Year' was held immediately after school. Tutors wrote down each other's howlers on scraps of paper which were read out by two staff after the fashion of the 'two Ronnies'. There were team as well as individual entries and a visitor's prize. The award of the grotesque plaster shape was not easily won for there was so much stiff competition. Memorable, for brevity at least, was the drama tutor's remark to the adult, under cloth cap, who was carefully reading a poster with his index finger:

'It's a question of *literacy* darling', she said to the Chairman of the Education Committee.

The cabaret later that evening had husbands, wives, all manner of staff and parents laughing at a deputy in drag as Marlene Dietrich, songs and sketches which went on with varying degrees of professionalism for at least an hour. Very few foibles, if any, were missed in the barrage of direct humour.

Incorporation for members of all groups meant being a participant in informal events as well as engaging in activities which were bound to bring them into contact with others in different ways. The effects were felt as far as the governing body. The governors were six councillors, three staff, three parents and two pupil observers. At the governors' meeting on the 20th June 1977 the Chairman regretted that they had to disband because of the local government elections. He said, 'It's a sad day, we've made great strides. We'll see some great sparks from this school'. A district councillor continued the theme: 'No governing body has done things like this one . . . We've done things that most have not attempted. It's the one meeting that I've enjoyed'. Stewart Wilson replied 'We've had the governing body behind us. I hope that you will still look on it as your school whatever happens'.

The very informality of incorporation had its problems though. Almost because people identified so strongly and talked together often, the relationship between pieces of officialdom was not really worked out. Four distinct bodies existed; school council, staff meeting, users' association and governing body. To be sure, there were overlaps but there was also a sense of 'hit and miss' about the future. When initiatives failed, like the Community Newspaper, it was obvious to some that the collective energies of all four bodies could have been enough to make it a regular publication.

But tribes are noted more for ceremonies rather than for constitutions. Incorporation worked for the tribe by making first impressions an elaborate experience. It also stunted the development of a bureaucracy and the deadening effects of departmentalism. Clearly tutors thought well beyond their immediate interests; beyond the goal of pupils being successful in their own subjects.

Idealizations

Sutton Centre's 'philosophy' was spoken calmly and firmly; yet within the reasonableness there was the glint of a determined ideological struggle. Stewart Wilson and his staff knew there was bitter opposition, particularly within the 'profession' to their ideals. By 1977 the ideals were obviously more than passing fancies. There were proofs; a pupil began 'A' level work in his fourth year, music and athletics competitions were invariably won and eighteen parents stood for parent governor. One candidate's self description read:

Daughter in her fourth year at Sutton Centre. Now a member of SCUA Education Committee, Rambling Club, occasional coffee bar helper. Have attended Family German course, now attending Sociology course. I have spent two holidays with Sutton Centre children.

According to Stewart Wilson:

> Perhaps most fundamentally of all, we are starting to persuade and con-
> vince the wider public that a school is their building as well as their
> children's building and that they have the right of access and a right to the
> vast range of facilities and interests which a school, through its buildings
> and staff, can provide.[17]

Opponents, though, were convinced that such ideals were a direct and an indirect
threat. The direct threat was to show others up; so many teachers elsewhere wanted to
be with children as little as possible and far away from the building as much as possible. As MacDonald neatly puts it:

> One man's bandwagon is another man's hearse.[18]

The real challenge was over the idealization of pupils. Kids came first, not last. In
essence Sutton Centre philosophy was wholly opposed to there being classes of
citizens; to streaming either by ability or specialization. The idea began from a different position altogether: every pupil should get a lot out of school. The Profile cards
then went one stage further:[19]

> Home Management's first aim was to:
>   encourage pupils to become critical consumers.
> Environmental Studies' aim was to:
>   study the world and man's place in it, and to encourage in all of us an
>   appreciation of the environment and a sense of responsibility towards
>   it.

Getting something out of school developed, therefore, into the right to be critical
and creative. The ideal was that pupils were to grow to be sexually mature not sexist
and immature. A Nottingham Head complained that a girl whose parents had
moved insisted on doing woodwork in her fourth year.

The children were not being educated *in order* to be productive, they were *being*
productive. Productiveness was regarded as an attitude of mind upon which the
quantity and quality of output depended. The pupil was presented as imaginative,
trustworthy and responsible, a person to be encouraged into a competent co-
operation with others. No pupil was said to be automatically interested largely in sex-
based pursuits, lazy, limited, dishonest or only stimulated by competition. Pupils
were said to have potentials rather than be bundles of problems. An ideal which
emphasizes potentials, of course, directs attention to what to do next and to the sensitivity felt at all times by the pupil. Put another way the ideal was to avoid alienating
the pupil; to avoid the authoritarian alternative at all costs.

Equal value was given to expressivity (thinking), instrumentalism (doing) and
involvement (power sharing). Usually pupils are described as either inclined to the
Arts or to the more 'practical studies'. These two capabilities are often regarded as
'either/or' gifts which are rarely found in equal strengths in a single person. Sutton
Centre's ideal was that because of power-sharing both thinking and doing would
flourish.

> Of course, as a society we would all like to write well and with correct spell-
> ings but let us first make sure that we can read well and speak with

confidence . . . Above all, will the young people . . . be allowed some real
say in what we are planning to do with them?[20]

The ideal of involvement has many layers: it readily corrects any suggestion that
incorporation is a subtle silencer of true opposition; that resistance is bought off with
the bangles of a colonial trader.

An organic meaning of community was put forward: of co-operation between
people with different skills, a force for good and a good experience in itself. If the
townspeople assumed that community referred to their hierarchy – to the natural
pecking order from rich down to respectable and on to ragged – then involvement cut
across *their* barriers. A consequence of incorporation *and* curriculum would be an
active, aware and articulate working class. The Centre experience was intended to
equip pupils to play a part in the town; not to leave it at the earliest opportunity.
Pupils were not to be discouraged from being miners and hosiery workers but equipped to express themselves at work and at home.

Sometimes, though, the ideals were being subverted whilst at other moments
there were compromises of priority. Ideals were held but not always equally and
consistently. There was the use of setting for languages in European Studies. The
problem of priority referred to was the competition between the aims of 'fill the
building' and 'let's take education out whenever possible'. Stewart Wilson did not
feel the latter as strongly as many of his staff. The common ground, though, between
Head and staff felt firmer by the term. They shared the idealization of the pupil.

This idealization was given the most full, public exposure. Sparks could be
expected but the very unity of the staff prevented the onset of serious fear. The
idealizations were an achievement in themselves. Stewart Wilson had challenged this
much in his talk at Hartlepool:

> Now I know that many of you would like to say 'Yes but we are doing this
> or we are doing that in our schools already. Some of the things you are
> advocating are common practice in many of our schools'. But how many
> schools are there, I wonder, where the Head and his staff have ever really sat
> down to consider what their total philosophy should be – or if they have,
> have then published it for everybody in the school and the surrounding
> community to see.[21]

The Tensions of a Distinctive Form

Whereas schools rarely define and make public their 'total philosophy' those in the
youth and adult education services often do. The latter, in fact, often base their purpose on dealing with the casualties of the secondary school system. They write of providing a sanctuary where people can put their self-esteem back together. They, too,
think there is a great deal in every individual; a potential that is ever-present.[22]

Immediately one outside criticism of Sutton Centre becomes apparent, 'you can
do what you like, there's no discipline, it's not a school it's a community centre . . .
Tutors are not teachers at all. They are social workers'. Thus, there was less of the
usual mistrust and distance between the two Cinderella services and their ugly sister, a
secondary school. And, almost because of this compatibility and subsequent working
relationship, Sutton Centre was steadily and heavily criticized. Staff could not say

there was discipline because there was no provision for pain and discomfort. When progressive definitions of discipline were advanced some professional colleagues and local politicians could not, or would not, see the point. The tag of 'social workers' was one which the tutors had to live with. The principle that 'as teachers we must undertake a far wider pastoral role than we have done hitherto' did, after all, lend itself to such criticism. The criticism was founded upon deeper suspicions too, for to what extent was Sutton Centre recognizable as a secondary school at all?

Visitors were met with a style which combined a form more like that of primary schools and a content more akin to adult education. Pupils worked in groups around tables within walls covered with their displays. Close examination of the syllabi showed many controversial issues being openly discussed. Health education, for example, included an examination of swearing. Pupils were actually learning about taboo subjects. Sutton Centre was an alternative community centre rather than a mirror image of the community's views – the pleasure of purposeful play combining with the potency of questioning the world as it is.

It was, therefore, the claim of community education and at the same time standing against some of the community's taken for granted values, that brought into question the Centre's real relationship with the town. By giving power to pupils and parents the town's status-divisions of age and occupation were challenged. Problem families were not treated with disdain but welcomed into a haven from the hostile world. Both 'problem' and respectable families could develop within the Centre strengthened by access to the power of all its plant and facilities. The haven was not meant to be a quiet retreat but to play an active part in community development. Roughly translated the result was a new power base with more people involved than there were active in local political circles. National and international interest made matters worse because the glare of publicity inflated the special status of the Centre that bit more. Parents and pupils took such attentions remarkably well. For even if they felt poked and provoked there was still the effect of a pride in their own place. They frankly found many of the idealizations rather daunting, if not actually embarrassing. The idealizations were teachers' words to transform education rather than everyday Sutton speech. A man, regularly in the Reprographics department to do publicity for his Club, was asked by a visitor how he felt about the Centre's commitment to community education:

'I've had some use out of it', he said.

A fifth former helping in the PHAB club said,

It saves you money on a Friday night.

The Chairman of the School Council said,

I'm not a guinea pig. I'm working hard to get to Oxford.

A mother in class said:

I work part-time but manage to fit in one evening at the Centre and with luck I might even make it two. Occasionally I go in on a Tuesday morning to do some extra learning but I hasten to add that the teacher does not let my presence interfere with the children's education.

When asked if he thought the Centre was too lavish a man replied:

> After all this place is an educationally deprived area. So all these things they've put here *should* be free or nearly so. We've had nothing for so long.

Sutton Centre's participants were busy making their own daily increments of proof in a matter of fact way. Overall vandalism and truancy rates were much lower than might be expected. The acid test was waited for with bated breath, academic attainments were expected of the first full fifth form.

The parent's news-sheet in October 1977 included the following items:

11th Sessions
Our evening 11th sessions are again proving extremely popular with our pupils and with quite a number of pupils from our feeder Primary Schools. *Some pupils come back to the Centre five nights a week for various activities.* Visitors to the Centre never cease to be amazed at seeing 40 to 50 youngsters working away at their Maths or Science every evening and the Centre library is so popular with pupils doing follow-up work that we may sadly have to start having a rota system for library use. *Can we remind all parents that you are welcome to come along to 11th session activities with your children and to join in if you wish.* There are, incidentally, vacancies for adults in several of our Family classes and in our 'A' level classes in Mathematics, Literature, History, Environmental Science, Physics, Art and Economics.

Our school attendance for the half-term has been good – averaging out at 92.7%. In fact many tutor groups regularly average over 95% and we have a large number of pupils who have set their sights on being members of the 'One Hundred Percenters' Club at the end of the year.

The Save Our Schools Campaign.
The Director of Education has recently launched a Country-wide appeal entitled 'Save Our Schools' – (SOS for short) in an effort to halt the damage caused to many of our schools by vandalism and fire . . . The Director of Education also recently publicly commended Sutton Centre for having the lowest rate of vandalism of any secondary school in the county.

When all the facts and trends were shown to the County Architect he exclaimed,

> Good Lord the thing is actually taking off.

And so it was – only to be shot down on the runway a month later in November 1977.[23]

A Brief Review

The story abruptly ends when the 'tribe' was beset by two enquiries. The school was put on trial just four years after it began. There was then the story of a trauma to be told; which, needless to say, is being done.[24] The three 'I's of initiation, incorporation and idealization proved useful and illuminating here because of what people were doing. The organizing idea characterizes the period in such a way that the original claim can be repeated. At Sutton Centre comprehensive education developed because of an ethos of community education. Content was more important than form. How people got on with each other was rated more highly than how they were separated into tasks and statuses. In sum, rather than a replica of a secondary modern or grammar school or a little of both there was a different kind of school.

It is difficult to do something and to argue the right to do it at the same time; one usually manages to stop the flow of the other. This paper is an existential sociology of one school, its teachers and their teaching. The idea of there being a tribe helped to recall an exciting story; a story made exciting by the collective effort to work in a community school.

The case for, and characteristics of, an existential sociology have not been spelled out. In its present form the paper leaves it to the reader to use the evidence in different ways and to decide between the alternative forms of relationship which can exist between sociological work and the world of education. Being at Sutton Centre made that choice much less difficult than it might otherwise have been.

Acknowledgements

I would like to thank Richard Taylor, Martin Galloway, Bob Mahy and David Purseglove for so many comments which literally took my breath away. The paper was first well criticized by D.A. Jones, A. Clifford and H. Rée. The editors of this book then manfully edged me back to the drawing board when I thought to disappear off into fieldwork. This fine force-field of friends is not responsible for the weaknesses which still exist.

Notes

1   DALE, R. (1979) p. 95.
2   'Man first of all exists, encounters himself, surges up in the world – and defines himself afterwards . . . man is before all else, something which propels itself towards a future and is aware that it is doing so. Thus, the first effect of existentialism is that it puts every man in possession of himself as he is and places the entire responsibility for his existence squarely on his shoulders'. SARTRE, J.-P. (1948) pp. 28–29.
3   BLAKE, W. (1810–1866) p. 597.
4   WILSON, S. (1980) p. 126.
5   The profile card on Personal Relationships introduces the course to pupils, parents and other adults as follows:
>   Included within the scope of the Department are the often separated areas of study
>   – health and sex education, religious education, careers guidance, social and community service.
>   These elements are integrated into a continuous course over five years leading up to a choice of CSE awards. Further opportunity to develop aspects of the course will be available in our 11th sessions and sixth form courses.
>   In the first year we shall help our new entrants to understand the Centre community, the family unit, their personal development and a code of living based upon the concept of 'Consideration for Others'.

The second year develops the study of health and welfare for the individual and the community, including the work of the Church, National and Local Services and Voluntary Organizations.

Third year work concentrates upon the changing relationships, needs and problems associated with adolescence.

CSE Courses in the fourth and fifth years allow choice between 'Relationships and Responsibilities', 'Health and Welfare', or 'Religious Studies'.

Careers guidance will be offered at appropriate stages.

6 WILSON, S. (1980) *op. cit.* p. 126.
7 *ibid.* p. 130.
8 *ibid.* p. 128.
9 ELSEY, B. and THOMAS, K. (1977).
10 WILSON, S. (1980) *op. cit.* p. 115.
11 RÉE, H. (1977) p. 189.
12 RÉE, H. *op. cit.* p. 189.
13 'We aim to encourage . . .
     Awareness of the *SENSES* mainly to do with sight, sound and touch.
     Success in some form of *COMMUNICATIONS* through the use of verbal, visual and written material and the presentation of work to each other.
     A sense of *RESOURCEFULNESS,* the how and where of finding information.
     Some understanding of *MASS MEDIA* of advertising, pop culture, television, newspapers, achieved by mounting advertising campaigns, planning discos, making television programmes, producing magazines and then examining the results.
     Involvement in the running of the *CENTRE* with the setting up of pupil run services.
     SELF MOTIVATION DIRECTION RESPONSIBILITY in a non-pressurized situation.'
14 'Profiles are part of a grounded alternative'. FLETCHER, C. (1980) p. 46.
15 'The School Council is representative of every tutor group and its terms of reference are that it is free to discuss anything concerning the Centre (and this includes the freedom to criticize the Head and the way the Centre is run)'. 'Basic Philosophy Document'.
16 WILSON, S. (1980) *op. cit.*p. 131.
17 *ibid.* p. 142.
18 'It is naïve to think of educational change as a game in which everybody wins, seductive though that is'. MACDONALD, B. (1976) p. 131.
19 Tony Benjamin (1978) made a content analysis of courses in relation to the characteristics encouraged.
20 WILSON, S. (1980) *op. cit.* p. 124.
21 *ibid.* p. 117.
22 'Without *some* notion of moral worth education becomes a sterile game'. EASTHOPE, G. (1980) p. 165.
23 *Vide,* FLETCHER, C. (1978).
24 FLETCHER, C. *et al* (forthcoming).

References

BENJAMIN, T. (1978) 'The school as it was: 1976–77' – Community Education in Sutton Centre – 1976–77, Sutton Centre Research Project, Department of Adult Education, University of Nottingham.
BLAKE, W. (1810–1866) *Complete Writings* Oxford University Press.
DALE, R. (1979) 'The politization of school deviance: Reactions to William Tyndale' in BARTON, L. and MEIGHAN, R. (Eds) *Schools, Pupils and Deviance,* Driffield, Nafferton Books, pp. 95–112.

EASTHOPE, G. (1980) 'Curricula are social processes' in BARTON, L., MEIGHAN, R. and WALKER, S. (Eds) *Schooling, Ideology and the Curriculum* Lewes, The Falmer Press, pp. 153–167.

ELSEY, B. and THOMAS, K. (1977) *'The School and the Community* School of Education, University of Nottingham.

FLETCHER, C. (1978) 'Assessing school performance: The background of an inquiry at Sutton Comprehensive School', *British Educational Research Journal* Vol. 4, No. 2, pp. 51–61.

FLETCHER, C. (1980) 'The Sutton Centre profile' in BURGESS, T. and ADAMS, B. (Eds) *Outcomes of Education* Macmillan, pp. 46–55.

FLETCHER, C., FISHER, M. and WILLIAMS, W. (forthcoming) *Schools on Trial* Lewes, The Falmer Press.

MACDONALD, B. (1976) 'Evaluation and the control of education' in TAWNEY, D. *Curriculum Evaluation Today: Trends and Implications* Macmillan, pp. 125–136.

RÉE, H. (1977) 'What it means to others' in WATTS, J. (Ed) *The Countesthorpe Experience* Allen and Unwin, pp. 185–190.

SARTRE, J.-P. (1948) *Existentialism and Humanism* London, Methuen.

WILSON, S. (1980) 'The School and the Community' and 'Eleventh Sessions at Sutton Centre as a Community Involvement' in FLETCHER, C. and THOMPSON, N.T. (Eds) *Issues in Community Education* Lewes, The Falmer Press, pp. 115–132, 139–142.

The Teaching Nexus: A Case of Mixed Ability

Stephen Ball, University of Sussex

There are a growing number of discussions and studies which are addressed to the problem of constraints upon teaching. These can be divided, with some admitted degree of injustice, into two main camps. There are those which give stress to a view of constraints as primarily structural phenomena, constituting a field of determinations within which teachers must work and to which they must accommodate their practices (e.g. Sharp and Green, 1976; Hargreaves, 1979; Hunter, 1979). And there are those which, while cognizant of the limitations of social structure, attribute to the teacher a degree of knowledgeability in the skilful construction of strategic responses to constraint (e.g. Lacey, 1977; Woods, 1981). However, neither camp has yet had a great deal to offer in the way of empirical analysis to match their theoretical elaboration. Certainly, there has been little attempt to investigate and plot teachers' own perceptions of the constraints which they confront in their work. It is with these perceptions that I am concerned here.

I am not proposing a new approach or some kind of theoretical breakthrough in the study of teaching, but I do want to address the problem of constraints upon teachers from a somewhat different position. That is, *in terms of* the perceptions, experiences and perspectives of teachers as social actors. These might be summarized as what Reynolds (1981) refers to as *phenomenological constraints*. These to be related in turn to the teacher's construction of a subject identity, negotiation of career and management of classroom activities. The whole to be explored in the context of a case study of innovation in a comprehensive school. The innovation is mixed-ability grouping and the school I shall refer to as 'Beachside Comprehensive' (Ball 1981).

According to Hunter (1979, p. 130), the existence of taken-for-granted parameters, which constitute the ideological and socio-political constraints upon decision-making in schools – the 'third' face of Power – 'becomes apparent only when they are breached or challenged'. The occurrence of a fundamental institutional innovation of the kind discussed here provides a fruitful empirical case of such breaching and challenging. Several analytically separable levels and dimensions of constraint are exposed to view. As will become apparent, however, the aspects of constraint to be dealt with cannot and will not be treated as mutually exclusive, neither does the concentration on the teacher exclude the consideration of the specific role of structural features.

Sociologically, teaching cannot be viewed simply as a technical work process that requires the selction of 'appropriate' practices in the light of given working conditions. As work, teaching characteristically involves various degrees of personal involvement, ideological commitment and, correspondingly, investment of self (Becker, 1964). An adequate account of innovation in or constraints upon teaching must therefore, in some way, recognize the implications *of* and *for* 'the development and sustenance of the self' (Hargreaves 1979, p. 148). In the everyday lifeworld of school it is the teachers' sense of self and work identity which underpins the meanings and interpretations attributed to educational phenomena and work problems. This relationship was evident in the case of the mixed-ability innovations at 'Beachside' in the range of orientations to and interpretations of it held by the staff. From these orientations and interpretations it was possible to identify three relatively coherent group perspectives among the staff as a whole (Becker, 1961). The issues raised by the constitution of these *perspectives* and the conflicts between their adherents delineate the major areas for analysis in the following sections of the paper.

Thus, the first part of the paper contains a brief analysis of the mixed-ability debate in the school, which was a preamble to, *and* continued for a time alongside, the implementation of the new system of grouping. This may be considered as the *educationalist phase* of the innovation (to adapt Keddie's 1971 terminology), but nonetheless it reveals some of the taken-for-granted working premises and background expectancies which underlay the previously undisturbed working practices of groups of teachers in the school. The second part of the paper looks at the implementation of the innovation; that is, the actual preparation for and teaching of mixed-ability classes. This may be considered as the *teacher phase* of the innovation. It is here that available 'possibilities for action' were considered in the context of constraints deriving from four major sources.

1   The teachers' perceptions of social context.
2   The limitations of subject sub-culture and subject identity.
3   The demands of career and collegial evaluation.
4   The problems of survival and the maximization of personal satisfaction (in dealing with the situational realities of the mixed-ability classroom).

To reiterate an earlier note, these are heuristic and analytical categories and as such they cannot be dealt with as mutually exclusive.

The debate

The proponents of mixed-ability were a small group of teachers, centred on the Head of English, whom I identified as representing an *idealist* perspective. They saw mixed-ability as an important part of what a comprehensive school should be concerned with, and as offering each child a greater degree of equality of opportunity than was possible within the existing system of 'banding' pupils.

It's to keep all their options open for as long as possible, not judging them too early. Most of the judging that goes on is concerned with verbal ability and fluency and I don't think that that necessarily has all that much to do with intelligence or endowed ability.

The teachers teaching English, many of us in the department, are ideologically opposed to the competitive ethos of the school and work positively against it. (mixed-ability) . . . is an answer to the idea of what I think a comprehensive school is and the way I think it should be going.
Head of English (interview)

The Head of English forcefully articulated these views to other members of staff and most particularly in the staff meetings at which votes were taken on whether to introduce mixed-ability grouping. At the other extreme there was a slightly larger group of teachers, centred on the head of Languages, but also taking in Science and Maths staff, who were opposed to the introduction of mixed-ability grouping in the school generally and in their subjects specifically. I identified this group as representing an *academic* perspective. The concerns of this group centred around 'standards' and 'maintaining academic excellence' and the problems of the 'brighter child' and the 'demands of the subject'. Mixed-ability was seen to be a threat to these concerns and the sort of school that they felt 'Beachside' had become. Some of those adhering to the academic perspective explained their oposition to mixed-ability in the following ways.

> I felt that there might be a lowering of the higher academic standards due to the less pressure being exerted on the brighter children.
>
> Science teacher (interview)

> I'm concerned about the problem of the more able children.
>
> French year (interview)

> I'm not convinced that the most able child gains from it; I have no evidence for that and I shall want to see improved exam results. But I don't think the 'high flyers' get enough out of it.
>
> Technical Studies teacher (interview)

The staunch opposition of the Languages department, and to a lesser extent Maths and Science, led to a negotiation of the terms of the innovaton which involved compromises on both sides. The Languages Department agreed to accept mixed-ability in the first year, but were allowed to 'set' in the second and third. Maths were given the same concession but eventually decided to extend mixed-ability into the second year on their own initiative. Science, willingly agreed to mixed-ability in the first two years (with some dissent from the Physics teachers) but were adamantly against it in the third and were allowed to 'set'. Also the climate of concern for the 'brighter child' which emerged strongly in the debate, led the headmaster to create a post of special responsibility 'for the most able child', which was given to a senior member of the Science department, an ex-grammar school teacher, who was a vociferous opponent of mixed-ability. These compromises may be seen as attempts to assuage the degree of threat that the mixed-ability innovation constituted to the self conception held by those teachers committed to their work role primarily as subject-specialists. For these teachers, the maximization of personal satisfactions was predicated on at least some teaching to receptive and committed pupils capable of high levels of academic achievement. For these teachers their subjective self-interests and their associated concerns for the 'standards' of their subject led to an implacable opposition to mixed-ability.

In the construction of their careers, these subject-centred teachers had built up a commitment to teaching which involved a whole set of sidebets made to a *substantial* academic identity (Ball, 1972). Their commitments to teaching were almost entirely based on the rewards and personal satisfactions accruing to them through these aspects of their work. The teaching of low stream, remedial or non-examination classes was regarded as an onerous task, a form of 'dirty work'.

The possibility of the introduction of mixed-ability wholesale through the school represented for the subject-centred teachers the threat of a spoilt professional identity (Goffman 1963) and of deskilling. As they saw it, their skills lay in teaching languages, or whatever, to the academically able and committed, not in struggling to control and interest the resentful, less able pupils, who did not possess, as they saw it, 'the necessary *skills and abilities'*.

From the institutional point of view the compromises made to the academic opponents of mixed-ability not only allowed the innovation to go ahead but they also served to retain the commitment – 'the willingness of social actors to give their energy and loyalty to social systems, the attachment of pesonality systems to social relations which are seen as self-expressive' (Kanter 1974, p. 126) – of these teachers to their work roles in the school.

But, given this strong opposition to the introduction of mixed-ability, the question then is how did it come about that mixed-ability was accepted by a majority of staff in a free vote. The answer lies in the disposition and attitudes of the third and largest group of teachers, in fact a group which included just about all of the rest of the staff. I identified this group as representing, for want of a better term, a *disciplinary* perspective. The support of this group for mixed-ability was founded on one straightforward principle; their belief that the introduction of mixed-ability groups would bring about a reformation of the 'social atmosphere' of the school through the elimination of troublesome low-stream anti-school classes. Thus in interviews and staff meetings these teachers spoke of mixed-ability being 'necessary from the disciplinary point of view' (Geography teacher: staff meeting) and in order 'to rid ourselves of the very few disciplinary blackspots' (Technical Studies teacher: interview). The rationale behind this particular brand of support for mixed-ability was of two kinds. There were those teachers who worked with a labelling account of the causes of indiscipline in relation to mixed-ability:

> Well the idea seems to be that everyone is equal and to separate people on an academic basis or level is bad and gives the children inferiority complexes . . . 'we are in band two or three' . . . and they give up because they don't think anything is expected of them.
>
> Physics teacher (interview)

Others worked with a notion of the inherent nature of bad behaviour, so that mixed-ability was seen to provide 'A dilution really. You don't get 35 kids who don't like school, all in one form, it spreads the butter very thin' (English teacher: interview).

I have introduced the group perspectives here to illustrate the particular nature of the innovation process at 'Beachside' and the extent to which the innovation brought out into the open significant differences between members of staff in their hopes for and conceptions of comprehensive schooling. The debate over the innovation may be seen, with regard to the idealists and academics at least, as a conflict between competing definitions of the school. As Lacey (1977, p. 136) suggests, such fundamental conflicts are normally 'reconciled but they remain as subterranean issues, part of the backcloth against which other dramas are enacted and other battles (such as interdepartmental issues) are fought out. Very, very occasionally these subterranean issues erupt'. The innovation itself can only be analyzed in terms of the divergent interpretations, meanings and significances it had for the different groups of teachers identified. The course of the debate and the process of implementation only makes sense in relation to the threat perceived by the *academics,* the potential seen by the *disciplinarians* and the principles held by the *idealists*. The innovation cannot be taken to be a commonly understood proposed change in existing practices.

Rather it is a socially constituted 'product of interaction' within the separate groups of supporters and opponents.

However, the teachers at 'Beachside' were not merely required to take up a position towards 'the idea' of mixed-ability grouping but once the innovation was accepted by a majority vote, all teachers, at least in teaching the 1st year, had to construct or select strategies for the organization and management of mixed-ability classes. While there was no open debate about teaching methods, there was a widely expressed view in the school that mixed-ability teaching required the reconsideration of existing methods. In particular the old saw 'you cannot class teach to mixed-ability groups' achieved considerable currency. Perhaps not surprisingly, it was possible to discern a rough relationship between the responses of the different subject departments to mixed-ability teaching and their original orientation to the innovation proposal. As Havelock (1970) suggests 'group membership and reference group identifications are major predictors of individual adoption of innovation. This is summarized in figure 1 (page 164).

What emerged from my initial examination of the responses of the various departments to the teaching of mixed-ability groups was a continuum of positions between the original polarization of the English and Languages departments. With the English department represented by a cluster of attitudes and commitments that may be summarized as child-centredness and the Languages department represented by a cluster of attitudes that may be summarized as subject-centredness.

But it is important to stress that the perspectives identified represent priorities on the part of most teachers, even the most committed proponents and opponents, and they are priorities constructed at a particular point in time for particular purposes. They were articulated for the most part in the educationalist context (Keddie, 1971) of staff meetings, etc.

The importance of other considerations tended to emerge in the implementation stage, in the teacher context (Keddie 1971). Thus, typically from an opponent:

> Mixed-ability would have been impossible in the second-year, although I am glad that there will be mixed-ability in the other subjects because the social atmosphere has definitely improved.
>
> Maths teacher (interview)

And proponents:

> It does worry me to some extent that the brighter ones are still being held back. I know that this is being catered for in other ways, but it does worry me when I see them switching-off and being bored.
>
> Geography teacher (staff meeting)

> We have had mixed-ability for some time in the sense that we do individual teaching. There has not been much difference in practicals but in theory work we have trouble in lessons to keep up the slower and stretch the brighter but socially it's a very good thing.
>
> Head of Home Economics (staff meeting)

Thus it was that at certain times almost all the staff expressed their concern over the implications of mixed-ability for the 'brighter child' and almost all were willing to testify to their pleasure at the improved 'social atmosphere' in the mixed-ability cohorts.

Figure 1   *Views of and Implementation of Mixed-Ability Grouping*

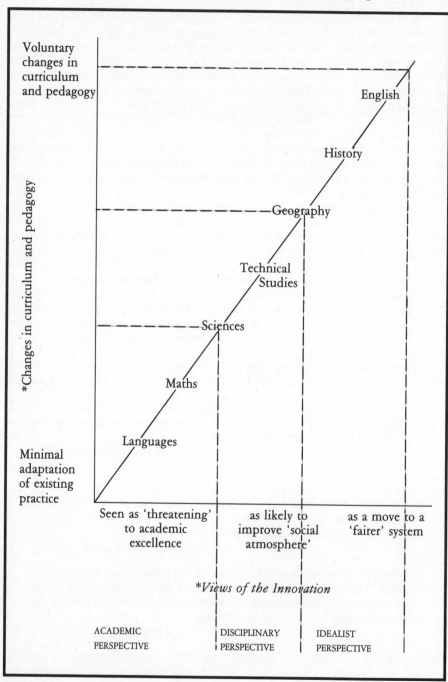

*These are not quantitative variables.

Social Context

Also in the teacher context, at the implementation stage, the staff perceived the 'possibilities for action' available to them to be limited by a national climate of educational accountability, by the demands and expectations of parents and other members of the local community and by more abstract and generalized public or societal expectations of the role of schooling. The Headmaster put it this way:

> We cannot take up the possibilities of mixed-ability at this stage because we would be doing a dis-service to the kids and have their parents in uproar because they are not doing exams, we can't do that locally until the system of 16 + examinations changes nationally.
>
> (interview)

This comment by the Headmaster is worth considering in some detail because it throws up a number of points about the nature of *constraints* as perceived by the 'Beachside' staff. First, we should note that the Headmaster is *anticipating* a *possible* reaction of parents rather than reporting an actual reaction. The possible consequences of policy decisions have become a part of the decision-making process. But second, it is also apparent here that the 'possibilities of mixed-ability' are viewed as inopportune not simply in a political sense but also in their implications for the futures of the pupils. In this sense, as the Headmaster goes on to explain, the major limiting factor here is taken to be the existing structure of the examination system nationally. Thus, we have a complex interplay (between the structure of the examination system, the reactions of parents and doing best by the pupils) invoked to account for the parameters within which decisions are made in the school. Other teachers provided much simpler models of the limitations within which they framed their responses to mixed-ability.

> There are constraints upon us to get good results. There are demands from society. We are expected to get good 'O' and 'A' level results, and, for ourselves as subject specialists, we want to maintain the level of achievement in our subject.
>
> Head of Maths (interview)

> The thing (mixed-ability) on the public side has got to be justified . . . you can't say well we are turning out kids who are more socially adjusted – they are probably not anyway – but if we could say that, it's intangible. Whereas the tangible proof that you've got comprehensives that work is this examination business, isn't it? I mean it was like that in Thameside, quoting exam figures . . . Manchester were in favour of grammar schools and said that they had terrible results from the comprehensives. How must you justify the school to the public? This is it?
>
> History teacher (interview)

Here the teachers are influenced by and responding to, in part at least, the public controversies surrounding the examination achievements of comprehensive schools. But this form of public accountability is not treated simply as an imposition; both teachers who are quoted talk as though they find this form of evaluation of their work acceptable and appropriate, in as much that the school must be justified to the public.

All of these three comments were recorded after the implementation of mixed-ability was under way in the school. It is significant that none of these comments are concerned with the decision to introduce mixed-ability but with the form of its introduction. For this school at least, it was the nature of mixed-ability teaching and the curriculum that were subject to constraint rather than the actual organization of pupil groups, although, as public relations officer for the school, the Headmaster took great pains not to draw public attention to the grouping innovation. He also attempted to maintain a public 'facade' (Smith and Keith 1971) which laid stress upon the level of examination performance in the school. At Speech Days and in Governors meetings he presented detailed breakdowns of steadily improving percentage pass-rates in public examinations and took pains to highlight the number of sixth form leavers obtaining university places.

Subject Sub-culture and Subject Identity

However, given this awareness of social context, in focusing on the actual selection of curricular and pedagogy from the available 'possibilities for action' for teaching mixed-ability classes, the most immediate and specific source of parameters for the teachers is not the lay audiences of the local community or the national educational climate but the professional audiences of school colleagues and the subject community.

We have already had one indication of the importance of *subject* as a limiting factor in mixed-ability teaching in the comment quoted above from the Head of Mathematics. He is expressing here one of the tenets of the *subject-centred* response to mixed-ability. Specifically, he draws attention to the importance of *subject identity* for the secondary teacher and, thus, the importance of the *subject-community* as a reference group for personal values and as a source of norms delineating appropriate and acceptable teaching methods and curricular content. Thus, for some of the 'Beachside' teachers, maintaining the integrity of their subject provided both a set of responses to the proposed innovation and, once it was accepted, a set of definite limitations to the form of its implementation. The comments made by the Head of Mathematics can also be taken to refer to a second agenda of concerns relating to the status of Mathematics in the school, as reflected in 'O' and 'A' level results, and, thence, as relevant to the competition between subjects for access to resources and policy-influence in the school.

As regards the first level of interpretation (the orientation of teachers to their subject community beyond the school as a source of identity, norms and values), Gouldner's (1957) work on 'Cosmopolitans' and 'Locals' can be seen to be relevant. The problem with applying Gouldner's model in this case is that the subject communities and their *sub-cultures* do not produce the same orientations towards the innovation in each subject. It is not possible to identify opponents of the innovation and reluctant implementers as *Cosmopolitans* and proponents as *locals*. Where the subject sub-cultures of Mathematics and Languages *were* a source of opposition, the sub-culture of English, in this case orientated to the 'radical' position dominant at the time within NATE, was a source of support.

I want to concentrate on the sources of opposition, particularly in Languages, Science and Maths. The pervasive influence of subject sub-cultures has been noted and recorded in a number of studies (Lacey *et al* 1973; Lacey 1977; Esland 1971; McLeish 1970; Ball and Lacey 1980) and all tend to attribute this to the centrality of subject specialization in the latter years of school and teacher-training courses. Thus, Lacey (1977) argues, the process of becoming a teacher can be best understood as 'multi-stranded'. At 'Beachside', the most substantial aspect of the intrusion of these subject sub-cultures was that which highlighted the 'given' nature of the subject in terms of its conceptual structure and curricular organization. Thus, in the first instance, the proposed innovation presented a threat to the maintenance of these structures and organizational forms. Later, once the innovation was to be implemented, these structures and organizational forms were presented as inevitable limitations upon the range of possible curricular and pedagogical responses. This inevitability was often specifically related, once again, to the dictates of the examination system. In the case of French, the Head of Department explained of his subject:

> I think it's got to be a building up subject, it's the most building up subject of all, possibly more so than Mathematics. Now in the country as a whole only one or two people have done mixed-ability teaching; but it usually comes down to some sort of group work, worksheets and self-correcting worksheets, which I think are a nonsense . . . I think that French in itself is not interesting above a certain point, it's interesting to be able to count up to 20 in French, to say 'Je m'appelle Louise', that sort of thing. But you can't say the sorts of things you want to in English. Therefore I think class teaching, where you're standing in front of the class reading a piece from a text or talking, is what makes the thing work.
>
> (interview)

This comment is interesting in a number of ways. Initially, the Head of Department makes clear the conceptual structure of French as a school subject: 'it is a building up subject'. He goes on to link this to the appropriate pedagogy but in doing so he also emphasizes the inappropriate, and deviant, nature of attempts to change the pedagogy, 'which I think, are a nonsense'. He reaffirms the norms of the subject community and places the deviants beyond the boundaries of good practice. He also emphasizes the essentially uninteresting nature of French as a school subject; this again is used to emphasize the inevitability of a recitation method of teaching. In this also, he demonstrates the boundary between French as an academic subject and the world of everyday English talk: 'you can't say the sorts of things you want to in English'. All of these indicators serve to define and reaffirm the academic nature of the subject. This was elaborated further as the interview continued.

> You see children who can't write it very well, and can't read it very well, they can't pronounce it either, they have poor oral discrimination . . . I suppose some people would work out their Mode III 'O' level as we have our Mode III CSE, in fact some people would be happy with a French Studies curriculum, but that's not French to my way of thinking. If you were going to do that you would really lower the already not very good language ability of English people.
>
> I can't see how it could be changed, I can't envisage how one would change the sort of thing one is trying to achieve. I could imagine one could produce masses and masses of different graded work sheets on certain topics, the thematic approach. But so much is linear, the tenses are the problem. They're a big problem. Children have a poor conception of what a tense is in English, and this is a big stumbling block. I can't conceive how it

would change. It's changed a bit over the years, recently there's been more
emphasis on the oral and listening and understanding.

Here, the Head of Department again uses a form of description of the conceptual and curricular structure of French that was also employed widely in Maths and
Sciences; that the subject is 'linear'. In other words, it is necessary to learn the basic
concepts before more difficult concepts can be tackled. This progression tended to be
linked in a number of ways to the problems of mixed-ability, as we shall see, but was
of special concern in terms of measuring the accepted pacing of the subject, and that
demanded by the starting point of the 'O' level syllabuses, against the range of
speeds of working of the pupils in a mixed-ability group. Again the deviant nature of
some pedagogical innovations is identified in the work of 'some people' and this is
related to the ultimate compromise, 'French Studies'. The extract also illustrated the
nature of school French as essentially a written rather than an oral subject.

There is also some indication of the view that was frequently proposed, that the
linguistic abilities of the pupils are fixed; those who have poor oral discriminations or
whatever, tended to be regarded as unable to learn French. This notion of fixed
linguistic ability was specifically used to facilitate the intensive process of selection
and cooling out which reduced a first year intake of 300 pupils all taking French, to a
single 'O' level group in the fifth year with a yearly pass-rate of over 80%. Finally,
the extract highlights the finite range of thinking or imagination that is possible
within the tenets of the subject sub-culture. The subject sub-culture constitutes in
effect a 'finite meaning-structure' (Schutz and Luckmann 1974) with a limited
'horizon of experience' and 'institutionalized stock of knowledge'.

Only that which appears essential for the theme of the experience is a possible determination relevant for the stock of knowledge. The explications
necessary in the situation *and* those foreseen as necessary for a subsequent,
typically similar situations are based on this.

(pp. 149–50)

Many of the themes illustrated in the Head of French's interview were reiterated
in the accounts provided of their subject by members of the Maths and Science
departments. In particular, many of these teachers argued for the necessity of early
setting in their subject because of what they saw to be the inability of some children
to understand concepts introduced at these times as a preparation for 'O' level work.
There was frequent reference to the second and third year as a crucial period in the
cognitive development of pupils, when 'abilities diverge'. The teachers portrayed
their subjects in terms of an inevitable and necessary ordering and pacing of content.
This ordering and pacing was often, but not always, related to the demands of external examinational syllabuses. For example, in Chemistry, Atomic Structure was introduced in the third year 'as a necessary preparation for 'O' level'. Thus, the Head of
Science explained in a staff meeting:

Mixed-ability is working socially, but I don't see how we can carry it on in
the third year, if we are going to teach it properly and get through the
material necessary as a foundation for 'O' level. By the time we get into the
second term of the third year the kids are so strung out in their level of
achievement. I don't see how we can keep them together.

Again, it is possible to view this kind of structuring as imposed and maintained by the requirements of the external examination, but that oversimplifies the situation. Most of the 'Beachside' teachers saw the ordering and pacing of their subject not simply as artificially maintained by the Examination Boards but as having some degree of intrinsic logic related to the nature of the subject itself and/or the conceptual development of all, or some particular groups of, pupils.

Indeed, most of the teachers had been socialized into their subject through the same order and pace in their own schooling. To some extent they are involved in replicating their own experiences of the subject (at least for the most successful pupils) (Mardle and Walker 1980).

Career and Collegial Esteem

Having acknowledged the influence of external audiences, lay and professional, upon the responses of the Beachside teachers to mixed-ability grouping, it is necessary now to return to those expectations which emerged internally as criteria for assessing the adequacy of these responses. It is important though to recognize that these institutional expectations emerged informally and that they must be set against the entrenched subject affiliations already discussed and the headmaster's commitment to departmental autonomy in curriculum decision-making. Nonetheless, the individual departments found themselves confronted with a number of often conflicting pressures; the demands of the subject itself, on the one hand, set against the problems of teaching in a classroom containing a wide range of 'ability' on the other; and the expectations of a professionally competent response to the new teaching situation over and against the need to maintain academic standards (measured in terms of 'O' and 'A' level passes) and additionally, in some cases, the limiting effects of scarce financial or personnel resources.

For some individuals the decision-making involved in the resolution or accommodation of these conflicting pressures can be expressed in the relevant terms of Berlak and Berlak's (1981) 'language of dilemmas' which provides 'a way of formulating a broad range of tensions and controversies in teachers and in society . . . that are deliberately or sub-consciously being played out by teachers as they go about the daily job of teaching' (p. 6). They postulate that the observable behaviour of teachers may be viewed 'as the "product" of the pulls of many dilemmas' (p. 68) and stress 'the creativity that may be involved in this process' (p. 68). But they also make the point that 'teachers' resolutions are neither totally in one direction or in the other but a combination of opposites' (p. 22). Perhaps all these elements are evident in this comment by Mr. Card, a History teacher:

> I feel that what we have done is that we have reappraised as we've gone along, we haven't just done worksheets and left it. We've not only reappraised the worksheets at History meetings, we've also discussed how they've come across and how we can improve them. And certainly in the third year, there's been much more flexibility and we haven't necessarily used worksheets for all the topics. We've devised what we're going to do and talked over some ideas and we'll do it our own way and use whatever we want to use . . . but no one has had the time, or whatever, to sit down and actually plan and say 'we must use this and this, and we've got all these resources available'. We could use drama ideally but is the room you're in

suitable? You know it's pathetic things like this. It seems pathetic on the surface but you've got the trouble of changing rooms and organizing timetable changes. You've only got the kids for a double lesson a week and there's a certain amount of work we've got to get through. In the third year, for example, for them to take their exams and choose their options so if I spend a month and say 'well I'm going to scrap this and do a bit of drama and make it more interesting', which it probably would be – if all the kids muck up their exams and get low marks, where do I stand then? You know, you've always got this dilemma, on the one hand you're torn to do something, on the other you've got certain commitments to the school philosophy. It's a dilemma which is very difficult to solve, probably not solveable unless you say, well I'm going to damn the exams and we're going to go our own way.

In History and several other departments the apparent solution to mixed-ability grouping lay in the use of home-produced worksheets or commercially produced workcards or workbooks. By these means it was possible to bring about a reorganization on the socio-spatial structure of the classroom by individualizing pupil's work. This provided for both a shift in the 'symbolic imagery' (Hargreaves, 1976) of lessons and a strategy for coping with variations in pupils' speeds of working while, as Hargreaves suggests, producing little change in the 'pupils' and teachers' constructions of school reality' (1976) (for a full account of this see Ball, 1980 and 1981). However, in the Science Department the adoption of the School Council Integrated Science Project, which they saw as the best possible response to mixed-ability classes, was prevented by the costs that would have been incurred in re-equipping the laboratories. One teacher at least was unhappy with the 'second best' arrangements of using home-produced worksheets. He reported in an interview:

> The Chemistry Science course is too staid and too academic for me, there's not enough entertainment or project work in the course and we've got kids who have scientific hobbies at home who are doing very badly in Science at school. And we haven't changed anything for mixed-ability really, it's more or less the same course as Band 1 had.

According to the assessment of this teacher, the response of the Chemistry Department was not a professional, competent one. For him the dilemmas created by the introduction of mixed-ability grouping were not adequately resolved. He left 'Beachside' soon after, moving to a school with mixed-ability grouping and an integrated science course. For his colleagues, though, the accommodations arrived at in the department proved acceptable in themselves or they were able to accomplish their own personal coping strategies in the mixed-ability classroom. Thus, another Chemistry teacher explained:

> When we were preparing for mixed-ability we produced lots of workcards and projects, but I haven't felt that they have been necessary. I feel that we can stretch the brighter kids by stimulating their minds in open-type lessons.
>
> (aside in lesson)

The further point to be drawn from this difference of opinion and difference in strategy is the necessity of taking into account the variations, that occur even in a single department, in the subject identity, job commitment, personal priorities and institutional involvement of individual members of staff. Thus, not only do we find differences in educational philosophy between teachers but also differences in the nature, or overall level, of their commitment to teaching in general or to teaching at 'Beachside' in particular. Some departments were inhibited in constructing a response to or in implementing mixed-ability because of the unwillingness of members to engage in curriculum development work. Some teachers had limited time and energy to devote to such work in the face of other role requirements in the school. Again we must take account of the priorities held by those involved. For some staff the lower years were not a very significant part, quantitatively or qualitatively, of their teaching load. Their major commitments were in fourth, fifth or sixth form teaching or to Pastoral Care or Careers or Community Liaison. The allocation of personal time and effort is invariably decided according to the perceived worthwhileness of the task (Hoyle 1974). For a few, the daily round of teaching was dominated, as Woods (1977) described, by the problems of *survival* with little energy or enthusiasm left over for curriculum development.

Together with constraints inherent in particular ideological commitments and subject identities, the teachers at 'Beachside' carried with them the personal baggage of experiential limitations. Few teachers had had previous experience of mixed-ability teaching. This was often expressed to me as the problem 'we don't know what we don't know'. Interestingly, one part-time History teacher who did have such experience found himself totally at odds with his colleagues as far as appropriate techniques for the organization and management of mixed-ability classes were concerned.

> My understanding of mixed-ability teaching is not the same as the rest of the department. Having worked in a Middle School and having had groups working on different topics. There was no suggestion of a rotation system of different work-cards so you can have low ability groups and faster groups or mixed-groups. There was no idea that we should move away from class-teaching. It's not mixed-ability. It's just class-teaching with a wide ability range . . . I don't like these worksheets.
>
> (Interview: Mr. Daniel)

Mr. Daniel stood outside of the range of 'typical biographies' (Schutz and Luckmann, 1974) to be found among the 'Beachside' teachers. His views on mixed-ability teaching serve to illustrate the limiting effects of those stocks of knowledge and relevance structures associated with the typical biographies of his colleagues. As Schutz and Luckmann (1974) argue 'plan systems' devised to deal with current problems emerge 'by means of memory and my past, of past decisions, of acts undertaken, of incompleted projects'. The experiences and meanings acquired from previous classroom experiences produce their own inertia and restrict the adoption of novel strategies (Denscombe 1980).

Satisfactions and Survival

Taking into account the social-structural, cultural and experiential forces indicated here and the contingencies of social action and concomitant level-one decisions which bring about their modification in the classroom, the outcome in terms of mixed-ability teaching at 'Beachside' is best represented as a 'move along a continuum from conventional schooling rather than a "successful" or "unsuccessful" break from traditional principles' (Denscombe 1980, p. 51). The management of classroom activities which constituted mixed-ability teaching was still firmly oriented to and embedded in the assumptions of what Willis (1977) calls, *the dominant teaching paradigm* which 'locates all others – even as they attempt to go beyond it' (p. 63). The 'idea' that is, of 'teaching as fair exchange', 'of knowledge for respect, of guidance for control' (p. 64). Indeed, as I have indicated, for a significant group of 'Beachside' teachers, the introduction of mixed-ability grouping was seen to be a means to reassert and reinforce those basic tenets of the paradigm. (Improvements in social atmosphere and the classroom behaviour of the pupils emerged as *the* major feature of the innovation both in the precursory debate and in the teachers' evaluation of it.) (See Ball 1981, p. 235).

In effect the 'Beachside' teachers were faced with the problem of incorporating mixed-ability teaching in some form into the *dominant teaching paradigm* as defined by institutional and collegial views of 'good practice', at the same time ensuring their own *survival*. On both counts the social construction and material conditions of the mixed-ability classroom threw up difficulties. In terms of social construction the individual teacher was confronted by the significance of differences in pupils' 'abilities' and in the form of variations in speeds of working and differences in 'motivation' and in the form of variations in attitudes to school. The accounts offered by the 'Beachside' teachers of their mixed-ability teaching are replete with references to the former as their major concern in the organization and management of learning. Those departments which chose to employ worksheets, etc., may be seen to be responding directly to the 'problems' of coping with variations in pupils' speeds of working and thus the pacing of task work, by differentiating the classroom curriculum and weakening the *frame strength* of lessons. These particular pedagogical strategies also provided ways of responding, both practically and symbolically, to the climate of concern for the 'brighter child', referred to previously.

Indeed, the need to identify and understand the 'individual differences amongst children in the class' (Wragg 1978, p. 40) is given impetus and emphasis in the growing body of 'methods' literature on mixed-ability teaching. Student teachers are encouraged 'to anticipate difficulties by knowing' (Wragg 1978, p. 40) about such differences. Identification and differentiation, as a result, are quickly becoming accepted as constituting 'good practice' in the mixed-ability classroom.

However, for inexperienced teachers, the shift in socio-spatial classroom structure to accommodate mixed-ability groups highlighted the presence of pupils with low motivation. This produced a potential increase in *survival threat* (Pollard 1980) through increased difficulties in *policing* (Hargreaves 1979) the classroom. Curbishley and Evans (1980) have documented one example of such problems in the teaching of SMP mathematics to mixed-ability classes using workcards to individualize learning. Denscombe (1980) also illustrates the ways in which the open classroom increased the possibilities of negotiation, misrepresentation and frittering by pupils. But there is a paradox here, in that, for some 'Beachside' staff, the solution to the management problems of the mixed-ability classroom also lay in the use of pedagogical strategies, such as worksheets, which individuated pupils' learning. Such strategies could reduce the overall frequency of pupil misbehaviour and localize what misbehaviour there was to a few highly visible pupils. This may stand as an empirical example of what Reynolds (1981) called 'coercive individualism' at work in the immediacy of classroom interaction. Although this is clearly a matter of *situational control* rather than *social control* (Woods 1977).

A concomitant factor to the increase in *survival threat*, brought about (for some teachers at least) by mixed-ability grouping, was the increased threat to collegial status and situated identity (Ball 1972). Both classroom noise and pupil progress were taken as measures of professional competence and apparent classroom management problems could result in a damaged professional identity. As Willis (1977) again indicates:

> It should also be noted that the basic framework and the teaching paradigm stretch upwards as well, and that any deviation from it amongst the staff is regarded as equally pathological.
>
> (p. 66)

For a few, the *survival threat* inherent in mixed-ability grouping was that of *de-skilling*. The introduction of worksheets, or other similar methods of individuation, threatened to eliminate the recitation method that was relied on by particular groups of teachers as their sole pedagogy. It was such de-skilling that was resisted by the academic opponents of mixed-ability. However, the working isolation and relative classroom autonomy of teachers at 'Beachside' allowed for the destandardization of worksheet teaching (see Ball 1980) and thus the accommodation of a wide variety of different pedagogical techniques and teaching styles, even within a single department. In this respect the use of worksheets in the mixed-ability classroom can be seen to provide a viable action framework for the 'juggling of interest priorities' (Pollard 1980), both in the immediacy of classroom interactions with pupils and in the longer term pursuit of collegiate status, promotion and career and the development of self *via* work identity.

Figure 2   A Model of Constraints upon Teaching

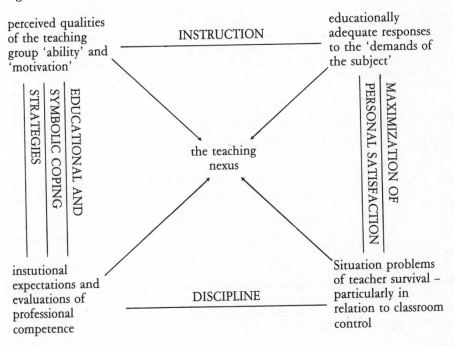

This 'juggling of interest priorities' represents the teachers' strategic management of the teaching nexus – that is the situation that teachers confront when attempting to resolve the demands upon them made by pupils, parents, employers, politicans, superiors and colleagues. This is portrayed in figure 2 (page 173).

As we have seen, these constraints and pressures need not be consonant and compatible in themselves. They are often experienced as dilemmas and contradictions by the teacher. This is especially common in the confrontation between the situational features of the classroom and the teacher's commitment to communally adjudged criteria of professional competence. Figure 2 also illustrates the basic tension between the demands of the instructional and disciplinary roles of the classroom teacher. However, it must be borne in mind that the teacher's work identity and self-conception, which derive in part from previous work and training experiences, are also modified and developed in relation to new experiences. A coherent model for the analysis of constraints upon teaching must not only take account of the complex and multifaceted quality of teaching as work but also its contextual and emergent nature.

References

BALL, D. (1972) 'Self and identity in the context of deviance' in SCOTT, R.A. and DOUGLAS, J.D. *Theoretical Perspectives on Deviance* New York, Basic Books.
BALL, S.J. (1980) 'Mixed-ability teaching: The worksheet method' *British Journal of Educational Technology* 11 (1) (January) pp. 36–48.
BALL, S.J. (1981) *Beachside Comprehensive* Cambridge, Cambridge University Press.
BALL, S.J. and LACEY, C. (1980) 'Subject disciplines as the opportunity for group action: A measured critique of subject sub-cultures' in WOODS, P.E. (Ed) *Teacher Strategies* London, Croom Helm.
BECKER, H.S. *et al* (1961) *Boys in White* Chicago, University of Chicago Press.
BECKER, H.S. (1964) 'Personal change in adult life', *Sociometry* 27 (1), pp. 40–53.
BERLAK, H. and BERLAK, A. (1981) *The Dilemmas of Schooling* London, Methuen.
CURBISHLEY, P. and EVANS, J. (1980) 'Teacher Strategies and Pupil Identities in Mixed-Ability Curricula – with special reference to Mathematics', Paper delivered at the BERA Annual Conference, University College, Cardiff, September 2–4.
DENSCOMBE, M. (1980) 'Pupil strategies and the open classroom', in WOODS, P.E. (Ed) *Pupil Strategies* London, Croom Helm.
ESLAND, G. (1971) 'Teaching and learning as the organization of knowledge' in YOUNG, M.F.D. (1971) *Knowledge and Control* London, Collier-Macmillan.
GOFFMAN, E. (1963) *Stigma* Harmondsworth, Penguin.
GOULDNER, A. (1957) 'Cosmopolitans and locals' *Administrative Science Quarterly* 2, pp. 381–306 and 444–80.
HARGREAVES, A. (1979) 'Strategies, decisions and control: Interaction in a middle school' in EGGLESTON, J. (Ed) *Teacher Decision-Making in the Classroom* London, Routledge and Kegan Paul.
HARGREAVES, A. (1976) 'Progressivism and pupil autonomy' *Sociological Review* 25.
HAVELOCK, R.G. (1970) *A Guide to Innovation in Education* Ann Arbor, Michigan, Center for Research on Utilization of Scientific Knowledge.
HOYLE, E. (1974) 'Professionality, professionalism and control in teaching', *London Educational Review* (Summer), 3 (2) pp. 13–19.
HUNTER, C. (1979) 'Control in the comprehensive system' in EGGLESTON, J. (Ed) *Teacher Decision-Making in the Classroom,* London, Routledge and Kegan Paul.
KANTER, R.M. (1974) 'Commitment and social organization' in FIELD, D. (Ed) *Social Psychology for Sociologists* London, Nelson.

KEDDIE, N. (1971) 'Classroom knowledge' in YOUNG, M.F.D. (Ed) *Knowledge and Control* London, Collier-Macmillan.

LACEY, C. (1977) *The Socialization of Teachers* London, Methuen.

LACEY, C. *et al* (1973) *Tutorial Schools Reseach Project Volume I: Teacher Socialization/The Post Graduate Training Year* London, SSRC.

McLEISCH, J. (1970) *Students' Attitudes and College Environments* Cambridge, Institute of Education.

MARDLE, G. and WALKER, M. (1980) 'Strategies and structure: Some critical notes on teacher socialization' in WOODS, P.E. (Ed) *Teacher Strategies* London, Croom Helm.

POLLARD, A. (1980) 'Teacher interests and changing situations of survival threat in primary school classrooms' in WOODS, P.E. (Ed) *Teacher Strategies* London, Croom Helm.

REYNOLDS, D. (1981) 'The Comprehensive Experience'. (This volume).

SCHUTZ, A. and LUCKMANN, T. (1974) *The Structures of the Lifeworld* London, Heinemann.

SHARP, R. and GREEN, A. (1976) *Education and Social Control* London, Routledge and Kegan Paul.

SMITH, L.M. and KEITH, P. (1971) *An Anatomy of Educational Innovation* New York, John Wiley.

WILLIS, P. (1977) *Learning to Labour* London, Saxon House.

WOODS, P.E. (1977) 'Teaching for survival' in HAMMERSLEY, M. and WOODS, P.E. (Eds) *School Experience* London, Croom Helm.

WOODS, P.E. (1981) 'Strategies, Commitment and Identity; making and breaking the teacher role'. (This volume).

WRAGG, E.G. (1978) 'Training teachers of mixed-ability classes: A ten point attack', *Forum,* Summer.

Teacher Strategies and Pupil Identities in Mixed Ability Curricula: A Note on Concepts and Some Examples from Maths*

P. Corbishley, J. Evans, C. Kenrick, and B. Davies
Chelsea College, University of London

In this article we present some exploratory descriptions of mathematics teaching in mixed-ability secondary school classrooms. Central to them is the understanding that classrooms cannot be studied without reference to the history of a subject area within the overall organization of the school. The relations of pupils and teachers in the classroom are framed by themselves, by the larger school and even LEA and DES practices and organization.

The techniques used to gather information were marked by eclecticism. They consisted of conversation, observation by note-taking not on a schedule, semi-structured interviews, questionnaires, statistics compiled from files, and standardized tests. In two case study schools we have several hundred 'lesson' observations from first to third year teaching groups mainly in the broad academic curriculum. These, initially, concentrated on the teachers' 'use of time' to be complemented later by closer observation aspects of the activity of individual or groups of pupils in particular forms (teaching groups) who were followed through their timetable. Questionnaire returns were collected for whole year groups. Our aim was to explore, define and clarify what was involved in mixed-ability teaching.

Almost certainly, the only rules of methodological purity which we did not breach (to our knowledge) were those respecting anonymity and confidentiality. The pressures of spending a year, virtually full time, as an observer in many contexts in a school opens up friendships, draws down requests for help and information, sets up demands on objectivity that deny simple injunctions about keeping data clean. What does need to be recorded, however, is the incredible courtesy with which the temptation to 'use' or 'lean upon' us was resisted, especially in respect of the detailed and uninhibited information which we collected from children about 'school'.

The descriptions of classrooms which follow cannot be judged by the degree of naturalistic correspondence they have with the situations from which observations and information were drawn. No methodological techniques can satisfactorily encapsulate classroom practice, mood, and interaction. The originating classroom situations have gone, traces remain as raw information not all of which can or needs to become part of any description. Descriptions can however be judged on whether they are spuriously or reasonably evidenced patterns of the working of classrooms; on whether they clarify a complex social reality, given the existing state of classroom research; on whether they provide a basic sketch which enables readers to go on to spot what has been overlooked or judge it as irrelevant.

---

* This paper refers to material which is part of a broader study of mixed ability grouping and curricula, financed by SSRC in two stages as *A Preliminary Study of Unstreaming in London Secondary Schools* and *Teacher Strategies and Pupil Identities in Mixed Ability Curricula: A Case Study Approach*.

For the sake of commonsense clarity rather than for any theoretically laden purpose we first distinguish classrooms in terms of how the available curriculum material is presented to pupils. We distinguish between *whole-class, individualized, individuated* and *small group* modes of introduction.[1] Each will have relation to a range of other factors which include curriculum content for the subject, the number of periods given by the timetable, the discipline situation in the school, the range of pupils to be taught and teachers' own articulated and unexpressed ways of teaching and handling relations with those pupils. Choice of such modes of transmission is a factor to be considered in its own right, contributing alongside others to any given classroom.

The SMP scheme was used in both schools in the form of workcards. It has two main sections each corresponding to a year's work for a pupil going on to do 'O' level. It implies a particular pacing of work if the scheme is to be completed. The scheme can be used for three rather than two years for the remainder of the pupils who also fall into the top 80% to 85% of the ability range. Pupils in the bottom 15% of the range would find difficulties with completing the scheme at all in such time.

A pupil can enter section 1 (equivalent to a year's work towards 'O' level) at any of ten topic points. There are 28 topics in both sections so that the range of starting points is comparatively broad. Most of the topics are subdivided into units which offer material at different levels of competence/ability. The first section contains 38 such units with 5 possible levels of difficulty, the second 46 with 6 levels. There is some overlapping of levels between section one and two. The scheme combines choice of topic to be followed, with some discreteness from other topics, and an inbuilt hierarchy of difficulty. It represents, therefore, a considerable restructuring of the straightforward linear and sequential view of mathematical curricula. One could, for instance as a first year pupil, do all ten starting topics in turn as none assume or lead on to another. Additionally there are preliminary materials (mainly arithmetical) to section 1 and supplements to both 1 and 2. The individualized character of the scheme lies in the fact that each pupil works on a separate set of cards on a unit not necessarily being done by any other pupil.

The decision to use this scheme is inevitably a departmental one because of the resources involved. But individual teachers can deviate, e.g. by sticking to book-based, whole-class teaching, though this would tend to require some kind of seniority as the basis on which to evade departmental policy. The mathematical content of the scheme comes at the 'newish' end of the spectrum but teachers can operate their own strategies here too. Teacher 1, for example, in school V, removed the cards dealing with the topics Arrow Diagrams, Maps, Measuring Polyhedra, Statistics and Tessellations arguing that the variety of materials did not leave 'enough time for practice, for fractions, to go back and grind it into them'. In the view of the head of department, however, these same topics were useful in motivating pupils and rekindling an interest in mathematics.

Each unit of the scheme contains different numbers of individual cards. Some of these may be marked with an asterisk, signifying the need to have work looked over. Each unit also contains a checkcard for the pupil's own self-monitoring, and a test card the results of which are to be marked by the teacher. The teacher must therefore direct and redirect each individual pupil's work as they demand. The monitoring built into the system recreates a recurring demand for teacher attention from the whole range of pupils. In the words of the SMP's 1973 *Teacher's Notes,* 'the teacher sees children often but briefly'.[2] In contrast, in whole-class presentation, a teacher need not question or talk to all pupils, nor do pupils have to answer a teacher's question because normally answers are volunteered. In the SMP workcard scheme, if a pupil does not contact a teacher, at least occasionally, it is a positive sign of non-work. Furthermore, as the expectations that a pupil will contact teacher is built into the scheme, different ranges of pupils (in terms of work or ability) can create very different demands on how a teacher allocates time between them.

Changes, in contrast to whole class teaching, occur also in the social and disciplinary relationships of teacher and taught. The traditional social relationship of teacher to the whole class as a social unit is broken up. The curriculum content of the scheme requires the provision of different types of paper and equipment which have to be administered by the teacher, some of whom feel they have ceased to 'teach' and become managers instead. Statements to the whole class tend to retain only their disciplinary character. Didactic pedagogical talk moves from the public arena into the immediate one-to-one situation. The teacher's role becomes internally more differentiated.[3]

Changes also occur for pupils, as the same scheme is designed for pupils to work singly or in groups as the teacher prefers. The variety of cards and ancillary equipment generates talk about who has got what when the materials of the scheme are not in their accustomed place. Further discussion may or may not be encouraged by the teacher. If discussion in groups is permitted or even encouraged by teachers in other subjects the imposition of silence can be resented. Teachers will distinguish between conversation about 'work' and 'interest' talk. 'Interest' encompasses a wide range of pupil behaviour. It might be paralleled with Goffman's[4] side involvement or with what Stebbins[5] calls 'away behaviour'. It is 'not-work'. Interest behaviour is common to all classrooms. In an individualized scheme which builds in self-pacing by the pupils, his/her level of involvement, attitude, motivation, ability to work independently of teacher attention, their absorption in work, now becomes more crucial to classroom management. The teacher's own biography and experience of schooling can also crucially affect decisions on what work and interest are, as can a pupil's own sense of identity. The individualized mode allows for new and differing individuality of teacher styles. Likewise the behaviour of pupils reveals features of classroom life which can be overridden in whole class presentation.

Categories such as 'work', 'interest', 'ability', teacher and pupil 'talk' as well as sex, age and some notion of social class are part of the commonsense of researchers and directly useful in classifying and ordering information. Terms like 'piloting'[6] and 'steering groups'[7] are drawn from previous analyses. The latter corresponds to the teacher commonsense need to 'pitch' lessons at a particular level. It originated with work on whole-class presentation in mixed-ability classrooms. Talk in whole class presentation tends to be steered by the teacher in a question and answer format requiring 'closed' answers from pupils. It was found that teachers using this mode tended to have a particular repertoire of questions for pupils in the just below average 10th to 25th percentile.[8] Largely unconsciously, teachers were using this group to determine whether it was time to transfer to a new content. The concept of steering group and the work associated with it links teacher talk, the range of pupil abilities, the amount of time given to a topic within a lesson over a year or the years of schooling, and the structure of the curriculum.

The concept of frame, as we develop it, addresses even more general issues in recent empirical and theoretical work. It includes a family of meanings which still await systematic inter-relation. Within them, there is the idea of 'boundary' as well as 'limitation'. The word frame itself has several colloquial meanings which are interesting for their analogical properties. Frame as in 'picture frame', for instance, invokes the boundary element which Bernstein uses in talking of the separation of school based and commonsensical knowledge.[9] His work tends to suggest that the dissolution of boundaries between subjects alters the mode but not the fact of identity formation. He argues that in weakly framed teaching situations pupils are less tightly tied to the boundaries and hierarchies of knowledge identities but that such frames make for greater intrusion into personal identities.[10] Frame as in 'frame-up' can imply an illegitimate social control.[11] Labelling theory in education also raises these issues Frame as 'boundary' extends into the area of identity formation as an integral aspect of social control.

Frame as 'limitation' has been developed by Lundgren, especially in relation to school administration.[12] Limitations on time, space and other resources are the product of national and local political decisions; policy is mediated through organizational frames (previously emphasized by Dahloff[13]) and becomes part of curriculum with its internally sequenced content unit. Proceeding from rather different metatheoretical assumptions his work, like Bernstein's, is deeply concerned with the organization, pacing and timing of knowledge contents.

A further sense of frame, which is roughly 'to give a perspective, a framework (not necessarily fully conscious) on the world' is found in Mary Douglas's[14] explorations of ontologies. She argues that the perception and valuation of frame in the above senses vary according to the social contexts in which human beings centre themselves. She offers a quasi-structuralist analysis of the image and metaphor of boundary, control and limit. Her analysis allows us to hypothesize differences so that what one teacher regards as an alienating boundary is for another simply an occasion for action or for another a misplaced and ungrounded temporary restriction which simply has to be put up with.

We do not undertake empirical analysis of all these senses of frame. Rather it provides us with a flexible way of indicating how the specific factors of classroom life are interrelated. Limit, boundary and control are experienced in all aspects of life. Our descriptions are intended to show how different combinations of specifically educational factors become differently framed and framing. The word frame is then a shorthand for an under-formulated theory of the social as control and the differing ways in which the social is constituted as sometimes determined and sometimes determining. In general, the direction of determination is downwards through hierarchical levels but recent sociology of education has been overly pessimistic about countervailing pressures even when expressed passively. For example, a school policy on mixed-ability grouping has often been regarded negatively by modern language departments as an illegitimate and intrusive use of a Head's authority which undermines their capacity to shape the subject identities of pupils and produce sufficient specialists in the time available. One consequence can be that appropriate curricula are not developed and a self-fulfilling prophecy of low performance sets in, on the basis of which the department negotiates a change of policy. Such forms of resistance deserve more attention in education. In general we would argue that school policies on timetabling curriculum and 'schooling' have strong bounding and limiting effects on classrooms. They are teacher strategies and affect pupil identities, generalized at the level of school organization, and are nearly always ignored in classroom studies.

At the school organizational level we delineate three major aspects of framing. The first is curriculum, which we have illustrated in our reference to SMP. The second can be regarded as the *timetable* which puts groups of pupils together with teaching staff and resources within designated curriculum areas. It generates planned diversity in the context of order. It decides the social and physical space of pupils, subjects and teachers. 'Rich' core departments, such as mathematics, with lots of space can plan on the assumption that pupils come often enough to remember what was taught last time. Poor neighbours with minimal allocations per week cannot afford such an assumption, particularly on the part of the 'less-able' in mixed-ability classrooms. There is pressure to 'topic-ize' content as the time taken by different pupils to work through given materials becomes central. In some modes of transmission some pupils can suffer endemically from 'not finishing' or 'being behind'. Teacher strategies and pupil identities are directly affected by timetabling procedures.

Schooling, in our view, is not synonymous with all that goes on in school which also includes timetabling and the curriculum. It is a complex phenomenon which will only be sketched in here. It refers to the homogenizing and differentiating patterns of access which pupils have to the timetabled curriculum. These can be administrative – as given by mixed or single sex, grammar or comprehensive – or intra-school – as with grouping for pastoral or teaching purposes. Schooling in this restricted sense includes the 'hidden curriculum' and is strongly formative of pupil identities.

Mundanely, attempts are made to socialize pupils into routines of concentration, industry, quiet behaviour and movement. Differential success in these attempts produce school variation quite close to what Rutter *et al*[15] referred to as 'ethos' – the hidden curriculum made policy-amenable flesh. We are not convinced that this is any more telling than other explanations that fail to root themselves in an understanding of the realities of learning in the classroom. Our work is essentially preliminary and dogged by the struggle to name the relevant parts. But we are inclined to argue that to be schooled is best viewed as having the cognitive and emotional attitudes prerequisite to learning in large classes. Within them different modes of transmission will have specific effects, e.g. workcards make demands in terms of reading ability. In turn the number of children with functionally 'poor' reading ages varies with intake, and within that by form group, creating demands on pupils and teachers. In our case studies in two comprehensives, school V, with a largely 'balanced' intake and a broader parental occupational spread, sought in remedial work to improve pupil self-organization for work in 'ordinary' classrooms. It sought to provide remediation as, what might be termed *reschooling,* i.e. the making-up of skills not yet learnt. In school H, with a predominantly 'low ability intake, remedial work exhibited a far larger element of *resocialization,* i.e. compensation for real or imagined defects in home culture. For us, questions of whether there are processes skills and attitudes, which are constantly required by pupils to facilitate movement into curriculum content whatever one's measured ability, became of increasing importance as the research progressed. One reason why we investigated mixed-ability practice was the belief that its demands on pupils would be 'different'. Our evidence suggests that we must inevitably allow for more complex ideas of what it is to be able in school. Teaching, or teacher strategies in the classroom, falls under the rubric of schooling as a further element in what determines access to the curriculum. Our evidence shows that pupils' perspectives upon or consumption of teachers is highly sophisticated. Teacher is intensely scanned for signs of whatever is of importance to the individual pupil or the class. In contrast, teachers only come to know something of pupil's reactions to *them* and *their* subject materials. Within the classroom, pressures which create the steering group tend to limit many teacher's awareness of others. Teachers cannot be taken for the simple agents of social control they appear to be in some overdetermined and morally crusading versions of schooling.

Grouping pupils is a further aspect of 'schooling' as we are defining it. In the first phase of the project, we approached 'unstreaming' in secondary schools as a phenomenon not confined, but apparently highly related, to comprehensive re-organization in the late 'sixties and early 'seventies. There was a parallel phenomenon in America in the 'twenties and in Sweden in the 'sixties. The research literature which has grown out of these changes, is larger than on school differences and ability but no clearer as to whether measured abilities are enhanced by changes of variation in school organizations.[16] Both push us to the view that grouping, as such, does not 'promote' learning. Much of the literature appears to be about how patterns of grouping are imagined to mirror particular forms of society and somehow to prepare pupils for that society. Grouping becomes centred on socialization. Ability grouping *is* the school's basic form of pastoral grouping; what is called pastoral grouping corrects for or builds upon it.

School organization level frames – in terms of schooling, time-tabling and the curriculum – become, at the classroom level, curriculum content, mode of transmission, time, the pattern of discipline, teacher strategy and pupil identity. Pupils appear to have the least autonomy in the classroom, teachers the most, as they make the immediate decisions on discipline, content and timing and so forth. Teacher decisions at the administrative level, however, more or less constrain those with scale 1 grades who largely carry out school policies in the face of the range of pupils. Pupil identities are often not immediately affected by school policies or individual teachers; outward conformity often suffices. In the longer term, though, over the life of their careers as pupils they are more deeply and permanently influenced. Teachers and pupils have different forms of autonomy in front of the curriculum, the timetable and schooling and, so, are differently constituted in terms of frames and framing.

The four empirical vignettes which follow describe some of the strands woven in the complexity of individualized teaching in mixed-ability mathematics. Table 1 outlines intake and organizational differences between the two schools in which observations were made.

Table 1   School Differences

	SCHOOL H	SCHOOL V
No. of pupils in 1977 intake	198	195
No. of forms in year 1	8	6
Year 1. Test score distribution NFER AH 2/3 (10–20–40–20–10) high low	2–7–28–32–30	13–30–43–10–3
% of children with RA less than 9 years on entry	40	12
Ability grouping in years 1 – 3	Mixed ability except Modern Languages after Yr. 1. Term 1, and Maths, Science and Humanities from beginning year 3	Mixed ability throughout, except Maths, French in Year 3.

Schooling and Curriculum Change in School H (Example 1)

Schooling, as has been argued, refers to the modes of entry to curricular knowledge. It is variably constituted by, among other things, LEA decisions on re-organization, pupil grouping and by teacher strategies required for presenting novel curricula to the range of a pupil intake.

The history of the Maths Department in School H must be seen first in the context of the change from a non-selective secondary of 500 pupils to a comprehensive of 1600. The existing Head of Department was appointed in 1969, two years prior to comprehensivization. He found

> a syllabus that didn't come to anything: it was not imaginative, arithmetical using various sets of books. Pupils were streamed.

In order to modernise existing practice he adopted a new scheme. Two years after comprehensivization the syllabus was again changed, this time to SMP. The decision arose from a complex of factors. We have outlined the history of the school as it became a comprehensive elsewhere.[17] More immediately, the academic board in the school was persuaded to adopt a general policy of mixed-ability in the first year in the hope of ameliorating discipline problems.[18] The school simultaneously went to a four period day to cut down movement. These were changes in the schooling-frame affecting both pupils and teachers. The head of Maths was not sympathetic to the change to mixed-ability.

> I resisted it, we weren't prepared . . . I abstained on the vote, the whole department had just left the previous summer.

The last comment reaches out to wider LEA and national decisions on resources and staffing particularly in what could now be called inner city schools. The year of mixed-ability change, 1974, was also the pre-Houghton period.

> In the summer of 1974, I spent time looking through SMP . . . staff were employed during the summer; I was only one short. I presented them with a complete system.

SMP had several advantages. It seemed suitable for a range of abilities both in terms of content and mode of presentation and so it seemed to deal with the 'mixed-ability problem'. It also effected greater control over teachers. It was an attempt, in the face of severe teacher shortage (partly the result of badly planned LEA changes), to establish order and continuity of teaching method and content.

> I never liked the (old) books. It left too much to the teacher . . . there was a great deal of tension because of staff problems – problems because staff were given the choice to come here or some other school. Many of the staff only had Junior school experience.

The Head of Department recognized the discrepancy between both the content and organizational style of the workcards and teacher perspectives.

> One of the problems is . . . you need to be more highly specialized to get

the best from the situation. It needs taught organizational skills which many teachers don't have.

And again

Their knowledge of maths is how they've been taught in school. They have fixed ideologies about how maths should be . . . which contrasts the maths we have. There's conceptual barriers to be broken down. They saw silent pupils, the blackboard and class teaching . . .

The teachers themselves, however, focused on problems of pupil control. The one teacher who did not use the scheme as the Head of Department recommended (he included opening and ending phases of 'tables' to cover the basics), was also a senior member of the pastoral staff and so could 'resist'. He noted that

It doesn't allow the teacher to have the appearance of authority. A lot of movement. A lot of chatting.

The remaining teachers endeavoured to follow the modes of working into which the Head of Department, by co-teaching, socialized them. Perhaps this, too, led to their own emphasis on establishing competence among first year pupils as can be seen from Table 2.

Table 2   Contrast in the talk of first and second year teachers over seven periods of 40 minutes, excluding beginnings and endings. School H.

	First year		Second (2)/Third (3) year	
	Public	Immediate	Public	Immediate
Teacher A (R)	15	44		
Teacher B (R)	19*	42*	5	40 (3)
Teacher C (R)	22	43	7	41 (2)
Teacher D (D)			6	18 (2)
Teacher E (R/D)			6	38 (3)
Totals	56 (30%)	129 (70%)	24 (15%)	137 (85%)

D = at the desk   R = going round the room

Each count from which these percentages were constructed refers to a complete interaction as judged by the fieldworker and not to a speech utterance of a specifiable length. Each count is a categorization of a 'piece' of teacher action which potentially carries a number of messages. We were concerned primarily but not solely with disciplinary and diagnostic meanings as given by the commonsense of the conversation. In individualized instruction, with worksheets mediating between the teacher and pupil, the centralization of talk, *via* the teacher, of whole-class presentation is not prevalent. Occasions when it was required tended to occur during the brief 'opening' or 'closing' phases of the lesson. In the main body of the lesson, teacher-pupil interaction was mainly at an immediate face-to-face level, interspersed with the issuing of public regulative messages. Individual help, with the teacher talking to a pupil at the desk or moving round to lean over the pupil's desk, becomes the salient phenomenon. The normal practice in school H, with first year pupils, was for teachers to move round the room (R) rather than have pupils queue at the desk (D). The tendency for teacher rather than pupils to move decreased slightly in school H with the age of the teacher, length of stay in the school and hence experience of SMP workcards. Differences between schools and, within school H, between teachers, reflect different discipline frames.

The major difference between older and younger pupils occurs in the amount of public regulation of pupil behaviour and in a way which inverts the expectation that older pupils would receive more regulation for their greater indiscipline. Overall some 30% of teachers' talk in the first year is public. This amount is halved in succeeding years. Only teacher D teaching from the desk in the third year registers a higher share (25%).

Pupil Identities in the Economy of Teacher Interaction (Example 2)

Table 3 outlines how teacher talk-in-action is a fixed quantity (determined by the timetabling) of which different types of groups receive a bit more or a bit less. Pupils in groups 2 and 3 receive more public regulative talk than those in 1 and 4, and also slightly more of the immediate contact with the teacher.

*Table 3   Teacher B talk in one 40 minute period, marked * in Table 2.*

(a) as percentage of teacher talk across four groups

	Public	Immediate	Total
GP 1 (5 pupils)	5	24	18
GP 2 (4 pupils)	32	21	25
GP 3 (4 pupils)	37	26	30
GP 4 (7 pupils)	26	29	28
	100	100	101

(b) as average per pupil in each group

	Public	Immediate	Total
GP 1	0.2	2.0	2.2
GP 2	1.4	2.3	3.7
GP 3	1.8	2.8	4.5
GP 4	0.7	1.7	2.4

There are further regularities which are, we would suggest, functional expressions of the situation in which this teacher find herself. On the one hand the teacher controls the teaching process (at classroom level resolving and having to resolve problems of discipline, pacing and content), on the other the teacher is herself controlled or constrained by related factors (by the interplay of pupil identity, content, time and mode of transmission which enter into the teaching process, having first arisen at the level of administrative decision making, and the wider LEA situation). Discipline and instruction is structured in interaction with specific groups of pupils. Regularities are expression of a teacher's perception and interpretation of pupil abilities at the point of interplay of framing relationships. They are related to specific pupil identities which, we suggest, are thereby given further impetus to closure in a partly self-fulfilling process.

The groups referred to in Table 3 are analytical and fieldwork constructions. Knowledge of steering group phenomenon pre-disposed us to focus on how teachers distribute their attention across the ability range. Ability as given on pupil records, by teacher ratings and standardized tests was our first criterion in characterizing groups. The second was how the fieldworker perceived the pupils' involvement in work or interest activity, and the third was the element of teacher interaction indicated by the fieldwork notes on with whom, about what, teachers talked. Figure 1 sets out a simplified form of the first two dimensions. It is clear that interest activity on the part of pupils interacts with both public and immediate teacher talk. The numbers in brackets are those of pupils who fall in each category.

Figure 1   Pupil categories by ability and work orientation.

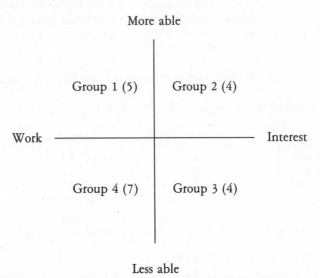

Group 1 refers to a small group of 5 pupils who are characterized by their apparent commitment to work, their ability/willingness to portray behaviours appropriate to the context defined by the scheme and teacher. This is reflected in the almost total absence of public (regulative) messages addressed to them. In marked contrast are the pupils of groups 3 and 2, whose behaviours are extremely problematic as the teacher endeavours to maintain an appearance of classroom order and productivity. They account for 69% of all public messages. Between the excellence of the 'total worker' and the indifference ('interest') of groups 2 and 3 falls the behaviour of group 4. Less committed than group 1, and less difficult than groups 2 or 3, they achieve identities more anonymous (in the perspectives of researcher and teacher) than those groups. They tend to be described by teachers (as pupils 'normal' for school H), as average in behaviour and attainment. The grouping described, however, belies any straightforward polarization of identity according to a behavioural/academic dichotomy. Pupils of group 1 are rated by teacher assessments and on NFER AH2/3 test as amongst the most able in the class. They are able and willing to portray behaviour which facilitates the realization of potential. Group 2, however, are similarly described as able children but are also likely to be described as under-achieving in respect of their perceived unwillingness to meet the behavioural requirements of the scheme. Given their 'ability' and behaviour, such pupils are unable to maintain skilfully 'successful' pupil identities in the perspectives of both teachers and their peers.

Group 3, in their pattern of work, are (to observation) in direct contrast to group 1. Whereas the former tend to work and see themselves as working solidly, the interest behaviour of group 3 calls for the highest proportions of both public and immediate teacher talk. In contrast to group 2 such pupils are defined as less able rather than *unwilling* to work independently, consequently their progress is seen as dependent upon teacher intervention. Group 3 is of some interest. We suggest they constitute a 'counter-steering group' which emerges as the frame of teacher distribution of knowledge is transposed on to the workcard (which becomes the main vehicle of the individualized mode of transmission) and as a pupil's learning problems tend to become surface features of interactions. A crucial factor in this process is the time frame of SMP in which, for an individual pupil, there is no specified time by which a task must be completed. The constraints for teacher and taught of finishing a topic within the lesson or the week are removed and transposed to the two (or three) years the department allocates for this form of curriculum material. In return, in marked contrast to whole class mathematics teaching governed by a tightly structured pacing of the syllabus, less able pupils are never removed from their learning problems with a particular topic. They never have the luxury of being removed from at least the surface features[19] (in terms of a particular topic) of their learning problems as the class moves *en masse* to the next unit of curriculum. Pupil progress through content thus becomes more dependent upon an intervention of teachers at the point at which the learning problem is experienced. In such circumstances, we suggest, the learning problems of pupils (who would under conditions of whole class teaching fall beneath the steering group and who would have missed out on learning) become more apparent to the teacher. A counter steering group phenomenon emerges. Unable to progress without teacher help, their learning problems are increasingly expressed in 'active' forms of behaviour, to the extent that teachers are unable to meet (i.e. supplement worksheet instructions) their learning requirements. Teacher B, for example, on whom we are commenting, comes into this context of constraints and limitations. Her frame of mind is committed to the scheme though with reservations. She finds her actions bounded in particular by this group of pupils.

> SMP is supposed to be for mixed groups but there's about six pupils who are really weak I can't get to them because it takes about 10–15 minutes each time. There's M demanding attention. I have to deal with her and I have to keep discipline.

We see then, that there is a group of pupils falling towards the bottom 15% of a standardized ability range who thereby fall outside the curriculum content of SMP and whose needs cannot be met in the available time. (Despite changes in the organization of curricula, *time* thus remains a frame factor for teachers in respect of pupil abilities.) Four of the six pupils referred to are pupils of the counter steering group. Their distinguishing feature is their tendency, unlike the other two pupils, to express their learning problems in active forms of behaviour. In turn these pupils rate themselves as below average in interest, behaviour, work and ability. The teacher's and pupils' perceptions overlap, though as we shall see not totally, with each other and those of the researcher.

As mentioned earlier, the interest behaviour of the pupils of group 3 (counter steering group) calls for highest proportions of both public and immediate teacher talk. (Although the differences between groups in the amount of immediate talk received is only slight we are suggesting that even *comparability* is significant. That pupils receive as much, and more, of the teachers attention as an 'able' child, constitutes a significant re-focusing of teacher attentions when considered against the background of whole class method.) The pupils themselves, however, do not consider that they receive sufficient attention. 'Teachers should stay with you longer and explain things to you.' In this respect it is clearly necessary to consider the duration as well as the incidence of interactions. A characteristic feature of immediate talk is its brevity (30–90 seconds). Whether or not time, as given at the level of immediate interaction, is experienced as a frame, as limit or possibility, will thus depend upon the levels of ability with which pupils are pre-disposed. For the pupils of the counter steering groups, despite a personalized time frame, time remains as a constraining factor. Indeed, given the brevity of interactions (in respect of pupil ability) we would suggest that such pupils are involved in a process of individual piloting, and meta-learning, (i.e. they learn that they have received instructions but that they have not undestood, a process reflected in and intrinsic to, their identity construction). The teacher finds them 'lacking in concentration', they're 'so easily disturbed'. The pupils however expect a teacher to impose concentration 'she doesn't tell you to sit down . . . she just waits to let you make a noise and then when it gets bad she just shouts at you'. In the teacher's view they 'give up so easily and waste time, if they can't do it they get silly half hours' or 'they just skim over the work and get annoyed when you tell them to go back and do it again'. In the pupils' perspective 'if it's easy . . . it's not so bad, but when it gets hard you just give up and you just get fed up . . . muck about'. Concentration is one factor, then, confidence another. 'They have to have confirmation of everything before they go on.' In whole class method such a group would rarely take up this amount of immediate teacher attention, they would exist below the steering group created by curriculum and time frames, though they might be the focus for public statements of a disciplinary nature. The re-focusing of teacher attention, however, as far as this is contingent upon behavioural non-conformity, occurs *pari passu* with increasing negative identification of such pupils as social types in a teacher's perception. The behaviours thus described have their origins in the interplay of frame factors (time, control, ability, etc.) and are, we are suggesting, context specific. Changes in frames signify changes in the learning opportunities experienced by pupils. This is illustrated in the identity of one of the pupils of the counter steering group (group 3). This pupil does not rate himself as below average in terms of ability, work, behaviour and interest in mathematics. The more favourable self conception can be explained by the learning opportunities made available during the Autumn term *via* remedial extraction. He himself notes

> You can't concentrate . . . you feel like mucking about, when you see someone mucking about you want to join in . . . In maths I work better. out of class . . .

This raises the much broader issue of what abilities are required to work under mass schooling even when the presentation is individualized. It is important to note that group 2 also receives high proportions of teacher attention. They are an abler group so their difficulties of working in the classroom cannot be just passed over as lack of intelligence. The interests and attitudes of such groups have received little attention in the literature. Their existence needs to be emphasized if only to prevent over-simple dichotomies being accepted uncritically. The pupils' own explanation for their situation is made in terms of the softness of teacher discipline. Such incompatibility between pupil outlook and teacher strategy may reflect a wider clash between home and schooling. The mother of one of the group 2 pupils says of the school on report evening that 'it's not strict enough . . . I'm very disciplined in the house so I can't understand how he's so bad'.

Finally, one further important comment needs to be made on Table 3 (b). As has been noted teacher B gives disproportionate amounts of attention to groups 2 and 3. She also gives very similar amounts of total attention to groups 1 and 4. But the internal relations of the total is not the same in both cases. For groups 2, 3 and 4 there is a constant relationship between public and immediate talk. In each case the difference is unity or near unity (e.g. group 4 – 1.7 minus 0.7 equals 1). This is not so for group 1 where the difference is 1.8, or nearly twice that of the other groups. It can be seen that this group is treated very differently from all others: the experience of being able pupils is markedly more positive. This evidence is similar to other studies and adds weight to the picture given for other pupils.

Curriculum Change and Teacher Perspectives (Example 3)

From the descriptions drawn from school H pointing to the interaction of schooling and curriculum, we now go on with data from school V to indicate what part teacher perspectives can play in shaping curriculum change. The different staffing and pupil intake positions in the two schools contribute to the different ways in which the same curriculum package is implemented. Our previous example focuses on the schooling of pupils, this one to resistance on the part of teachers, especially in the instance of one teacher deeply embedded in his own biography as a learner at school.

School V suffered none of the traumas over reorganization experienced in school H. Mixed-ability was gradually introduced across the subject range as a feature of school policy on how it was appropriate for pupils to be schooled. There was however no thought of dispersing difficult-to-control pupils across different classrooms.

The Head of Department appointed in 1975 inherited the curriculum and grouping organization. He also inherited a department which had never had a 4, 3, 2 points structure. Staff turnover has 'always been quite high' according to a previous Head of Department, pushed partly by the search for promotion outside the department. Due to LEA policies on advertising, recruitment tended to be a last minute affair leaving a feeling that the department was not getting the best teachers as the pool had been scooped. The new Head of Department thought that 'large turnover' also prevented the establishment 'of a developmental thread', 'a uniform approach' in the vocabulary used by teachers or in particular methods: e.g. for doing subtractions.

He did not find SMP books in particular a totally acceptable curriculum package.

I'm not all in favour of SMP materials in general though the workcards are a reasonable success.

In the fourth and fifth year he introduced MEI (Maths in Education and Industry).

The biggest problem in the department however, he felt, was the pupils' motivation – 'the few who do not respond, of all abilities'. This reflects a concern within the school for what was called under-performance. (The effect of these nebulous pressures as mediated through Teacher 1 is the main focus of the analyses in the last example below.) He felt that motivation was intrinsic to the workcards, its lack is 'revealed by workcards', 'they can help to reveal it'.

The question of the classroom organization of the workcards had, however, generated discernible divisions within the department. The story begins in 1975 with a teacher teaching 35 pupils in the smallest room available to the department. This teacher 'stressed he had to be firm . . . wanted it highly organized'. He made tables responsible for cards. '. . . if a card was not available . . . ask permission of another.' Four separate but complete sets of workcards were allotted to four separate groups of pupils, under the control of what Teacher 1, the direct inheritor of this arrangement and the focus of the final study below, was to call 'captains'. In the Head of Department's view this system in the way it was enforced 'held up kids'. This too was noted by the group of pupils studied from Teacher 1's classroom. The emphasis was on keeping track of the cards rather than on the pupils who 'had done very much less work'. This pattern of strong control over the organization of the workcards was continuous with the emphasis taken over or reinforced by the wider school ethos, especially as experienced by first and second year pupils.

A second teacher, regarded as having a negative influence by the Head of Department, 'detested the workcards . . . and didn't feel the pupils were learning anything'. Teacher 1 didn't share this view 'in general they learn as much as they would any other way'. However, he admitted the influence of this teacher. Because of the effects of the points structure in the department, there was 'not a lot of help from above. There was no second in the department then'. The probationers, especially, talked among themselves and listened to the advice of someone who had been teaching elsewhere without the workcard system. An alternative reality had credibility. So Teacher 1 would have preferred a whole class presentation because 'it makes marking easier, if there's a problem point one can go over it, reinforce for the less able and see where the brighter slipped up'. Teacher 1 had devised his own mode of marking the test card in SMP without the pupil present *via* sheets of paper additional to the normal exercise book. These he need only check for reasons of presentation and so forth, as the pupils realized. His abstraction of the marking of the test from the pupil's work reduced the problem of queueing. It was a solution to a felt difficulty which, by anticipation only, he thought whole-class presentation to a mixed-ability group would solve.

One relatively experienced teacher observed teaching second year classes tried actively to incorporate elements of whole-class presentation. Probationers in the year of observation, chiefly under the influence of this teacher and Teacher 1, made different alterations. Differences in practice continued to be handed on informally. Teacher 1 was, by now, what counted for an experienced teacher, though without a scale 2, and feeling not quite fairly treated. He reflects that at first the demands in the classroom

> come from all angles. When you were trying to help someone, always a queue built up for niggly little things which were not mathematical. You spent your time as an administrator. Now very little time is taken up with

administration; you may help with problems, there are the tests and, you know, keeping an eye on them.

The concern for keeping an eye on them echoes Teacher B in school H's problems on keeping discipline. The meaning of order, however, was somewhat different in the two schools. Teacher 1 who emphasized administration and ended several lessons with the pupils sitting in silence, argued that the class had 'got very chatty' and 'more boisterous', so some remedial action was required. He chose to take this *via* detentions for the whole class rather than singling out the individuals (mainly boys) who was observably the source of the difficulty. This particular attitude to discipline could have been a reflection on how he took the pastoral system to delimit the classroom teacher's job. It may also have reflected his perception of pupils in the school as compared with his own history.

In his view, which echoes the Head of Department's, the pupils were 'very complacent, most are from reasonable homes', '. . . the reputation that the school's got adds to the complacency'. They expect that 'teachers will do it for you', whereas, in contrast 'when I was at school we knew we had to work for what we got, the teachers wouldn't do it for us'. The attitude he criticizes was one of passivity, 'they won't sort of look at it and think for themselves . . . they seem to want it on a platter rather than seeing the core of a problem and weeding out all the bumf around it'.

But, in contrast to the Head of Department, he prefers 'the ones who are doing the work. It's getting the responses from them'. 'The ones who are willing to try the hardest. If you're doing your best for them they can only do their best'. In all this he is consciously or not refracting his own experience of being taught maths at an East-End secondary modern. 'At times it was hard-going, looking back he was good . . . being in the academic stream there was a lot of work. It was a very intensive course. I enjoyed maths so there was a lot I wanted to take in and not just get by.' He thought his own teachers – in marked contrast to his own view of his pupils – saw him as 'reasonably bright with a fair amount of effort made in my work'. He saw himself 'as a worker with a drive to be first if I could make it'. The contrast between his autobiography of motivation and social mobility and the complacency of pupils from reasonable homes is the context for a study of a small group of girls in the final section.

Teacher Biography and Pupil Identity (Example 4)

In the second description of the formation of pupil identities in terms of the economy of the distribution of time available, the teacher was responding to the constraints of time, curriculum materials and the range of pupil identity. In the example which follows it is suggested that teachers can shape the identity of pupils out of their own identity as a pupil and a learner.

We have already seen how Teacher 1 was socialized into a pattern of working in the classroom as a probationer, elements of which he passed on to other probationers. At its core was the attempt to keep track of the curriculum materials *via* the cards rather than *via* the pupils' progress, which he considered to be less than it could be judging by his own schooling. Just under 25% of the class were judged by the teacher to be working less well than they could. Two boys fell into this pattern. One was able and, like the teacher, came from a skilled working class background. They both defined themselves as model pupils. Six girls, however, who included all the ablest girls in the class, matched the teacher's negative judgement in their own self-ratings.

The question is why did these girls have negative self-identities which matched the perceptions of the teacher?

From fieldwork observations it was clear that these six girls worked separately sitting in different places in the front of the class near to the teacher's desk, one group to the left, the other to the right. If we take the group on the right their low behavioural self-rating could have been part of their social identity as a chatty work group. In one lesson their 'interest' talk included discussion of a sister, the brownies in preference to a Judo club, a mother's relation to another, detention for the class, teacher sarcasm and favourites, *Panorama* and whether another girl was in love with one of them. This conversation was mainly carried out by two of the group while the third worked solidly. The behaviour of the group to the left was such that it was scarcely possible to call them a group as they hardly interacted. Their pattern of work and concentration was so total as to be distractingly boring to observe. For three of the six pupils then our observations did not agree with either their own or the teacher's estimation. It can be added that their pattern of total work was followed in other lessons also.

On the Hope-Goldthorpe scale[20] of the 'social desirability' of jobs the teacher's father had a less desirable job than 80% of the class. His score at 33 was close to the group of six's average score of 34. The group to the left of the teacher scored 45 which was the average for girls (boys 49). So it was the group to the right whose fathers had the less desirable jobs, though all six fell in the bottom half for girls. The group of six pupils then fell within the teachers's own experience of social mobility to a teaching job. Is it possible that, however obscurely, he saw these pupils in danger of failing to make the transition that he had made in the general atmosphere of complacency, and so was marking them down in order to further motivate them?

The context in which the group of three to the left, especially, came to agree with him, is the variations on SMP, including captains, etc. which this teacher had learnt when a probationer. First, there is the emphasis on pupil control. The pupils sat at hexagonally sided tables which were to encourage conversation (the maths classrooms were the only ones equipped with such tables). There was general pupil resentment at what they took to be his illegitimate interference in their conversation. Instead requests for help or with equipment were to be routed through him.

> One time he was in a really bad mood for about two months. He was knocking off merit points and everything. You know, just for saying 'can I borrow your scissors?' or something and B. was explaining to S. how to do this card and he said 'you've lost a merit point, he should come up to me, that's what I'm here for'.

> Sometimes you get so frightened of going up to him because (another pupil chips in) he's more of a threat (and another) than a teacher.

And so the teacher's chosen strategy for dealing with the curriculum package together with a particular emphasis on discipline becomes a damper on work.

Central to his strategy, as noted in the previous section, was the fact that the pupils did work on the test element in each unit on pieces of paper separate from their ongoing class and home work done in exercise books. He needed, therefore, only to look at these books every so often. Pupils continued sitting at their desks while their test was being marked. Queues were reduced. But again the pupils' perceptions make the strategy counterproductive.

When he marks the book he just ticks it, just to see if it's neat or not. It's only really the test he looks at.

Their classwork is made less significant; teaching more mechanical. As one pupil from the group of six noted

Once I even left a page free and he just ticked it. I once did a whole card wrong and he just put a tick by it.

Events like this did not encourage in the girls the feeling that the work was relevant. But the context of this quotation in the interview is important. It was the way they expressed their answer about how they were not working hard in the classroom. Further elements of this teacher's classroom organization add to the impression. The Head of Department has already been quoted to the effect that it 'held up kids'. One of the group of six agrees

I prefer a book because you've got to get them all, the workcards, the tests. I don't like the tests, you've got the check and the test, it's kind of annoying that when you've finished one workcard you've got to go all the way back, climb over a 100 chairs, get the workcard and start again, and it's kind of – it's a bit of a drag.

This able pupil has got up and moved over to where the cards were stored eight times in the lesson in which she was most closely observed. She is articulating how a mode of teacher-inspired organization which permits just one card to a pupil at a time (instead of all or part of a unit) slows down the pace of work.

In summary, we can suggest that, first, the teacher (consciously or not) sees that certain pupils from similar occupational and ability backgrounds to his own, relative to the rest of the class, need pushing. Second, these pupils perceive themselves to be working less well than would be possible because of the teacher's own strategy of organization. Dissatisfaction with how the curriculum scheme is implemented translates itself into low estimations of how hard they work and how deeply they are interested. The third element which bring the other two together is that of sexual differences linked to the girls' perception of differences in primary and secondary schooling. It seems that it is the girls who were more open to negative self-identity.

The group of three, to the right of the teacher, who perceived themselves to be less well behaved, discussed the ease of the work they were variously doing on Arrow diagrams, Angles and Decimals. The work was considered easy or a repetition of primary work. In general, in contrast to the boys, girls in the class felt they worked less hard in the secondary school than they had expected. In interview they commented unfavourably, too, on the size of the school, the problems of not knowing everyone, of the teachers not knowing you and on having to change classrooms. Boys, in contrast, favoured size, favoured room changes, and favoured having more than one teacher (because you could escape unfair treatment). Some girls noted the advantage of subject teachers who are more specialized and who met you less frequently and so tended to be less bored and bad tempered. The division, therefore, is not totally general or fully clear cut. There does seem a preference, however, especially marked in the group of six, for the primary school atmosphere. Only girls, too, wanted whole class presentation. The general comments on not working as hard marks a 'distance' from the secondary school. Boys regarded themselves as having worked harder. Perhaps for the boys it is the real beginning for as one noted 'secondary school's more important for when you grow up and get a job and so you have to learn more'. The girls' openness to Teacher 1's concern with pupil motivation is dependent, perhaps, on a sexually defined unease with the secondary school. Sexual divisions intertwine with those of status or class.

In this group of girls we can see how the broader frame factors of schooling, including that which transfers pupils at 11, interact with identities formed prior to and outside of schooling. Further comments from this group of six suggest that the question of ability as perceived by the teacher also enters in. So, finally, the teacher's administration of the supplementary materials provides further evidence of how the classroom situation and teacher behaviour is 'read' by pupils. One of the group of six asked the teacher why only particular pupils had received these materials

> and he said well they're the ones who get the high on their test. And I don't think that's fair . . . because that means he's been helping them, he's been paying more attention to them than anybody else.

The question of supplementing the work of the able is an issue raised in broad-ability classrooms. This teacher judges on test performance alone.

Conclusion

We have presented four descriptions as explorations of how the concrete life of classrooms is created in its idiosyncracy and its complexity. The systematic aspects of classrooms have been indicated by the ways in which framing of classroom factors takes place. Four descriptions, of themselves, are insufficient to determine which of the senses of frame recur predominantly across a school (and by inference across the system of education). A greater degree of system will be seen when we report on the modes of presentation used by other subject areas in the curriculum.

Notes

1 The terminology is used in confusing fashion in the literature: we settle for individualiz*ed* = every pupil has something different provided, individu*ated* = every pupil has his own copy of the same thing.
2 SMP Teachers' Notes Cards p. 7.
3 In this sense, we would argue that BUSWELL'S (1980) argument about the *de*skilling effect of the workcard-based curriculum 'package' upon teachers is partial. Acute shortages of subject teachers in certain areas, both numerically and qualitatively, have been, in our view, an important force behind the development and diffusion of many of our curriculum packages, especially in Maths and Science. Their adaptation can quite clearly constitute a *skilling* of teachers. Moreover, it is part of our argument (running through the three examples below) to show that the workcard and package require no less but, rather *different* skills from teachers, to an extent as yet barely realized either by themselves or analysts of their classroom tasks. In this respect, APPLE, M. (1980) is glib.
4 GOFFMAN, E. (1963).
5 STEBBINS, R. (1975).
6 LUNGREN, U.P. (1977).
7 DAHLOFF, U.S. (1971), LUNGREN, U.P. (1972).
8 BELLACK, A. *et al* (1966).

9   See especially 'On the classification and framing of educational knowledge' in BERNSTEIN, B. (1977).

10   See his 'Pedagogies visible and invisible' in BERNSTEIN, B. (1977).

11   For example, see HARGREAVES, A. (1972) and HARGREAVES, A., HESTOR, S. and MELLOR, F. (1975).

12   LUNDGREN, U.P. (1972).

13   DAHLOFF, U.S. (1971).

14   See DOUGLAS, M. (1966), (1973).

15   RUTTER, M. *et al* (1979).

16   CORBISHLEY, P. in DAVIES, B and CAVE, R.G. (1977) reviews the UK/US literature, DAHLOFF, U.S. (1971) and LUNDGREN, U.P. (1972) take a wider perspective.

17   Our analysis of the pastoral systems of our two case study schools can be found as CORBISHLEY, P. and EVANS, J. 'Teachers and pastoral care: An empirical comment' In BEST, R. *et al* (1980).

18   *ibid*

19   EDWARDS, A.D. and FURLONG, V.J. (1978).

20   GOLDTHORPE, J.H. and HOPE, K. (1974).

References

APPLE, M. (1980) 'Curricular form and the logic of technical control' in BARTON, L., MEIGHAN, R. and WALKER, S. (Eds) *Schooling, Ideology and the Curriculum* Lewes, Falmer Press, pp. 11–127.

BELLACK, A., KLIEBARD, H., HYMAN, R. and SMITH, F. (1966) *The Language of Classrooms* New York, Teachers College Press.

BERNSTEIN, B. (1977) *Class, Codes and Control, Vol. 3.* London, Routledge and Kegan Paul.

BEST, R., JARVIS, C. and RIBBENS, P. (1980) *Perspectives on Pastoral Care* London, Heinemann Educational.

BOWLES, S. and GINTIS, H. (1976) *Schooling in Capitalist America* London, Routledge and Kegan Paul.

BUSWELL, C. (1980) 'Pedagogic change and social change' *British Journal of Sociology of Education* 1 (3) pp. 293–306.

DAHLOFF, U.S. (1971) *Ability Grouping, Content Validity, and Curriculum Process* New York, Teachers College Press.

DAVIES, B. and CAVE, R.G. (Eds) (1977) *Mixed-Ability Teaching in the Secondary School* London, Ward Lock.

DOUGLAS, M. (1966) *Purity and Danger* London, Routledge and Kegan Paul.

DOUGLAS, M. (1973) *Natural Symbols* London, Barrie and Jenkins.

EDWARDS, A.D. and FURLONG, V.J. (1978) *The Language of Teaching* London, Heinemann.

GOFFMAN, E. (1963) *Behaviour in Public Places* New York, Free Press.

GOLDTHORPE, J.H. and HOPE, K. (1974) *The Social Grading of Occupations: A New Approach and Scale* Oxford, Clarendon.

HARGREAVES, D. (1972) *Interpersonal Relations and Education* London, Routledge and Kegan Paul.

HARGREAVES, D., HESTER, S. and MELLOR, F. (1975) *Deviance in Classrooms* London, Routledge and Kegan Paul.

LUNDGREN, U.P. (1972) *Frame Factors and the Teaching Process* Stockholm, Almquist.

LUNDGREN, U.P. (1977) *Model Analysis of Pedagogical Processes* Stockholm, Gleerup.

RUTTER, M., MAUGHAN, B., MORTIMORE, B. and DUSTON, J. (1979) *Fifteen Thousand Hours* London, Open Books.

SCHLECHTY, P.C. (1976) *Teaching and Social Behaviour: Toward an Organizational Theory of Instruction* Boston, Allyn and Bacon.

STEBBINS, R. (1975) *Teachers and Meaning: Definitions of Classroom Situations* London, Brill.

Towards a Sociology of Assessment

Tricia Broadfoot, Westhill College

This paper is entitled 'Towards a Sociology of Assessment'. As a result it has probably already offended a significant proportion of readers who see in such grandiose claims a desire for instant glory based on superficially appealing, but essentially glib, analyses put forward at the expense of genuine, patient and detailed scholarship. We have become familiar with the necessity for specific sociologies such as those of religion or education whose legitimacy is testified to by the existence of courses and posts in appropriate departments of higher education. This is because, as in any other discipline, there is continual pressure for greater specialization – the application of the rules of the subject to ever more finely demarcated aspects of social life. Thus in recent years we have seen the emergence within the sociology of education of identifiable sub-areas of concern – the sociology of deviance, the sociology of teaching, the sociology of curriculum, and the sociology of school organization – to name but a few.[1] Each of these specialist areas has had to justify itself in terms of its independent contribution to the parent discipline, to the substantive area of concern, or both. Thus too, the sociology of education must justify itself in terms of the insights it can afford into general areas of sociological concern, whether this is the construction of social action at the micro level or, at the other extreme, the nature of advanced capitalist societies at the macro level. Alternatively, it must justify itself in terms of the insights it affords those involved in the practice of education itself – notably teachers.

If this is the justification in general terms for a sociology of education, it is also the rationale for the collection of papers in this volume which, in considering various aspects of education, seeks to fulfil a twofold function of both contributing to the development of the sociology of education as an academic study, and helping to provide insight into teachers' everyday, practical problems. Thus the claim for a sociology of assessment *per se*, rests on whether a case can be made that such a study provides unique insight for the sociology of education and/or for teachers' understanding of their day-to-day situation.

Stage One: The Need for Definition

The first step towards the justification of a sociology of assessment is to define precisely what is meant by the term 'assessment'. For teachers this is likely to include a whole range of activities concerned with evaluating pupils' progress – the routine marking of exercises and essays, class tests, standardized tests, periodic school examinations, public examinations, a variety of different school records, reports to parents, testimonials and references, as well as the more rare formal evaluations by outside bodies such as school psychologists.

This already lengthy list would be further added to by the senior management of the school in their concern for the way in which 'the consumers' outside the school – such as the parents of actual and prospective pupils, the local community in general, employers and further and higher education establishments – would judge the products of the school and, hence, its activities. Equally, senior management at least will be concerned with the assessments upon which the management hierarchy outside the school – local education authority (LEA) advisers and officials, and the education committee of the local council – come to form their judgements about the quality of education provided in that particular school. There is also a third level of concern, typically of much less interest to the individual school or even LEA, which preoccupies those charged with national responsibility for educational provision and standards – the Department of Education and Science (DES), Her Majesty's Inspectorate (HMI) and, ultimately, Parliament.

Thus, a sociology of assessment must comprehend the whole range of evaluative activity within the education system from the judgements teachers form in the classroom about individual pupils through to the way in which various, more formal ways of judging pupils' progress in the school as a whole provide for the accountability of the individual teacher, the school, the local authority and, ultimately, national educational provision as a whole.

If the first step towards the justification of a sociology of assessment is a definition of the range of activities which would fall within such an analysis, the second must be to recognize how central these assessment activities are to the form and organization of education as typically practised today in most societies with any kind of fairly well developed mass education system. The logical third step would then be to establish *why* assessment has become so integrally connected with the business of mass teaching and learning and, hence, what significance this integral relationship has for the way in which the processes of contemporary schooling relate to, support, contradict or are independent of the society in which they are situated. This then is the scope and the task for this paper.

Stage Two: The Central Role of Assessment

I have suggested elsewhere (Broadfoot, 1979) that the institution of formal evaluation procedures in education which was contemporaneous with the institution of mass education systems *per se* was directly instrumental in rationalizing educational provision into a system. In particular, it emphasized four themes which have become dominant in the provision of schooling as we know it – 'competence', 'content' (rationalization of), 'competition' and 'control'.

The idea of 'competence' was reflected in the institution of qualifying examinations for various professions such as medicine.[2] The consequences of the institution of such exams were much more far-reaching, however, since the existence of such tests rapidly came to legitimate the idea of the written, theoretical test – a legitimacy it still retains today. This, in turn, became a major factor in determining the content and style of the curriculum – a movement away from 'on the job' training in favour of formal qualifications. Clearly such a movement was central to the growth of bureaucracy which necessitated, among other things, a change from ascribed to achieved roles based on merit.

A changing emphasis in the 'content' of schooling was clearly the other side of this coin since, whilst a few élite schools continued to be preoccupied with the development of personal qualities such as leadership, for most pupils the aesthetic, the practical and the non-cognitive aspects of education came to take a very back place in comparison with the acquisition of academic skills and knowledge.[3]

'Competition' is an even more far-reaching theme since it was not long before it was recognized that if examinations were useful in ascertaining competence, they were even more useful in regulating the growing pressure for entry into élite positions in the labour market. In this sense examinations, and indeed a whole range of other assessment procedures such as the intelligence tests first developed around the turn of the century, came to play a quite crucial role in the regulation of access to privilege and, more importantly, in legitimating the basis for selection. Where, previously, wealth and breeding had been the unquestioned criteria for all but an exceptional few to gain entry to the élite, the institution of formal educational assessment procedures allowed for the identification and recruitment of suitable individuals for the increasingly complex and mobile division of labour whilst reassuring those not so selected that they had failed in a fair competition.

This historical analysis is readily reinforced by a study of teachers' perceptions and school processes today. In a recent study of teachers' perceptions of control, extensive open-ended interviews revealed that virtually the only formal constraint on their autonomy of which secondary school teachers at least were aware, was the existence of public examinations.[4] It is the exams that determine the content of the curriculum, particularly for senior forms, and the exam results on which teachers hold themselves accountable – on which they expect to be judged.

> In the past it was very much the class teacher and the class and as long as the results came out right in the end, the way in which we did things was left to the individual . . .
>
> (primary school teacher, England)

The attitude of the authorities, in the eyes of one teacher is:

> We don't know what's going on in there, but it gets the results at the end so we might as well leave it alone.
>
> (secondary school teacher, England)

For those teaching senior pupils, especially, classroom autonomy is a hundred per cent, within the relatively tight constraints of an imposed syllabus and provided the examination results are satisfactory. Teachers recognize that they operate within a web of constraints composed of the interacting influences of their pupils, their training, the available resources, time, the expectations of colleagues and the head, the school's organization and ethos, and public opinion, especially that of parents. In practice, however, the principal effect of this web of constraints is to reinforce the pressure for results whilst helping to determine the ways in which teachers can set about achieving them.

> As long as a subject doesn't have a particularly bad record of exam passes – I'm afraid that is how we are made accountable – then you are left alone.
>
> (teacher at sixth form college, England)

> Apart from the exams, I have total autonomy.
>
> (teacher at sixth form college, England)

Schools obviously vary in the extent to which it is true to say 'exams rule the school' (secondary school teacher, England). The stage of schooling and the ethos of the institution will provide for significant differences in the relative emphasis given to co-ordinated curriculum planning, pedagogic style, pastoral care, social and emotional development – in short, those areas where it is not sufficient or possible to leave control of teaching activity to the arbitration of the exam result. Nevertheless, it is clear, both from what teachers say and from overt government and local authority initiatives, that currently there is increasing pressure on schools from community and management alike for standards, for qualifications – for visible, quantifiable testimony of pupil achievement. If parents and pupils themselves are worried about getting qualifications at a time of acute youth unemployment, their political representatives are increasingly concerned that through, for example, the publication of public exam results[5] or various kinds of standardized local and national tests of standards, they should be able to oblige schools to compete in demonstrating their quality as measured in such formal assessments.

The rights and wrongs of this trend from an educational point of view are largely beyond the scope of this paper, as is a detailed accounting for such contemporary developments.[6] Rather, for the purposes of this paper, the utility of picking out one or two of the distinctive characteristics of the contemporary teaching situation, particularly those concerned with assessment, lies in the way in which such an analysis can demonstrate how assessment procedures are still the main determinants of the four principle themes in the provision of schooling – 'competence', 'competition', 'content' and 'control'.

'Competence' in, for example, reading, is determined by testing; the existence of such tests more often than not identifying a particular set of norms of performance as appropriate standards. 'Competition' is clearly manifest in the intense pressure experienced by teachers for those exam passes which will enable pupils to compete in the employment and higher education markets. The ever increasing proliferation of formal exams since the institution of the GCE in 1951 is further testimony to the increasing pressure on schools and colleges to provide the currency for such competition. If the introduction of the CSE in 1965 was the first major manifestation of this kind of pressure across an ever widening ability band, the currently mooted 'voc' and 'I' levels are the most recent.[7] So imbued is the education system with the desirability of such competition between pupils that, although the influence of external exams may be deplored in the constraints it effects on the ability of individual teachers to decide for themselves how to respond to the idiosyncratic needs of pupils in a particular school or area, teachers actively encourage competition in the classroom, frequently in terms of future exam hurdles to be surmounted, as one of their major aids to motivation.

Likewise 'content' is more or less determined by public examination syllabuses for at the very least these provide an imposed definition of the appropriate kinds of activity for any particular subject which any in-school innovation must take into account and relate to. Indeed the influence of public examinations in legitimating a particular approach to curricular organization (namely subject-based) and encouraging a particular form of pedagogy (essentially didactic) is much greater even than their not inconsiderable formal role. Put another way, what schools (and especially secondary schools) teach today, how they are organized and how success is recognized – the whole familiar pattern of contemporary schooling (and, for that matter, teacher socialization) – is arguably a direct product of the external examinations first introduced in this country in the mid nineteenth century.

Finally, 'control'; it is this issue which comes over perhaps most clearly from the brief statements by teachers quoted earlier. Overt, explicit control of what teachers do is largely unnecessary because of the accountability provided for by formal assessment procedures. This is recognized by teachers, officials and educational consumers alike. Just as significant, however, is the fact that this widespread acceptance of the legitimacy of judging schools' and pupils' performance in terms of what can be measured by various kinds of tests and examinations, is a crucial source of social control. Pupils and their parents, teachers and the public in general have come to accept that school assessment is a fair basis on which the doors of future opportuniy should be opened to some and closed to the majority of others who do not manifest equivalent merit when measured in these ways. The fact that pupils typically accept the stereotype meted out to them by the education system – 'low achiever', perhaps, or 'less able' – is crucial to the selection and allocation function of schooling in advanced industrial societies. Certainly such pupils may manifest individual disaffection and prove troublesome. But it is extremely rare for any serious or concerted challenge to be made of the legitimacy of the criteria upon which assessment and, hence, the education system itself is based.

Clearly, it is not hard to make a case for the centrality of assessment activities to the way in which schooling is organized and practised today in societies with any kind of fairly well developed mass education system[8] – the second step towards a sociology of assessment identified earlier. Indeed the effects of assessment practices briefly collected here under the four themes of 'competence', 'competition', 'content' and 'control' have already begun to attract the interest of sociologists and social psychologists interested in the evaluative relationship between teachers and pupils (e.g. Rosenthal and Jacobsen, 1968; Fleming and Anttonen, 1971; Morrison, 1974; Nash, 1976) and those concerned with studying the effects of the resultant stereotyping (e.g. Hargreaves, 1967; Lacey, 1970; Rist, 1970; Keddie, 1971; Sharp and Green, 1975; Willis, 1977). Writers such as Jackson (1968) and Holt (1969) have been concerned to describe the way in which the ethos of the school, whose activities are dominated by a rationality which emphasizes competition, achievement, selection and motivation based on marks and grades, provides a hidden curriculum which conditions pupils in an even more fundamental way:

> In school he learns like every buck private or conscript labourer . . . how not to work when the boss isn't looking, how to know when he is looking, how to make him think you are working when you know he is looking.
>
> (Holt, 1969)

It is a short step from such micro concerns to the more macro analyses of, for example, Hextall and Sarup (1977) whose concern is with the social origins of the standards upon which assessment is based or the importance of the correspondence between the hidden curriculum of school and the qualities which must be fostered in the future worker (Bowles and Gintis, 1977; Willis, 1977).

> This process of sorting, shifting and positioning prepares pupils for being sorted, shifted and positioned in world society, a process which it both anticipates and legitimates through the frequently mutually reinforcing cognitive and behavioural criteria involved.
>
> (Dale, 1977)

Finally, a sociology of assessment is already implicit in those studies concerned with demonstrating the way in which school assessment disguises social inequality in the rhetoric of the meritocracy. By so doing, an assessment allows both for the identification of an élite and acts as a powerful means of legitimation and, hence, social control. Indeed this legitimation role is highlighted by the consistent failure of researchers to find any very significant correlation between school assessment and future performance – even where the activities are as closely related as school and university examination performance (e.g. Powell, 1973; Murphy, 1981). If, as in the case of many jobs, school assessment actually predicts *negatively* (e.g. SCRE, 1976; Williams and Boreham, 1972) its continued predominance can only be attributed to its legitimation function – that it provides a largely uncontroversial basis for the necessary sorting and allocation of pupils to future social and occupational roles.

The intelligence testing movement is a particularly interesting example of this function in this respect and has aroused a good deal of research interest (e.g. Simon, 1953; Karier *et al*, 1973; Kamin, 1974). The prevailing scientific-technical rationality of modern industrial society gives the apparently objective, scientific judgements of intelligence tests a particular force.

> I would suggest that the powerful pronouncement of science sanctifies common-sense prejudice and legitimizes the production of persons whose qualifications (or lack of them) block them from anything but menial or semi-skilled jobs. But it is a vicious circle since the objective test started from these prejudiced beliefs about the world. The tests are used by test constructors, teachers, administrators and politicians to support their own beliefs and value systems . . . In *use* measures of performance relative to some unexplicated standard (usually face validity, i.e. constructor's common-sense view of the world) become an objective measure of competence that have a determinative impact on students' lives . . . hanging on this thin thread is the entire occupational and status structure of society.
>
> (Mackay, 1974)

Important as these analyses are, they do not in themselves constitute an adequate sociology of assessment. It still remains to go on from specific studies of the ways in which school assessment practices operate in relation to mass industrial society to the third and fourth stages of a justification identified earlier. Namely, why has assessment become so integrally connected with the business of teaching and learning in contemporary mass education systems, and what significance does this integral relationship have for the way in which the processes of contemporary schooling relate to, support, contradict, or are independent of the *particular* societies in which they are situated? The first of these questions which form the focus for the rest of this paper requires an exploration of some of the central characteristics *common* to that type of society which gave birth to mass schooling. The second question, by contrast, requires a much more specific, substantive discussion of the way in which the *different* characteristics of particular societies mediate these general features into the idiosyncratic educational practices of any one society.

Stage Three: The Prevailing Rationality of Assessment

Assessment has become integrally connected with teaching and learning as we know it in contemporary educational practice simply, yet fundamentally, because in its broadest sense of evaluation – to make reference to a standard – assessment is one of the most central features of the rationality that underpins advanced industrial society itself. Assessment procedures are the vehicle whereby the dominant rationality of the corporate capitalist societies typical of the contemporary western world is translated into the structures and process of schooling. As Cherakoui (1977) suggests, the system of assessment that emerged with mass education systems must be understood as 'organically connected with a specific mode of socialization'.

Sociology has been much concerned to conceptualize the difference between 'traditional' or 'pre-modern' and industrial societies. Although varying widely in their perspective on central issues such as the basis for social order or the scope for creative social interaction, sociologists spanning the whole range of the structural-functionalist/conflict – system/action continua find substantial areas of common ground in their discussion of the changing basis for the allocation and performance of key social roles in the emerging industrial society. Crucial to Weber's analyses was the growth of a rationality that informed both the scientific-technical progress of the age and the associated bureaucratic institutional structures. Durkheim's very different social system perspective nevertheless emphasizes the same ideas of rational, individual, hierarchical and specific allocation of roles in his distinction between mechanical and organic solidarity.[9]

More recently, Parsons has reiterated this theme in what is its perhaps most explicit and detailed form to date, in his pattern variables. Whilst this categorization has many shortcomings,[10] Parsons' distinctions between the growth of value orientations such as affective neutrality, universalism, achievement and specificity at the expense of affectivity, particularism, ascription and diffuseness, respectively, enunciate very clearly some of the key characteristics of prevailing modes of social organizations. Actors will be chosen to perform specific, defined roles on the basis of their demonstrated competence as measured by some rational criterion.

The move from a collective, communal basis for social order to one based on individual interdependence, which so preoccupied Durkheim, was made both possible and necessary by the practical and ideological demands of the emerging capitalist order. Under 'practical' would be included the necessity for a mobile workforce in which the individual – not the family or the community – would take responsibility for a particular unit or stage of production, the whole process of which he might not even be able to conceptualize. This in contrast to the hitherto prevailing work organization in which one individual was typically responsible for the whole task. 'Practically' it was essential that this new type of worker should be prepared to accept the legitimacy of a system in which he was paid a money wage that was only a proportional return for his contribution to a system he was powerless to control. Herein lies the link between the changing 'practical' demands of a new economic order and the necessarily associated changes in the prevailing ideology,[11] if ideology is taken here in its most general sense to mean the accepted bases for social order. If a change in ideology with the advent of an industrial, capitalist order was legitimized and reinforced by the hegemonic domination of a new entrepreneurial class, the most central theme in the changes taking place went far beyond class in both its origins and its implications. This was the theme of individualization.

An individualistic orientation came to embrace the whole range of social institutions, not least the major value systems of religion and politics which saw at this time the rapid growth of protestantism and liberal democracy respectively in both of which the idea of the rights and responsibilities of the individual is central[12] (Smith, 1980).

By the same token, it is hardly surprising that the various ideologies of schooling that have developed – the developmental, child-centred, the moral and the meritocratic (Hargreaves, 1979) – are all options within an individualistic rationality which emphasizes personal needs, personal responsibility and personal reward. Such an orientation in turn implies the necessity for some agreed criteria against which need, responsibility and reward can be judged. The notion of rational criteria for judgement is embodied not only in the idea of the evaluation of a pupil's need or progress, but clearly extends to more impersonal issues such as school and classroom organization, unit costs or teacher inspection. Evaluation – the accountability of an individual unit – permeates every aspect of systemic provision and practice and is particularly visible in the various administrative bureaucracies which have grown up as an integral part of educational provision.

If sociologists of all shades of the conflict-consensus continuum have agreed that the change from traditonal to industrial society necessitated fundamental changes in the basis for social organization, conflict theorists have been particularly interested in the way in which the growth of the post-feudal economic order of capitalism necessitated alternative forms of social control which would legitimate the dominance of the emerging bourgeois class. Central to Marxist theory, in particular, is the relationship that emerged between the instrumental or productive 'base' and the expressive or legitimating 'super-structure'. The precise conceptualization of this relationship has many different portrayals – Gramsci's notion of 'hegemony', Althusser's 'Ideological State Apparatuses' and Bourdieu's 'cultural arbitrary' being among the most familiar to sociologists of education.

Although these concepts distinguish between the economic and the social order, they are much less helpful in situating the concept of evaluation than Habermas's distinction between 'the practical' and the 'purposive rational'. Habermas defines the 'practical' (praktisch) as the basis for symbolic interaction within a normative order – the level of feeling, consciousness and volition and the associated level of ethics and politics (loosely, 'super-structure'). The 'purposive rational' (zweck-rational) is action which is directed towards specific purposes (loosely the economic and administrative 'base'). Habermas's 'zweckrational' links closely with Weber's concept of rationality which he used to define the form of capitalist economic activity, bourgeois private law and bureaucratic authority. Habermas (1968) argues that, as social labour is increasingly industrialized, the criterion of rationality penetrates even further into other areas of life – urbanization, the technification of transport and communication. Indeed it may be argued that the growth of rationality has been of far more importance than that of capitalist production itself and that the story of modern history is the growth of bureaucracy: 'apart from the opaque line of technological rationality, social life is drift and habituation.' (Gerth and Mills, 1952).

This argument is perhaps most clearly set out not in any sociological work but in the popular classic 'Zen and the Art of Motor Cycle Maintenance', in which Pirsig (1976) distinguishes between the technological, rational, scientifically-organized 'classical' mode and the imaginative, emotional, aesthetic, intuitive, 'romantic' mode – the motor-cycle and the 'unlogic' of zen. Pirsig suggests that history may be in large part understood in terms of the shifting balance of power between these two cultures. At the present time the prevailing rationality is 'classical' – the 'person' is excluded in favour of the abstract 'operator'; notions of 'good' and 'bad' are replaced by 'facts'; and the organization of reality itself is an arbitrary but significant 'carving up' of perception.

Thus the progression from feudalism to capitalism and, in particular, from entrepreneurial to corporate capitalism, is bound up with the ever increasing power of technical-scientific rationality which structures not only the ideology and organization of production, but is more and more pervasive in the ideology and organization of social life as a whole. In particular, Marcuse (1964) argues that the classic class antagonisms identified in Marxism become increasingly hidden as the ideological power of technocratic consciousness provides for an unacknowledged political domination.

> In industrially advanced capitalist societies, domination tends to lose its exploitative and oppressive character and become 'rational' without political domination thereby disappearing.
>
> (Marcuse, 1970)

The legitimation for this process, according to Marcuse, is the constantly increasing productivity which keeps individuals living in increasing comfort.

> In this universe, technology also provides the great rationalization of the unfreedom of man and demonstrates the 'technical' impossibility of being autonomous, of determining one's own life. For this unfreedom appears neither as irrational nor as political, but rather as submission to the technical apparatus which enlarges the comforts of life and increases the productivity of labour . . .
>
> (Marcuse, 1964)

Following Marcuse, Habermas suggests that in advanced capitalist societies, deprived and privileged groups no longer confront each other *as* socio-economic classes. Although class distinctions still persist in the form of subcultural traditions, life style and attitudes, the scope for normative activity – political initiatives, debates about the nature of the 'good life', the ability for conscious action as a class, are increasingly drowned in the technocratic consciousness:

> Today's dominant, rather glassy background ideology, which makes a fetish of science, is more irresistible and farther-reaching than ideologies of the old type. For with the veiling of 'practical' problems it not only justifies a particular class's interest in domination and represses another class's partial need for emancipation, but affects the human race's emancipatory interest as such . . . technocratic consciousness reflects . . . the repression of 'ethics' as such as a category of life.
>
> (Habermas, 1971)

What is being described here then is the phenomenon of 'one dimensional man' – the logical development of the process of individualization and rationalization associated with the development of capitalist economic relationships. As capitalism has itself become more and more institutionalized, into various kinds of state and corporate capitalism, its ideological legitimation has equally moved from any kind of class hegemony to the predominance of a common prevailing rationality *per se,* where science and technology are both base and superstructure. If earlier, ownership and control of the means of production were crucial to effective domination, increasingly it is the bureaucracies of production and of administration which have become both controlling and self-determining. The rise of corporate capitalism has witnessed on the one hand the growth of a new 'technocratic' middle class of bureaucrats and technicians and, on the other, a related shift in power from the legislative to the executive branches of government in the rise of corporate management styles (Gerth and Mills, 1952).

What started as a desire to understand and, hence, harness the material/natural world for the means of production is increasingly being extended by both technocrats and bureaucrats alike into an attempt to extend 'technical' control into the realm of social life itself. This takes the form of new and more pervasive techniques for the surveillance, monitoring and control of both individuals and organizations.

> The economic take-off of Western Europe began with techniques that made possible capital accumulation, methods for the accumulation of men made possible a political take-off, as the traditional, ritual, costly, violent forms of power were superseded by a subtle calculated technology of subjection . . . The establishment of a coded, formally egalitarian constitution supported by a system of representative government. But this 'Enlightenment' politics had its dark underside in the ever-proliferating network of disciplinary mechanisms . . .
>
> (Sheridan, 1980)

Foucault (1975) suggests that the 'scientific method' of observation and evaluation was related to a growing post-enlightenment preoccupation with rules and normality. It was this tradition, in its extreme form giving rise to the Inquisition, which has also come to underpin the acceptability of making judgements on others in relation to prevailing norms. It is this aspect of scientism that has become a characteristic feature of contemporary, social institutions such as schools, prisons and hospitals. More significant even than the evaluation of individuals according to some arbitrary social standard disguised in the language of apparently objective science is the bureaucratic style of administration that this makes possible. In practice, this means that issues which are, in reality, questions of alternative values are perceived as technical problems to which a 'right answer' – an 'optimum solution' exists, waiting only to be discovered.

School assessment procedures are no exception to this pattern and, as Berger[13] has pointed out, are particularly revealing of changes in the basis of social order taking place at the present time *within* the prevailing rationality. The 'ever-proliferating network of disciplinary mechanisms' to which Sheridan (1980), citing Foucault, refers, the supersession of costly, violent forms of power by 'a subtle, calculated technology of subjection' may be identified as a relatively new feature of school assessment techniques. Hitherto, Berger suggests, the dominant form of evaluation was a *visible* form of social power in which the teacher or the examiner was vested with the personal right to pass judgement on a pupil's performance. Although open to all the vagaries of arbitrary personal preference, this system did at least allow some comeback by the individual pupil if he disagreed with the assessment because the judgement was clearly, in the last resort, the inevitably personal judgement of an individual. This system also allowed a good deal of diversity given the equally inevitable differences in the personal predilections of examiners, often much to the candidate's chagrin.

The trend in recent years, however, has been to deplore the various injustices inherent in such an approach and to seek a more 'objective', scientific and thus fairer approach to assessment. This has led to the increasingly sophisticated identification of behavioural norms upon which to base both teaching – as in the 'behavioural objectives' movement[14] and assessment –as in the current criterion-referenced[15] approach to testing. Linked as this movement is, both practically and ideologically, with the growth of corporate management strategies at every level of the educational bureaucracy,[16] it is a short step from the replacement of the traditional subjective assessment, by the more 'objective' technically sophisticated 'monitoring' as a pedagogic strategy, to its use as an administrative strategy – a means of individual and, indeed, system control. As the assessment is increasingly oriented to explicit norms of performance, to centrally or perhaps regionally generated criteria rather than, as hitherto, to the largely implicit criteria of the individual assessor, the social power which the imposition of those norms represents becomes increasingly invisible, hidden in the disguise of a bland and neutral technology in just the same way that 'corporate planning' disguises value judgements as scientific, rational, objective solutions to problems.

This, then, is another example of that suppression, in Habermas's terms, of 'ethics' (praktisch) as a category of life referred to earlier. If the implications are currently more visible at the more explicitly scientific end of the assessment scale, such as the psychological labelling of children with learning or behavioural difficulties or adults in mental institutions,[17] examples of this trend, which will affect all teachers and pupils and which are likely to become increasingly significant, are not hard to find.

In England, for example, the current government requirement on the combined GCE/CSE Examination Boards to furnish standardized criteria of performance for each subject in the new 16 + public examination, is a clear step in this direction. The government's Assessment of Performance Unit and similar moves towards monitoring school and system performance on the part of local authorities are equally, manifestations of the same trend.[18]

In France, to cite another contrasting example, because of the very centralized nature of the administration in which the institution and even the region are relatively insignificant as independent units of account, the trend towards normative assessment control has been much more at the level of the individual rather than the institution. Although pressure group opposition has rescinded, for the time being at least, the decision to pursue the computer-storage of elaborate individual records of personal academic and family background data for each child throughout his school career (a procedure which was instituted for a time following the 1975 Haby reforms), teachers in French schools have nevertheless found themselves almost totally responsible for that process of assessing and channelling pupils formerly performed by the now largely defunct examination system. This theoretically more efficient system of 'orientation' informed by national standardized tests, in which a panel of teachers *collectively* decide on the recommended future courses for each pupil, has the dual effect of being very much harder for the pupil to dispute and of encouraging conformity of standards. There is less and less place for the vagaries of the individual teacher or for the pupil to resist the label in a way he might have done in the one-off attempt of a formal examination. Because standards and recommendations are collective, they are impersonal and 'objective', their arbitrary nature so well hidden as to be removed from the agenda of discussion (Bachrach and Baratz, 1962).

These examples show clearly how the emphasis on understanding the nature of the prevailing ideology in the theories of continental Marxists and social philosophers such as Marcuse, Habermas and Foucault is central to the delineation of a sociology of assessment. Indeed, in recognizing the limitations of existentialism, structural

Marxism and, in particular, of analyses that take class conflict as their central theme, they have made a major contribution to the sociology of education as a whole which has latterly become so preoccupied with issues of class and inequality that other equally fundamental issues about the relationship between schooling and the nature of social life as a *whole* – of which assessment is just one – have not received the attention they deserve.

If the general basis for a sociology of assessment is now identified, the above discussion of changing styles of assessment procedure makes clear the need for the fourth stage of analysis identified earlier, in which such general trends are situated in the specific social settings of individual societies. A short summary of the arguments so far may help to clarify the need for this fourth step. Briefly what is being suggested is that school assessment – defined in an inclusive sense as all that activity in the education system upon which decisions about the performance of pupils, teachers, institutions and, ultimately, the education system as a whole are based – is central to the contemporary process and organization of schooling in mass, industrial societies. An explanation of why such assessment is so central to contemporary schooling is offered in terms of the form of rationality which emerged with the industrial revolution – itself closely associated with the new economic order of capitalism. This rationality emphasized, on the one hand, individualism and, on the other, a scientific-technical approach to both management and production. Thus, not only did it celebrate technology as the chief instrument of progress, it provided for the development and proliferation of various kinds of administrative bureaucracy through which the burgeoning infrastructure of the state could be provided and controlled.[19] One element in this infrastructure was the innovation of state provision for mass education.

However, whilst the institution of such provision is common to all industrial societies, there is clearly a good deal of variation between societies in the way in which the national educational system is organized. If elements of Weber's 'ideal type' of bureaucracy are necessarily manifest in every national education system, there are equally significant variations in bureaucratic style so that notions of hierarchy, general rules, continuous and impersonal offices and the separation between official and private life must be inter-related with historically specific social situations (Gouldner, 1948).

> No attempt has been made (by students of bureaucracy) to show the socio-psychological and institutional differences in the process of bureaucratization in so far as it can be attributed to a retarded breakdown of feudal institutions and traditions. As a result, little attention has been given to the effect of noncontemporaneous industrialization in different countries on the rise of their respective bureaucracies. It would be very important to investigate the effect of such factors on the pattern of obedience to authority and of the degree of spontaneous public co-operation which characterizes the different 'bureaucratic cultures' of the Western world.
>
> (Bendix, 1952)

Thus, there are different styles of bureaucratic provision just as there are significant differences in all the other social institutions in countries which nevertheless share a common capitalist and industrial development. An adequate sociology must thus be able to explain the particular practices of specific societies within this general theoretical framework. As far as the specific issue of assessment is concerned, it must provide a purchase on questions such as why some schooling systems place greater emphasis than others on public examinations or why some countries are currently greatly preoccupied with identifying formal bases for accountability whilst others are not.

Stage Four: Common Problems, Different Solutions

Any explanation of the way in which educational practices vary between societies which share a common capitalist order must be grounded in an historical analysis. Any one point in time witnesses the interaction between objectively changing social, political and economic conditions and the purposes and perceptions of individual and, hence, groups of actors, which are both structured by and in turn serve to structure the changing social reality. Thus, the precise form of national educational problems, how they are perceived and the range of potential solutions that may be considered, must be understood as the general problems of education within capitalist societies, mediated by the constraints of existing social forms – geographical, cultural, legal, economic, socio-political and religious – which together build up the patterns of meaning and perception at national, institutional and individual levels. Thus to understand sociologically the differences in assessment practice of two countries such as England and France – to use the examples quoted earlier – it is necessary to consider the whole fabric of their respective social orders. Clearly this is an enormous task and the brief substantive discussion offered here is only intended as an illustration of the kind of analysis that would be involved.

England and France: Two Different Traditions

In France, the contemporary approach to educational provision finds its origins in an administrative style already firmly established before the 1789 revolution (Halevy, 1960; Halls, 1976). This style was readily harnessed in the service of the twin ideologies underpinning the foundation of the education system – the one, equality (the legacy of the 1789 revolution) and, the other, administrative efficiency and national homogeneity (dating from the marginally later era of Napoleon). These two ideologies have traditionally found expression in an extremely centralized administration. The monopoly over public examinations and certification instituted by Napoleon is typical in this respect and very different from the proliferation of examining bodies in England. But examinations are only one of a variety of bureaucratic procedures such as the provision of detailed performance criteria of the expected outcomes of each stage of schooling, the close control of educational publishing, the central provision of detailed timetables and syllabuses, manuals on pedagogy and national provision for the inspection of individual teachers which manifest the centralized nature of the administration of education.

By contrast the English education system is decentralized to an extent that has at times bordered on anarchy. Born of a very different feudal legacy and political and ecclesiastical power bases (Veulard,1970; Archer, 1979), the establishment of a legal basis for a system of education in 1870 was more an act of recognition than the result of any very deliberate attempt to create such a system. The power of local interests (Simon, 1965) and an ideology of grassroots autonomy has meant that control of the English education system has had to be largely informal, principally and most successfully through public examinations (Broadfoot, 1980).

Explanations of these differences require a socio-political perspective which contrasts the cross-cutting effects of class, clerical and geographical interests in France with the fact that, in England, politics are dominated by class issues simply 'because nothing else is important' (Finer, 1970). The relative homogeneity in the values of the English bourgeoisie in contrast to those of the French has allowed the development of a stable two party system and democratic state (Smith, 1980). The gradual political transformation from absolutism to democracy in England versus the abrupt transition on the continent has, in turn, affected the nature of the administration. If, in England, the central administrative machinery has traditionaly grown according to need, in contrast to the purposive modelling (in the tradition of Napoleon in France – Laqueur, 1973), the bureaucracy has also grown in proportion to the weakness of the political structure. In France the administration has tended to be 'above politics', many decisions being taken under the pretext of administration which are in fact political. It is both deconcentrated – giving it a great deal of power locally – and specialist. In England, by contrast, the administration is generalist and centralized and, thus, less directly powerful. Yet this is itself the 'genius of the English'.[20]

The increasing complexity and diversity of contemporary social formations makes problematic traditional forms of bureaucratic control which depend on the application of pre-determined rules through a hierarchical structure of neutral officials. Increased 'steering capacity' depends on the substitution of a more 'managerial technology' which emphasizes *outcomes* rather than *processes* (Dale, 1980). Such a capacity depends on the creation of a network of reciprocal evaluation and communication systems which can loosely be subsumed under the rubric of 'accountability' procedures. The operation of this control is clearly evident in the quotations from the English teachers at the beginning of the paper who, whilst feeling formally free, know they will be held accountable *'post hoc'* on their results.

This very brief sketch of some of the more significant historical differences in the development of two education systems illustrates the fact that individual actors in an education system – administrators or teachers, for example – whilst standing in an objectively similar relationship to the problems of the development of the corporate capitalist state are likely to experience those problems very differently. A sociology of assessment would thus address, for example, the significance of process versus product forms of control as it affects the changing conditions under which teachers in classrooms have to work. In England, the APU, the 1977 government Green Paper, the growing power of school governors, local authority testing, central government directives to publish public examination results, and attempts to exert increasing control over the curriculum would be examples of such a study. In France the issues would be different – the events of 1968, teacher strikes, the moves to deconcentration, the abolition of formal assessment except for the Baccalaureat in favour of 'orientation', the new emphasis on vocational courses – but the perspective would be the same.

As far as the justification for a sociology of assessment is concerned, the arguments of this paper might well be left here. Although the analyses have been largely in terms of macro social theory and comparative systems theory, the utility of the concept of assessment or evaluation as a means of understanding some of the central and common aspects of contemporary schooling practices, how these relate to the general context of industrial capitalist society and the reasons for specific national variations in such practices, should now be clear. But if the analysis so far has gone some way towards fulfilling the remit set out at the beginning of this paper in terms of making a contribution to the development of the academic sociology of education, little has been said so far on the bearing such an analysis might have on 'teachers' private troubles'. Thus a brief consideration of how a sociology of assessment may help to shed light on the day-to-day dilemmas of the classroom forms the final part of this paper.

Teachers' Troubles – Personal or Public?

In any country the classroom situation in which an individual teacher finds him or herself will be determined by the interaction of a number of consistent factors. These are likely to include the age, ability, previous experience and expectations of the particular group of pupils concerned. Also relevant is the physical layout of the classroom, the available resources and equipment, and the size of the class. The time of day and the length of lessons are significant features, as is the extent to which the teacher is free to determine his or her own pedagogy and curriculum content. Teachers are likely to experience various forms of influence and control – from training received, from colleagues, from the management hierarchy in the school, from advisers and inspectors, subject associations, examination syllabuses, from national pronouncements on priorities and desirable practice and from the local community, notably school governors (where they exist), parents and employers.

This constellation of influences will not be the same for any two teachers anywhere. To the extent that similarities exist, however, one of the main sources is likely to be a common situation within a particular national education system. The way in which the provision of education is organized in any one country is likely to include a fairly close determination of the training and qualifications of teachers, the resources available for the provision of teaching posts (affecting such things as class size), school buildings and equipment, the organization of the different ages and abilities of pupils into various types and levels of school and class groupings, the amount of central control over the content of teaching as against the degree of autonomy enjoyed by the school and its personnel, the provision for in-service training and guidance and the scope for the local community either formally (through local officials and politicians) or informally (through various kinds of pressure group) to influence any or all of these features of school life. To this long but by no means exhaustive list must be added the more amorphous but very powerful influence of ideology and national educational tradition which gives rise in France, for example, to strong teacher support for centralized control as the basis for equality of opportunity and in England, by contrast, to strong teacher support for 'grass roots' autonomy in order that the maximum scope may be given to teachers' professional judgement.

In a decentralized country such as England, the relative weakness of such central influences, in comparison with a formally centralized one such as France, is complemented by the relatively greater power of the local education authority and the school institution itself. In England, teachers make little mention of the official administrative structure outside the school in defining their accountability, but rather define their responsibilities as to their department and the headteacher on the one hand, and to the pupils on the other.[21] This is an important difference, in terms of teachers' day-to-day activity between English and French teachers since the latter typically hold a strongly contrasting perspective in which their civil servant status in particular leads them to a perception of accountability as first and foremost to the national organization in the person of the inspector, rather than to the school as an institution, the head, colleagues or, indeed, pupils.

But this sort of systematic similarity in the objective conditions which surround teaching or the subjective perspectives which condition it, may be swamped by variations in the personal characteristics of teachers in terms of, for example, career stage, age, sex, class background, geographical location, race or qualifications. It is quite possible to find as much diversity between teachers *within* any one national education system as between teachers in different national education systems. One teacher in France may say,

> the teacher is absolutely free in his class . . . it's the results that matter not how they are achieved
>
> (primary school directrice, France)

or

> everybody teaches what he is in the final analysis
>
> (primary school teacher, France)

whereas another may say

> a teacher in France has no right to teach according to his own ideas . . .
>
> (lycée teacher, France)

or

> a teacher is a civil servant and his job is to adapt to the level of his class what he has to teach them.
>
> (former lycée teacher, now in local administration of education)

By the same token, one teacher in England may say

> I would say we've now reached an all time low in formal accountability
>
> (teacher, sixth form college, England)

whereas another says

> the change to freedom came slowly but it is moving back at a much quicker pace
>
> (primary school teacher, England)

Equally it is possible to find teachers in two different national systems talking in a very similar vein:

> We know what we're supposed to cover and how we do it is up to us. Really the responsibility is to ensure the exam sets reach as high a standard as possible and that the non-exam sets, I suppose I cynically say, are kept quiet – but I'd like to think they got something out of it.
>
> (secondary school teacher, Devon, England)

> In France there is a policy of producing academic failures, as a function of the needs of the national economy. A minority élite of the workforce – the technicians – are trained to control them.'
>
> (secondary school teacher, Calvados, France)

The typicality of these quotations, or of any others that might have been cited, is not the issue. They are sufficient to illustrate the difficulties inherent in any systematic, sociological analysis of teachers' practice; a difficulty which is clearly exacerbated when the further sources of variation, which a comparative perspective reveals, are recognised (as happens all too rarely).

All a sociology of assessment can hope to do is thus (1) to seek to identify, within the wealth of empirical variation, typical manifestations in classroom practice of the domination of the assessment rationality discussed earlier; and (2) aim at a greater understanding of the way in which this same rationality informs different styles of administrative organization and control as these affect classroom practice. Under (1) would be included those aspects of assessment which have already received most sociological attention – teacher-pupil interaction and evaluation in terms of expectations, labelling, stereotyping and conditioning through both the overt and the hidden curriculum. To this might be added less well explored areas such as the changes effected by different examination styles on teacher-pupil interaction and pupils' self-perception, the effect on teacher activity of the growing school self-evaluation movement or the relationship between national and local testing initiatives and curricular and pedagogic change in the classroom.

Patient and perceptive interactionist and ethnographic studies of this kind by sociologists have not so far typically been linked into a broader analysis of the origins and effects of such practices in the relationship between schooling and its historical and contemporary social context. Thus, a sociology of assessment which articulates these various levels can help to provide for both a much more penetrating sociology and for greater insight into why teachers find themselves subjectively or objectively constrained into adopting some of their most typical forms of behaviour.

Aim (2) fulfils a similar rationale from a rather different perspective. This is the way in which the educational policies which directly affect classroom practice are the product of those historically determined structural and ideological constraints which operate interactively at institutional, local, and national level. This currently very neglected area would include studies of the actual or perceived formal and informal constraints on teachers' practice arising out of particular features of educational administration. These might include public examinations, standardized tests, central curriculum directives, textbook control, financial policies, staffing policies or inspection procedures. Although many of these areas have nothing specifically to do with assessment, they are relevant to a *sociology of assessment* in that they represent the way in which the administrative bureaucracy – a device which finds its inner logic in the notion of individual responsibility and evaluation as discussed earlier – relates to the practice of teaching.[22]

It may well be that it is substantive sociologies of this kind which focus upon a particular aspect of school practice such as assessment or curriculum or teacher socialization that prove most helpful in overcoming the widespread dissatisfaction with macro structural theory on the one hand and empirically impeccable, ungeneralizable case studies on the other. If it does prove possible to overcome the now strongly institutionalized, as well as conceptually difficult, divisions between micro and macro perspectives, it should be increasingly possible for sociologists to direct their attention towards a better understanding of some of the fundamental changes currently confronting capitalist societies and the various ways in which such societies are seeking to respond to these more or less critical developments through their education systems. If, as Marcuse would have us believe, the growing domination of the scientific-technical rationality over every aspect of social life, whilst essential to capitalism, is also fundamentally destructive to society as a whole, the questions at issue are not simply niceties of sociological analysis but fundamental problems about the direction of social change. In relation to assessment in particular it may well be that, as Habermas suggests, the assessment which was so instrumental to the formation of contemporary society, proves in the long run also to be its undoing in a growing

> lack of understanding why despite the advanced stage of technological development the life of the individual is still determined by the dictates of professional careers, the ethics of status competition, and by values of possessive individualism and available substitute gratifications: why the institutionalized struggle for existence, the discipline of alienated labour, and the eradication of sensuality and aesthetic gratification are perpetuated. To this sensibility the structural elimination of practical problems from a depoliticized public realm must become unbearable. However, it will give rise to a political force only if this sensibility comes into contact with a problem that the system cannot solve. For the future I see one such problem. The amount of social wealth produced by industrially advanced capitalism and the technical and organizational conditions under which this wealth is produced make it ever more difficult to link status assignment in an even subjectively convincing manner to the mechanism for the evaluation of individual achievement.
>
> (Habermas, 1971)

If the need for a sociology of asessment is increasingly pressing, as teachers experience more and more corporate management in the classroom, such a sociology may equally be necessary to explain the progressive breaking down of the traditional methods of legitimation and social control provided by the institution of mass schooling.

Notes

1 This is well illustrated by the range of titles in Methuen's 'Contemporary Sociology of the School' series.

2 For example, in England, qualifying examinations for doctors were instituted in 1815 by the Society of Apothecaries, for solicitors in 1835 and for accountants in 1880.

3 This is illustrated in England in the 1917 institution of the first School Certificate Examination in which candidates were required to pass in five or more *academic* subjects drawn from each of four groups of English, languages, science and mathematics, with music and manual subjects a fifth optional group.

4 These interviews which involved 43 teachers drawn from two primary and four secondary schools in one English local education authority, were part of an SSRC research project under the direction of the author which was concerned to analyse different modes of accountability in England and France.

5 This practice, already widespread among schools in one form or another, will shortly become a statutory obligation on schools.

6 I have dealt with this issue at more length in my paper 'Assessment, curriculum and control in the changing pattern of Centre-Local relations', *Local Government Studies*, November/December 1980. There is now a considerable literature in this area to which the Open University Course 'Curriculum Evaluation and Assessment in Educational Institutions', Block I, provides as good an introduction as any.

7   The Certificate of Vocational Eduation (the Voc) is intended for sixteen year olds with low grade CSEs who combine further general education with vocational study. The 'I' level, as currently conceived, will be a means of broadening the curriculum for highly academic, A-level students.

8   In this paper the terms 'advanced industrial society' and 'advanced capitalist society' are used for the most part interchangeably, depending on the emphasis required. Some confusion arises from the fact that many nominally socialist societies such as the Eastern Block, and China, have education systems which are essentially similar to those of capitalist societies as far as the issues raised in this paper are concerned. A full explanation of this would be very complex and it is probably sufficient to recognize that these common features arise partly because, whatever the political ideology, the features of industrial production are in many ways very similar and partly because the form of production in many socialist societies is state capitalism. More generally still, many of the functions of assessment in particular, as is argued later in the paper, are a necessary feature of any society characterized by a division of labour.

9   Tönnies' analysis in terms of 'gemeinschaft' and 'gesellschaft' provides another example. A good general introduction to Durkheim's work is provided in Giddens, A. (1978) *Durkheim,* London, Fontana, and to Weber in MacRae, D. (1974) *Weber* Glasgow, Fontana. For Durkheim, Weber and Parsons see also Raison, T. (Ed) (1969) *The Founding Fathers of Social Science* Harmondsworth, Penguin, for a general introduction and further references, also Gramsci, A. (1974) *Prison Notebooks,* Harmondsworth, Penguin. One of the more accessible introductions to the work of Althusser may be found in Althusser, L. 'Ideology and Ideological State Apparatuses' in Cosin, B. (Ed) (1972) *Education Structure and Society,* Harmondsworth, Penguin. The most comprehensive statement of Bourdieu's work may be found in Bourdieu, P. and Passeron J.C. (1977) *Reproduction* London, Sage, and of Bernstein's in his *Class Codes and Control* Vol. 3 2nd edition, London, R.K.P. (1977).

10   Parsons' work is currently very much out of favour since many sociologists consider it manifests the worst kind of structural-functionalist stasis originating from the kind of 'armchair sociology' which pays little regard – unlike the founding fathers referred to here – to the insights to be obtained from empirical study. Recently however some of Bernstein's work has used some of Parsons' pattern variables in a way that indicates they may still have a useful role to play.

11   Habermas (1971) suggests that pre-industrial society was also pre-ideological society since ideologies are only necessary when the social order is problematic. It is thus particularly interesting that the term was invented in 1795 during the French Revolution by Antoinne Destutt de Tracy and from its original association with radical scientific thought, took on a perjorative meaning after Napoleon as 'thought which refuses to understand itself as historical' (Matthews, 1980).

12   Weber's discussion in 'The Protestant Ethic and the Spirit of Capitalism' of the vital contribution of the motivation provided by a new individualist religious ethic for the development of capitalism is central here in testifying to the fundamental change in modes of rationality and of association which took place at this time.

13   From an interview with Guy Berger, Départment de Sciences de l'Education, Université de Paris, Vincennes, in connection with the above mentioned SSRC project (note 2).

14   This movement, now gradually going out of fashion again, gained most support in the United States.

15   This movement is, by contrast, very much with us. See, for example, POPHAM, W.J. and HUSEK, T.R. (1969) 'Implications of criterion-referenced measurement', *Journal of Educational Measurement,* 6 (1) pp. 1–9.

16   Examples of this growth are readily apparent in, for example, the post-reorganization style of local government decision-making in England or the recent institution of the Service de Statistiques et Sondages in France which is charged with the collection, and transmission, of computer-stored data as a basis for more efficient educational administration.

17   The commission of dissidents to mental hospital in Eastern Block countries is one of the clearest examples of this. The Open University course E202 also provides a good discussion of this issue in its unit on 'Diagnosis and Testing'.

18   The 'Assessment of Performance Unit' (APU) was set up within the DES in 1975 to monitor national standards in each of the major curricular areas and 'to identify areas of underachievement'. It seems likely that the monitoring will in practice be confined to maths, science, English and modern languages owing to the technical problems other curricular areas present. The APU model has been taken up by several local authorities for their own purposes whilst others are involved in the LEASIB project being developed at the National Foundation of Educational Research to provide item banks which local education authorities can draw upon for standardized testing purposes.

19   I am not arguing here that there were no bureaucracies in pre-industrial society – ancient China provides one of the most classic examples in its civil service – merely that, with industrial society, bureaucracy became increasingly the norm, just as 'the State', defined as the administrative and political functions of government, came to accept as 'normal' that it should be charged with the provision of an increasing variety of services ranging from transport to law and order to public health to education which had hitherto been provided privately, if at all.

20   A term used in an interview by a French Inspecteur Generale in connection with the research cited in note 2.

21   Source: see note 2.

22   The work of writers such af Offe and Crozier are relevant in this respect, as well as that of Habermas himself.

References

ARCHER, M. (1979) *The Social Origins of Education Systems* London, Sage.

BACHRACH, P. and BARATZ, M.S. (1962) 'The two faces of power', *American Political Science Review* 56, December.

BENDIX, R. (1952) 'Bureaucracy and the problem of power' in MERTON, R.K. *et al* (Eds) *Bureaucracy* New York, The Free Press.

BOWLES, S. and GINTIS, H. (1977) 'IQ in the U.S. class structure' in GLEESON, D. (Ed) *Identity and Structure* Driffield, Nafferton Books.

BROADFOOT, P.M. (1979) *Assessment, Schools and Society* London, Methuen.

BROADFOOT, P.M. (1980) 'Accountability, Social Forms and System Control: A Comparative Perspective', Keynote Paper for the International Sociological Association (Education Sub-Committee) Annual Conference, Paris 1980.

CHERAKOUI, M. (1977) 'Bernstein and Durkheim: Two theories of change in education systems' *Harvard Educational Review* 48 (4) November, pp. 556–564.

CROZIER, M. (1964) *The Bureaucratic Phenomenon,* London, Tavistock.

CROZIER, M. (1969) 'The vicious circle of bureaucracy' in BURNS, T. (Ed) *Industrial Man* Harmondsworth, Penguin, pp. 250–62.

DALE, R. (1977) 'Implications for the rediscovery of the hidden curriculum for the sociology of teaching', in GLEESON, D. (Ed) *op. cit.*

DALE, R. (1980) 'Education and the Capitalist State – Contributions and Contradictions' in APPLE, M. (Ed) *Cultural and Economic Reproduction in Education* London, Routledge and Kegan Paul.

FINER, S.E. (1970) *Comparative Government* London, Allen Lane.

FLEMING, E.S. and ANTTONEN, R.G. (1971) 'Teacher expectancy or my fair lady' *AERA Journal* 8, p. 106.

FOUCAULT, M. (1975) *Surveiller et Punir,* Paris, Callimard.

GERTH, H. and MILLS, C.W. (1952) 'A Marx for the managers' in MERTON, R.K. *et al* (Eds) *Bureaucracy* Free Press.

GOULDNER, A. (1948) 'On Weber's analysis of bureaucratic rules', in MERTON, R.K. *et al, op. cit.*

HABERMAS, J. (1968) 'Technology and science as "ideology"' (for Herbert Marcuse on his seventieth birthday) later published in *Towards a Rational Society.*

HABERMAS, J. (1971) *Towards a Rational Society* London, Heinemann.

HALEVY, E. (1960) *England in 1815*, Vol. 1 of History of the English People in the 19th Century London, Benn.

HALLS, N.D. (1976) *Education, Culture and Politics in Modern France* London, Pergamon.

HARGREAVES, D.H. (1967) *Social Relations in a Secondary School* London, Routledge and Kegal Paul.

HARGREAVES, D.H. (1979) 'Individuality in Education' Paper given to the Standing Conference on Studies in Education (London).

HEXTALL, I. and SARUP, M. (1977) 'School knowledge, evaluation and alienation' in YOUNG, M. and WHITTY, G. (Eds) *Society, State and Schooling* Lewes, The Falmer Press.

HOLT, J. (1969) 'Schools are bad places for kids', *Saturday Evening Post* February 1969, reprinted in *The Underachieving School* Harmondsworth, Pelican (1970).

JACKSON, P.W. (1968) *Life in Classrooms* Chicago, Holt, Rinehart and Winston.

KAMIN, L.J. (1974) *The Science and Politics of IQ* New York, Wiley.

KARIER, C.J., VIOLAS, P. and SPRING, J. (Eds) (1973) *Roots of Crisis* Chicago, Rand McNally.

KEDDIE, N. (1971) 'Classroom knowledge' in YOUNG, M.F.D. (Ed) *Knowledge and Control* London, Collier Macmillan.

LACEY, C. (1970) *Hightown Grammar* Manchester, Manchester University Press.

LAQUEUR, T.W. (1973) 'English and French education in the nineteenth century', Review Essay, *History of Education Quarterly* Spring.

MACKAY, R. (1974) 'Standardized tests: Objective/objectified measures of competence' in CICOUREL, A.V. *et al, Language Use and School Performance* New York, Academic Press.

MARCUSE, H. (1964) *One-Dimensional Man: Studies in the Ideology of Advanced Industrial Society,* London, Routledge and Kegan Paul.

MARCUSE, H. (1970) 'Freedom and Freud's theory of the instincts' in *Five lectures* translated by Shapiro, J.J. and Weber, S.M. Boston, Beacon Press.

MATTHEWS, M.R. (1980) *The Marxist Theory of Schooling* Brighton, Harvester.

MORRISON, A. (1974) 'Formal and informal assessment in the classroom', *Education in the North* pp.63–67.

MURPHY, R.J.L. (1981) 'O-level grades and teachers' estimates as predictors of the A-level results in UCCA applicants' *British Journal of Educational Psychology* February.

NASH, R. (1976) *Teacher Expectation and Pupil Learning* London, Routledge and Kegan Paul.

OFFE, C. (1975) 'The Capitalist State and the Problem of Policy Formation' in LINDBERG, L.J., ALFORD, R., CROUCH, C. and OFFE, C. (Eds) *Stress and Contradiction in Modern Capitalism* Lexington, Mass. Lexington Books.

PIRSIG, R.M. (1976) *Zen and the Art of Motor Cycle Maintenance* London, Corgi.

POWELL, J.L. (1973) *Selection for University in Scotland* Edinburgh, University of London Press for SCRE.

RIST, R.C. (1970) 'Student social class and teacher expectations: The self-fulfilling prophecy in ghetto education', *Harvard Educational Review* 40 (3).

ROSENTHAL, R. and JACOBSEN, L. (1968) *Pygmalion in the Classroom* New York, Holt, Rinehart and Winston.

SCOTTISH COUNCIL FOR RESEARCH IN EDUCATION (1976) *Wastage on National Certificate Courses* Edinburgh.

SHARP, R. and GREEN, A. (1975) *Education and Social Control* London, Routledge and Kegan Paul.

SHERIDAN, M. (1980) *Foucault - the Will to Truth* London, Tavistock.

SIMON, B. (1953) *Intelligence Testing and the Comprehensive School* London, Lawrence and Wishart.

SIMON, B. (1965) *Education and the Labour Movement 1870–1920,* London, London University Press.

SMITH, G. (1980) *Politics in Western Europe* London, Heinemann.

VEULARD, A. (1970) 'Centralization and freedom in education', *Comparative Education* 6 (1) March.

WILLIAMS, I.C. and BOREHAM, W.I. (1972) *The Predictive Value of CSE Grades for Further Education* London, Evans/Methuen Educational.

WILLIS, P. (1977) *Learning to Labour,* Farnborough, Saxon House.

Known and Understood: Problematics in Developing an Understanding of the Social Effects of Schooling

Paul Olson,
The Ontario Institute for Studies in Education

Vignette and Plot: The Problems of Organizing the Meaning of the Whole from the Parts

The debate among critical theorists about the socio-political and structural economic aspects of education has now produced a variety of accounts of how schools – through hidden curricula – subvert their officially stated goals of allowing each individual to reach Carlyle's ideal of becoming 'all that (s)he may'. The evidence has mounted that in advanced industrial capitalist countries the functional relationship of school and society is such that the dream of schooling as a catalyst to mobility and achievement will largely remain a dream for whole classes of our youth.

The arguments criticizing school and society, and the role of teaching as a profession, especially in schooling's treatment of race, class, and gender, are as varied as they are voluminous. Illich, for example, (1970) assures us that liberation, regardless of class, will remain illusory until we wrestle education as a learning process from the control of the schools, or 'deschool' society.

Weinberg (1975), Holt (1964), Kohl (1970) and MacLaren (1980), among others, assure us that education is a 'shuck'. Bowles and Gintis (1976); with Jencks (1972); (1979); (1980); raised empirically documented arguments for a neo-Marxist conception of the institutional and ideological role of the schools as a service sector to the dominant economic order. Jencks, in his most recent monograph (1979), provides compelling statistical data to the effect that social class background (and other trappings entailed in stratified social structure) is the primary causal determinant for what individuals will achieve or fail to achieve in cognitive, economic or political terms, despite liberal claims of a 'meritocracy'.

Such empirically based interpretations of schooling do not, though, exhaust the field for contending candidates. Castells (1980), for instance, postulates that contemporary capitalism is facing a fiscal 'crisis of the state' and that, while corporate and governmental responses to it have been disjunctive and contradictory, it is probable that they will become increasingly repressive, especially for the most marginalized members of society. It seems a logical extrapolation from this model to assume that schools will mirror this repressive possibility.

Amid this flood of conceptual models, demographers such as Jackson (Jackson *et al*, 1978) complex and confound this picture in their analyses of declining enrolments. What their analyses raise are implications for the political economy and role of the school. Braverman (1975), focusing on the workforce, in general, and Apple (1979), focusing on the school context, in specific, argue that the mandarins of social control (whether by calculated design or by consequence of policies put unthinkingly into place) have initiated programs that act both to deskill workers and to preempt the traditional self-direction of the teacher.

These macro-structural analyses are complemented and counter-pointed by micro-interactional analyses of classrooms. Bernstein (1971), as an instance, shows how a speaker's linguistic style is used in the school situation to sort, reify, and legitimate such practices as 'tracking'. Amplifying the finding that linguistic style is a function of class, he argues that the development of an affinity between teachers, middle-class children and their families is insured by virtue of the template (or identity) in their linguistic styles; middle-class children will tend to express themselves in 'universalistic' codes, the linguistic modality of the ruling class, while working-class children and their families will tend to express themselves through 'particularistic' linguistic styles. One can readily infer the interactive and cumulative effects of this rift between the *Gesellschaft* institution of the school and the *Gemeinschaft* unit of the family (particularly the working-class family) upon the child's ability and willingness to learn. Bourdieu and Passeron (1977a, 1927b, 1977c, 1979), again assessing class influences on individual cognitive differences, argue that 'cultural capital' of the society is made differentially available to various social groups. These 'assets', they argue, are crucial to the understanding of how our social order both maintains and reproduces endemic inequality and power differentials insofar as access to them is both controlled by dominant power groups and conforms to sanctioned patterns of institutional mobility.

Even these levels of micro-interactional analysis seem abstract, though, when compared with those of classroom ethnography. Philip Jackson (1968) and Sharp and Green (1975, 1980), to name but two sets of researchers, suggest that the very physical organization of schooling, e.g., schedules, physical orientation of desks, etc., inculcates in children the *gestalt* elements of power, reward, and denial; they argue that the physical detail of the classroom simply mirrors at a microcosmic level the individualist ideology and hegemonic structure of our social order.

This litany of analyses is indeed abbreviated and incomplete; theories of cultural production and reproduction, for example, have only been touched upon. But the thread to be drawn from this small and tangled web of examples is that while it is clear that schools as agents of social change and justice are hardly deserving of 'top grades', what is less than clear is how all the various accounts of schooling and its social effects can be drawn together to provide a unified account of how schools actually function to achieve the effects they do.

Contextual Limits and Epistemological Problems in the Production of Our Conceptual Models

The examples I shall present here deal with seemingly trivial, but nonetheless real, limits to any effort to develop a concept of schooling's effects. The first example is drawn from the everyday world of direct participants in schools, i.e. students, teachers, parents. Schools, on the surface, appear to many of these participants to function more or less successfully. For whatever reason, many, if not most, students muddle or troop through the school fulfilling its requirements without further ado. This may appear to radical educators and sociologists, including myself, a hopelessly naïve interpretation of schooling, but I submit that it is critical for understanding why many teachers intuitively resist radical models: the conception that schools function as institutional agents of the reproduction of class structure runs counter to teachers' own intuitively felt and experientially desired understanding of teaching from which, despite adverse conditions, they gain both joy and dignity. It is useful to remember this as a critical point of pedagogy and praxis, since it is at this moment of *conscientizacao* (Freire, 1970, 1973, 1978) that many teachers begin, as we attempt to explain our theories to them. Teachers resist critical models largely because the ethos of critical explanation defies their memory and their grasp of their own lived experience.

The second and equally naïve example, drawn from UNESCO sources, is that models that focus on the school's failure to liberate individuals from influences of class, race and gender are empirically limited because the majority of the world's school-age children are not in what are traditionally labelled as schools (UNESCO, 1980). Schools as a common modality for processing youth exist most prevalently in advanced industrial societies. The analysis of schooling outlined above assumes implicitly not only that 'schools' belong to contemporary advanced industrial societies, but to capitalist societies. Our models, therefore, apply to no more than one in ten of the world's youth and their historical applicability spans, generously speaking, no more than two centuries (Berkeley, 1978). Again, this may seem a boorishly obvious point, but there is a more general point to be accrued.

Heidegger (1975) reminds us that all social relations are embedded in historically specific junctures of time and space. Additionally Schutz (1971) and Husserl (1973, 1969) remind us that these social relations are themselves always 'transcendent' of all possible analyses of them; as phenomena, they embed all possible analyses and, no matter how 'artful', any particular analysis must remain that of a partial recovery.

These phenomenological principles have several interesting corollaries. First, they imply that scientific inquiry cannot provide 'truth' in any absolute objectivist sense, since even the most eloquent conceptual reconstruction features of the phenomena, explanatory or otherwise, will have to be left out. Secondly, there must exist a tension between phenomena and analyses since any analysis always engenders a phenomenal reduction. Thirdly, phenomena always contain potential empirical resistance to our conceptual reconstructions. These phenomenological insights are backed by the more general canons of science: empirical texts *given* theoretical models become a possibility if, and only if, their conjectures are logically capable of refutation (Popper, 1972). Conjoined, these insights suggest that inquiry must be comparative in nature and that the parsimony of theory must be continuously checked against the alternatives within the evidence. Otherwise, knowledge becomes arbitrarily reified and loses its representational character.

Known and Understood: Sorting out Methodological, Conceptual, and Practical Tensions in our Understanding of Schooling Effects

This condensed *exegesis* of phenomenology provides a much more concrete focus for our understanding of schools than it might, initially, appear able to do. But first consider the distinction drawn by hermeneutical phenomenology (von Wright, 1971) between two types of knowledge, that is, between 'explanation' and 'understanding'. Basically, the former is conceived as oriented to achieving a description of a phenomenon's underlying structure and functional order and the latter, an interpretative grasp of a lived situation. The underlying problem expressed in this distinction expresses itself in a variety of contrasting forms: experiential versus causal analysis; objectivity versus subjectivity; the postulate of adequacy of actors' accounts versus etiology; ethnography versus structural and functional analysis; naturalism versus functionalism.

These contrasting forms, or orientations to the recovery of the social world, tend to govern the type of work researchers find it sensible to take on. For example, those who believe in etiological, causal, objectionist and functional accounts of the world tend to do structural analysis, functional analysis and/or class analyses of society. Those who believe in ethnography, naturalism, subjectivity, and the experiential knowledge argue that all possible meanings are encoded in actual situations. Examples of the latter approaches can be found in Thomas (1979), Robinson and Sullivan (1979), and Hookway and Pettit (1978). The perspectives affiliated with this general methodological *zietgiest* vary as much among themselves as they do *vis à vis* the structural and functional approaches. Ethnomethodology, as developed by Garfinkel (1967), Cicourel (1964), and McHugh (McHugh *et al* 1974), and heurmeneutical analysis, following Gadamer (1975) and Giddens (1979), offer, essentially, formalist criteria for interpreting experiential knowledge, while symbolic interactionalism offers a more content-based analysis of emergent meanings (Blumer, 1969) (Meltzer *et al*, 1975) (Shaffir *et al*, 1980).

Despite their differences, each of these qualitative analytic forms advances a general critique of the reification, rigidification, and anti-reflexivity of the etiological approach (Blumer, 1969) (Giddens, 1976, 1979) (McHugh *et al*, 1974); each have argued that the postulate of functionalism artificially imposes telology upon action.

Countering this experientially based understanding of the social world, causal analysis raises, in one form or another, the Marxian notion of false consciousness. (Althusser, 1971) (Aronowitz, 1973) (Habermas, 1970, 1971). This notion assumes that there are functionally objective elements of historical experience that have consequences for actors even when they remain undetected in subjective experience. Ideological domination (Horkheimer, 1947, 1972a, 1972b) and the operation of the state (Althusser, 1971), for example, have effective repercussions upon our action without necessarily being represented for us at a cognitive level. One *must*, according to social determinists of left or right, understand the objective relations that constitute the social collectivity if we are to evade a solipsistic relativism.

But which of these approaches to the social world is right and adequate? I would like to argue in the remaining sections of this paper that the recovery of social knowledge, in general, and our understanding of society, classrooms and schooling in particular, ought necessarily to involve a comparative *and* reciprocal exchange between both types of knowledge. I would like to suggest that this approach is more than a simple avocation of an eclectic approach but, instead, prepresents a methodological prerequisite for the production of adequately representative work.

Sorting Things Out

How do methodological habits come to play a part in our understanding of schooling? How do we become ensnared by our own analytic reductions? In order to make some suggestions about how methodological and theoretical positions come to manifest themselves in practice, I shall attempt to look again at some theories that have been critical of schooling's effects. Included in this review are: (i) arguments that schools simply reproduce social order; (ii) models of hegemony and symbolic domination; (iii) models of cultural production and symbolic domination; (iv) models of the fiscal crisis of the state; (v) arguments of cultural production and resistance.[1]

(i)   Reproduction Models

Work on the relation between schooling and the reproduction of the social order has been launched at an empirical level by American social scientists. In educational circles it is most closely identified with Jencks, Bowles and Gintis (1976), and Carnoy and Levin (1976). The target of this work has generally been to assess and, ultimately, to debunk as myth or ideology a public policy of 'equal' opportunity in the schools.

The historical specifics of the American context have made it embarrassingly clear that systematic inequality, at virtually all levels, but particularly of Black Americans, is a deeply ingrained feature of the society. Authors such as Rist (1978), among a multitude of others, have demonstrated that what Myrdal (1962) had so understated, as 'the American dilemma', was a deep and untenable set of social contradictions that had been left largely unaddressed. The response of official public policy was the development of 'equal opportunity' programs. Education was to be this policy's vehicle, for if Blacks were downtrodden and oppressed, the official rationale went, it was because as a collective they had been denied *individual* opportunity, most notably, access to education. Inequality, in a generic sense, was not viewed as undesirable since, in a 'meritocracy', stratified inequality would have to maintain. Just as the bees in Mandabel's classic piece 'Parable of the Bees, or Knaves Made Honest' strive selfishly, individually for as much honey as each can collect but, in returning to the hive, make it a part of the collective wealth, so, within society, would individual acts of ambition and greed be transformed into altruisms and collective good. While this type of rationalization for inequality finds contemporary root in the work of American functionalists, notably Parsons (1977), the most extreme and curious extension of it is found in Hernstein's (1972) notion that by virtue of American society's stratified form, it is efficiently 'husbanding' its gene pool.[2]

The problem with inequality, according to official policy, comes not with individual inequality but with *systematic* inequality of groups. The chronically downtrodden fail, according to this view, because they lack access to 'good schools' and proper education. Both militancy by Blacks in the civil rights movement and subsequent Supreme Court rulings helped to force some social policy changes. What was deemed most unacceptable by all was the principle that class- and racially-based inequalities would be intergenerationally transmitted. Equal access to schooling was to be the freedom train, delivering America to the promised land of 'justice for all'.

What Jencks, Bowles and Gintis did, using already available statistical data (e.g., the work of Duncan and Blau (1967) at Michigan; Sewell and Hauser (1975, 1976) at Wisconsin, as well as their own), was to demonstrate that schooling's influence on both cognitive and non-cognitive performance was marginal when compared to the impact of family background, intelligence and other variables. Schools, they illustrated, were neither likely nor appropriate agencies of social change because educational inequality was itself minor compared to income and other social factors. Schools were more accurately conceived, they suggested, as processing units, the effects of which were reproductive of social structure rather than transformative. This model's apparent applicability to other institutions that maintain inequality has not been restricted to the United States. Crysdale (1975, and with Beattie 1977), for example, provides data that in Canada the job obtainment of sons reflects that of their fathers.

Reproduction models, however, have been criticized by Giroux (1981a) and others for their *passive* conception of social action. This kind of critique is especially true with regard to Jencks who, focusing exclusively on relations between race and class background and school performance, failed to note the action and the interactional schemes that transpire in schools. This critique may be further strengthened by its reformulation in logical terms – that schools do not *seem* to influence cognitive performance (be the performance 'good' or 'bad') does not *analytically* warrant the conclusion that: (a) schools might not act as agents of such transformation, or (b) schools might not themselves *produce,* and not merely *reproduce* by virtue of their own practices, conditions of inequality. The reproductionists' logic, therefore, risks making unwarranted inductive leaps from *post hoc* to *ergo hoc* assumptions. Methodologically, this would be equivalent to a simplistic reductionism.

Ideologically, the adoption of this strategy is not without its consequences. By assuming that schools themselves are not active agents in social production, that the various social casts in society are fixed as to their character and identity, the theory implicitly endorses the power of the ruling strata; schools must and do mirror the substantive forces of society.

Given this analysis, what can and should educators do? Even the invectives of Bowles and Gintis to resist schooling and capitalism ring hollow. For theorists of social change, I would like to suggest, their hearts are in the right place but their heads are not. Their *moral* choice of social action, coupled with their own structural analysis, give rise to what Paul Willis has aptly dubbed a 'cowboys and indians' approach to social change. Because their statistical analysis is devoid of any microanalysis of how schooling actually operates, we are left strategically impoverished, without any notions as to what effective alternative action we might take. Thus, even the 'radical' forms of reproductionist theory leave us like Sancho Panza, ready to follow any Quixotian rebel who is courageous or mad enough to attempt the reform of the educational system.

(ii)   Models of Hegemony and Symbolic Domination

A variation of the theme of social reproduction is offered by Althusser (1971) who begins with a reformulation of the Marxian problematic: how does a society reproduce itself? How are material and ideological forces managed such that social order is maintained? Althusser (1971), like Gramsci (1971) and Giroux (1981a) and others (Karabel and Halsey, 1977; Gellner, 1974; Geertz, 1964), insist on the central role of ideology in the maintenance of control, not only of the workplace in the training and subordination of workers, but also in terms of the conscious and unconscious values, norms, and attitudes of the members of society. This line of argument parallels Marx's development of the notion of the historical boundedness of ideological hegemony; according to Marx, in any political epoch, the *apparent* 'natural' values of a society will correspond to those of the dominant ideology. Althusser's analysis is also surprisingly close to Etzione's (1961) functional account of social power; namely, that to be effective it must operate simultaneously at the normative, ultilitarian and coercive levels. Giroux (1981a) points out that these elements correspond to functional requisites for: '(1) the production of values that support the relations of production; (2) the use of force and ideology to support the dominant classes in all important spheres of control; and (3) the production of knowledge and skills relevant to specific forms of work'.

The base/super-structure relationship in Althusser's model is not absolute in a deterministic sense. Although Althusser (1971) acknowledges the primacy of the economic base, he conceives the ideological mechanisms of the *state* as governing and mediating economic relations in specific historical contexts. Assuming that one of the most dominant roles in this work of mediation is the school, Althusser argues '. . . one ideological state apparatus certainly has the dominant role, although hardly anyone lends an ear to its music, it is so silent! This is the school' (1971, p. 155). The school, far from being passive in this analysis, is the potent 'captain of consciousness'.

What Althusser thus contributes to reproduction models is a notion of social actions organized through an omnipotent system of symbolization. In these terms, the function of schooling can be seen as socialization, geared to the child's adoption of role models and internalization of rationales for social action. Jean Anyon (1981a and 1981b), while not necessarily an Althusserian, can be read as lending support to an Althusserian view of her ethnography of schools in New Jersey; she found that cognitive models, difficulty of material, and presentation of images of self varied, depending upon whether the child was from a working-class, middle-class, managerial-class, or ruling-class background. In the same vein, Robert Connell (1977) illustrates in an ethnography of Australian youth that dominant social values become a child's implicit assumption at an early age. And Madeline Grumet (1981) suggests that gender differences are reified for the child in school by the contradiction between the male/female *stated* role of the primary teacher as the authoritative representative to the child contrasted with the female teacher's *actual and practised* passive and submissive social role *vis à vis* the social structure. All these analyses could be seen to support the position that Gestalt-like learning of what should really be *understood* transpires in schools despite what is officially *taught*.

This position, taken to its Althusserian extreme, has been recently critiqued in the work of Richard Johnson (1979), Rachael Sharp (1980), and Henry Giroux (1981a). They claim that while Althusser raises the spectre of how individual consciousness is formed in classrooms, he fails to ground his analysis in any actual account of schools. Instead, he assumes *prima facia* the dominance of a school and classroom ideology. In so doing, he denies himself the twin possibilities that: (1) other modes of social relations exist and might predicate and penetrate social action; (2) that within the formation of both school and society there might be dialectically emergent elements, already transforming consciousness and social relations. While Althusser, in contrast to Jencks, and Bowles and Gintis, sees the *school as active,* the individual is still recycled more or less as society's clone. Rachael Sharp notes this contradiction:

> It suggests a determinist reproduction of the relations of production by the education system which tends to contradict Althusser's own thesis of the relative autonomy of the ideological and political levels and leads to a form of reductionism. It also provides no hope that subjects can ever escape from ideology. (1980, p. 163)

And so, Althusser's model improves on basic reproductionist models by reminding us of the active ideological components of schooling. However, in introducing ideology as an unanalyzed (or at least undocumented) element, he makes the subjugation of consciousness to ideology as mechanical as a vulgar Marxist reading of the base/superstructure relationship. It is as if Althusser has read half of Marx: while he realizes the historically specific functions of economic base and its derived ideology, he fails to recall that historical forces and cultural processes are always dialectically emergent and potentially resistant to domination. Ed Silva (1981) has noted that intellectuals on the left, however unwitting, contribute to the mystification that aids ruling class domination by not taking popular resistance movements seriously. Althusser, too, may have collaborated in this process.

Another model of hegemony is provided by the neo-Frankfurt theorists in their critique of Weber's distinction between value reference and value freedom (Marcuse, 1968) (Horkheimer, 1972) (Adorno, 1972). They argue that Weber's attempt to relegate values to an area external to scientific evaluation was a ploy designed to mask the ideological hegemony of 'value free' science and to insure *de facto* technical control of social organization. While the critical theorists did not directly address themselves to the institution of the school, the implications of their theory for schooling require little in the way of leaps of imagination. For schools, dating from Dewey (1902), have been viewed as morally and politically neutral institutions that, if managed properly, will produce benign effects. One might well speculate that the fundamental ideological tenet of liberal schooling is to deny that it is an ideology. Weber's solution for handling the difference between facts and values, between the 'known' and 'understood' – by simply denying that values and understandings are the proper subject for serious analysis – provided a model for hegemony of liberal schooling strategy which maintains its universalistic applicability by treating its 'failures' as individual accidents and its critics as biased representatives of minority opinion. What is missed in this seeming pluralist and liberal approach is the possibility that the *collective* effects of social relations might imbue implicit moral judgements and that, in fact, there is virtually no way in which social action could be otherwise. Analogously, liberal models of mass schooling claim universalistic applicability, but as Jencks, Bowles and Gintis, Carnoy and Levin (1976) and others are so helpful in illustrating, their effective results are anything but random.

The Frankfurt School has contributed to our understanding of liberal forms of knowledge, including schooling, by pointing to the ideological character of the scientific stance of value neutrality. Their arguments, like Althusser's, however, offer little effective contribution to the possibility of real resistance. For their dialectics seem to be largely applied to the mystifying powers of the ruling class. How else, for example, can one sensibly interpret Marcuse's (1964) notion of 'one dimensional man'? The transformations in the forms of symbolic domination, while almost infinitely flexible for the ruling economic group, are hardly symmetrical possibilities for other classes if one were to read only this position. This conception of history, I submit, is not only short-sighted but entails an over-romanticization of the creative powers of capitalist society. While it would be a critical mistake to underestimate the mesmerizing power of capital as a flexible system, it would be equally ill-conceived to see it as the immortal magician able to escape the consequences of its own contradictions.

(iii)   Models of Cultural Production and Symbolic Domination

What I have been trying to illustrate is how all the models are themselves necessarily limited in the level of verisimilitude they embody. In illustrating this by specific examples, it is hoped that the ways in which the methodological tensions representing the known and understood work their way into theory may be exemplified. I have also tried to show that in spite of these limits, the knowledge and understandings of various theories can and, I would submit, should complement each other to produce a balanced picture of social phenomena. I shall try later to suggest some examples of how work is and is not helped by correspondingly realizing and failing to realize these points.

A variation on the theme of ideological control, or symbolic domination, is provided in the works of Bernstein (1971) and Bourdieu (1977a). For Bernstein, as previously mentioned, variations in linguistic styles, insofar as they are embedded in class structure, contribute to the reification of the universalistic codes and the legitimate achievement agendas of the school. For these codes and agendas, in largely mirroring middle and ruling class values, both weaken and deny the life world expressions of the underclasses of society. In other words, the fit between class background and school expectation insures that one form of knowledge will be counted as valid and the clearly understood practice of the school will be to invalidate working class speech and, by implication, knowledge. This particular device insures not only class separation but illustrates the validity of Althusser's idea that the school, within the context of the classroom, functions as an agent of ideological domination. Bernstein's work therefore adds flesh to the Althusserian frame by showing how knowledge is transmitted in the classroom such that the school itself can be used to subvert, legitimate, and perpetuate class difference. What is central to this fit between family and the school is an asymmetrical distribution of power.

This latter point is useful to recall since Bernstein (1971) rejects mechanical notions of correspondence between codes and control. Changing the *form* of speech acts does not endanger the dominant social order in any serious way since such transformations, one might conceivably argue, may even act to supply the ruling classes with an expanded managerial base, through employing those individuals from the working class who are lucky enough, or clever or brow beaten enough, to become effectively 'bilingual' in the codes. To appreciate Bernstein's logic, it is important to remember that Bernstein, like Chomsky, does not see working class language as inherently 'inferior' in magnitude of content to any other type of speech. It follows from this that the relation between speech and performance is not a causal one or that one's linguistic style will not determine one's cognitive performance. The variations, though, are not accidental but, according to Bernstein, are perpetuated politically. Changing the form of children's speech does not change the structure of social power. This insight suggests real limits to liberal reform efforts to 'wash' the unwashed working masses in school.

This logic of the role of power as the real determinant of why children are tracked is carried out systematically throughout Bernstein's analysis.

An analogous argument (Giroux, 1981a) can be drawn from Bernstein's (1971) distinction between collection codes and integrated codes. While integrated codes are potentially more pedagogically progressive, their introduction will not alter the underlying power, class and structural relations in society. A similar argument might be made about the liberating potential of 'free' schools and 'open classrooms' as collective social transformers.

Bernstein is not alone in his emphasis on the importance of cultural and power factors. Bourdieu (1977a) offers another variety on the theme of how cultural domination is reproduced. The ideas of hegemony and domination, with Bourdieu, are given redefinition within the context of the school (1977a, 1979). Bourdieu rejects both rigid reproductionist models of cultural domination and liberal idealist conceptions of the neutrality of the schools. Instead, while Bourdieu argues for the relative independence and autonomy of schools from the economic, social and state apparatuses, he stresses that they embody arenas in which 'cultural capital' is transmitted; they are a 'habitas' in which value formation occurs. Schools, although structurally autonomous, transmit values that mirror class interests and provide experiences that are geared to maintaining differential access to cultural capital.

Schools are, in this analysis, places of 'symbolic violence'. Coercion is neither direct nor mechanically achieved, but consonant with dominant class interests. The relationships of state and economic domination symbiotically coexist by compatible, systematic, potentiating covariation rather than by direct causal manipulation. Schools, then, at the effect level are hardly innocent dupes, because what they achieve is analogous to what more obviously coercive means would achieve.

Keddie (1977), Mehan (1979), and Wexler (1981) have emphasized that it is classroom interaction that mediates and makes sensible the 'text' of curriculum. Bourdieu's theory of 'symbolic violence' presumes also this kind of naturalistic account of how social definitions are implanted in consciousness. Political, economic and cultural elements exert their power at the interactional level of symbols and rituals.

Bernstein and Bourdieu provide us with tenable accounts of how class difference is unconsciously but violently stamped into the minds of individuals from all classes. Their arguments, however, reinforce a model of self-contained dominant order. Where, for example, does social change fit into their accounts? Both theorists underline the importance of power for cultural reproduction, yet manifest class tensions, contradictions, and/or conscious action on the part of individuals to understand the typing and the violence inscribed upon them are not presented as serious. Both theorists grasp the immense importance and potential for psychological control in symbols, but are less salutory in amplifying for us how symbols hold the potential for reordering, subverting, and ultimately liberating individuals and collectives from their ideological doldrums. It may be a painfully banal example, but I do not believe that either theorists could account for a 'declassed bourgeois intelligentsia' or 'militant class resistance'. Perhaps it is unfair to consider their research in terms of Parsonian socialization paradigms, but the fact remains that they, like Parsons, ultimately employ an imprinting model of socialization to account for how actors learn roles, values, and norms.

(iv) Models of the Fiscal Crisis of the State

In the analysis of the fiscal crisis of the state (O'Connor, 1973; Castells, 1980; Mosley, 1978) the state's welfare functions are seen as operating to legitimate and cushion social relations. Functionally, the state and its apparatus form one of the three crucial sectors of society (the others being monopoly and competitive capital). As the economic order enter a fiscal crisis, or 'the tendency or government expenditures to outrace revenue' (O'Connor, 1973, p. 3), pressure increases and dislocations occur in the social order; however, momentum mounts from the private sectors to reduce the 'luxuries' of welfare, to cut down on the state budget for indirect and intangible mechanisms of social control. In terms of this analysis, one can easily speculate how education, as one such appendage of state control, becomes doubly threatened, due to (1) declining enrolments and (2) a relatively older population that is creating an increased competition for scarce resources between health and education sectors. Bourdieu and Bernstein's analyses read like sheer optimism compared to the bleakness of this view: as the crisis increases, the social order will be increasingly unable to 'afford' schooling as a tool of social control and legitimation. To use Althusser's analysis (1971), the coercive control model will take increasing precedence over the utilitarian and normative modes.

Concretely, this produces a situation in which teachers are being asked to take extra loads, support programs are being cut (especially those aimed at the underclasses), 'back to basics' are pushed over more liberal models of education. In the United Kingdom, for example, 'school milk' programs are now questioned as 'luxuries'.[3] In a word, the 'hidden' curricula of schools and their supporting myths are becoming displaced by more nineteenth century and more direct devices of social control. Iron displaces velvet as the guiding metaphor of social control.

Certainly economic crisis has consequences that ripple through all sectors of the social order – including schools. But are the doomsday scenarios, implied in the models of the fiscal crisis of the state, warranted? Schooling, after all, *does* produce 'human capital' (O'Connor's term) directly supportive of the whole industrial/social order. Also, it is questionable whether the poor, minorities, women and other groups in struggle could be expected to cheerfully and dutifully accept an increase in repressive measures. In Canada, at least, teacher unionism (Martell, 1974) and community organized resistance to school budget cuts are on the rise. The push by the private sector to attack the welfare state – evidence recent elections in the UK, the US, and Australia – suggest the pressures anticipated by O'Connor on the state apparatus may be real. The jury is still out, however, on whether such a reversal of decades, if not centuries, of social struggle can be effectively realised.

(v) Arguments of Cultural Production and Resistance

The history of theories of resistance is a venerable one. Lukács (1979) argues a version of Marxism, in which the relation between the working class and industrial capital is such that it generates inherent tensions. He develops a constructionist position that echoes Marx's observation, 'the definite social relations are just as much the products of men as linen, flax, etc.'. (Marx, n.d.) (Lukács, 1967, p. 48). Ideological control or false consciousness, according to Lukács, is always problematic, but must be understood, as (1) set against the larger objective relations of class and economy, and (2) set against the ideal of the full and objective understandings of society that dialectically emerge from particular social networks and the inherent tensions between clases. Lukács is thus important because he reminds us that the processes of ideology are epiphenomenal to the economic base and that the economic base is itself rife with potential for contestation and resistance.

That hegemonic and class functions are met with resistance within schools is the major postulate developed in the work of educators like Michael Apple (1979), Philip Wexler (1976), Jean Anyon (1981a), Henry Giroux (1981b), and William Pinar (1979), to name but a few. However, the resistance model examined here is drawn specifically from the work of Paul Willis (1975, 1977, 1978).

Willis' analysis of resistance is based on the notion that historically grounded culture plays a central role in both producing and replicating class relations. (As such, it may be seen in some respects as providing a counter thesis to Althusser's and certain versions of Lukács' critique of theories of cultural relationism). Willis accepts the fundamental Marxist tenet, of the primacy of base to superstructure, as a *general context* or backdrop for social analysis. The relationships of social production, however, Willis argues, transpire because of particular cultural relationships that emerge within, but also potentially transform, the larger social context.

Willis, by example, in *Learning to Labour* (1977) provides us with an eloquent and detailed analysis of how working class youth resist official school ideology. Ray Rist (1978) and Jean Anyon's (1981b) account of urban working class schools in the

US, in much the same vein as Willis' ethnographic work, contribute to a growing literature that suggests that schools become places just short of combat zones, when official social and school ideologies clash with students' class backgrounds.

Willis argues that the class-based resistance of British working class youth to school culture actually contributes to the *production* of a class relation, not merely the hegemonic reproduction of social order. He reasons, from his observations, that such resistance leads at least some working class boys to develop a legitimized counter cultural position to official school ideology. This part of his theory closely resembles Becker's (1963) and Friedenberg's (1963) analyses of the role of subcultures as normative units for ordering 'deviants'' mores. The plot of this resistance thickens, however, when we recognize that the youths' collective solidarity comes to be identified with machismo, violence, racism, sexism, anti-intellectuality and other regressive social elements that, according to the school, are not in the 'lads'' best interest. This pattern of internal solidarity with one's peers and radical exclusion of others (women, minorities, non-working class) is a twin-edged sword. Swung in one direction, it ensures that the sons of the working class will acquire the norms and mores they need to become integrated into the workshop culture of the factory. The school, ironically, despite the protestation of school officials and the resistance of the 'lads', conjoins with the lads themselves to produce a labour force through the inculcation of a masculine identity that is tied to solidarity with the workplace and pride in performance. Swung the other way, the culture that is learned at school predisposes one to resist authority and to be predisposed to trade unionism. Lysgaard (1961) and Cohen (1955) provide data to the effect that working class men identify with the family more strongly than do their managerial counterparts who tend to anchor their sense of self in the workplace. Working class youth, therefore, as well as learning to labour, learn to resist social and ideological tendencies towards individuation.

Methodologically, Willis' fusion of cultural ethnography with structuralist analysis is useful because it illustrates how the requirement to come to grips with real people and their situations leads to observations and conclusions that might not have been anticipated had we indulged in assuming the undocumented efficacy of our theoretical models (e.g., reproductionism; ideological hegemony; cultural hegemony; fiscal crisis of the state, etc.). The reliance on deduction, uninformed by first-hand empirical accounts, presents an interesting inversion of the dichotomy of the known and the understood: undocumented etiological models (usually associated with the 'known') confuse their 'understandings' or interpretations with reality itself, hence eluding the very knowledge they purport to seek. This inversion may really be another form of the problems of reductionism and reification discussed earlier. Alternatively, it may be a rediscovery of the scientific injuncture to develop empirically grounded theories.

In Willis' practice, the fusion of macro-theory and micro-methodological analysis is informed by a structuralist understanding of school and society. The utility of this underlying element may be illustrated if we compare Willis' work (1975, 1977) with some of the work on drug culture delinquency done by Young (1971). Young,[4] in carrying out his ethnography, employed notions of class structure and culture that were based primarily on actors' definitions of the situation. Class structure and culture, therefore, were *inductively* derived; they were not, that is, deductive elaborations from a theoretical understanding of stratified capitalist and working class culture as is found in Willis' work.

Young's finding now seem dated. He argues eloquently how leisure time at school and university facilitated for middle-class youth the luxury of drugs and counter culture. What he did not anticipate, though, was the mass use of drugs by working class youth. And thus, while his work is still illustrative of how and why differential access to resources may provide middle-class youth with less violent ways for channelling their frustrations *vis à vis* working class youth, it generally fails to hold up against comparative and longitudinal data. There are two points to be made here: (1) if Young had understood class theoretically, he might have been less susceptible to seeing affectations of form as primary when they were more probably aberrant or secondary; and (2) our understandings of phenomena, which I believe Willis both understands and embodies in his work, are not, in the final analysis, reducible to *structures* because cultural relations are *process* phenomena; our interpretation and comprehension of them are contextually contingent. This is not to say that cultural relations are independent of structural relations; structural relations compose the historical context from which cultural relations emerge and dialectically evolve; structural relations provide the backdrop against which action and understanding transpire.

This point may be further illuminated by comparing Willis' ethnography of Hammertown Boys in the UK with Elliot Leyton's (1979) insightful ethnography of the inmates of Hillview industrial training school in Dartmouth, Nova Scotia. Leyton's analysis of delinquency curiously blends a proto-Marxist analysis of marginalized class status, and a Laingian anti-psychiatric analysis of marginal family relationships. Family marginalization, Leyton notes, is not a class independent phenomenon because the child rearing practices of the underclasses tend to mirror their own social marginalization. Thus, manifest delinquency, according to this account, is neither nihilistic nor counter-cultural nor economically rational but is, rather, a desperate expression of youths, frustrated over their personal rejection by their own families.

While Leyton does talk to class and social structure, he does so in a relative void from any comparative context. This results in Leyton missing one of the most striking differences between his and Willis' subjects and, hence, in their respective ethnographies. The difference relates to the way in which Leyton's subjects, as opposed to Willis' 'lads', treat violence and 'blame' for their plights. The differences are almost ideal-typically Durkheimean. Leyton's youths tend to blame *themselves* for their downfall. They commit acts of self-violence (burning, cutting themselves, writing on the wall 'Lord give me a new life'). Willis' students direct their aggression largely at school and society. They blame others. To understand the difference in the ways in which the boys define their situations, one needs to understand the difference between the British working class history of *collective* resistance (E.P. Thompson, 1963) and the individualistic models of self-determination in the Canadian Maritimes. For, if you begin with a model of class conflict rather than a model of individual achievement as your basic assumption, you will arrive at very different conclusions about your lot in life. Just as Durkheim's individualistic Protestant *tends* to commit suicide as a response to crisis, so do Leyton's Canadian youths *tend* to blame themselves for their supposed 'failure'. Contrastingly, Willis' 'lads' are attuned to a collective logic that dictates that they act out a resistance model. It seems unlikely, at least to me, that this contrast could be recovered from a situationally focused analysis devoid of an understanding of historical context.

Two examples from my own work may be helpful in illustrating how structure and lived experience complex and conjoin in our understanding of social phenomena. The first example is drawn from an evaluation carried out by myself and a colleague (Burns and Olson, 1981) of a 'French Immersion' program in Northern

Ontario. Although Canada is a bilingual country, 'bilingualism' has largely meant that Francophones speak French, and usually English, while Anglophones, especially outside the province of Quebec, usually speak only English. As such, French Immersion is a curriculum innovation designed to immerse *Anglophone* children in French at school, while English remains the language of their home. The stated ideal of the program was to produce bilingual Anglophones and, in so doing, help to ease tensions between the country's two major traditional ethnic groups.

The programs themselves have been judged by *curriculum* evaluators (Swain and Berik, 1975), (Irvine, 1977) as successful in terms of high levels of cognitive achievement. Our sociological studies suggest more complex results. It turns out that program recruitment is largely by word of mouth, and that these informal networks tend to reach, by Northern Ontario standards, upper socio-economic background children. The reasons for this are that these strata are generally the best educated and most susceptible to innovation and, more importantly, most high salary jobs in the North, both in the private sector and even more so in the civil service, require bilingualism. Bilingually educated Anglophone children are at a distinct advantage for access to higher education and for maximum upward job mobility. This fact does not escape the parents of immersion students.

The French Immersion student is generally surrounded by peers who both best fit and are most motivated to succeed within the school structure. His or her parents tend to be the most active at the Board of Education level and the most successful in organizing 'community' control of curriculum. For example, they usually insure the transfer of the best teachers into the French Immersion Program. The tracking process is further compounded by teachers who frequently engage in the crassest form of labelling. French Immersion is functionally the only elementary school program in which teachers have the option of recommending that a child not be in the program. 'Slow learners' and anyone not deemed productive enough are very likely to be sent back to regular English language classes. The cumulative effect is that French Immersion in Northern Ontario, operating under the egalitarian label of a public program, functions as an élite school system.

The conflict generated by these *de facto* implementation procedures is marked in Northern communities. The English-speaking teachers we interviewed felt threatened about their job security because (1) immersion programs were depleting their classes of potential students in a time of declining enrolment, and (2) younger immersion teachers, because of their bilingualism, were likely to be kept on while senior English-speaking teachers were likely to be released. Trade union principles were therefore functionally violated. The English teachers we spoke to were also resentful of being 'stuck with the dregs', or the poorer students. In addition, working class parents expressed dismay that teachers and funds were going to the 'French'. (Programs are, in fact, for Anglophones but are perceived to be 'for the French'; the logic is that if the French weren't there, the problem would not exist; this perception does *not* escape the French.)

The problem becomes more pronounced in French Catholic Separate Schools that, in Ontario, have an open-door policy and are publicly funded. French separate school administrators *publicly* deny that French Immersion Programs exist in their schools. This denial largely stems from not unwarranted fears that the Francophone constituency would resent their schools being used for the benefit of largely upper income Anglophones. *Privately,* administrators will tell you they welcome the immersion students because, in times of declining enrolment, their admission often spells the difference between a school remaining open and being closed down.

The immersion children themselves confound and add to administrators' paranoia by systematically outperforming Francophones *in French*. This result is probably the result of four factors: (1) first, the children are generally upper socio-economic background; (2) as a result of the first, the fit of their family support system with the school is generally better than most other children; (3) in the French Immersion classes, there is a high motivational solidarity among peers. In school yards, we observed that Immersion children typically spoke in French, while Francophones sometimes used a mix of both languages, but generally spoke in English; and (4) most determinantly and ironically, Immersion children generally speak a Parisienne dialect of French. Teachers generally favour Parisienne as 'correct' French. Francophones' 'inferiority' in French, therefore, is largely due (1) to their subjugated class background as a group, and (2) to the fact they embrace their own national linguistic culture. Our studies provide preliminary data to the effect that upper socio-economic background Francophones are also beginning to enrol their children in the French Immersion Program.

How should we interpret our findings? It seems clear that the ways in which French Immersion programs have been implemented have done anything but reduce group tensions which, after all, was their stated goal. But it would be erroneous to see this as a deliberate class plot. Most of the parents, teachers and principals we interviewed worked hard and generally had the children's best interests at heart. One can hardly fault parents for wanting 'the best' for their child. On the other hand, if one does not realize the macro-structural roles of school in tracking, class mobility, linguistic sorting, ideological hegemony and the like, one cannot appreciate why and how French Immersion Programs function as they do. Elements of class reproduction, the fiscal crisis of the state, racial tensions, and so on, enter and affect the programs because they prefigure and predefine the roles and 'interpretive frames' of those involved in the situation. Class structure is, thus, a powerful limiting context and, in that sense, a determinant of the program's various conflict points; W.I. Thomas' situationally contingent definitions then function in this context to bind actors to one course of action rather than another.

The second example of how structure relates to lived experience is drawn from field work done in an Ontario elementary school. While touring the school with the principal, I inquired as to whether the school had open area classrooms. I believe even Sharp and Green (1975), who have emphasized that classroom's physical organization can impress a line/staff model of social control in children's consciousness, would have been shocked by the classroom I was taken to. The center of this open area classroom was occupied by a walled-in, and all but fortified, library area with controlled and limited access for children. The walls, the principal volunteered on his own, had been installed on the insistence of the librarian. He also commented, somewhat sheepishly, that 'we teachers find we don't work well in open area classes'. This was not surprising, since around the central library, facing in opposite directions, were four classrooms arranged in traditional fashion with the teacher at the front and the children sitting in neat rows. All four teachers were simultaneously shouting over one another, trying to teach their classes. The principal, again spontaneously, informed me that the teachers had voted to have walls installed, but that the local board had refused to fund their request since it had expended funds several years earlier to take the walls out. It was quite clear that the 'innovation' had been imposed from above and that, in actual practice, both children and teachers would have been better off in a more conventional walled-in setting. The worst of this tragi-comedy was yet to come.

I observed several children at the back of each class wearing headphones. Naïvely, I asked the principal if they were learning French. I was informed that the children with the headphones were 'hyperkinetic', and that these problem children 'learned better' if music was piled into them by earphones. I think it is fair to describe my immediate reaction as shock. Upon reflection, however, I realized, as Jackson, Sharp and Green and others before me had in different ways, that there are logical sensibilities that are set up by, and make sense only in the special context of, classrooms and schooling. If you were a teacher in a classroom trying to reach thirty children, eight hours a day, needing to shout in order to be heard over three other teachers, whom you could not will away, and there were a few children who systematically appeared to be disruptive, a functional logic would tell you instinctively: 'write off the few: try to save the many'.

I believe that it would be an error to assume that what I observed in the open area classroom was in any direct sense 'caused' by the social structure of capitalism. If one reads Hargreaves, Hestor and Mellor's (1975) useful book on delinquents in the classrooms, one gets an excellent ethnographic picture of how classrooms are places of literally hundreds of rules for possible understandings for appropriate situational action. One improves upon this understanding if one has also read Jackson's (1968) *Life in Classrooms* and realizes that the features of authority, denial, and reward – the political economy of the classroom – derive at one very basic level from the structural dynamics of crowding and consequent competition for attention. One does better still if one realizes the political realities of how schools function in relation to the rest of the socio-economic order: the *interaction* to change the structural relations of the classroom mirrors a power decision about how one ought to run a social institution and society as much as it does a conscious decision to subjugate possible actualization. Social structure does not make individual action but it does make the particular context in which, wittingly or unwittingly, we all negotiate for our individual identities.

In this presentation, I have tried to develop some examples of how lived experience and structure penetrate one another in our conceptual recovery of the social world. Causal analysis, I have tried to suggest, is never adequate because cultural relations, their emergence from and their fit to context, are incessantly dialectical and reflexive processes. Lived experience offers us empirical resistance to our reductions of phenomena to fixed origins and ends. Structuralist accounts, however, help us to recover the *collective* understandings and contents against which all social action is set. To assume that individual action can be analysed apart from social structure is to deny the historical, the situational and the constructional character of social action. The denial of the situational and the constructional character of social action prevents us from seeing the possibilities for alternatives that exist at a collective level rather than at the level of everyday experience and empirical observation. By successive and continuous seeking of the boundaries and overlaps of our models, we begin to develop a strategy of inquiry which allows us sensibly to stake out what is 'known'. To me, this is an intelligible 'understanding' of how to proceed.

Notes

1 My own analysis here closely parallels Henry Giroux's (1981a) clear piece on reproduction models. Those interested in a more comprehensive overview and strategy should consult his work.

2 For a review and counter argument, see Chomsky's (1972) piece.

3 I wish to thank Roger Dale for bringing this debate to my notice.
4 This section is an elaboration of a discussion with Steven Hester around his paper (1980).

References

ADORNO, T. (1972) *Aspects of Sociology* Boston, Beacon Press, pp. 183–205.
ALTHUSSER, L. (1971) 'Ideology and ideological state apparatuses' in *Lenin and Philosophy and Other Essays* London, New Left Books, pp. 123–173.
ANYON, J. (1981a) 'Elementary schooling and distinctions of social class' *Interchange* 12 (213), Sept.
ANYON, J. (1981b) 'Social class and school knowledge' *Curriculum Inquiry* (in press).
APPLE, M. (1979) *Ideology and Curriculum* Boston, Routledge and Kegan Paul.
APPLE, M. (1979) 'Curricular form and the logic of technical control: Building the possessive individual' in BARTON, L., MEIGHAN, R. and WALKER, S. (Eds) *Schooling, Ideology and the Curriculum* Lewes, Falmer Press.
ARONOWITZ, S. (1973) *False Promises* New York, McGraw-Hill.
BECKER, H. (1963) *The Outsiders* New York, The Free Press.
BERKELEY, H. *et. al.* (Eds) (1978) *Children's Rights* Toronto, OISE Press, Symposium Series 19.
BERNSTEIN, B. (1971) *Class, Codes and Control, Vol. 1–3* London, Routledge and Kegan Paul.
BLUMER, H. (1969) *Symbolic Interactionisms* Englewood Cliffs, Prentice-Hall.
BOURDEIU, P. (1977c) 'Cultural reproduction and social reproduction' in KARABEL, J. and HALSEY, A.H. (Eds) *Power and Ideology in Education* New York, Oxford University Press.
BOURDIEU, P. (1977b) *Outline of Theory and Practice* Cambridge, Cambridge University Press.
BOURDIEU, P. (1979) 'Symbolic', *Critique of Anthropology,* 4 (13) and 4 (14) pp. 77–85.
BOURDIEU, P. and PASSERON, J. (1977a) *Reproduction in Education, Society and Culture* Beverly Hills, Calif., Sage.
BOWLES, S. and GINTIS, H. (1976a) 'Schooling and inequality from generation to generation' *Journal of Political Economy* 80 (S) pp. 219–251.
BOWLES, S. and GINTIS, H. (1976b) *Schools in Capitalist America: Educational Reform and Contradictions of Economic Life* New York, Basic Books.
BRAVERMAN, H. (1975) *Labour and Monopoly Capital* New York, Monthly Review Press.
BURNS, G. and OLSON, P. (1981) *Sociological Effects of French Immersion in Northern Ontario* Toronto, OISE Report.
CARNOY, M. and LEVIN, M. (Eds) (1976) *The Limits of Educational Reform* New York, D. McKay.
CASTELLS, M. (1980) *The Economic Crisis and American Society* Princeton, Princeton University Press.
CHOMSKY, N. (1972) 'IQ tests: Building-blocks for the new class "System"' in *Ramparts* 11 pp. 26–30. Reprinted in COSLIN, B., DALE, R., ESLAND, G., MACKINNON, D. and SWIFT, D. (Eds) *School and Society* (2nd ed.) London, Routledge and Kegan Paul. pp. 244–250.
CICOUREL, A. (1964) *Method and Measurement in Sociology* New York, Free Press of Glencoe.
CONNELL, R. (1977) *Ruling Class, Ruling Culture; Studies of Conflict, Power and Hegemony in Australian Life* Cambridge, Cambridge University Press.
CRYSDALE, S. (1975) 'Aspirations and Expectations of High School Youth', *International Journal of Comparative Sociology* XVI, pp. 1–2.
CRYSDALE, S. and BEATTIE, C. (1977) *Sociology in Canada: An Introductory Text* Toronto, Butterworth and Company.
DEWEY, J. (1902) *The Child and the Curriculum* Chicago, University of Chicago Press.
DUNCAN, O. and BLAU, P. (1967) *The American Occupation Structure* New York, Wiley.
ETZIONI, A. (1961) *A Comparative Analysis of Complex Organizations* New York, Free Press of Glencoe.

FOUCAULT, M. (1970) *The Order of Things* London, Tavistock.

FOUCAULT, M. (1972) *The Archaeology of Knowledge* New York, Pantheon Books.

FREIRE, P. (1970) *The Pedagogy of the Oppressed* New York, Seabury Press.

FREIRE, P. (1973) *Education for Critical Consciousness* New York, Seabury Press.

FREIRE, P. (1978) *Pedagogy in Process* New York, Seabury Press.

FRIEDENBERG, E. (1963) *Coming of Age in America* New York, Vintage Books.

GADAMER, H.G. (1975) *Truth and Method* BORDEN, G. and CUMMINGS, J. (Eds) New York, Seabury Press.

GARFINKEL, H. (1967) *Studies in Ethno-methodology* New York, Prentice-Hall.

GEERTZ, C. (1964) 'Ideology as a cultural system' in APTER, D. (Ed) *Ideology and Discontent* Glencoe, The Free Press.

GELLNER, E. (1974) *Legitimation of Belief* Cambridge, Cambridge University Press.

GIDDENS, A. (1979) *Central Problems in Social Theory: Action, Structure and Contradiction in Social Analysis* Berkeley, University of California Press.

GIDDENS, A. (1976) *New Rules of Sociological Method* London, Routledge and Kegan Paul.

GIROUX, H.A. (1981a) 'Hegemony, resistance, and the paradox of educational reform' in *Curriculum and Instruction: Alternatives in Education* in GIROUX, H., PENNA, A. and PINAR, W.F. (Eds) Berkeley, McCutcheon Press.

GIROUX, H.A. (1981b) *Ideology, Culture and the Process of Schooling* Lewes, The Falmer Press.

GRAMSCI, A. (1971) *Selections from Prison Notebooks* HOARE, Q. and NOWELL-SMITH, P. (Eds and Trans) New York, International Publishers.

GRUMET, M. (1981) 'Pedagogy for patriarchy: The feminization of teaching' *Interchange* 12 (2) & 12 (3).

HABERMAS, J. (1970) *Towards a Rational Society* (trans J. Jeremy) Boston, Beacon Press.

HABERMAS, J. (1971) *Knowledge and Human Interests* (trans J. Jeremy) Boston, Beacon Press

HARGREAVES, E., HESTER, S. and MELLOR, F. (1975) *Deviance in Classrooms* London, Routledge and Kegan Paul.

HEIDEGGER, E. (1973) *The Phenomenology of Internal Time-Consciousness* HEIDEGGER, M. (Ed) and CHURCHILL, J.S. (trans) Bloomington, University of Indiana Press.

HERRNSTEIN, R. (1972) 'IQ' *Atlantic Monthly* 228:43–58 + 5; 110D.

HESTER, S. (1980) 'Ethnography and Social Structure: Methodological Issues' Unpublished paper.

HILGUR, V. (1977) 'Class and gender: Role model considerations and liberations in advance capitalism' Originally in BERG, A.M. and FORLAG, P. (Eds) *I Kvinner bilde* in *Interchange* 12 (2 & 3), 1981.

HOLT, J. (1964) *How Children Fail* Harmondsworth, Penguin.

HOOKWAY, C. and PETTIT, P. (Eds) (1978) *Action and Interpretation: Studies in the Philosophy of the Social Sciences* Cambridge, Cambridge University Press.

HORKHEIMER, M. (1947) *Eclipse of Reason* New York, Herder and Herder.

HORKHEIMER, M. (1972a) *Critical Theory: Selected Essays* New York, The Seabury Press.

HORKHEIMER, M. and ADORNO, T.W. (1972b) *Dialectics of Enlightenment* New York, Herder and Herder.

HUSSERL, E. (1969) *Formal and Transcendental Logic* (trans D. Cairns) The Hague, Martin Nijhoff.

HUSSERL, E. (1973) *Explorations in Phenomenology: Papers* (trans D. Carr and E. Casey) The Hague, Martin Nighoff.

ILLICH, I. (1970) *Deschooling Society* New York, Harper and Row.

IRVINE, D. (1977) 'Evaluation Methodology for a French Language Immersion Program' Paper presented at the Evaluation Workshop on the French Language Immersion Program, (SUC at Plattsburg), March 17–18, 1977.

JACKSON, P. (1968) *Life in Classrooms* New York, Holt, Rinehart and Winston.

JACKSON, R. (Commissioner) (1978) *Final Report: Implications of Declining Enrolment for the Schools of Ontario: A Statement of Effects and Solutions* Toronto, Ministry of Education, Ontario.

JENCKS, C., SMITH, M., ACLAND, H., BANE, M.J., COHEN, D.K., GINNS, H., HEYNS, B. and MICHELSON, S. (1972) *Inequality: A Reassessment of the Effects of Family and Schooling in America* New York, Basic Books.

JENCKS, C., BARTLETT, S., CORCORAN, M., CROUSE, J., EAGLESFIELD, D., JACKSON, G., McLELLAND, K., OLNECK, M., SCHWARTZ, J., WARD, S. and WILLIAMS, J. (1979) *Who Gets Ahead? The Determinants of Economic Success in America* New York, Basic Books.

JENCKS, C. (1980) 'Structural versus individual explanations of inequality: Where do we go from here?' in *Contemporary Sociology* 9:6:762.

JOHNSON, R. (1979) 'Histories of cultural theories of ideology: Notes on impasse' in BARRETT, M., CORRIGAN, P., KUHN, A. and WOLFF, J. (Eds) *Ideology and Cultural Production* New York, St. Martin's Press.

KARABEL, J. and HALSEY, A.H. (Eds) (1977) *Power and Ideology in Education* Oxford, Oxford University Press.

KEDDIE, N. (1971) 'Classroom Knowledge' in BELLACK, *et. al. (Eds) Curriculum and Evaluation* Berkeley, McCutcheon Publishing, pp. 280–316.

KOHL, H.R. (1970) 'Examining the Crisis in Education' Berkeley, Pacifica Tape Library (phonotape, 1970).

LEYTON, E. (1979) *The Myth of Delinquency: An Anatomical Juvenile Nihilism* Toronto, McClelland and Stewart.

LUKÁCS, G. (1967) *History and Class Consciousness: Studies in Marxist Dialectics* (trans R. Livingstone) Cambridge, MIT Press.

LYSGAARD, S. (1961) *Arbeiderkollektivet* Oslo.

MACLAREN, P. (1980) *Cries from the Corridor: The New Suburban Ghettos* Toronto, Methuen.

MARCUSE, H. (1964) *One Dimensional Man: Studies in the Ideology of Advanced Industrial Society* New York, Beacon Press.

MARCUSE, H. (1968) *Essays in Critical Theory* (trans J.J. Shapiro) New York, Beacon Press.

MARTELL, G. (Ed) (1974) *The Politics of the Canadian Public School* Toronto, J. Lorimer and Co.

MARX, K. (n.d.) *Poverty of Philosophy* (with introduction by Frederick Engels) New York, International Publishers.

McHUGH, P. *et. al.* (1974) *On the Beginning of the Social Inquiry* London, Routledge and Kegan Paul.

MEHAN, H. (1979) *Learning Lessons* Cambridge, Mass., Harvard University Press.

MELTZER, B. *et. al.* (1975) *Symbolic Interactionism: Genesis, Varieties and Criticism* London, Routledge and Kegan Paul.

MOSLEY, H. (1978) 'Is there a fiscal crisis of the state?' *Monthly Review* 30 (1) May, pp. 34–45.

MYRDAL, G. (1962) *An American Dilemma: The Negro Problem and Modern Democracy* (Sterner and Rose, Asst.) New York, Harper and Row, (20th anniversary ed.).

O'CONNOR, J. (1973) *The Fiscal Crisis of the State* New York, St. Martin's Press.

PARSONS, T. (1977) *Social Systems and the Evolution of Action Theory* New York, Free Press of Glencoe.

PINAR, W. (1979) 'The Abstract and the Concrete in Curriculum Theorizing' Unpublished paper.

POPPER, K. (1965) *Conjectures and Refutations* 2nd Edn. New York, Basic Books.

RIST, R. (1973) *The Urban School: a Factory for Failure* Cambridge, Mass., MIT Press.

RIST, R. (1978) *The Invisible Children: School Integration in American Society* Cambridge, Mass., Harvard University Press.

ROBINSON, P. and SULLIVAN, W.M. (Eds) (1979) *Interpretive Social Science* Berkeley, University of California Press.

SCHUTZ, A. (1971) *Collected Papers* Natanson, M. (Ed) The Hague, Martin Nijhoff.

SEWELL, W. and HAUSER, R. with ALWINARD, D.F. *et. al.* (1975) *Education Occupations and Earning in Early Career* New York, Academic Press.

SEWELL, W. and HAUSER, R. with FETHERMAN, D. (Eds) (1976) *Schooling and Achievement in American Society* New York, Academic Press.

SHAFFIR, W. *et. al.* (1980) *Fieldwork Experiences: Qualitative Approaches to Social Research* New York, St. Martin's Press.

SHARP, R. (1980) *Knowledge, Ideology and the Politics of Schooling* Boston, Routledge and Kegan Paul.

SHARP, R. and GREEN, A. (1975) *Education and Social Control: A Study in Progressive Primary Education* Boston, Routledge and Kegan Paul.

SILVA, E. (1981) 'Making Hegemony Problematic: Power, Knowledge and the Current Centre' Working paper to be presented at the 1981 American Educational Research Association conference in Los Angeles, California.

SWAIN, M. and BERIK, H. (1975) *Bilingual Education Project: Evaluation of the 1974-75 French Immersion Program in Grades 2-4, Ottawa Board of Education* Available through the Ontario Institute for Studies in Education.

THOMAS, D. (1979) *Naturalism and Social Science: A Post-Empiricist Philosophy* Cambridge, Cambridge University Press.

THOMPSON, E.P. (1963) *The Making of the English Working Class* London, Gollancz.

UNESCO (1980) *Statistical Yearbook: 1978-79* Section 2.8 of the 'Education' section Paris, UNESCO.

WEINBERG, C. (1976) *Education is a Shock: How the Educational System is Failing our Children* New York, William Morrow and Company.

WEXLER, P. (1976) *The Sociology of Education: Beyond Equality* Indiannapolis, Bobbs-Merrill.

WEXLER, P. (1981) 'Structure, Text, and Subject: A Critical Sociology of School Knowledge' Working paper.

WILLIS, P. (1975) 'The cultural meaning of drug use' in JEFFERSON, T. (Ed) *Resistance Through Rituals* Birmingham, Centre for Contemporary Cultural Studies.

WILLIS, P. (1977) *Learning to Labour* Lexington, Heath.

WILLIS, P. (1978) *Profane Culture* London, Routledge and Kegan Paul.

VON WRIGHT, G.H. (1971) *Explanation and Understanding* Ithaca, New York, Cornell University Press.

YOUNG, J. (1971) *The Drugtakers: the Social Meanings of Drug Use* London, MacGibbon and Kee.

YOUNG, M.F.D. (Ed) *Knowledge and Control* London, Collier-Macmillan.

3

Contemporary Concerns
and the Work
of Teachers

Introduction

At the beginning of this book the claim was advanced that a major theme which provides a unifying link between the different papers included in the collection is a concern to extend sociological analysis of the world of *teachers*, a concern which could be addressed, it was suggested, through the establishment of a more dynamic sociology of teachers' work. Whatever other concerns this sociology would have to include – and we have argued that historical and structural conditions should feature prominently – there is little doubt that consideration of the interactional practices teachers undertake to accomplish what they and their co-interactants recognize as 'teaching' will need to be accorded a very high priority. Fortunately, during the last decade there has been a steady stream of publications in this country and in America which provide ethnographic accounts of classroom life or which present interactional analyses of the social construction of classroom relations – accounts and analyses in which various dimensions of the work of 'teaching' have been chronicled. At first, because this particular research approach was developed as part of a movement away from what was seen by many as the dire consequences of a 'problem-orientation' in the discipline, work was characterized by an enthusiasm for the production of detailed descriptions of routine classroom practices and a reluctance on the part of writers to get involved in the provision of critical commentary. However, as this type of research has developed, though its advocates have not lost their basic commitment to a micro-sociological approach, the relevance such work has for pressing *analytical* problems of wider significance in the sociology of education has become increasingly clear. This is largely because one· of the most tangible outcomes of this kind of research has been a more certain demonstration of the recognition that how educational activities like 'teaching' are accomplished is first and foremost a consequence of the participants' perceptions and definitions of the situation and of the acts they perform in direct response to these understandings. Now, whilst this emphasis upon the subjective dimension of action is not to deny that the form and direction of these interpretations and interactions *might be* strongly influenced by 'external' factors embedded in the contexts in which they originate or operate, it does mean that the legitimacy of certain practices in sociological analysis of education is thrown into sharp relief.

It is this concern, the question of the legitimacy of certain forms of analysis, which is discussed in this section of the book through a consideration of certain fundamental strategies and conditions which constitute and structure the activity 'teaching', or, more succinctly, through an examination of models of teacher action. The section begins with papers by Stebbins and by Walker which involve demonstrating the ways in which the assumptions and perceptions of the analyst can so deeply penetrate description and analysis of the world under investigation as to jeopardize the chances these analysts have of presenting a 'truthful' account. Stebbins, using a review of different attempts to describe how classroom situations get defined, indicates how the appreciation gained from a synthesis of data suggested in these different approaches can be used to inspect *theories* about how 'teachers' . . . strategies relate to structural and ideological aspects of society'. Walker, through a critical examination of approaches to the analysis of classroom conversation seeks to identify the *analytical* conditions which would have to be satisfield if a defendable description of how 'actors in schools *announce* their sense of structure (and) orient their behaviour to this sense' in communicative interaction is to be established.

Albeit indirectly, the first two papers in this section touch upon a question to do with the legitimacy of analytical methods which is developed as a major theme in the last three papers in the volume. The detailed examination which has been developed in micro-sociological research of teachers' daily activities has led those researchers promoting this approach to take a very critical stance indeed towards all explanations of educational affairs based on descriptions or concepts which lack reference to the significance of human agency. The basic criticism involves the view that if, on the one hand, it is evident that the interpretations individuals bring into schools have significant influence on the construction of reality in classrooms then it is difficult to accept, on the other, any description which fails to show how the categories and concepts the analyst uses to capture this reality refer to some property or other to which participants themselves orientate. The authors of the last three papers in this section have refined this criticism and used the insights such a development offers to tackle what seems to be one of the most important analytical concerns in contemporary sociology of education – the question of the extent to which participants in educational processes have choices. Although the practical instances covered here range through a case-study of the impact of personal biography on teacher action (Woods); a case-study of the processes of curriculum decision-making in a suburban middle-school (Hargreaves); and an ethnographic study of talk in staffrooms (Hammersley), all three papers present evidence to support the general claim that the *power* teachers have to act upon their personal understandings or to implement their individual strategies is differentially distributed. The authors, however, caution against the temptation of importing over-simplistic theories to explain these differences in which the origins and mechanism of this power distribution are attributed to ideological formations, the constraining influences of which are assumed rather than confirmed. We hope that the stimulus provided in the contribution the papers collected in this volume will make to the establishment and development of a sociology of teachers' work will provide for such confirmation.

Classroom Ethnography and the Definition of the Situation

Robert A. Stebbins, University of Calgary

In the social sciences at any rate, it seldom takes long for the new to grow old. For instance, the recent proliferation of interpretive studies of the classroom was one of the 'new directions' in the sociology of education listed by Young (1971). This trend has been with us for approximately a decade, and already there is talk of its obsolescence and, hence, of its fall from grace in the scientific community. Only seven years later Delamont (1978) made an eloquent plea for a stay of execution of this fledgling. After all, it is a mere child in educational research, when compared with the other approaches followed there. Certainly it is deserving of an extended life so that we may see what its maturity will bring.

One way to effect this reprieve is to attempt a theoretical integration of the many disparate interpretive classroom ethnographies which, as David Hargreaves (1978) has correctly noted, is an outstanding item of unfinished business:

> In a sense I am making a plea for tenacity among adherents of the perspective . . . It is clear that among the most important tasks is the generation of better theory, at both the substantive and the formal levels, and greater attention to the production of empirical and conceptual generalizations in place of the proliferation of unique, isolated case-studies with their *ad hoc* employment of minor concepts.
>
> (D. Hargreaves, 1978, p. 19)

As fruitful a way as any to embark on the theoretical mission of this paper is *via* the theory of the definition of the situation. Though the use of the term 'theory' may appear to some as an excessive claim for a degree of coherence presently lacking in this line of thought, there has been, nonetheless, an accumulation of data and propositions amounting to a theorylike structure. This accumulation has been under way for better than sixty years. Its central concept, the definition of the situation, remains, even today, at the core of the interpretive sociologies as these are applied to educational phenomena:

> Whilst there are divergences between the various schools of interpretative sociology there have been methodological convergences. All in similar ways lay stress on the study of everyday life and on actors' own interpretations and definitions of the situation; social order is seen as the accomplishment of actors through their interaction; social life is thought of as process.
>
> (Delamont, 1978, p. 60)

In this paper many of the studies dealing with the meaning or definition of major classroom situations (e.g., academic performance, disorderly behavior) are reviewed to identify their particular theoretical concern with and general location in the theory of the definition of the situation. Attention is centered on the overall meaning of these situations, as established through conscious interpretations and syntheses of the relevant personal, social, physical, and temporal considerations and through the relevant preformed cognitive structures that teachers and pupils carry with them from one school day to the next.

In conducting this review, two criteria were used to determine which studies should be included and which excluded from this paper. First, each study had to be demonstrably about how either teachers or pupils or both define a major recurrent classroom situation or about how their definitions lead to the emergence of a larger social fact, be it a fleeting group definition of what is happening or something more enduring, such as a behavioral norm, personal or collective identity, or established sequence of activities. Put otherwise, the studies examined here had to have as one of their primary aims the explanation of situated behavior, an explanation that is predicated on the outlook (which may be framed by the structural properties of the situation) of one or both sets of classroom members. Or these studies had to explain the rise of some social fact or social reality which starts in the definitions of particular situtations produced by some of all of those members. In research terms the definition of the situation had to be either a main dependent variable or a main independent variable.

Second, those studies treating the definition of the situation as a dependent variable had to be implicitly or explicitly organized around a type of teacher or pupil goal or 'principal action orientation' (Stebbins, 1975, pp. 7–9) to be implemented in a recurrent classroom setting. Which is to say that such studies also concentrated on at least some of the means these actors use to reach their ends and / or on at least some of the conditions (elements in the situation over which they have no control) affecting their chances of reaching their ends. In short, the modern theory of the definition of the situation is a detailed version of the basic 'unit act' in the theory of social action synthesized by Parsons (1937, pp. 43–45) better than forty years ago.

Application of these criteria led to the exclusion of several kinds of classroom studies. Among them are the purely descriptive works, including those attempting to identify types of teachers or pupils or types of behavior in which they engaged. Also excluded are the studies measuring the attitudes and opinions of those in classrooms, except where these orientations are tied in some way to the pursuit of situated goals. Such investigations are usually concerned with an undifferentiated range of situations, instead of their specific types. Studies aiming to uncover the latent or manifest consequences of teacher or pupil actions in the classroom, as these sustain a larger social system, are also beyond the scope of this paper. Here the observer's understanding of the consequences of the actors' behavior is scientifically more significant than their viewpoints and intentions. Those studies of the definition of the situation that do follow the ramifications of a given definition beyond the awareness level of the actors involved, do so by taking those actors' outlooks as the starting point. Finally, studies attempting to plot and analyze the interaction patterns of teachers and pupils, as epitomized in the investigations of Ned Flanders (1970), are excluded, chiefly because of their scant concern with the subjective side of schoolroom life. In sum, the theory of the definition of the situation is clearly too limited to organize all classroom research.

Research on classroom interaction is spread unequally across the areas of definition of the situation theory mentioned earlier. Hence this review identifies not only the theoretical foundation of each study surveyed, but also the areas of the theory in need of additional empirical attention. Moreover, it makes possible a rich explication of some of the theory's more general propositions, which furthers its development.

There has been a sizeable number of investigations of classroom interaction carried out over roughly the past ten years concentrating in one way or another on the meanings of situations. They can be classified according to the part or parts of the theory of the definition of the situation they explore. The plan in the following sections is first to summarize one of the theory's segments and then to present the main observations to emerge from the classroom ethnographies done in the past decade or so pertaining to it.[1]

Symbolic Interactionism

Most of today's symbolic intractionists explicitly or implicitly treat the definition of the situation as the central concept in the sociological theory of motivation (e.g., Stone and Farberman, 1970: pt. 8). The motivational approach is summarized in the following sequential model, which locates the definition of the situation in relation to the initial reaction of the individual teacher or pupil to the classroom setting:

1 Typical actors in a given identity enter a typical setting with a particular action orientation (i.e., intention, goal, interests at hand) in mind.
2 Certain aspects of these surroundings, some of which relate to the orientation, activate or awaken some of the predispositions the actors characteristically carry with them.
3 The aspects of the surroundings, the orientations, and the activated predispositions, when considered together, initiate further selection of a cultural or habitual definition.
4 This definition guides subsequent goal-directed action in the situation, at least until reinterpretation occurs.

Thirteen indicators operationalize, in a general way, our definitions of any situation. Five of these concern our *perceptions of others:* their social identities and present behavior; evaluations (rational and affective) of the present situation; action orientations; plans of action (strategies for reaching their action orientations); and justifications of those plans. The next five operationalizations center on our perceptions of ourselves as reflected in the social *looking glass* by means of the reactions of those others: our reflected identities and behaviors; our evaluations; action orientations; plans of action; and justifications. The final three operationalizations refer to our own *reactions* to these ten perceptions: our evaluations of them; plans of action; and justifications.

In actuality, choosing standard cultural and habitual definitions takes place in two artificially demarcated phases occurring in rapid succession. Phase I is that of identifying the ongoing events as an instance of some category of situation (e.g., tardiness, academic performance, pupil illness). However, recurrent situations are never free from associated meanings in the individual mind; they never occur as neutral, uninterpreted happenings. In the very process of identifying the category of setting we are in, we have also selected a portion of our cultural or habitual definition because it is associated through socialization with the events at hand. In other words, some or all of the first ten indicators appear simultaneously merely from identifying a set of events as of a particular kind.

Phase II of the selection of a cultural or habitual definition amounts to choosing a standard personal evaluation, plan of action, and justification (last three indictors). This can only be done after answers have been provided to at least some of the questions posed by the indicators that constitute Phase I. There must be a modicum of information about the situation to evaluate and respond to with a plan of action. In Phase II, choice is guided by the action orientations of the actors, their identification of the setting in Phase I, and the activated predispositions resulting from this identification.

It is more difficult to conceive of unique definitions of the situation in terms of these phases. Once people realize they are unable to identify the setting in which they find themselves (Phase I), that they are in unusual circumstances for which there is no standard meaning, they begin to construct a makeshift definition out of whatever information they can gather along the lines of the indicators.

The motivational approach is distinguished from its sister approaches in the symbolic interactionist segment of the theory by its concentration on the interpersonal processes operating during the selection or construction of a suitable definition. Among these processes, which unfold prior to any action directed by that definition, are role taking, self-reflection (looking glass self), and perception of others.

Perception of Others

We turn first to the five operationalizations pertaining to the perception of others. The main research interest in this area of the theory during the time period under review has been on the typifications teachers and pupils develop of one another.[2] Starting with the teacher's standpoint David Hargreaves (1967, chapter 5) sets the stage for this work by observing how the teachers in the school he studied classify their charges according to (1) those who conform to expectations (academic and orderliness), (2) those who fail to do so, and (3) those who fit neither category. This taxonomy comes into play when the teachers deal with actual instances of misbehavior and intellectual performance. Likewise, McPherson (1972, pp. 84–88) reports that pupils identified as behaving or performing below expectations are seen as caring little about school (imputed pupil evaluation). Her teachers' perceptions of academic performance and misbehavior are frequently dependent on their awareness of their pupils' social class and sex. Teachers may also 'show up' (teacher plan of action, Phase II) pupils whom they dislike, while sparing their pets this sort of publicity (Woods, 1975, pp. 136–138).

Pupils, of course, are inclined toward the same practice. Two dimensions along which teacher classification occurs have emerged from recent ethnographic research: that of ease of interaction with a teacher and that of his or her ability to control and teach (e.g., Corrigan, 1979, pp. 60–61; Delamont, 1976a, p. 74). Woods (1976, pp. 183–184) and Furlong (1977, pp. 171–175) have found that these two dimensions intersect to form a fourfold typology of teachers as seen through student eyes; strict-good teachers, easy-good teachers, strict-bad teachers, and easy-bad teachers. So far as the symbolic interactionist segment of the theory is concerned, these generalizations about the pupils' classification system have yet to be joined to the types of definitions of the situation they use in the classroom. At present these types exist in an interactive and theoretical vacuum.

A handful of studies concentrate on teachers' evaluations and identifications of pupil *behavior* (instead of the pupils as persons). Hammersley (1977, p. 10) describes his teachers' concern with whether misconduct is simply a lapse in student self-control or an intentional challenge. Different reactions in Phase II of the teachers' definitions are predicated on such evaluations. And teachers' perceptions of pupil boredom lead the former to the conclusion (evaluation, Phase II) that they are doing a poor job and that they must quickly think of some way to correct this deficiency (McPherson, 1972, p. 85). In an essay on teachers' adoption of the humorist role, Stebbins (1980, pp. 89–90) explains how they identify both the pupils and their behavior prior to their humorous reaction in the situation. Certain categories of pupils acting in certain ways help determine the form of humor a teacher will enact.

The only study to assess all the operationalizations dealing with the perception of others is Metz's (1978, pp. 132–140), which was conducted in a racially mixed school. She observed that black pupils are especially sensitive to equal treatment, for they constantly compare their interactions with the teacher with those of their white peers. For example, black pupils predominate in the low ability groups at that school. They resent the teacher's imputation that they are incapable of learning (identification, evaluation) and that his goal is one of being a custodian instead of a teacher. They further resent his use of this imputation to justify the decision to cease teaching them (plan of action). Corrigan's (1979, pp. 64–65) work, though it encompasses fewer operationalizations than Metz's, shows how pupils variously perceive their teacher's justifications for punishing them as retribution, deterrence, maliciousness, or anger. On a different theme Woods (1976, p. 181) noted that pupils see an over-zealous teacher as violating their rules when he or she curtails classroom laughter and thereby removes their only escape from boredom.[3] Pupils also decide whether to involve themselves actively in a lesson on the basis of their perceptions of the teacher's talk – as warm and encouraging or cold, inflexible, and discouraging (Barnes, 1969, p. 64).

The Looking Glass

The operationalizations subsumed under the heading of the social looking glass have always received the least scrutiny from classroom ethnographers. This unfortunate oversight persists to this day. The perspective required of teachers and researchers to gather data in this area is difficult to establish and hold in retrospective interviews about schoolroom incidents (Stebbins, 1975, p. 121). The only examination whatsoever of this part of the definition of classrooms situations is that of the author (Stebbins, 1975, pp. 57–59, 75, 85, 109–110).

Teachers' Reactions

Phase II of the definition of the situation consists of the reactions of teachers and pupils to their perceptions as manifested in the first ten operationalizations. The evaluation of these perceptions by teachers is seldom, if ever, treated separately in the classroom ethnographies. Rather, it is either assumed (e.g., teachers dislike disorderliness once they have identified it in their presence) or lumped together with the plan of action selected to deal with the unfolding situation. One rare exception is McPherson's (1972, p. 105) observation that, at least in the school she studied, teachers are shocked and hurt by pupil hostility. Pupils are expected to keep such feelings to themselves. Another exception comes from Hargreaves and his associates

(1975, p. 225). The seriousness with which an infraction of classroom rules is held is a form of evaluation. Different degrees of seriousness lead to different plans of action.

It should come as no surprise, however, that one of the subjects of greatest interest in this field is the plans themselves. In recent years these have come to be known as 'teacher strategies' (also referred to as coping strategies, survival strategies, and techniques of classroom management). Teacher strategies are patterns of 'specific and repeatable acts chosen and maintained in logical relationships with one another to serve the larger and long-term rather than the smaller and short-term objectives' (Paisey, 1975, p. 14). Initially these strategies are constructed by teachers (later they are selected from a pool of strategies) in response to the ways their personalities mesh with each class they are put in charge of (Hargreaves, A. 1978, pp. 75–77).

Woods (1979, pp. 150–165) has developed the most complete list of strategies. It is used here as the basis for presenting the diverse plans of action which teachers select and implement in the schoolroom.

(1) *Domination* is a common strategy, particularly for teachers of low ability pupils. It hinges on physical force (for a classic example, see Becker, 1952), vocal superiority, bluff (Lacey, 1970, pp. 174–175), rigid discipline (Hargreaves, D. 1967, pp. 103–104; Gouldner, 1978, pp. 30–31), establishing rules (Delamont, 1976b, pp. 94–99; Hammersley, 1976, p. 110), continuous surveillance (King, 1978, p. 51; McPherson, 1972, p. 89), 'showing them up' (Woods, 1975), and so on. The essential process in domination appears to be the maintenance of what Lacey (1970, pp. 174–175) calls 'role distance', wherein teachers try to keep an emotional and personal gulf between them and their pupils.

(2) *Negotiation* is another widely used strategy, which rests on the exchange of valued things, privileges, opportunities, and relationships. Martin (1976, pp. 60–67) observed teachers using group pressure, comparisons with other classes, and social-emotional tactics of various kinds (appear sad, be ingratiating) to negotiate with pupils for improved orderliness or academic performance. Bribery and relaxation of classroom rules may become part of a negotiation (Hammersley, 1976, p. 113). Flattery is also used sometimes (e.g., Metz, 1978, p. 115). Teachers soon learn, however, that some pupils are 'non-negotiable' while others are only 'intermittently negotiable' (Martin, 1976, pp. 37–41).

(3) Some teachers attempt to win control of their pupils by *fraternizing* with them, by sharing their interests, their styles of speech, their fashions in clothing, and so forth (e.g., Denscombe, 1980a, pp. 60–61). At times teacher initiated humor has fraternization as its aim (Stebbins, 1980; Walker and Goodson, 1977; Leacock, 1969, pp. 94–97). Levity and permissiveness may be regarded as instances of either negotiation or fraternization, depending on the circumstances surrounding their use (King, 1978, pp. 50–51; Leacock, 1969, pp. 94–97).

(4) Physically or psychologically *removing* oneself from the classroom is a way some teachers evade its problems. In modified form this strategy includes ignoring minor infractions of schoolroom rules (Hammersley, 1976, p. 114). David Hargreaves (1967, pp. 103–104) observed the occasional teacher sitting at his desk calmly marking papers, seemingly oblivious to the hubbub around him. Woods mentions daydreaming, falling asleep, leaving the room, absentation, and wasting time as additional expressions of this strategy.

(5) *Routines* serve as a means of control, since they help pace the activities of the classroom. They include structured exercises, group activities, audio-visual techniques, programmed learning, and work cards. The student is carried along through the lesson with scant opportunity for side involvements.

(6) *Occupational therapy* (Woods, 1979, p. 164) is based on a similar restriction of attention. Here pupils are told to draw maps, pictures, or patterns; do individual experiments in science; or carry out projects in industrial arts.

(7) *Controlling talk* through questioning, lecturing, limiting spontaneous pupil commentary, and related maneuvers is still another strategy by which teachers pursue their twin goals of intellectual training and maintenance of order. Gouldner (1978, p. 38) watched her teachers keep trouble down by refusing to let certain pupils participate in the classroom discussion. Teachers may rely on different 'participant structures' (Phillips, 1972, pp. 377–378) to foster the sorts of verbal interchanges they want with their pupils. These include interacting with the class as a whole (see also Payne and Hustler, 1980), or with part of it, while the others work quietly at their desks. Stubbs (1976, pp. 159–161) lists eight forms of 'metacommunication', which teachers use to advance their instructional aims: getting pupils' attention; controlling pupil talk; checking on understanding; summarizing; defining; editing pupil answers; correcting their answers; and specifying the topic of discussion. As Barnes (1969, p. 27) points out 'teachers are covertly signaling to their pupils what their role as learners is to be' (see also Keddie, 1971, p. 45).[4]

(8) *Avoidance of provocation* (Stebbins, 1975, pp. 66, 91–92) is yet another strategy, and one that is particularly familiar to those teachers who must routinely confront the low ability, chronically misbehaving pupil (Metz, 1978, pp. 107–110; Hargreaves *et al,* 1975, pp. 239–249; Denscombe, 1980a, pp. 65–66). Presumably, teachers who succeed in dominating their classrooms with iron fisted tactics have little call for this strategy.

Like the evaluations preceding these plans of action, the justifications for them have only rarely been considered separately by classroom ethnographers. The few they have considered are usually related to plans for handling misconduct. Woods (1975, p. 130) examined the reasons teachers give for 'showing up' their pupils: depending on the situation, they say this practice helps sustain orderliness, dramatizes schoolroom rules, serves as punishment (sometimes including revenge), and induces greater academic motivation (by shaming the pupil into a better intellectual effort). In the classroom of a Canadian free school, the curriculum is used to justify actions taken by the teacher against those who are uninvolved in it (Novak, 1975, p. 58). Justifying disorderly behavior related plans of action highlights the teacher's quandary about how to handle this situation. The 'moral principle' or justification that it is right and proper to punish misbehavior and the 'pragmatic principle' that punishment must be efficient and effective, but not disruptive of classroom activities, are in conflict whenever teachers contemplate intervention in pupil deviance (Hargreaves *et al,* 1975, pp. 221–222).

On a more abstract level, the solutions to three dilemmas commonly found in the elementary classroom also serve as justifications for certain plans of action (Berlak and Berlak, 1976, pp. 16–19). First, there is the dilemma of 'childhood continuance vesus childhood unique', or the view that the differences between children and adults are chiefly quantitative versus the view that children are unique. Second, is the dilemma of 'holistic versus molecular learning', or the belief that learning proceeds from knowledge of the whole to knowledge of its parts versus the belief that it proceeds from knowledge of the parts to a knowledge of the whole. Third, is the dilemma of 'public versus personal knowledge'. The first horn of this dilemma is that each pupil ought to know a minimum body of knowledge whether or not he or she perceives it as relevant at the time it is being learned. The second horn is that knowledge is worth acquiring if so perceived by the pupil. Such knowledge is introspective and reflective; it promotes understanding. Teachers were observed by the Berlaks to solve these dilemmas in several ways, depending on the requirements of teaching and managing their classes at the moment.

Pupil Reactions

Turning to pupils' reactions to their perceptions of what is going on in various classroom situations, we find more or less the same pattern of research interests; namely, the greatest attention has been given to plans of action. So far as this review is concerned, only Metz (1978, pp. 123–133) has dealt directly with pupils' *evaluations* as a component of their definitions of the situation. Some of those whom she interviewed feel their teachers default at times on their obligation to maintain classroom control or to act as the academic authority there. At other times these pupils are dismayed by teachers who demand order for order's sake. Here, they may resort to such plans of action as rebellion or mucking about (Furlong, 1977, p. 170), both of which are covered shortly. Mucking about may also follow on an evaluation of the classroom proceedings as tedious or confining (Woods, 1976, p. 185; Furlong, 1977, p. 164; Bird, 1980, pp. 99–100).

Moving on to *plans of action,* as based on evaluations like those just described, it is doubtful that pupils develop strategies in service of long-term objectives as teachers do (see preceding definition of strategy). Pupils' classroom action orientations are usually situationally limited and evanescent. The concept of 'strategy' is used here with this reservation in mind.

As Denscombe has noted, pupil strategies are, in many respects, 'counter-strategies':

> Whatever the extent of pupil influence . . . it clearly takes the form of a *re*action to a situation not entirely of their own making and one in which they suffer a lack of institutionalized rights. Much of their activity, in consequence, takes the form of *counter-strategies* through which teacher strategies can be baulked and through which acquiescence to teacher control can be traded-off against aspects of lessons which pupils find preferable.
>
> (1980b, p. 56)

Six such strategies have so far been discovered through ethnographic research, while a seventh strategy is cooperative in nature.

First, there are the forbidden acts of *talking* and *eating* in the classroom. The pupils observed by Corrigan (1979, pp. 56–57) justified these strategies as ways of making school more enjoyable or at least tolerable. At times it is simply good fun to flaunt the rules.

Next is the *noise* strategy (Denscombe, 1980b, pp. 57–59) which is implemented mostly in closed or traditional classrooms. The purpose of the noise is to disturb the flow of lessons or annoy the teacher or both.

A third strategy is to engage in *humor.* Woods (1976) identified two subtypes: 'mucking about' and 'subversive humor'. The latter is aimed at undermining the image of the school and the teacher. Denscombe (1980b, p. 63) explored a third subtype, which uses humor to avert threatening classroom situations or divert the teacher's focus of interest. The respite thereby gained from the tedium of the lesson or from an unpleasant task (e.g., a test or recitation) is the justification for this counterstrategy.

Fourth is *negotiation*. While the outcome of the negotiation process is taken up later in this paper as a form of reality construction, the plan of one or more pupils to try to negotiate with the teacher over some value falls within the motivational approach. Fraternization, which can be used by pupils too, is one subtype of this counterstrategy. Flirtation, ingratiation, and friendliness are among the tactics available to the would-be negotiant. Like teachers, pupils may try personal or group comparisons, expressions of emotional states, humor, and playing off one pupil against another in their attempts to bend the circumstances to their advantage (Martin, 1976, pp. 62–67; Denscombe, 1980b, p. 63).

Fifth, is what may be called the *exploitation* counterstrategy. Here pupils take advantage of the teacher's fraternization or avoidance of provocation strategies to shirk their assignments or gain a brief respite from them. No negotiation is involved here; the teacher, it is hoped, will remain ignorant of what is happening.

Still another counterstrategy is that of *rebellion*. It commonly occurs when pupils evaluate the teacher as incompetent; as unable to teach effectively or control the class sufficiently or fairly. Martin (1980, p. 26), for example, found a link between disorderliness and pupils' perceptions that their teachers categorize them as dull, as behavioral problems, or simply as unfavored (when compared with teachers' pets). Severe sanctions for objectionable demeanor, dress, or language outside the classroom may so anger pupils that they skip school, vandalize its property, or steal, all of which they justify in terms of the unfairness of the sanctions (Reynolds, 1976, pp. 135–136). Metz (1978, p. 133) recorded a similar reaction among the students she observed when their teacher insisted on order for its own sake.

A seventh strategy, which is not a counteraction to a plan the teacher just implemented, is that of *academic cooperation*. Pupils try to determine (evaluation) what teachers want in the way of an academic performance and give it to them. For instance, they ask questions to improve their knowledge or to confirm their interpretation of a point (Barnes, 1969, pp. 44–46). This they justify as an effective way to achieve good grades and avoid trouble (Delamont, 1976a, pp. 99–100). But even here Hammersley (1974, pp. 360—361) found that pupils occasionally succeed at breaking the rules of participation (e.g., shouting out the answer or not 'sirring' the teacher) in their enthusiasm to demonstrate their learning or understanding of some part of the lesson.

Before moving to the next approach, mention should be made of the sole study to concentrate on unusual definitions of classroom situations. Moore (1978), who studied an alternative school in the United States, noted that its pupils were confronted with considerable ambiguity. Their understandings of schoolroom life gained through previous experience in traditional institutions were inappropriate. Even as the academic year progressed some forms of interaction failed to crystalize into a recognizable pattern. Both pupils and teachers were often forced to construct makeshift definitions (which frequently conflicted) from bits of past experience and present perceptions of self and others.

Personality Approach

The personality approach of the theory of the definition of the situation deals with the characterological side of the defining process. Values, goals, attitudes, beliefs, and the like constitute its main focus, but only to the extent that these mental states are also treated as activated predispositions in actual types of situations.

The main goals in the classroom for the teacher are intellectual training (and sometimes moral and social training) and maintenance of order (Stebbins, 1975, p. 45). These goals gain more concrete expression as principal action orientations in countless everyday situations in the school, such as keeping noise to a tolerable level or inculcating the concept of whole numbers. Recently, a third goal has been identified, which remains unfulfilled if one of the first two is not met. Pollard (1980, pp. 49–50) refers to it as 'survival' (see also Denscombe, 1980a). It is possible that a teacher could even train her students intellectually *and* maintain order, but be so bankrupt from the experience that she failed to survive in the role of educationist.

The pursuit of these goals in ongoing situations is justified by certain values (or 'relevance structures', Furlong, 1977, pp. 175–183) and beliefs. The aforementioned goals indicate that teachers usually want their pupils to learn and to behave themselves while doing so. Although scant attention has been given to this facet of the defining of situations, it is evident from the classroom ethnographies that many teachers also want their pupils to regard them as fair-minded and pleasant individuals, to enjoy their educational experiences, and to come away from them with feelings of accomplishment. The strength with which the value of orderliness is held among teachers is recognized by some scholars as highly variable (e.g., McPherson, 1972, p. 90; Leacock, 1969, pp. 107–113). Hence, teachers' levels of tolerance for disorderliness are quite divergent.

Classroom research to date provides only a hint as to what the *situationally related* belief structure of typical schoolteachers looks like. Rist (1973, pp. 48–53, 95, 200), in his observations of instructors in an American inner-city school, concluded that they see the majority of their pupils as losers, as wanting in self-control, as possessing a low attention span, and as lacking the integrity to return borrowed items. The teachers studied by McPherson (1972, p. 87) believe boys are more disobedient than girls. Teachers in a mixed Indian-white school in the United States hold that white pupils are interested in, desire, and have the ability to internalize and act in accordance with the basic rules for orderly classroom interaction noticeably more than Indian pupils (Phillips, 1972, pp. 376–377).

Such beliefs influence teachers' evaluations of certain classroom situations as well as their subsequent plans of action there. For instance, Rist (1973, p. 95) observed how his teachers tended to work only with those pupils whom they felt could succeed; namely, the ones who were middle-class. The presumed low attention span of the losers also led these teachers to chop up their teaching units into small periods to help prevent potential misbehavior.

Even less is known about the personality side of pupil definitions of classroom situations. Only three values have been identified so far. McPherson (1972, pp. 106–107), among others, observed that pupils want order in the classroom and want their teachers to treat them equitably. It is clear from research by Metz (1978, pp. 121–122) and Woods (1976, p. 178) that pupils also want to engage in pleasant activities and to avoid boredom while at school.

Reality Construction Approach

The dramaturgical, motivational, and personality approaches to the definition of the situation are chiefly concerned with explaining the situated behavior of individuals.

The reality construction approach picks up where these three leave off. Its primary questions are (1) how the definitions (which may be tentative) of already interacting or behaving individuals coalesce into a collectively recognized understanding of what is happening and (2) how personal and collective definitions spawn new social forms and modifications of existing ones? Classroom ethnographers working within the symbolic interactionist segment of the theory have restricted themselves to Number 1. Lest there be any confusion, it should be pointed out that consensus is a quintessential property of collectively constructed definitions. Therefore, conflicting pupil and teacher definitions are beyond the scope of this approach.[5]

The reality construction approach has so far taken three forms in the ethnographic exploration of classrooms: negotiated arrangements, self-fulfilling prophecies, and working agreements. Only a short summary of the complicated conceptual framework of negotiation is possible here (see Martin, 1976, pp. 3–13). Negotiation is an interpersonal process whereby those involved in it arrive at the settlement of some issue by means of various exchange tactics. After presenting the preconditions and extent of negotiations, Martin (1976, pp. 11–12) described the ideal typical stages of this process:

> (a) communicating goals of the interaction, (b) defining and redefining the situation, (c) attempting to put alter on the defensive by drawing his attention to new materials and/or using other persuasive tactics, (d) displaying one's bargaining counters and evaluating those of others, (e) reevaluating alter's position to see whether what has been done thus far has achieved the desired ends, (f) going through these stages again, (g) reaching a working agreement concerning the issue(s) negotiated, and (h) solemnizing the agreement.

There are three possible outcomes to a negotiation. A compromise may be struck in which each negotiator gives a certain, albeit not necessarily equal, amount. Or, secondly, one of the negotiators compromises little or none at all; even after considerable negotiation he has enough power in the situation largely or completely to get his own way. This outcome is won at expense of the other negotiator (zero-sum game). In the third outcome the same circumstances pertain, except that winning in the negotiation has been accomplished without cost to the other parties involved in it (non-zero-sum game). To avoid possible confusion, it should be reiterated that the decision to negotiate some issue, as a teacher or pupil strategy (plan of action), is different from the negotiation process itself, from which a new social reality emerges.

The literature divides roughly into two parts: negotiation by teachers and pupils wherein both try to make classroom life more tolerable or workable; and negotiation where ambiguous teacher-pupil relations must be clarified, because one or both parties want clarification. Making life in the classroom more tolerable or workable is usually carried out by means of 'closed negotiations' (Martin, 1976, p. 34). Here the teacher announces explicit directions and consequences for failing to heed them. This form of closed negotiation is instantiated on page 57 of Martin's monograph.

Peter Woods (1978) applies the label of 'closed negotiation' to a different form which, unlike Martin's, hinges on nonverbal interaction. That is, a settlement is reached indirectly without overt recognition (or at least without overt acknowledgement) of the negotiated nature of the outcome by the parties concerned. In Woods' form the parties independently try to maximize their own interests in opposition to and conflict with each other. Concessions are made, but grudgingly. When skipping school, pooling knowledge and resources for examinations, cribbing, mucking about, and so forth become unchallenged parts of the classroom routine, they are concessions won from the teacher by the pupils through nonverbal closed negotiation (also see Woods, 1977).

Reynolds' (1976) discussion of 'truces' among teachers and their delinquent pupils further illustrates the nonverbal form; such as when the staff he studied learned to accept the fact that their authority ends at the classroom door, after pupils caught fighting and drinking outside it refused to come to school when disciplined for these misdemeanors. Wegmann (1976) watched pupils directly challenge their teacher with repeated disorderliness, while the teacher indirectly handled the situation much of the time by ignoring the challenge, treating it humorously, or feigning personal hurt by their acts. The pupils soon developed a new and more precise outlook on the applicability of their classroom's orderliness rules (i.e., a new social reality took shape). Additional examples of the indirect closed negotiation may be found in McPherson's fieldwork (1972, pp. 105–106).

New social realities enabling a more tolerable, workable classroom milieu are not always grudgingly negotiated. Open negotiations also occur from time to time (Woods, 1978). Here the contending parties meet each other openly and willingly to arrive at a consensus they both more or less favor. Reynolds (1976), for example, describes how the teachers of the delinquent boys he observed voluntarily relaxed their classroom goals to permit more football offset by less schoolwork.

The other focus, negotiation for the purpose of clarification of teacher-pupil relations, is characteristic of the early days and weeks of each academic year when pupils are adapting to the routines, rules, and dispositions of their new teachers. Inevitably, both sides bend somewhat as they try to negotiate a consensus sufficient to guide their behavior for the remainder of the time they are together (Pollard, 1980, p. 44; McPherson, 1972, p. 112). As Ball (1980, pp. 146–151) has noted, this occurs in two stages: the first is passive, purely observational, and short; the second involves testing out the teacher's rules, routines, and the like, usually by a few pupils. 'A sense of community' (consensus) arises as the class considers the response of the teacher to the testing initiatives of its representative members. Ball argues that teachers and pupils are aware of this process; in other words, negotiation is open in the sense intended by Woods.

In the alternative school studied by Moore (1978), clarifying negotiations can be observed throughout the year and take up much teacher-pupil energy. The unfamiliarity of the setting for all participants means that understandings about classroom life developed in traditional educational institutions no longer apply.

Self-fulfilling Prophecies

Hargreaves *et al* (1975, p. 141) summarize the self-fulfilling prophecy as follows:

1 Teacher believes X about a pupil (e.g., that he is very intelligent).
2 Teacher makes predictions about the pupil (e.g., that he will make outstanding academic progress).
3 Change in teacher attitude and behavior towards the pupil.
4 Change in pupil self-conception and behavior in line with the teacher's attitude/behavior.
5 Fulfilment of the prediction.

In short, founded on the interaction between teacher and pupil, a new social reality arises depicting the latter's academic abilities.

Unlike the Rosenthal and Jacobson (1968) studies, which were experimental, classroom ethnographers have been able to demonstrate through rich accounts of the self-fulfilling prophecy the proposition that this form of reality construction may be favorable or unfavorable (e.g., D. Hargreaves, 1967, p. 106; Delamont, 1976a, chapter 3; Rist, 1973, pp. 164–195). One of the current questions in this area is just how widespread and inevitable is this process: the answer may turn out to be that it is less widespread and inevitable than conventionally thought. The teachers studied by Bird (1980) were inclined to see their pupils as unique. Labels placed on them during a crisis were forgotten, unless the critical behavior persisted for many months. Until this happened and they became fixed in the teacher's mind, pupils tended to live in ignorance of the sorts of feelings their teachers momentarily had about them. Likewise, McPherson (1972, pp. 99–100) found that teachers do reclassify pupils along academic and orderliness dimensions, although reclassification along the second is less common than along the first.[6]

Working Agreements

For lack of a more suitable term, 'working agreement' is the one chosen here to refer to those constructed realities and the processes by which they are accomplished that are neither negotiations nor self-fulfilling prophecies. Research on reality construction outside education concentrates almost exclusively on this kind, paying rather little attention to the other two. The classroom ethnographic literature, however, contains only one study of the working agreement. Furlong (1976) observed 'interaction sets', or groups of pupils who, at any one time, perceive what is happening in a similar way and, by various means, inform each other of their perceptions. In this fashion they reach a consensus on how to act together. Furlong provides several examples of working agreements about disorderly behavior and academic performance developed in interaction sets. The case of Carol's misconduct is one of them.[7] Carol had been told by her teacher to leave because she had been rude to her.

> She (Carol) wanders out slowly, laughing and looking around at Valerie and Diane, who laugh as well. She stands outside the door, looking through its window for a few minutes . . . trying to catch the eyes of the people inside the room.
>
> (Furlong, 1976, p. 27)

As she leaves the room Carol makes continual non-verbal contact with Valerie and Diane. Moreover, she keeps doing this through the window in the door. Valerie's and Diane's laughter communicates to Carol the degee to which the three of them share a definition of the immediate situation.

Dramaturgical Approach

According to the dramaturgical approach life is theater and people are its playwrights. They use communicative techniques to express their definitions of the situation to others in the same setting. That is, they dramatize their evaluations, plans of action, and justifications as based upon their perceptions of what is happening. In this fashion, activated predispositions (e.g., values, attitudes, beliefs), moods, and intentions gain expression through such techniques as facial expressions, gestures, vocal intonation, words, posture, clothing, physical location, props, and the like.

Classroom ethnographers have all but ignored this approach to the theory. One paper by the author (Stebbins, 1980, p. 89) deals briefly with it in connection with the use of humor in the classroom . The definition of the situation of the humorist (usually the teacher) is expressed histrionically. By this means the audience for the humor learns of the humorist's predisposition to jest, his or her mood at the moment, and how he or she judges or evaluates the immediate situation. For pupils such information is sometimes obscure and so may be welcome, especially when conveyed in a pleasing manner.

Ethnomethodology

Lacking a better one, the label 'ethnomethodologist' is used here to identify those scholars who have shown a direct interest in the definition of the situation from a cultural perspective, in contradistinction to the consciousness perspective of the symbolic interactionists. Definition of the situation as a concept has always been more peripheral to ethnomethodology than to symbolic interactionism. Today's ethnomethodologists search for sets of constitutive rules or sets of cultural practices called *frames*. Behind every definition of the situation lies a frame which, even though the individual is unaware of it, shapes his or her behavioral response to the events of the immediate present. There is a cultural system of categories and rules governing the creation and communication of meaning. In Goffman's (1974) terms, human beings are the 'resources' who manifest the hidden rules and categories.

In contemporary educational research the search for frames as an important condition in the creation and communication of meaning has been extended to the study of 'structuring activities that assemble the social structures of education' (Mehan, 1978, p. 32). Structures are the 'objective and constraining "social facts" of the educational world' (Mehan, 1978, pp. 35–36). They include pupil intelligence and scholastic achievement and patterns of behavior, such as the interaction between teacher and pupil, tester and pupil, and principal and teacher. Furthermore, these structures are no longer treated separately from structuring. Rather they are treated together and equally, 'by showing how the social facts of the educational world emerge from structuring activities to become external and constraining as part of a world that is both of our making and beyond our making' (Mehan, 1978, pp. 60–61).

The present compass of the ethnomethodological segment of the theory of the definition of the situation is at least as wide as that of the symbolic interactionist segment. In the language of the latter it runs from the definer's personality (especially its cultural background) to the social realities constructed through the interpersonal relations of those in the immediate setting.

The search for assumed rules and categories, represented here by the phrase 'frame analysis', has been going on for some time in the field of classroom ethnography. Nell Keddie (1971) conducted one of the first studies of this genre. She concentrated on the category of 'normal pupil', or the teacher's taken-for-granted image of her pupils in different ability groups. Keddie found that the 'normal attributes' of pupils in each group are used by teachers to render invalid certain comments the pupils tend to make. The former control the latter in this way. For example, when pupils in the C stream (the lowest group) voiced a complaint about a lesson, their teachers responded with: 'he is just trying to get out of work' or 'they'll try anything on' (Keddie, 1971, pp. 139–140). By contrast, such comments by pupils in the A stream are taken seriously.

Lundgren (1974) sought to explain the teaching process in terms of rules govern-ed by frames. He sorted frames into two groups: organizational (e.g., class size, ability composition of the class) and temporal (amount of time at one's disposal). The teaching process is defined as a system of transformations according to a set of rules. These rules are manifestations of the organizational and temporal frames of the classroom and the school of which it is a part. The teachers' actions constituting the transformations are understandable in relation to their intentions and goals. In the terminology of the present paper, their actions may be understood by discovering their definitions of the situation.

Time frames play a similar role in Novak's (1975) study of the free school. The temporal order enforced by the curriculum is a taken-for-granted constraint on teachers and pupils. In addition, the curriculum sets limits on human action by requiring particular spatial arrangements (e.g., seating plans, seatwork groupings) and interpersonal relations (e.g., teacher questioning practices, restricted interaction in a testing situation). As mentioned earlier, the curriculum also helps identify deviance in the classroom and justifies action taken against it as part of the motiva-tional approach to defining such situations.

Another prominent theme in the frame analytic classroom ethnographies is the constraining nature of the assumed rules and categories underlying teacher-pupil relations. Edwards and Furlong (1978, chapter 6) found that teachers assume they share the definitions of proper classroom behavior with their pupils. They also assume they are viewed as the authority in intellectual and orderliness matters. And they assume later lessons can build on knowledge inevitably acquired in earlier ones. Edwards (1980) goes on to note in a subsequent article that teachers 'own' the classroom interaction, since they manage and organize it. The organization of much of classroom talk can be explained by this structural fact. Furthermore, teachers govern the knowledge their pupils ultimately gain. What they learn and how the learning is accomplished is greatly affected by this condition. McHoul (1978) comes to a similar conclusion: the rules for differential participation rights of teachers and pupils to talk rests on teachers' exclusive control over who shall speak next.

Mishler (1972) treats the background rules and categories of the classroom as teacher 'cognitive strategies' (these strategies differ from the ones referred to in the motivational approach). Cognitive strategies are composed of three components: (1) rules on how attention is focused; (2) rules on the search and evaluation procedures used in teaching; and (3) rules on the structure of alternatives presented while teaching. Teachers were found to vary extensively in their linguistic expression of these strategies.

And pupils have rules, too, which they expect their teachers to honor. Nash (1976, pp. 86–91) lists five of them: teachers are expected to keep order, teach well-defined and specific subjects, explain difficult parts of each lesson, be interesting, and be fair. The consequences may be unpleasant for teachers who ignore these expectations. Though not a rule among the pupils studied by Nash, he also found they are grateful when a teacher is friendly.

Structuring

'Social competence' (Mehan, 1978) is a key concept in the subtle, but significant, shift in emphasis to structuring from the earlier frame analysis. Effective classroom participants have the requisite skill and knowledge to interpret the speech and behavior of other participants there and to respond sensibly (as defined by the others). In the classroom this implies the integration of academic knowledge and interpersonal skills, some of which are unique to that setting. Socially competent teachers and pupils when interacting share meanings at a level sufficient to generate structures of the sort mentioned earlier in this section.

The concept of social competence appears to have grown out of Mehan's (1974) and Cicourel's *et al* (1974) older interest in the problem of how teachers and pupils acquire the ability to interpret rules and categories (an interest different from the interests pursued by the frame analysts):

> The acquisition of interpretative abilities enables a member to create cultural and normative sense in on-going settings and to make judgments about the meaning of information, thus helping him to decide what is 'normal', 'bizarre', 'threatening', 'humorous', etc . . . Normative rules are like prescriptive and proscriptive recipes for deciding what is socially acceptable and unacceptable behavior . . . Social and psychological cognitive processes must be acquired to articulate immediate experiences with normative rules governing formal language use, legal codes, implicit social activities like rules of etiquette, games, and kinship relationships.
>
> (Cicourel *et al*, 1974, p. 301)

To achieve this articulation teachers must supply unstated background features when the applicable rules are in play in a situation. This is necessary because rules are incomplete (Mehan, 1974, pp. 125–126). The same holds for teachers' instructions, for they, too, are incomplete. The child must locate additional defining information in other aspects of the immediate setting (e.g., instructional materials, facial features of the teacher, behavior of classmates). Moreover, pupils must learn to disregard as unimportant the superfluous language of teachers, while attending closely to their important statements (Barnes, 1969, p. 62). Social competence, however, never comes naturally; it develops slowly over the years at school through the progressively more complicated tasks set for pupils by their teachers (Dore *et al*, 1978, pp. 383–384).

Some social competence is actually 'procedural competence' (see Edwards and Furlong, 1978, chapter 6). Development of the procedural type begins with the onset of the child's school career:

> Administrative, disciplinary, and instructional rules are announced, refined, and repeated so that pupils come to accept certain ways of doing things as normal in that context. As the process continues, the rules largely sink out of sight. Explicit descriptions become implicit prescriptions and teachers can refer more and more obliquely to how things are (and ought to be) done . . . A procedural map is being drawn, the salient features of which will later be taken for granted.
>
> (Edwards and Furlong, 1978, p. 83)

Procedural settling in involves learning rules on getting down to work, working on one's own, talking, and paying attention. Pupils must know these rules and when and how they apply.

The notion of social competence can also be profitably applied to deviance in the classroom, which is the violation of the rules in force there. Deviance, Hargreaves *et al* (1975, p. 55) point out, hinges on imputations made by the teacher about the behavior of one or more pupils. The meaning of these imputations depends on teachers' and pupils' *competent* understanding of the rules appropriate to the situation in which the infraction takes place and of events preceding that infraction. These rules are generally beyond the participants' awareness; they are assumed to be operating in certain contexts.[8] Subtle implemental rules are used by teachers to accomplish a classroom task. Violation of these constitutes deviance (Hargreaves *et al*, 1975, chapter 5). For example, among the sub-rules implementing the larger rule of pay attention are (in the situation where the teacher is reading a passage to the pupils), no looking around the room, keep eyes open and on the teacher, refrain from side involvements with the hands, and no talking. With respect to the motivational approach, the pupil's identity as troublemaker or good student helps the teacher impute deviance where evidence of it is ambiguous.

Much of the time, acquiring social competence takes place through discourse, which is undoubtedly one of the main reasons for the recent shift to conversational analysis in classroom ethnography.[9] Dore and her colleagues (1978, pp. 375–376) describe how the language or 'text' of pupils indexes the tasks they are doing by means of five methods. Pupils signal each other about the task they are orienting to, which they do by *displaying, announcing,* and *formulating* their actions. Moreover, they *repair* one another's misunderstandings about the nature and conduct of the task as well as hold each other *accountable* for accomplishing it. McDermott *et al* (1978) propose a similar model.

One of the many social facts to result from the structuring relations of socially competent teachers and pupils is the lesson; another is orderliness. Both are examples of a new social order made possible by the skilled articulation of assumed rules and the immediate experience of the participants. It follows that a lesson, for instance, is as much an accomplishment of pupils as of teachers, for the former make it happen by properly interpreting the latter's utterances (Payne, 1976). The 'properness' of the interpretation is a judgment of the teachers, of course.

In accomplishing a social fact, pupils also operate by their own rules of competence. These are arrayed along four dimensions (Pollard, 1979, pp. 79–81) (1) knowledge about the teacher; (2) understandings associated with particular subjects and activities in the curriculum; (3) flow through time of each lesson, school day, and school year; (4) physical characteristics of the school and classroom settings. Pollard (1979, p. 88) holds that pupils are aware of these rules and that they make effective use of them to judge the relevant actions of other pupils and the teacher.

Boggs (1972) has identified some of the rules in Pollard's second dimension. When queried by a teacher, it is safer for pupils to answer minimally, if at all. But other children can be queried, answered, and talked to at any time. So can adults when they are communicating with a group of children. When children sense an adult is receptive to interaction with them, they can individually volunteer information and possibly even initiate a conversation.

Building on Mehan's (1974, p. 126) pioneering statement, French and MacLure (1980) have added to this list of rules by setting out the unconscious 'strategies' pupils use to answer correctly their teacher's questions. One of them is to repeat the candidate answer of a classmate. Another is to retrieve items previously introduced into the discourse (usually by the teacher). A third strategy may be followed when the first two cannot be implemented. Here pupils draw on their stock of typical classifications of objects and events by trying to locate their answers within them. Some item in the question is selected as a superordinate concept for a class of items. Possible answers are then selected in terms of their membership in that class. The authors present two additional strategies, which are variants of the third.

Conclusion

This review gives substance to Delamont's (1978, pp. 67–68) observation that much work remains to be done in classroom ethnography. The review, I believe, also demonstrates the pivotal role of the concept of the definition of the situation in the interpretive sociologies. Andy Hargreaves (1978, p. 75) asserts that the teacher 'is the crucial linchpin in the wheel of causality that connects structural features of the society to interactional patterns in the classroom and back again, thereby reproducing those structural arrangements'. The definition of classroom situations is the social psychological process by which this link is effected.

Thus, the theory reviewed here can contribute, as David Hargreaves (1978) insists, to an understanding of how ideology is implemented (if implemented at all) on the behavioral level. For example, teachers' coping strategies relate to structural and ideological aspects of the society by underscoring some of the problems they have to cope with, including large classes, inadequate physical facilities, and seemingly unteachable slum children (A. Hargreaves, 1978, p. 78).

Meanwhile, on the social psychological side, the concept of the definition of the situation is indispensable to our understanding of the teacher-pupil relationship.

> It seems probable that the pupils who come to be perceived by teachers as the most able, and who in a streamed school reach the top streams, are those who have access to or are willing to take over the teachers' definition of the situation. . . . This is not necessarily a question of ability to move to higher levels of generalization and abstraction so much as an ability to move into an alternative system of thought from that of his [the pupil] everyday life.
>
> (Keddie, 1971, p. 150)

In conclusion, the time has come not to abandon the fledgling interpretive sociology of the classroom, but to forge ahead with a renewed effort fired by a sense of theoretical purpose. This should be the classroom ethnographer's most important mission in the immediate future.

Notes

1 Classroom ethnographies incorporated into the analysis in my monograph on teachers' definitions of classroom situations (Stebbins, 1975) have, for the most part, been omitted from the present review.
2 It should be mentioned that some of this research falls outside the scope of this paper, for the ethnographers fail to relate the categories they have identified to definitions of the situation (e.g., Gouldner, 1978, chapter 3; Rist, 1973, pp. 61, 113).

3   This is the point at which to note that imputed justifications may also help explain behavior in that they are seen by definers as its cause. But definers may also offer other causes. For instance, McPherson's (1972, pp. 84–85) teachers often blame parents and the 'changing times' for the unruliness of their pupils. Neither of these are imputed pupil justifications.

4   Despite the best laid instructional plans or strategies, teachers may be forced to modify them through combinations of teacher-pupil 'informing, directing and eliciting transactions' (Sinclair and Coulthard, 1975, pp. 59–60).

5   The conflict of definitions perspective of Waller (1932), which continues to stimulate research (e.g., Corrigan, 1979; Reynolds, 1976), is logically part of the motivational approach. As the opposition unfolds, teachers and pupils evaluate each other as engaged in behavior inimical to the definer's interests, interests that person is unwilling to compromise.

6   Studies of and theories about the typification of pupils and teachers, even though they also discuss the self-fulfilling prophecy, have been omitted from this part of this review (e.g., Hargreaves *et al*, 1975, chapter 6; Sharp and Green, 1975, chapter 6). They are mostly concerned with how types are formed rather than with how they serve in definitions of situations.

7   Following Goffman, Furlong uses 'definition of the situation' to refer to the phenomena labeled here as the 'working agreement'.

8   Kindergarten children are as yet socially *in*competent so far as schoolroom proceedings are concerned. Therefore the idea of deviance has little validity when applied to their behavior. As King (1978, p. 52) observes children of this age are capable of being naughty, but are unable to act intentionally naughty by knowingly breaking local rules.

9   Some of the conversational analysis ethnographies center largely or entirely on utterances, while searching the definition of the situation of the speaker for their meaning (e.g., Sinclair and Coulthard, 1975; Walker and Adelman, 1976; Stubbs, 1975; Torode, 1976; French and MacLure, 1979). Such a model is beyond the scope of the theory of the definition of the situation, although the latter could be of great use to the former.

References

BALL, S. (1980) 'Initial encounters in a classroom in the process of establishment' in WOODS, P. (Ed) *Pupil Strategies* London, Croom Helm.

BARNES, D. (1969) 'Language in the secondary classroom' in BARNES, D., BRITTON, J., ROSEN, H. and the LATE (Eds) *Language, the Learner and the School* London, Penguin.

BECKER, H. (1952) 'Social class variations in the teacher-pupil relationship' *The Journal of Educational Sociology* 25 (4).

BERLAK, H. and BERLAK, A. (1976) 'Towards a political and social psychological theory of schooling' *Interchange* 6 (3).

BIRD, C. (1980) 'Deviant labeling in school: The pupils' perspective' in WOODS, P. (Ed) *Pupil Strategies* London, Croom Helm.

BOGGS, S. (1972) 'The meaning of questions and narratives to Hawaiian children' in CAZDEN, C., JOHN, V. and HYMES, D. (Eds) *Functions of Language in the Classroom* New York, Teachers College Press.

CICOUREL, A. *et al* (1974) *Language Use and School Performance* New York, Academic Press.

CORRIGAN, P. (1979) *Schooling the Smash Street Kids* London, Macmillan.

DELAMONT, S. (1976a) *Interaction in the Classroom* London, Methuen.

DELAMONT, S. (1976b) 'Beyond Flanders' fields' in STUBBS, M. and DELAMONT, S. (Eds) *Explorations in Classroom Observation* New York, Wiley.

DELAMONT, S. (1978) 'Sociology in the classroom in BARTON, L. and MEIGHAN, R. (Eds) *Sociological Interpretations of Schooling and Classrooms: A Reappraisal* Driffield, Nafferton.

DENSCOMBE, M. (1980a) 'Keeping "em quiet": The significance of noise for the practical activity of teaching' in WOODS, P. (Ed) *Teacher Strategies* London, Croom Helm.

DENSCOMBE, M. (1980b) 'Pupils' strategies and the open classroom' in WOODS, P. (Ed) *Pupil Strategies* London, Croom Helm.

DORE, J., GEARHART, M. and NEWMAN, D. (1978) 'The structure of nursery school conversation' in NELSON, K. (Ed) *Children's Language* New York, Gardner Press.

EDWARDS, A. (1980) 'Patterns of power and authority in classroom talk' in WOODS, P. (Ed) *Teacher Strategies* London, Croom Helm.

EDWARDS, A. and FURLONG, J. (1978) *The Language of Teaching* London, Heinemann.

FLANDERS, N. (1970) *Analyzing Teaching Behaviour* Reading, Mass., Addison-Wesley.

FRENCH, P. and MACLURE, M. (1979) 'Getting the right answer and getting the answer right' *Research in Education* 22.

FURLONG, V. (1976) 'Interaction sets in the classroom. Towards a study of pupil knowledge' in STUBBS, M. and DELAMONT, S. (Eds) *Explorations in Classroom Observations* New York, John Wiley.

FURLONG, V. (1977) 'Anancy goes to school: A case study of pupils' knowledge of their teachers' in WOODS, P. and HAMMERSLEY, M. (Eds) *School Experience* London, Croom Helm.

GOFFMAN, E. (1974) *Frame Analysis* New York, Harper.

GOULDNER, H. (1978) *Teachers' Pets, Troublemakers and Nobodies* Westport, Connecticut, Greenwood Press.

HAMMERSLEY, M. (1974) 'The organization of pupil participation' *Sociological Review* 22 (3).

HAMMERSLEY, M. (1976) 'The mobilization of pupil attention' in HAMMERSLEY, M. and WOODS, P. (Eds) *The Process of Schooling* London, Routledge and Kegan Paul.

HAMMERSLEY, M. (1977) 'School learning: The cultural resources required to answer a teacher's question' in WOODS, P. and HAMMERSLEY, M. (Eds) *School Experience* London, Croom Helm.

HARGREAVES, A. (1978) 'The significance of classroom coping strategies' in BARTON, L. and MEIGHAN, R. (Eds) *Sociological Interpretations of Schooling and Classrooms: A Reappraisal* Driffield, Nafferton.

HARGREAVES, D. (1967) *Social Relations in a Secondary School* London, Routledge and Kegan Paul.

HARGREAVES, D (1978) 'Whatever happened to symbolic interactionism' in BARTON, L. and MEIGHAN, R. (Eds) *Sociological Interpretations of Schooling and Classrooms. A Reappraisal* Driffield, Nafferton.

HARGREAVES, D., HESTER, S. and MELLOR, F. (1975) *Deviance and Classrooms* London, Routledge and Kegan Paul.

KEDDIE, N. (1971) 'Classroom knowledge' in YOUNG, F. (Ed) *Knowledge and Control* London, Collier-Macmillan.

KING, R. (1978) *All Things Bright and Beautiful* New York, Wiley.

LACEY, C. (1970) *Hightown Grammar* Manchester University Press.

LEACOCK, E. (1969) *Teaching and Learning in City Schools* New York, Basic Books.

LUNDGREN, U.P. (1974) 'Pedagogical roles in the classroom' in EGGLESTON, J. (Ed) *Contemporary Research in the Sociology of Education* London, Methuen.

MACLURE, M. and FRENCH, P. (1980) 'Roots to right answers: On pupils' strategies for answering teachers' questions' in WOODS, P. (Ed) *Pupil Strategies* London, Croom Helm.

MARTIN, W. (1976) *The Negotiated Order of the School* Toronto, Macmillan of Canada.

MARTIN, W. (1980) 'Student perspective on categorizing in the school' *Research Bulletin* No. 80–012, St. John's, Newfoundland, Institute for Research in Human Abilities.

MCDERMOTT, R., GOSPODINOFF, K. and ARON, J. (1978) 'Criteria for an ethnographically adequate description of concerted activities and their contexts' *Semiotics* 24 (3/4).

MCHOUL, A. (1978) 'The organization of turns at formal talk in the classroom' *Language in Society* 7.

MCPHERSON, G. (1972) *Small Town Teacher* Cambridge, Mass., Harvard University Press.

MEHAN, H. (1974) 'Accomplishing classroom lessons' in CICOUREL, A. *et al* (Eds) *Language Use and School Performance* New York, Academic Press.

MEHAN, H. (1978) 'Structuring school structure', *Harvard Educational Review* 48 (1).

METZ, H. (1978) *Classrooms and Corridors: The Crisis of Authority in Desegregated Secondary Schools* Berkeley, California, University of California Press.

MISHLER, E. (1972) 'Implications of teacher strategies for language and cognition' in CAZDEN, C., JOHN, V. and HYMES, D. (Eds) *Functions of Language in the Classroom* New York, Teacher's College Press.

MOORE, D. (1978) 'Social order in an alternative school', *Teacher's College Record* 79 (3).

NASH, R. (1976) 'Pupils' expectations of their teachers' in STUBBS, S. and DELAMONT, S. (Eds) *Explorations in Classroom Observation* London, John Wiley.

NOVAK, M. (1975) *Living and Learning in the Free School* Toronto, McClelland and Stewart.

PAISEY, H. (1975) *The Behavioural Strategy of Teachers* Slough, NFER.

PARSONS, T. (1937) *The Structure of Social Action* Vol. 1, New York, Free Press.

PAYNE, G. (1976) 'Making a lesson happen: An ethnomethodological analysis' in HAMMERSLEY, M. and WOODS, P. (Eds) *The Process of Schooling* London, Routledge and Kegan Paul.

PAYNE, G. and HUSTLER, D. (1980) 'Teaching the class: The practical management of a cohort', *British Journal of Sociology of Education* 1 (1).

PHILLIPS, S. (1972) 'Participant structures and communicative competence' in CAZDEN, C., JOHN, V. and HYMES, D. (Eds) *Functions of Language in the Classroom* New York, Teacher's College Press.

POLLARD, A. (1979) 'Negotiating deviance and "getting done" in primary school classrooms' in BARTON, L. and MEIGHAN, R. (Eds) *Schools, Pupils, and Deviance* Driffield, Nafferton.

POLLARD, A. (1980) 'Teacher interest and changing situations of survival threat in primary school classrooms' in WOODS, P. (Ed) *Teacher Strategies* London, Croom Helm.

REYNOLDS, D. (1976) 'When teachers and pupils refuse a truce' in MUNGHAM, G. and PEARSON, G. (Eds) *Working Class Youth Culture* London, Routledge and Kegan Paul.

RIST, R. (1973) *The Urban School: A Factory for Failure* Boston, MIT Press.

ROSENTHAL, R. and JACOBSON, L. (1968) *Pygmalion in the Classroom* New York, Holt, Rinehart and Winston.

ROSSER, E. and HARRÉ, R. (1976) 'The meaning of "trouble"' in HAMMERSLEY, M. and WOODS, P. (Eds) *The Process of Schooling* London, Routledge and Kegan Paul.

SHARP, R. and GREEN, A. (1975) *Education and Social Control* London, Routledge and Kegan Paul.

SINCLAIR, J. and COULTHARD, R. (1975) *Towards an Analysis of Discourse* Oxford, Oxford University Press.

STEBBINS, R. (1975) *Teachers and Meaning: Definitions of Classroom Situations* Leiden, E.J. Brill.

STEBBINS, R. (1980) 'The role of humour in teaching: Strategy and self-expression' in WOODS, P. (Ed) *Teacher Strategies* London, Croom Helm.

STEBBINS, R. (1981) 'Definition of the situation: A review' in FURNHAM, A. and ARGYLE, M. (Eds) *Social Behaviour in Context* London, Allyn and Bacon.

STONE, G. and FARBERMAN, H. (1970) (Eds) *Social Psychology Through Symbolic Interactionism* Waltham, Mass., Ginn-Blaisdell.

STUBBS, M. (1976) 'Teaching and talking: A sociolinguistic approach to classroom interaction' in CHANAN, G. and DELAMONT, S. (Eds) *Frontiers of Classroom Research* Slough, NFER.

THOMAS, W. and ZNANIECKI, F. (1918) *The Polish Peasant in Europe and America* Boston, Richard G. Badger.

TORODE, B. (1976) 'Teachers' talk and classroom discipline' in STUBBS, M. and DELAMONT, S. (Eds) *Explorations in Classroom Observation* London, John Wiley.

WALKER, R. and ADELMAN, C. (1976) 'Strawberries' in STUBBS, M. and DELAMONT, S. (Eds) *Explorations in Classroom Observation* London, John Wiley.

WALKER, R. and GOODSON, I. (1977) 'Humour in the classroom' in WOODS, P. and HAMMERSLEY, M. (Eds) *School Experience* London, Croom Helm.

WALLER, W. (1932) *The Sociology of Teaching* New York, Wiley.

WEGMANN, R. (1976) 'Classroom discipline: An exercise in the manufacture of social reality', *Sociology of Education* 49 (1).

WOODS, P. (1975) ' "Showing them up" in secondary school' in CHANAN, G. and DELAMONT, S. (Eds) *Frontiers of Classroom Research* Slough, NFER.

WOODS, P. (1976) 'Having a laugh' in HAMMERSLEY, M. and WOODS, P. (Eds) *The Process of Schooling* London, Routledge and Kegan Paul.

WOODS, P. (1977) *The Pupils' Experience* E 202, Schooling and Society, London, The Open University Press.

WOODS, P. (1978) 'Negotiating the demands of school work' *Journal of Curriculum Studies* 10 (4).

WOODS, P. (1979) *The Divided School* London, Routledge and Kegan Paul.

YOUNG, M.F.D. (1971) *Knowledge and Control: New Directions for Sociology of Education* London, Collier-Macmillan.

Teacher-Pupil Question-Answer Sequences: Some Problems of Analysis

Stephen Walker, Newman College

Part 1: Classroom Talk and Research in the Sociology of Education

As competent speakers of the language natural to our particular social order, we have little difficulty in accepting the following, fairly self-evident observations. First, that there is a large number of social situations in which participants to the talk which forms the interactional bedrock of the situation perform conversational activities which might be grossly characterized as asking questions and giving answers. Secondly, that, in certain 'institutional' settings, engagement in these kinds of activities appears to be a major part of the business being conducted in the social encounters which are enacted in these settings. Thirdly, that the ways in which such conversational work is done in particular 'institutional' settings is audibly different from (a) the way it is accomplished in other such settings and (b) the way it is routinely 'brought off' or recognized as appropriate in 'naturally-occurring' stretches of talk.

Consider the following fragments:

Fragment 1. OU: 45, 3A[1]

C   And isn't it a *fact* (1.0) Miss Le Brette (1.0) where you (1.0) went to (1.0) on this evening (2.0) was at least *a* quarter of a mile (0.5) from the main highway? =
W   = I don't know.
    (2.5)
C   Some distance back into theuh (.) into the wood wasn't it?
    (0.5)
W   It was up the *path* I don't know how far.

Fragment 2. Frankel:TC:1:1:2 – 3[2]

S   = •hhh Uh:m, •tch •hhh who w'yih   ta:lking to.
    (0.6)
G   Jis no:w?
S   •hhh *No* I *ca*lled be- like between ele⌈ven on
G   ⌊I wasn't
    talkeen tuh a:nybuddy. (b) Be-oth Marla'n I slept 'ntil about *noo:n* =
S   O⌈h
    ⌊

Fragment 3. G80:F15.[3]

A You have never heard me describe myself •hhh er as a Marxist I have only been er er put in the position of answering that question when the specific point has been put to me •hhh about whether er I would call myself a Marxist •hh or whether or not I subscribe to Marxist economic philosophy.

I Do you ascribe to Marxist economic philosophy.

A I would say that there: ar: the(y) (.) philosophy of Marx as far as the economies of Britain is concerned is one with which I find sympathy and would support yes.

I Well that makes you a Marxi*st* doe⌈sn't it.
⌊Not necessarily

makes me a Marxist in the descriptive sense.

Fragment 4. McH 78:184[4]

A What's going *on* here
  (1.5)
A Yes
B Mining
  (1.5)
A Mining, what sort of mining?
  (2.0)
C Open cut mining
A Open cut?
  (0.5)
D Ir⌈on ore
E ⌊Iron ore
A Iron ore. Why iron ore?
  (1.0)
A Don't they mine other things (in) open cuts?

Even casual scrutiny of these extracts generates, I think, feelings of familiarity, a sense of situation. By making reference to certain resources we possess as competent speakers of the language being used, we can intuitively analyze the way in which the talk in these fragments has been designed and produced. By so-doing we identify certain features in this production which allows us, with some surety, to re-locate the four sequences within the settings in which they were spoken. Quite clearly, in fragment 1, 3 and 4 at least, discernible social identities are being assumed and displayed by the participants to the speech-exchanges. Although all the parties are engaged in the production of what we might call Question – Answer (Q – A) sequences, these are done in such a way as to make some minimal sense of discrete social identities and situations available to us. The question arises, however, as to what factors might be employed to firm-up our intuitive hearings or readings? How best can we manage a movement away from casual analysis of this kind of talk towards a level of delicacy which would enable us to expose and elaborate upon our tacit understandings in a manner which would provide some practical pay-off in the sociological quest for understanding the nature of social organization?

Before attending to this concern, however, it is necessary to address a more basic, though not unrelated, issue. This is the question of the justification for treating the phenomenon noticed above as a topic for investigation or, indeed, at a more general level, the question of the reasons for undertaking *any* kind of detailed exploration into the organization of spoken interaction. This latter issue, particularly with reference to investigations in the sociology of education, is crucial. First, this is because there is a tendency for much of the substantive work which is concerned with the systematic analysis of *ordinary* activities and practices in educational settings to be regarded, at best, as Hammersley notes (1980), as stubbornly 'empiricist' (and, hence, by implication, a-theortical and unsociological) or, at worst, as trivializing (Bernstein, 1977). Secondly, some clarification of interest is necessary because such interest inevitably has a methodological consequence. Analytical observers, whose curiosity about the nature of talk in school is stimulated, say, by a desire to describe the internal structure of a presumed grammar of discourse, are likely to focus upon different phenomena as data and to grant legitimacy to different strategies of investigation from, say, those whose interest is stimulated by a desire to explore the processs by which socially-situated meanings and identities are managed through classroom interaction.

It might seem entirely sufficient to defend an interest in such instances of interaction as classroom talk in terms of this activity being just one more aspect of social behaviour that is worthy of study in its own right. My own interest, however, goes beyond this and is based upon what I take to be some important contributions that analyses of this interaction can make to three more far-reaching and pressing problems currently confronting sociologists of education. The first of these is a purely pragamatic concern. As several commentators have observed (Reid, 1978; Strivens, 1980), the professional responsibilities of a good many sociologists of education involve them in work at both applied and descriptive levels; that is, they involve a commitment to a teaching role as well as to a research role. This dual involvement has advantages. Signficantly, it provides a basis from which sociologists of education can eliminate naïvety from the descriptions and analyses they make by relating these to their own or their students commonsensical understanding – or, to put it another way, it goes some way to promoting conditions for what Garfinkel calls the 'unique adequacy' requirement for sociological work. However, occupancy of this position is not without problems. Acute amongst these is the demand made by both initial training and in-service students for the sociologist of education to demonstate the usefulness of the discipline in terms of the contribution that the insights it generates can make to the practical problem of accomplishing and managing classroom order and the routine procedures of classroom life – the problem of being a teacher. Whilst the sociologist of education *qua* sociologist might argue that such prescription is not his or her concern, for the sociologist of education *qua* teacher this is not an easy issue to duck – especially if one wants to retain credibility and the opportunities for linking theoretical and applied aspects of the work which are afforded by the direct involvement by sociologists of education in teacher training. Atkinson and Heritage (forthcoming) have highlighted the particular problem which arises in confronting this demand, however, in their reminder that several years have passed since Cicourel (1973) commented:

> that despite the popularity of the role concept within sociology, practitioners (have) proved incapable of defining the particulars of individual roles, of developing manuals of instruction for specific role enactment or of

determining the interpretive procedures by reference to which roles are identified and accountably enacted.

Now, notwithstanding the valuable contribution which the work of writers like David Hargreaves (1972), Nash (1973), Hammersley (1976), Woods (1980) and the authors in the Stubbs and Delamont (1976) reader has made to our understanding of 'the particulars of individual (classroom) roles', there remains something of a lacuna in our ability to identify the strategic interpretive procedures used by teachers (and by pupils, for that matter) in accomplishing role performance. The impact this absence has upon the extent to which the student's challenge to 'tell it as it is' can be met, is, I think, sharply pointed in a recent comment made by Payne and Hustler (1980). They observe:

> The routine manner in which an experienced teacher handles and controls his pupils may well be so much a taken-for-granted aspect of his everyday life in a classroom that he cannot easily tell others how he does it. It is not unusual to hear student teachers enquiring of 'old hands' how they cope with classes so easily and complaining about the latter's inadequate or unhelpful responses. The novice teacher is as Schutz's stranger in the culture of the classroom order. When he is told to observe a lesson to see how it is done, frequently he simply does not know what to look for, what is worth noticing. Even when students are more specifically directed to pay attention to the classroom talk, just what it is they are to attend to often remains obscure.

There seems to me to be good reason for assuming that a sustained investigation of verbal interaction in classrooms is capable of providing considerable purchase for any attempt aimed at explicating the devices by which teachers and pupils successfully accomplish everyday life in classrooms. Although the specificities of these resources might be considerably opaque, they are not so deeply embedded as to make them inexplicable. To assume this would be to adopt a view of the organization of classroom life which participants themselves would find impossible to operate in the sense that the bases for action in the organization would be so ambiguous as to render attempts at sustained, orderly and regularized transactions totally unachievable. Central to the successful accomplishment of such interaction is that, for all practical purposes, teachers and pupils make their sense of the bases of their actions and their expectations available to each other as they set about producing and monitoring their affairs.

The rather obvious recognition that a great deal of this display is achieved through speech-exchange places the study of verbal interaction high on the list of research priorities for anyone motivated by an interest in producing authoritative descriptive of *how* classrooms work.

A closely related reason for being interested in the study of verbal interaction has to do with the contribution it seems such study might make to a more abstract concern in the sociology of education – that is an orientation to educational reform and change. The identification of this orientation in both the rhetoric and implicit motivations of many writers in the field, what Whitty (1977) has called the 'possibilitarian' position, is well-documented. Whilst I do not want to advance the claim that from the study, say, of classroom talk, one can derive programmes and projects for educational reform, I would suggest that research into this kind of phenomena can be used as a corrective, against some of the excesses of certain 'possibilitarian' proposals. When formulating policy proposals or considering the practical implications of sociological research an important question must be concerned with, as Atkinson and Drew (1979) have argued:

> . . . how far the knowledge of social organization being accumulated points to practical limitations on what it may or may not be possible to do in the social world.

And it may well be that in some cases reformist proposals emanating from sociology of education are open to a charge of being guilty of what these writers call 'the alchemists' mistake', the error of proposing ambitious practical goals without having some idea of what conditions would have to be met to accomplish these goals. To pursue this analogy, whilst 'iron cannot be transformed into gold, it can be turned into steel' and I would argue that one of the benefits of developing a more thorough knowledge of how talk is organized in classrooms as they are presently constituted is that it throws light upon the kinds of situational adjustments which would have to be taken into consideration to provide a discourse setting which would accommodate the key goals of any alternative proposals. Thus, for example, by determining the contextual features teachers are orienting to in the interactional work which leads to the massive production of Q – A sequences in classroom conversations and by isolating the kinds of modifications of features of 'naturally-occurring' conversational activities made to enable this kind of orientation, it is possible to be much more sensitive and precise about the contextual adjustments which would be necessary to reduce reliance on this conversational strategy and, hence, reduce some of the 'undesirable' consequences we might attribute to its use.

The third reason I have for defending an interest in educational discourse is one which I think carried most weight. It seems only a slight exaggeration to suggest that the most pressing concern which confronts sociologists of education is the problem of dealing with a proliferation of theoretical approaches championed within the discipline and, more particularly, of resolving the tension which arises in attempts to overcome what is coming increasingly to be represented as a basic issue of dualism in the discipline, the 'way of connecting social actions to structurally generated constraints' (Hargreaves, 1980) or an agenda for demonstrating an interdependence between voluntaristic and deterministic dimensions of social life. As is well known by now, at the heart of this tension is a concern to take seriously the recognition that sociological explanation which *fails* to show either, on the one hand, how what are taken to be structural or systemic properties penetrate practical social conduct and action or, on the other hand, how the practical accomplishment of everyday behaviour is socially situated, will be only partial explanations. Andy Hargreaves (1980) has provided a useful framework for inspecting a number of attempts to resolve this tension. He distinguishes between:

a 'the gentle incorporation stance' (which in attempting to pull together 'useful' elements from a variety of perspectives under the umbrella of a preferred standpoint is vulnerable to relative slippage)
b 'the necrolatry stance' (whose adherents seek for synthesis in the writings of the founding fathers but in so-doing tend to preserve a somewhat daunting gap between the discussions found in classical scholarship and more recent developments in the processes of schooling and findings of empirical enquiry) and,

c   'the splendid isolation solution' (which is characterized by disinterest in synthesis with the attendant danger that any taken-for-granted assumptions about either the impact of the externally objective upon the subjective experience or, conversely, the extent to which everyday thinking and practices are penetrated by cultural forces which will inevitably intrude into the analysis, remain unexamined).

In his reaction to these theoretical discussions Hargreaves is quite right, I think, in emphasizing the questions of the way the extent to which schools actually do serve as institutional settings in which the structure of social relations is reproduced as the central substantive concern for sociologists of education wrestling with the issue of dualism. He rejects approaches to this concern which attribute a direct reproductive function to schools by relying on a plausible but empirically unverified assumption about the correspondence between the social relations of schooling and relations within other social sites; (one is reminded here of Giddens' (1979) somewhat ribald observation that 'if Parsons's actors are cultural dopes, Althusser's agents are structural dopes of even more stunning mediocrity). Similarly, Hargreaves questions approaches which attribute a relative autonomy to schooling at the theoretical level but which then have difficulty in demonstrating which kinds of concrete educational circumstances provide for social reproduction and which do not, and, more importantly, which have difficulty in explaining how constraining properties persist in relatively autorious domains. Finally, Hargreaves expresses fears about the direction being taken in those accounts where aspects of school which emerge through attention being given to problems of *'social control'* are distinguished from those which merge in response to the problems of *'situational control'*, are held to be separate enterprises and, thereby, distract attention away from the issue of how situational properties emerge and change in response to actors' reactions to experiences in contexts *outside* the immediate school situation. Hargreaves' own solution to the problem of synthesis (involving a programme which he proposes will go some way towards redressing the omissions in analyses of which he is critical) rests upon a call for detailed studies of the *strategies* teachers (and pupils) use as they cope with the problems and dilemmas of everyday classroom life.

> We need to consider the possibility that teachers construct the world of the classroom through the employment of different styles but that this process of construction occurs perhaps in situations not of their own choosing and that there are a set of constraints in play which require some sort of resolution through the decisions that teachers are daily and repeatedly called upon to make . . . Coping with society in its institutional mediated form as a set of ongoing and perplexing problems provides teachers with the important yet frequently taken for granted challenge to devise and enact, creatively and constructively a set of teaching strategies which will make life bearable, possible and even rewarding as an educational practitioner.
>
> (Hargreaves, 1978)

Now, whilst I would agree that a proposal aimed at demonstrating that the practical activities which teachers and pupils creatively construct are responses to their needs to accomplish resolution of the dilemma of institutional restrictions offers attractive possibilities for revealing the constraints which frame classroom interaction in a manner which avoids crude reduction, I am rather unclear about how such a proposal would be translated into an empirical programme. To be sure, Hargreaves envisages studies in which accounts of differences betwen types of educational settings, between the ways differences in material provisions are treated, between pedagogical assumptions teachers articulate, between forms of grouping in classroom and the like are generated. Furthermore, all such accounts are to be constructed in terms which strive to show how the strategic responses which *realize* these differences are linked to less local constraining parameters identified and responded to by the social actors involved. My confusion, however, arises from not knowing how to identify accurately what constitutes a strategy; I am not clear about the criteria on which I could legitimately claim that such and such an observable instance of social behaviour in the classroom is an unequivocal instance of such and such a strategy and that this strategy can be regarded as a response to such and such a circumscribing social factor or contextual feature. My difficulty, then, is nothing more than a manifestation of that hoary old sociological problem of finding a descriptive apparatus which is capable of revealing key features of social action in a way which demonstrably preserves the sense, analysis and relevance which the acting subjects involved have for this phenomenon. In the present discussion, however, such a requirement is surely essential because such a complicated edifice of explanation is being built which depends upon the validity of the initial claim. My proposal is that the systematic investigation of verbal interaction in classrooms can give this research programme an instrument to cut into this difficulty.

In a sense it seems quite strange that a pointer in this direction comes from Gintis in his article 'Contradiction and Reproduction in Educational Theory' (1980). He emphasizes that:

> . . . it is the *form* of the educational encounter – the social relations of education – that accounts for both its capacity to reproduce capitalist relations of production and its inability to promote . . . healthy personal development. The actual content of the curriculum has little role to play in this process. The contradictory location of the education system can be described in terms of its characteristic *form* of discourse, as opposed to the actual *content* of the curriculum.

It is one thing to assert that the medium of communication affirms institutional restrictions and evaluations in schools but quite another to demonstrate how this affirmation emerges in concrete social interaction in classrooms. Fortunately, however, in the way Giddens' remarks on structures, system and action have been taken and shown to be appropriate to a conceptualization of classroom interaction by Edwards and Furlong (1978), such a goal has become more attainable. The basic proposal Giddens (1979) makes is that an analysis of productive and reproductive aspects of social life can be held together through the employment of the notions of the 'duality of structure' (or that 'social structures are both constituted by human agency and yet at the same time, are the medium of this constitution') in tandem with the notion of *structuration* (or that 'structure enters into the constitution of the agent and social practice, and exists in the generating moment of this constitution'). Edwards and Furlong translate this to apply to educational analysis by arguing that 'it is through recourse to their sense of a structural relationship that teachers and pupils repeatedly reconstitute that structure, which is both the *basis* for their interaction, and a *product* of it'. The logic of this argument, then, is that both structure and action *presuppose* one another and I would contend that, if we allow that conversational interaction is one of the major devices by which actors in schools announce their sense of structure, orient their behaviour to this sense and in so-doing *reproduce* forms of social relationship which comprise that structure, then there are good grounds for moving the study of this interaction away from being a peripheral concern in the sociology of education to a more central position.

Part 2: The Problems of Analysis

There is a good reason for having devoted a substantial amount of time to a clarification of interest in talk. It is that the admissions made place considerable constraint on the types of analysis which could be used to achieve the goals implicit in these interests. Such analysis would have to be capable –

1   of revealing with some precision the modifications of 'natural' discourse practices which teachers and pupils make to accomplish classroom life and how these modifications work as a central device for such accomplishment,
2   of showing how these modifications are sensitive to local contextual properties and, most importantly,
3   of demonstrating how the production of these transformations both constitute and are constituted by wider institutional restrictions.

Now, whilst it is not practical to consider the entire range of analytical strategies adopted in the study of educational discourse it is possible to introduce some consideration of three broad *trends* in analysis with a view to making some assessment of the potential these have for satisfying the requirements I have just set out.

A key problem facing analysts who wish to determine how institutional restrictions are constituted and re-constituted at the very basic level of speech exchanges, is of knowing how to determine the interactional work that is being done utterance by utterance. Consider, for example, the lines arrowed in fragments 5 and 6 below:[5]

Fragment 5. W/W 1

```
1→T   Would you mind time to stand still?
2  PP  °Mmm        °Na      ⌈Y
3  P                         ⌊I would if –
4  T   Pardon.
5  P   I would if it was Thursday cos we got games and everythink.
6  PP  (Laughter⌈)
7  T             ⌊Y'd lag a- you'd like evera everyday to be Thursday, a
8      Thursday lasting say for fifty years,
```

Fragment 6. W/W 1

```
1→T   What do you think festoon means then? (1.5) James.
2  P   Cover you
3  T   Ye:ss. A better word than cover (1.2) Karen.
4  P   Mek- garlands n =
```

5   **T**   Ye:ss, a better word than that, begin with a ↑ de::, they will =
6   **P**   = Decorate him
7   **T**   Thats right . . .

We have a clear sense of two different 'kinds' of questions being asked by the teacher. We might want to borrow Searle's (1969) distinction between 'real' and 'exam' types of questions to differentiate between them and argue that the first line in fragment 6 is an 'exam' type question. This would be entirely consistent with what both literature on classroom talk and our commonsense knowledge tell us. We have been assured that 'teachers ask questions to which they already know the answer' and regularly ask 'closed' questions as part of a strategy aimed at getting pupils to display understanding, memory, competence or whatever. The problem here is with the grounds we have for claiming that the utterance in line 1 of fragment 6 is one of these types, whilst line 1 of fragment 5 is something of a different order. Of course, one way of defending such a claim is by appealing to our awareness of the physical context of the accuracy. Here we have a teacher, in a classroom, conducting a lesson and we may, therefore, be reasonably assured that both ourselves and, more importantly, the teachers and pupils engaged in the interaction can use this knowedge as resource for interpreting line 1 of fragment 6 as an 'exam' type question. There are two objections to doing this. The first is that many other kinds of verbal interaction take place in classrooms other than those ostensibly licensed by the context. Even in 'lessons' pedagogical exchanges are regularly interrupted by casual conversations and the like. On what basis, then, could analysts or participants justify an interpretation of any particular utterance as being one that is constrained by the 'rules' of the context as opposed to one that is not. Secondly, one can wonder about the accuracy with which either analyst or speakers can interpret an utterance by relating its production to some precise, locatable feature of the activity context. If we interpret line 1 in fragment 6 as a question of a particular type on the basis of our awareness that it is being produced by a teacher in a lesson, which particular contextual variable, out of the many available, do we draw upon as a resource for making this claim. That he is a teacher? That he is teaching in a junior school? That it is a poetry lesson? That we know him to be a formal teacher? That he was emergency trained? And if this is a difficulty in respect of first parts of Q – A exchanges it is even more complicated when we confront the issue of interpreting other parts of such exchanges. Consider line 4 of fragment 7.

Fragment 7. W/W 1

1   **T**   What does the word ee aar ee mean, does anybody know,
2   do you Karen
3   **P**   After.
4→**T**   No. It means before.

The possible interpretations we could make of this line by making recourse to the activity-context can be even more numerous than those proposed as candidate descriptions for the teacher's question in fragment 6. We might want to say that, in rejecting the pupil's answer and in revealing an alternative solution, the teacher undertakes interactional work which both we and the pupil hearers can make sense of because we *know* teachers in classrooms assess, evaluate or comment on pupil's contributions to the talk. Or could it be that, for this instance we could invoke other aspects of the context which, with equal justification, we can imagine are being made to operate by the participants – even if in doing this we produce bizarre descriptions. The teacher doesn't like Karen because she is a pain-in-the-neck, or a girl, or working-class. Or the teacher is tired, anxious to rush off to make a phone-call, to get on with the written work or have a cup of tea. Now, the point for giving this list of frivolous interpretations is to emphasize the enormous difficulties which emerge if either observers or participants rely too much on their sense of context as a resource for rendering utterances intelligible. Descriptions based on this are, as Heritage (1980) shows *'indefinitely extendable';* as he observes:

> We still have no solid methodological precepts by reference to which we might ascertain just what the operative sense of context is for the partici-pants, and in the absence of such precepts, there will continue to exist the possibility of a process of slippage in which an observer's version of the operative context may be unknowingly substituted for the participants' version.

An alternative to using a sense of context as a device for generating descriptions of conversational interaction is to base descriptions of utterances produced in talk upon what competent speakers of a language reasonably know to be the distinguishable activities that can be attributed to the basic units of discourse which are put together to accomplish talk. The most developed and best known programme which applies this strategy to educational analysis is the work of Sinclair and Coulthard (1975) in this country, and the work of Mehan (1978) in the USA. In their 'discourse analysis' Sinclair and Coulthard employ speech act theory to gain access to the work being accomplished in each utterance and the notion of a rank scale as a tool for showing how utterances are related in the production of classroom interaction. Their procedure, crudely summarized, is:

a   to transcribe recordings of classroom discourse
b   to designate labels to each individual utterance isolated according to the function they attribute to these utterances by virtue of the *acts* we generally know these speech events to perform, and
c   to arrange these acts in larger categories so as to demonstrate how individual acts build-up into different and larger kinds of teaching 'moves' – 'opening' moves, 'answering' moves and 'follow-up' moves. In short, they attempt to show how teachers and pupils make particular use of a basic syntax of discourse.

As a programme for developing a systematic description of verbal interaction in educational settings, this type of technique has severe limitations, however; limita-tions which arise from the theoretical premises on which it depends. As Levinson (1980) has argued, the justification for basing description of discourse on the func-tions to which the language is being used in specific utterances, that is functions which are determinable in advance and outside any particular language activity-setting, relies on the validity of four assumptions. I will consider each of these four assumptions (all of which, Levinson argues, are untenable) separately and attempt to illustrate the issues raised by relating them to some classroom data. At the heart of the problem is the difficulty of the relation between two kinds of basic units used in the analysis – unit utterances and unit acts.

First, the programme assumes that units of talk uttered and the acts they perform correspond. Indeed, in so far as we do not need to question the perlocutory force (or speaker's intention) of every utterance directed towards us, this relationship is taken for granted. However, this is not to say that a whole utterance unit cannot either stand for two or more act intentions or interpretations at the same time or that the contents of a single utterance unit are in themselves the sole basis on which intention is attributed. The first point here is well illustrated by fragment 8, some speech occasioned by my entrance into a room in which a small group of pupils were working on their own:

Fragment 8. W/W 2

```
SW      Ow ya getting on?
Jean    ⌈⌈We nearly finished⌉⌉
Sally   ⌊⌊Alright. Thank you⌋⌋
```

Whilst Sally seems to have treated my utterance as some kind of question about their state of interest Jean has interpreted it as an inquiry about their state of accomplishment. However, to classify my question as 'Elicitation'

a   tells us little about the work the utterance did in its production,
b   ignores the possibilities that utterance units can be and are multi-functional, and
c   assumes that the structure of the utterance (question) will signify perlocutionary and illocutionary force.

Similarly, with regard to the second point just raised, teachers, often employ short utterance like 'Jones!', '4M' or 'Stop talking' in which not only is the direct force unclear, but which demonstrably actualize a 'hierarchy' of intentions and meanings ranging from immediate prohibition or deviance impution through indications of teacher's mood to statements of likely consequences of conduct to which they refer. The basic point here is that the flexibility of the grammatical rule-system, rather than constraining speakers to an extent which would permit classification of a finite range of perlocutions or intentions in speech, in fact enables speakers to extend this range indefinitely; therefore, we should question the status of an analytical model which attempts to reduce such speech behaviour to a limited range of speech act categories.

The programme secondly assumes that the indentification of the smallest section of some piece of talk to which function or act is attributable is unproblematic. But what is it, we may ask, which defines the parameters of an utterance unit as an act unit. Consider line 3 of fragment 6 (p. 272), 'feed-back' to a pupil's answer to a question about the meaning of a word. The teacher remarks

'Ye:ss, a better word than cover'.

How are we to treat this? Is the whole utterance simply a single unit 'response' or is 'Yes' a response unit and the rest an 'elicitation'; or does 'better' constitute part of an 'acceptance' whilst the intonation of the second part of the utterance also acts as an elicitation, (is intonation a definer of unit?)? Such questions may seem trivial but the fact that the teacher gets straightaway after this turn an offer of a further candidate answer suggests that some of his utterance has been taken as some kind of further elicitation. Which part of it? If all of it then it can't be simply called 'feedback', but the 'yes' indicates a link with the prior turn of talk. That this kind of rather futile speculation is possible indicates the difficulty one has in both ascribing unit utterance to acts and in defining the parameters of an utterance unit; as Levinson (1980) points out:

> Which unit is the relevant unit for speech act assignment cannot be determined in advance, for utterance units seem to be identified on functional grounds,

the function being tied to the context of production of an item.

The third assumption the programme makes is that there is a reliable procedure by which we can assign *acts* to *utterances*. Now, although in, say, grammatical analysis there are some specificiable procedures by which we can locate the function a word is performing in a sentence or a morpheme in a word, the same is not true of discourse. This is largely because of what Levinson (1980) calls the *'indirection* in human communication' or the indistinct relation between utterance and act. For example, in the utterance 'May I remind you that you've not paid your conference fees' the function or act is not self-contained since it could not possibly stand as a 'request to remind' since such permission has been taken as given by its production. We note at once, then, that there is no simple relation or procedure by which we can assign acts to utterance by virtue of what they 'literally' mean. That the utterance 'Would you like another drink?' is regularly followed by 'Thanks, I'd love one' indicates it has been understood and treated as an offer to buy another round and not as, say, an inquiry into the recipient's state of thirst. And yet there is nothing in the utterance itself to indicate it was functioning as an offer. I would not, then, want to claim that this 'indirection' poses extreme problems for speakers, nor that the way they deal with it is inexplicable, but simply that the act being performed is not analyzable in terms of some pre-determined convention. What speech-act analysts tend to do to dissolve the difficulty of this indistinct relation is to argue that 'local procedures' (like hearing a question as an offer) are explainable by 'situational' rules. The acts being performed in such utterances are identifiable, they propose, not by the 'literal' conventions they seem to obey but by ones established in the activity settings in which they are produced. But this is to turn the whole analytical procedure back upon itself and leaves us with the familiar problem of the infinite extendability of such descriptions.

The final assumption on which the programme rests, is that we can move from a description of single activities to a description of the ground rules which give these activities structure or continuity, that is, rules which give organization to single activities produced in talk. Here again, the tying of the theory to an 'act' base severely restricts the contribution such an approach can make to explanations of discourse. Consider fragment 9. A pupil has just told the teacher that he doesn't know if the life of a gypsy is any different from his own. The exchange below ensues.

Fragment 9. W/W 1

P He travels around
T He travels around Mister Jackson, do you?

P °°Sometimes, yeh hh°°
T What's your address?
P Ninety-two Linton-
T Pardon?
P Ninety-two Linton Way.
T Thirty-two Linton Way.
P *Ninety*-two.
T Ninety-two. And do you think ninety-two Linton Way (.) will be in the same place tonight as it was yesterday?
P ((Nods))
T Yes. Is ninety-two Linton Way in the same place now as it was last year?
P Yes.
T So you do not really travel around, do you? Is ninety-two Linton Way on wheels?

The kind of analysis speech act theorists would have to make of such an exchange would be to concentrate upon the individual acts speakers engage in to accomplish the sequence, treating each utterance as having a unilateral function – elicition, reply, check, evaluate, etc. etc. But the *function* of the whole series of questions, it could be argued, is not to ascertain or check-out specific information but rather to build-up *through* the *whole* sequence a 'natural' argument which demonstrates to both the individual pupil and to others in the class that the answer to the *first* question was not acceptable *in the* discourse structure the teacher wanted to construct (albeit not a 'wrong' answer in itself) and also to establish a general point by 'inference' about the differences between gypsys and ordinary mortals. The point here is that what was accomplished in this particular sequence was not determined by the function or even the structure of the speech acts but by how the sequence conformed to the conventions of a 'language game' collectively established by the participants to the discourse. Certaintly the conventions of the 'game' – as established – constrain the verbal contributions permitted but these are not conventions of speech acts *per se* and the model that relies on speech act theory, therefore, is unable to explain such structure.

There are dangers, then, in making too heavy a reliance upon two possible sources of reference, *context* and a *syntax of speech,* as points against which descriptions of verbal interactions can be confirmed. I should perhaps emphasize here that I am not discounting the possibility that a sense either of *context* or of *act* being performed in an utterance might be something that a participant to a speech-exchange is orienting to, but rather, that it is only when this orientation is reportably displayed in the flow of the interaction that it can be claimed to be an organizing feature of that interaction. To clarify this point, I should like to return to a consideration of line 1, fragment 6.

Fragment 6. W/W 1

1→T What do you think festoon means then (1.5) James.
2 P Cover you
3 T Ye:ss. A better word than cover (1.2) Karen
4 P Mek- garlands n =

```
5   T   = Ye:ss, a better word than that, begin with a ↑ de::, they will =
6   P   = Decorate him
7   T   Thats right . . .
```

By what token might it be legitimately claimed that this is an 'exam' type question, and, futhermore, that it is going for an answer that the teacher has prejudged as worthy of acceptance?

A first answer is, of course, that there are design features about the question which gives it this character. In the lesson from which the fragment is taken the teacher regularly uses a formula in designing questions which has features like 'Who can tell me . . .?' or 'What do you know about . . .?' or 'Does anybody know . . .' or, as in this case, 'What do you think . . .' In the sense that questions displaying these kinds of design features are treated as exam-type questions by pupils (as is revealed in the way the pupil frames her own response in line 2 here) and have that treatment confirmed as accurate (as in lines 4, 6 and 9 here), an interactional environment is progressively constructed and re-constructed against which the hearing of a question designed in a particular way as being one of a particular type can be quickly ratified. However, complete confirmation of such a hearing is not fully achieved until the interactional work being attempted through the production of the utterance is finally dealt with. Or, as Heritage (1981) has proposed:

> Whilst recipients may have plenty of *a priori* resources with which to infer the status of a question, its status is not fully decided until after the provision of a post-answer receipt.

Now, he further suggests that we can inspect this proposal by comparing the way a Question – Answer exchange like that in fragment 6 runs-off with ones produced in naturally occurring conversations. In fragment 2 on page 265 there is an example of one of these. In the last line of the illustration S produces 'Oh' in response to G's answer to S's first question, 'Who w'yih ta:lking to?'. Scrutiny of a host of transcripts in which this 'Oh' particle appears in similar conversational environments (i.e., post-answer position) indicates that it is commonly used as one resource by which an individual can mark the receipt of information about which they were previously unaware. The product of 'Oh' after an answer to a question is routinely used to indicate that the answer being attended to is 'news'. Leaving aside the issue of when the particle is used to accomplish this kind of work and when it is put to other uses, as undoubtedly it is, we can focus upon a more general observation. This is that, in the Q – A exchanges in fragments 6 and 2, the status of the initial question is displayed and confirmed across at least three turns of talk. A asks a question, B analyzes that question and produces an answer based on that analysis and A produces a third turn which confirms or denies the validity of the interpetation displayed in B's answer. Thus, in fragment 6, teacher produces an 'exam' question, the pupil reads it as an 'exam' question and exhibits this reading in the design of his or her answer and the teacher confirms that reading in the post-answer receipt.

What reason is there, however, for stressing this inter-relation between utterances. It is to demonstrate the more general but absolutely crucial recognition that both the utterances produced in verbal interaction and the practical activities they are designed to facilitate can neither be analyzed nor regarded as successfully accomplished as unilateral undertakings. Rather, they are sequentially organized events; both the utterance actors produce in talk and the interactional sequences these utterances generate are understood and brought-off as successful by social actors by reference to the place they occupy and the part they play in a *sequence* of activities. Moreover, an orderly advance of these activities is only *possible* by social actors displaying to each other their practical understanding of these sequential features and from these displays the non-participating observer/analyst is able to read-off organizing features of the interaction. Now it is because the approach to the study of interaction as Conversational Analysis makes this *sequentiality* its prime focus, that I wish to conclude this discussion by proposing that it is this approach to the study of verbal interaction in schools and classrooms which holds most promise for attaining the goals I set out earlier. Conversational Analysis, as initially developed by Sacks, Schegloff and Jefferson in a programme designed to meet the analytical constraints contained in the approach to social research proposed by Harold Garfinkel, takes as its organizing focus a simple but massively consequential recognition that has been concisely summarized by Schegloff and Sacks (1974) thus:

> We have proceeded under the assumption . . . that in so far as the materials we worked with exhibited orderliness, they did so not only to us, indeed not in the first place for us, but for the co-participants who had produced them. If the materials were orderly, they were so because they had been methodically produced by members of society for one another, and it was a feature of the conversations that we treated as data that they were produced so as to allow the display by the co-participants to each other their orderliness, and to allow the participants to display to each other their analysis, appreciation and use of that orderliness.

This orderliness in conversation is achieved through participants to conversations successfully and quite routinely accomplishing two objectives which must be fulfilled if the interaction is to proceed without the basis on which it moves forward being re-negotiated with every attempt to communicate. First, the regular and controlled transfer of the right to speak (or the allocation of turn at talk) and second, the demonstration of how successive utterance can be seen to be sequentually relevant. In actual practice there is a range of specific resources by which speakers meet these requirements but, basically, this is done in the way I suggested the exchange in fragment 6 was brought-off. Speaker A produces a first utterance which is designed to display who speaks next and the activities to be attended to in the next turn. Speaker B, having analyzed A's utterance, found him or herself as having the right to speak next, produces a turn of talk which exhibits an understanding of what was produced by Speaker A, which itself requires a response and which displays the basis on which who should take the next turn can be ascertained. And so on. Thus sequentiality is practically accomplished. But what advantages does this approach to analysis of interaction have in terms of the goals for sociology of education I have raised!

First, it avoids the problems of the 'infinite extendability of description'. By grounding description in what teachers and pupils '*demonstrate*' they are orienting to in the production of talk, this type of analysis removes the need to provide some kind of warrant against which descriptions are defended. This is no small advantage. If we can say with *surety* that *this* is what teachers and pupils in a particular setting are doing together through their talk, we are then provided with the basis for making many comparisons – not only between, for example, different phases in one lesson but between different classrooms, between different occasions when we think different teacher or pupil strategies are being employed, different curriculum objectives promoted, different groups of children being taught and so on. Furthermore, if we are sure of our descriptions we can safely move around to make comparisons between teaching situations and other educational encounters (for e.g., parent-teacher consultations, staff discussions, meetings of examination boards) and also between how these encounters are accountably accomplished across a variety of settings or periods of time. In short, the approach provides a firm basis on which to check theory.

The second advantage it has is that it can demonstrate how contextual features condition the accomplishment of educational encounters. Given, for example, a requirement on teachers and pupils to find a basis for 30 participants collectively to monitor speech and to manage taking turns at talk whilst preserving sequentiality, the reliance by the teachers on the production of Q – A sequences as conversational strategy is not surprising in that they provide a solution to both these constraints. In short, the approach helps identify local properties of social organization.

The third advantage it has is that by attending to the sequential nature of talk in educational settings, we can capture a sense of the ways in which such settings and the institutional restrictions and evaluations which are realized through the interaction are *collaboratively* accomplished. In designing and producing utterances which are sequentially related, teachers and pupils collaborate in a process in which they produce actions which show their mutually constraining analyses of each other's activities. These analyses may well involve all kinds of value-judgements based upon the participants' sense of structure. But if they are to operate as a condition of action they must be displayed and they are mostly displayed, to borrow a phrase from Perry Anderson, in the 'discrete, blameless gestures' of communicative interaction.

Notes

1 Fragment taken from ATKINSON, J. and DREW, P. (1979).
   Key to Symbols Used in Fragments.
   The transcribing system is that commonly used in conversational analysis and is one which has been extensively developed by Gail Jefferson.

Symbol	Example	Representation
Italics	isn't it a *fact*	Intonational emphasis
Brackets + Number	(1.0)	Pause/Gap of 1.0 seconds.
	(.)	Micro-pause.
Equal signs	=	Indicates that there is no interval between end of an utterance where it appears and on-set of next.
Colons	Jis no:w?	Sound which is prior to symbol is stretched.
Dash	I called be-	Word/sound cut-off.
Arrows	who w'yih ↑ ta:lking to.	Direction of intonational shift.
Extended brackets	Ir⌈on ore	Talk is overlapped
	⌊Iron ore	
Bracket + word	the (sound)	Uncertain hearing of word/sound.
Dot + hh	•hh	Inbreath.
	hh•	Outbreath.

2 Fragment taken from transcript Frankel:TC:I:I.
3 Fragment taken from transcript made by D. Greatbach, University of Warwick.

4 Fragment taken from McHOUL, A. (1978).
5 Fragments 5 – 9 are all taken from transcripts made from video-tape recordings of a class of ten and eleven year-olds in Birmingham, England.

References

ATKINSON, J.M. and DREW, P. (1979) *Order in Court* London, Macmillan.
ATKINSON, J.M. and HERITAGE, J.C. (in press) *Structures of Social Action* Cambridge, Cambridge University Press.
BERNSTEIN, B. (1977) *Class, Codes and Control: Vol III* London, Routledge and Kegan Paul.
CICOUREL, A.V. (1973) *Cognitive Sociology* New York, Free Press.
EDWARDS, A.D. and FURLONG, V.J. (1978) *The Language of Teaching* London, Heinemann.
GIDDENS, A. (1979) *Central Problems in Social Theory* London, Macmillan.
GINTIS, H. and BOWLES, S. (1980) 'Contradiction and Reproduction in Educational Theory' in BARTON, L., MEIGHAN, R. and WALKER, S. (Eds) *Schooling, Ideology and the Curriculum* Lewes, The Falmer Press.
HAMMERSLEY, M. and WOODS, P. (Eds) (1976) *The Process of Schooling* London, Routledge and Kegan Paul.
HAMMERSLEY, M. (1980) 'On interactionist empiricism' in WOODS, P. (Ed) *Pupil Strategies: Explorations in the Sociology of the School* London, Croom Helm.
HARGREAVES, A. (1978) 'The significance of classroom coping strategies' in BARTON, L. and MEIGHAN, R. (Eds) *Sociological Interpretations of Schooling and Classrooms; a Reappraisal* Driffield, Nafferton.
HARGREAVES, A. (1980) 'Synthesis and the study of strategies: a project for the sociological imagination' in WOODS, P. (Ed) *Pupil Strategies: Explorations in the Sociology of the School* London, Croom Helm.
HARGREAVES, D.H. (1972) *Interpersonal Relations and Education* London, Routledge and Kegan Paul.
HERITAGE, J.C. (1980) 'The Availability of Context: a Response to Levinson From a Sociological Perspective', Unpublished mimeo, University of Warwick.
HERITAGE, J.C. (1981) ' ' 'A change of state' ' token and aspects of its placement in repair' in ATKINSON, M. and HERITAGE, J.C. (Eds) (in press) *Structures of Social Action* Cambridge, Cambridge University Press.
LEVINSON, S. (1980) 'On the essential inadequacies of speech act models of dialogue' in PARRETT, H. (Ed) *Possibilities and Limitations of Pragmatics* J. Benjamin, B.V.
McHOUL, A. (1978) 'The organization of turns at formal talk in the classroom' *Language in Society* 7, pp. 183–213.
MEHAN, H. (1978) 'Structuring school structure' *Harvard Educational Review* 48, pp. 32–64.
NASH, R. (1973) *Classrooms Observed* London, Routledge and Kegan Paul.
PAYNE, G. and HUSTLER, D. (1980) 'Teaching the class: The practical management of a cohort', *British Journal of Sociology of Education* 1 (1).
REID, I. (1978) 'Past and present trends in the sociology of education' in BARTON, L. and MEIGHAN, R. (Eds) *Sociological Interpretations of Schooling and Classrooms: a Reappraisal* Driffield, Nafferton.
SCHEGLOFF, E. and SACKS, H. (1974) 'Opening up closings' *Semiotica* 8, pp. 289–327.
SEARLE, J.R. (1969) *Speech Acts,* Cambridge, Cambridge University Press.
SINCLAIR, J. and COULTHARD, R. (1975) *Towards an Analysis of Discourse: the English of Teachers and Pupils* Oxford, Oxford Univesity Press.
STRIVENS, J. (1980) 'Contradiction and change in educational practices' in BARTON, L., MEIGHAN, R. and WALKER, S. *Schooling, Ideology and the Curriculum* Lewes, Falmer Press.
STUBBS, M. and DELAMONT, S. (Eds) (1976) *Explorations in Classroom Observation* Chichester, Wiley.

WHITTY, G. (1977) 'Sociology and the problem of radical educational change' in YOUNG, M.F.D. and WHITTY, G. *Society, State and Schooling* Lewes, The Falmer Press.
WOODS, P. (Ed) (1980) *Teacher Strategies* London, Croom Helm.

Strategies, Commitment and Identity; Making and Breaking the Teacher Role

Peter Woods, The Open University

There has been much interest, of late, among sociologists in teacher strategies (Lacey 1977; Hargreaves, A. 1977, 1978 and 1979; Pollard 1980a; Woods 1977 and 1980). This is partly because the concept offers a way of getting to the heart of school action, until recently an under-researched area; and partly because it allows for the consideration of the influence of both structurally generated constraints and of individual biography.

Thus Hargreaves (1977) came to see strategies as the meeting point of societal determination and individual construction in the concept of 'coping strategies'. While this draws attention to what has to be coped with, to the problems and constraints that are externally determined, it also recognizes the act of creativity on the part of the teacher. Hargreaves (1978) argued that teachers are wrestling with educational goals in current capitalist society that are fundamentally contradictory, (e.g. 'egalitarianism' but 'socialization for the occupational order'), operating under material conditions which are a product of planning and politics, and assailed by a number of differing educational ideologies. Strategies are given a further twist by institutional mediation of these constraints.

However, to the extent that Hargreaves has developed the model (1977, 1978, 1979), he has so far tended to emphasize the constraints, at the expense of teacher creativity. We have adaptations, given in the examples of strategies of 'policing' and 'confrontation avoidance' (Hargreaves, 1979). But he does not discuss negotiations, which arise from a dialectical interplay of teachers' own intentions and resources and the structurally determined conditions that confront them.

In attempting to correct this imbalance, Pollard (1980a) makes two significant inputs, one at the middle level of the institution, in the form of the influence of children in interaction with teachers, teacher culture, and what he calls 'institutional bias'; the other in the area of teacher biography. He points out that while constraints are important, there are other, equally important issues of 'what it is that "coping" means, how coping is defined by the participants, what criteria are used to judge degrees of coping, what goals do the participants bring to the interaction?' (1980a, p. 13; see also Hammersley, 1980). In offering one kind of answer to these questions, Pollard has recourse to symbolic interactionist theories of the self. A key idea is that the self is not a constant, homogeneous whole, and different facets of it are realized depending on coping requirements. Pollard introduces Schutz' (1970) concept of 'interests-at-hand' to analyze these facets of self. In these, motivational relevance is governed by situational demands and interests, which are 'juggled' depending on how priorities are perceived as classroom processes evolve (see also Pollard, 1980b).

These are important developments, but they need to be taken further, and considered in relation to more teachers. For example, what governs interests and priorities? Again, while the self might not be a consistent whole, is there not some aspect of it that has more permanence, that has repercussions for our actions? One

283

possible kind of answer to such questions, which offers to elaborate the biography end of the model, was suggested to me while reconsidering some data on two teachers, gathered during a year and half's observation in their school in the mid-1970s. The method here is akin to that of analytic induction. It is assumed

> that the exceptional instance is the growing point of science and that cumulative growth and progressive development of theory is obtained by formulating generalizations in such a way that negative cases force us to either reject the generalization or to revise it.
>
> (Lindesmith, 1947, p. 37)

Such a strategy 'makes necessary the intensive analysis of individual cases and the comparison of certain crucial cases' (Denzin, 1970, p. 197). All cases should fit the theory or model, but if one deviant case be found, it should not be discarded, but rather the theory or model should be adjusted to accommodate it. By examining and comparing the two teachers in some detail, therefore, we can test some areas of the Hargreaves/Pollard model, and possibly suggest some refinements and additions. The comparison is not as thoroughgoing as I would wish it, for the analysis is being applied long after leaving the field, and the opportunity for theoretical sampling through 'pinpointing' (Glaser and Strauss, 1967) has passed. My analysis, therefore, has the status of a first enquiry, suggesting areas for future focused attention.

The two teachers were ideal for a critical case analysis for they were two remarkable men in a rather remarkable situation. The situation was a traditional secondary modern school ('Lowfield'), with an authoritarian-paternalistic head of very fixed views one year short of retirement. The school also was about to undergo a profound change in status, to comprehensive. It was not, in short, the most propitious moment to try to introduce radical change.

This was rather irksome for our two heroes, who held radical views. Tom was head of art, in his early fifties; Dick in his twenties, at the other end of the teaching career, taught social studies. The difference in age and career stage might appear to invalidate any one-to-one comparison, but in this particular instance, the data suggests that their different achievements may be a product of other differences between them. I shall suggest that one possible reason why Tom had survived for so long, despite his radical views, in what seemed a hostile environment, and that Dick lasted for so short a spell (one year at the school, though he had spent each of the two preceding years at two other schools) was to be found in their types of commitment and their conceptions of identity. I want, first, to establish their similarity in views of teaching, and to illustrate their different strategical orientations.

Views of Teaching

Tom and Dick were very similar in respect of their values and beliefs about teaching. They were contributors to that style of teaching that Hammersley (1976) has called, following Schur, 'radical non-interventionism', or that Dale (1978) has characterized as the 'hippy' strand of the progressive movement.

The most explicit example of this for both teachers was in their views of and approach to pupils as equals, their rejection of the traditional teacher role, and their dislike of institutional and bureaucratic aspects of the job. Tom compared himself with the headmaster. They had heated discussions on how and what to teach kids.

The head's line was 'when you go in there you should say "you *will* do this!"' But Tom preferred the gardening metaphor. He saw himself as a gardener – the seeds arrive and he will help them grow, now and then applying a little fertilizer (*cf* Parlett and Hamilton, 1972). He was a strong believer in community education. He was the only member of staff to live in the village, fraternizing with the kids and the parents, many of whom he had taught of course, out of school. For him, school had to be seen in this context – as part of the community life. There was frequent reference in his talk to kids as 'human beings' and as 'adults'. Thus, much of the organization of school and of the curriculum militated against treating kids as human beings (for example, there were inadequate resources to make the 'block system' work), and he was for 6th form colleges, for they allow kids to be more adult. He 'loved people'. But the more his love, the greater the frustration at the hundred and one petty administrative things like collecting money, answering letters, the caretaker (a 'union' man and a big problem), and poor teachers'.

Dick had the very same heroes – A.S. Neill in particular. He also articulated the philosophy – education from within, liberation, anti-bureaucracy, and anti-hierarchy. He had had some experience in a Village College, but in his view its pro-gressivism was only skin deep. He had heard some dockers talking about the Liver-pool Free School. He gave them A.S. Neill to read. 'If we can get through to parents like this' he said, 'it's a beginning'. He contrasted himself with his predecessor, whom he gathered was rather 'authoritarian'. His approach was rather different, more 'free and easy, trying to make *them* forthcome'. His whole efforts were devoted to try to get the kids to think for themselves, as opposed to trying to force them to do things. The answer was inside oneself, rather than seeking it outside. There was so much talking down to kids in the school – he tried to operate on the same level with them. One example of the elitism he so loathed was when he proposed taking a party to the House of Commons. The headmaster thought that a good idea, but of course 'he would have to take the more able ones, – the "other lot" the intellectual stuff of the House of Commons would go over their heads!'

Dick reiterated the Neill philosophy. The main point about it was *trust* of children. He was for 'living' as opposed to 'lessons', 'emotions' as opposed to 'head-work'. He had faith that Summerhill type schools would become more common. Though he did not doubt initial difficulties. Neill's success in getting kids ultimately to respond to their new found freedom by doing creative things and to change for the better, made him optimistic. They had free choice of lessons, no science (though there was a laboratory for 'discovery purposes'), and a far healthier attitude to sex. Above all, they had a large measure of self-government, which was the basis for social control in the school.

Despite the thirty years or so then that separated Tom and Dick in age, they were broadly of a mind as regards views of teaching and learning. How did they try to realize their aims and what did they achieve?

Strategies

This takes us to a consideration of strategies, and here they were remarkably different.

Dick's strategies took three forms:

a   constructive progress,
b   ambitious experimentation, and
c   radical departures.

Perhaps the most generally recognized constructive contribution Dick made was a brand new social studies CSE programme, carried through despite 'all the head-master's suspicions and growlings' (for example, he would not hear of Community Service carrying 30% of the marks). 'But he had worked on it with the head of department, Mrs. Lane and, indeed, with Tom, and eventually the head had agreed. It contained not only new subject matter, for example on consumer education and the running of schools, but also new methods, with much project work, a good deal conducted outside the school with the pupil as roving researcher. Interestingly, it was not acknowledged as Dick's invention. Once he had approved of it, the headmaster spoke of 'our brand new social studies syllabus, which Mrs. Lane and the humanities' department have devised'.

Dick's year at the school, however, was characterized more by frenetic and ambitious experimentation. For example, he was very keen on films, and not just ordinary films. Films in lessons, between lessons and in the evenings with the school's film club, which he founded and ran. Swedish sex education films, Dr. Martin Coles' sex education film, and the BBC film of Summerhill were all shown. But to what effect? The A.S. Neill film was shown to fourth and fifth years. The film shows pupil self-government, Neill himself being out-argued and outvoted, and nude bathing in the swimming pool. It also contains two clear messages for aspiring imitators. One was the time it took for the children to become socialized into the A.S. Neill frame of thinking. The other was a comment by Neill that we do not live in a free civilization. 'If I allowed my pupils double beds', he said 'the DES would close my school'. Even Summerhill has limits.

But those of Lowfield were much narrower, and Dick was in a much less power-ful position. He was working within a completely different world of meanings and values, where the general culture and other agencies of socialization were much stronger than him, and simply absorbed him within their framework. Thus the reac-tions of the class to the films were to titter at the bathing sequence, and to demand to see that particular bit again. More seriously, one opined 'It don't seem natural'. Another said 'what happens when they leave and come out into yer actual world? They'll be in a gap'. The tone of the whole discussion afterwards was critical. Asked by Dick if they would have liked to have gone to such a school, there was a massive 'no'. A spokesman declared 'you wouldn't learn anything. They don't have no lessons. You've got to have some order'. Some would argue that these pupils, whatever their lack of academic prowess, had learnt their lesson.

The pupils did not know how to respond to Dick's innovations. When he sent them out on projects some found it difficult to handle their new gained liberty. There were reports of shoplifting, and irate 'phone calls to the school from law-abiding citizens which caused the headmaster to hold an enquiry. When Dick gave them a comic strip sketch on consumer rights, and asked them to fill in the blurbs, they vied with each other in inventing obscenities. When they got bored during a part of one lesson when he was addressing the whole class, and began to talk, gradually louder and louder, *he* was the one who shut up, standing and facing them in silence for a full ten minutes while the storm raged around him. It was that master symbol of the institution, the bell, that brought the disorder to an end, not Dick's new technique.

It is possible to argue that he did achieve something through his approach. Some thought he was a 'great teacher' because he 'fixed things up' 'did interesting things' 'treated them like human beings'. Others however found him 'rather "queer"', not like a proper teacher – he never tells you off'.

The same is true of the staff, a few of whom were, for a time at least, captivated by his ideas and enthusiasm while the rest looked on askance. What could have been a forum for change became more of a caucus of malcontents, who steadily became more divisive and rebellious as the year progressed.

So Dick was eventually emboldened to try something more radical. He attempted to reform the government structure of the school by establishing a School Council. Its initiation was prepared by way of a press campaign through the school's new newspaper, whose editor was, of course, Dick.

The newspaper raised questions about corporal punishment, under the heading 'retribution by physical violence', urged pupils to help change the direction of power within the school structure, to join the School Council and the NUSS, advertised films like 'Strike' and pamphlets like 'Peace News', and advised, 'Don't let them get at you kiddo – come and see us at School Council'. The draft constitution when it appeared declared amongst other things that 'The School Council shall be responsible for making representations to the appropriate bodies on behalf of the students of the school on all matters affecting the day to day running of the school, and shall also act as a consultative body when new rules and regulations are deemed necessary'.

These were all, clearly, radical departures from the school's usual customs and structure. While it was going on, according to Tom the headmaster was girding his loins, going along with it in form if not in content. Thus, when he was asked to expound on his constitutional position to one of Dick's classes, he did so to the letter, reading out the articles of government for all but ten minutes of the period', and in a tone of voice and with a fixity of stare that dared anyone to challenge him. Tom reckoned the head was quietly but definitely preparing a dossier, including all the minutes of School Council meetings. Soon, he had more material available. Dick refused to attend a Speech Day evening. The head told him it was a required duty, but Dick insisted it was against his principles. Another member of the 'anarchists' trust' capitulated, because he was on a short-term contract and wanted the head's reference for a new job, but Dick refused to yield.

When the head tried to breathe life into the wilting house system, Dick entered into the spirit of it with his usual enthusiasm, spending over £7 of his own money to requisition badges for his house, bearing the name of the house and the motif of a black clenched fist on a red background. With this simple trick, it seemed to the head that Dick was threatening to subvert the most hallowed of institutions. After a day or two of furore and debate, during which another master proposed for his house the motif of a Churchillian cigar with a V sign on a blue background, badges were banned, apparently because of their 'communist implications'. Nobody could accuse Dick of being a retreatist or for lacking resource. He sat down immediately and began a long letter to the Chairman of the Governors.

Generally, Dick and the head began to clash more frequently, as when one of Dick's pupils allegedly set off the fire alarm, and had the whole school turned out on the field in a snowstorm. The head was heard by the multitude thundering at Dick to send the miscreant at once to his room, where he proposed to 'put him over his desk and thrash him'. Dick was heard by those near him to reply that he would do so only when the headmaster had 'calmed down a little'.

Eventually, however, Dick's resolution snapped and he resigned after a series of incidents, when the head had exerted himself and reinforced the *status quo*. An interruption of one of Dick's lessons to instil a different structure of expectations, an exertion of authority over the whole school in which the head caused everybody to suffer because he had been worsted in an incident with two errant fourth formers, and other such happenings, and Dick gave up with a suddenness that stood in stark contrast to the total vigour and resolution of his former application.

Tom seemed to have started out like Dick, but had modified his approach later. He told me about several incidents in his early career similar in spirit to those of Dick. For example, he had got the kids to produce a newspaper. They had a referendum on sport, and 99.9% of them had disapproved of rugby. This went up on the wall, with the other information, and the games' man of the day 'had apoplexy. He was soon round having a right do– ''you're undermining my authority'' – and only one person in the staffroom would speak to him'. Another edition had a Tarzan like picture, 'not particularly well endowed, a few hairs on the chest'. The senior mistress saw it and was horrified, fetched the head and down it came. On another occasion he initiated a 'great debate' about school uniform but he was the only one to speak out against it. They accused him of trying to sabotage the system, but 'no' he said 'I'm a democrat, I accept the majority vote.' Tom's libertarianism was contained. For instance, the examples above were on off attacks on parts of the system on opportunistic basis, in contrast to Dick's calculated, total assault. Also it could be argued that Tom by virtue of his subject was more peripheral to the main life stream of the school. A somewhat bohemian style could be functional for the school, offering pupils a form of therapy (Woods, 1977).

These days Tom takes it more quietly. But he has not lost sight of his vision and his ideals. Basically he says it's depressing. You just can't 'do it' in the state system. But he does what he can, speaking up now and again in Heads of Departments' meetings on the lines of more freedom, occasionally winning a small victory. Most of his colleagues think he's mad, so he shuts up, he knows he'll never get anywhere.

Just inside the Art Room door is a little sign – 'Conform or Else!' – mocking the system. It applies to staff as well as to pupils. He has learnt the art of compromise. When editing the school magazine, everything had to be submitted to the higher judgement and occasional censorship of the headmaster. He complained, the head insisted, he went through with it. There are, however, limits to Tom's tolerance, for example certain people, who in his opinion were inadequate, being made head of the forthcoming Faculty of Design. He did not necessarily wish it for himself, in fact he thought he had talked away his chances, but he did want somebody with vigour and vision.

Yet, though far from satisfied, Tom does enjoy a measure of achievement. He does teach his own kind of art. He likes the summer season best, when he can take the kids out. They get on a bus and go out to villages, have a snack out, go in a Wimpy and so on, escape the boundaries of school. Or he sends them in small groups to places, to colleagues of his, whom he has contacted beforehand. In school he creates his own kind of environment – informal groupings, pop music, coffee and so on. The Art room is a place where pupils like to go. He is always pleasant with them, laughing, joking, teasing, enquiring about family, extra curricular activities, softening the institutional boundaries, showing the human side of teaching.

Another feature of Tom's strategies that differ from Dick's is their range of application, for he teaches in evening classes, and fraternizes in the local pub, or elsewhere in the local community. To Tom, school is part of life, to be encompassed within the larger design. Dick also had a grand design, but in his spare time applied it to a different community. The close integration of the various compartments of life is an important factor for Tom. He can achieve things in his evening school and at large that he cannot in day school, but which he can nonetheless lay the basis for and form connections with.

Dick tried to revolutionize the power structure. Tom worked to gain power within the system, and to influence those in the upper hierarchy. Tom had gained a position. He was the senior Art Master and Head of Creative Design. He was a personal friend of the Chairman of the Governors, a local leader of the religion Tom shared with him. The chairman also shared with Tom his views of teaching. It was this very chairman who received Dick's letter of protest about the house badges and who could do no more than try to quieten the matter down. For Dick, therefore, he was the end of the road. But for Tom, he was an avenue to some accomplishment, over and above the power structure of the school, that could nonetheless be fed back into it.

Tom had not only an administrative influence, but also an academic one. For one of his old colleagues at the school, of similar views to his own, had been appointed a county adviser, and visited the school quite frequently when long discussions between them, often over a pint at the local, took place. The deputy head, heir apparent to the headship, was also a kindred spirit, up to a point, often calling in the Art Room for a coffee and a smoke. Tom, in fact, felt that he had helped secure his position as deputy head, by frequently alerting the head to the fact that he was doing all the duties required of such a position. He had also secured this man's appointment as staff representative on the steering committee to oversee the school's transition to comprehensive status, against the Head's initial wishes. In these ways, Tom made his influence felt, and got his views represented. This influence was within the legitimated power structure, and at some important and influential points. One should also note Tom's influence in the community in general, where he was well-known and respected. Parents, seeking a consultation about their children, often bypassed the formalities and went straight to him.

In summary, Tom's approach to teaching carries a veneer of compliance, but he provided therapy for the pupils, a sociation centre in the school, attempted and accomplished the occasional innovation, had an impact on some influential opinons, and linked these efforts with his wider concerns. It was through this partial accomplishment, I suspect, that Tom had managed to preserve his philosophy intact.

How can we categorize these differences between Tom and Dick? Lacey (1977) spoke of three modes of strategic orientation among teachers: (1) strategic compliance, wherein the individual accepts the prevailing system though entertains private reservations; (2) internalized adjustment, where the individual believes the prevailing system is the best; and (3) strategic redefinition, where individuals actually achieve change by 'causing or enabling those with formal power to change their interpretation of what is happening in the situation.' (p. 73). Tom's prevailing mode might be seen as an example of the third variety though with a large injection of the first at crucial points. Dick's might be seen as a 'failed' attempt at strategic redefinition.

Lacey gives an example of one such case among his sample of student teachers. 'Peter' had become vulnerable because of his espousal of the classic 'risk' syndrome of strategic redefinition, collectivizing strategies (i.e. where 'the problem is shared by the group whose collective opinions legitimize the displacement of blame', p. 86), and 'radical direction of displacement of blame'. In these situations, Lacey argues, success depends on the individual's ability to redefine the situation, and, if necessary, to employ compliance strategies at crucial points (ibid, p. 89). Lacey describes this ability as 'sensitivity to the environment and to significant others within it' (p. 90) and quotes extensively from Miller and Parlett (1974) on 'cue-consciousness'.

Kounin (1970) noticed a similar quality among teachers, which he termed 'with-it-ness'. There was, I feel, a marked difference between Tom and Dick in this apprehension, and specifically, to my perception, in sociological awareness. Dick's failure to draw the lessons of Summerhill, to appreciate the difficulties arising from the environmental and temporal circumstances of the school he was in, the limitations as well as possibilities of pupil and teacher cultures, the power vested in the ongoing organizational structure of the school – all this seems to suggest shortcomings of an awareness which was necessary in a situation where radical political change was being attempted. Tom, by contrast, appeared to have a sound theoretical knowledge of the situation geared to practical action which rose above the recipe knowledge one often finds in beleaguered schools. Time and again, in his discussions with me, he showed intuitive understanding of such refined sociological areas as labelling theory, the amplification of deviance and teacher typifications. I do not have space here to give examples, but there are plenty available in my fieldnotes. Also, the general strategical drift discussed above suggests a considerable sociological awareness.

However, to leave the analysis there would be a mistake. It would be to suggest that Dick was defective in either native ability or knowledge, and I believe neither to be the case. Other factors lay behind this apparent difference in awareness and, to identify them, it is helpful to characterize Tom's strategical orientation as pragmatic, and Dick's as paradigmatic. I borrow the distinction from Hammersley's analysis of teacher styles (1977)

> By paradigm I mean views about how teaching ought to be, how it would be in ideal circumstances . . . The pragmatic component of teacher perspectives is concerned with what is or is not possible in giving circumstances and with strategies and techniques for achieving goals.   (p. 38)

Hammersley draws attention to the difficulty of unravelling paradigmatically and pragmatically motivated elements of teacher perspectives. However, I would argue that in this case Dick was drawn towards an orientation that allowed no compromise on his views of how teaching should be, while Tom equally clearly shows a concern for 'what is or is not possible in given circumstances'. We can go further, and on the basis of the evidence that Tom and Dick afford us, claim that, in the paradigmatic orientation, as well as ideals and principles being uppermost, there will be little or no situational adjustment (Becker, 1977). Any 'collectivizing' (i.e. sharing problems with colleagues and seeking a collective view) will be undertaken in the service of those ideals and principles rather than in the more pragmatic teacher culture or subculture (Lacey, 1977). Inasmuch as the norms, rules and values prevailing in the institution are at variance with those of the ideals and principles, they will be subverted, not accommodated. In as much as the power structure is tilted against the ideals, attempts will be made to swing the balance.

In Tom's kind of pragmatic orientation, there is situational adjustment but also some partial redefinition. Tom has come to prefer 'privatization' of his problems, near-conformity of career structure, and acquisition of power within the prevailing framework. All this takes place without the loss of the vision of ideals, though inevitably there is compromise of principles in practice. The mode is characterized by opportunism, testing out chances on a limited front, and seizing whatever possibilities present themselves to further one's aims. They are not necessarily limited to the school.

The comparison of Tom and Dick is suggestive in the area of strategical orientations. Clearly, there is something interposing between ideology and strategy that causes Tom and Dick to go their separate ways. Differences in age and subject specialism may obviously be important. But, since Dick's teaching career came to such a sudden end, there would appear to be other factors. There was, I believe, a marked difference in 'awareness' between them in some respects. But the characterization of their strategical orientations as paradigmatic and pragmatic leads us to other areas on which this difference in awareness may be dependent. My analysis suggested the related concepts of commitment and identity.

Commitment

I have written elsewhere on a form of commitment known as 'career-continuance':

> One of the major social system problems involving the commitment of actors is its continuance as an action system. This involves cognitive orientations bearing on profits and costs, and generally implies commitment to a social system role. The individual who makes a cognitive continuance commitment finds that what is profitable to him is bound up with his position in the organization, is contingent on his participating in the system. There is a profit in his remaining there and a deficit associated with leaving. Continuance is accompanied by 'sacrifice' and 'investment' processes. As a price of membership, members give up something, make sacrifices, which in turn increases commitment. So does investment, which promises future gain in the organization. The member takes out shares in the proceeds of the organization and thus has a stake in its future. He channels his expectations along the organization's path, and the more he does so, the more he increases the distance between this and other possibilities. They grow more remote as his commitment grows larger. In this way the process is self validating, self-reinforcing and frequently irreversible. The member goes on further to lay down what Becker calls 'side-bets' as other, unanticipated, sources of reward appear, once the line of action has been chosen.
>
> (Woods, 1979, pp. 143–144)

In a study of a hundred primary teachers (30 men, 70 women), Nias (1980) has identified other forms of commitment. These are first, commitment as vocation – this involves a 'calling' to teach, and the examples include a missionary sense deriving from religion, or the promotion of other ideals, or 'caring' for children. Secondly, there was commitment as profession – a dedication to one's skill as a teacher, involving a continuous search to improve one's knowledge and abilities, and to do the job really well. Thirdly, there was commitment as identity – here, teaching offered people the opportunities to be the sort of people they wanted to be. Fourthly, Nias did recognize the 'career-continuance' kind of commitment identified in my previous research (see also Kanter, 1974). Of course there was overlap in practice among these four analytical forms.

Lacey also, from his questionnaire study (of students on PGCE courses) noticed differences in forms of commitment. One common form was to education in its broadest sense. Teachers with this kind of commitment 'acquire jobs in the schools which they feel will give them the freedom to teach in the ways they wish (comprehensive schools), and already see their careers taking them outside the classroom and ouside the school' (Lacey, 1977, p. 126). They are committed to a set of ideals about education and society, not to teaching as such and, if blocked from achieving their ideals through teaching, will explore other means of bringing them about. This roughly corresponds to Nias' commitment as vocation.

The other form Lacey noted, corresponding to Nias' second category (commitment as profession), was a professional commitment to teach, to a career in the school, and to subject-based teaching. They rated their teaching abilities very highly, and were dedicated to their advancement.

Nias points out that one of the differences between these two forms of commitment (vocation, profession) and the other two (identity, career), is the willingness of the individual to give scarce personal resources – time, energy, money – to one's work (see also Lortie, 1975). Tom and Dick would clearly both be included among the former categories on that basis. But there were, nonetheless, important differences between them.

It is not surprising that Nias, among primary teachers, and Lacey, among student teachers should find a preponderance of vocational and professional commitment, while in the beleaguered secondary modern school of my research, the prevailing mode was career-continuance. What is surprising, perhaps, is that we should find in the latter two teachers whose forms of commitment were more in line with those in the former categories. However, the type of school forced a crucial difference between Tom and Dick to be revealed. Both Tom and Dick showed 'vocational' commitment. But that does not get us very far, and it misses entirely the real point of contrast between them. For while Tom, by my estimation, was just as committed to ideals as Dick, he was also more committed to the principles and practice of teaching, and over a wider range of application. This enabled him to 'juggle' his interests. Pollard has demonstrated how teachers do this in the immediacy of the classroom situation (1980b). Tom illustrates how one 'juggles' or 'negotiates' on a wider front. I gained the strong impression from him that his own position in the school was always precarious, that is to say his sense of fulfilment, and confidence in what he was doing was perennially a matter of doubt for him. This was perhaps inevitable given the wide gulf between his views and those prevailing within the school at large, which yielded a reality far removed from that desired by Tom.

This position would have been intolerable were it not for those other two broad areas of commitment. The first was to the principles and practice of teaching. Tom was a professional, who, while seeing many faults in the system, nevertheless recognized the need for administration and bureaucracy, for control and examinations and the like. This is illustrated in Tom's approach to the subject choice process, which forces teachers and pupils alike to face the realities imposed on them by structural considerations. Though not a front-line subject, Art, by virtue of entering for 'O' level and CSE faces the same pressures:

A lot choose Art, yes, and you know why, don't you? I'm not fooled. I say to them, 'Why do you want to do Art'? I say, 'I know, but come on, you tell me', and they say, 'Huh, I don't want to do old biology or whatever, all that homework and so on'. It's an easy option, and they go for it on both lines. My results this year were pretty poor which rather proves my point. But what I do is this. I pick those with most artistic abilty and I like it to be seen to be fair. I don't spring this on them either. I tell them all this at the beginning of the third year. I tell them they'll be judged on the quality of work that goes into their folders, and then, towards the end of the year, I get them to lay it all out, so they can all see, and, of course, some are very good and some are pathetic. There's no other way, not if they want to take the exam. If they just want a skive, they can do it somewhere else.

Here, one might have expected a wholesale commitment to Tom's ideals to have operated against examination results leading the decision-making. The whole tenor of this statement, also, would have been different. As it is, it contains the vocabulary, idiom and implications of traditional teaching – pupils trying to outwit teachers for an easier time, the experienced teacher easily recognizing the attempted subterfuge, poor results, skiving, and the strategy that appear to bridge the gap between ideals and practice – the demonstration of ability by fair procedures.

Despite his own periodic fulminations against bureaucracy, Tom recognized the need for organization. He was himself Head of Art and first year tutor, the first carrying responsibilities for the subject specialism, the second involving important counselling functions. This latter post was another bridging device between ideals and practice, for it enabled Tom to indulge some of his most cherished ideas centred on interest in the person, including their whole background. But it also brought about frustrations when the channels of communication between Tom and parents were obstructed by the hierarchy.

Dedication to subject specialism was also prominent. Lacey (1977) identified strong student subject sub-cultures, and argued that these operated as latent cultures within schools. There were signs that Tom was influenced by and contributed to such a sub-culture, sustained by his relationships with other Art teachers in other schools and colleges. Its guiding feature is 'creativity'. Art is regarded as a creative subject – it comes from within. Techniques can be learned, but their deployment in the act of composition is fundamentally a creative process. There are certain implications for teaching style – a relaxed atmosphere, gentle encouragement, a removal of restriction, constraint and conflict, indeed the creation of an environment where pupils can find expression. Art has therapeutic qualities, therefore, both for pupils and for teacher, for whom it is another bridge between aspiration and accomplishment.

The point is neatly made again by the stark contrast between the views of Tom and those of the headmaster. According to Tom, the head was concerned 'only with the production of nice pictures'. He had 'no conception of what teaching art involves'. Having given this trenchant opinion, he would say 'I never bloody well could understand Art!'. He was interested usually only when visitors were coming. The Art room was one of the front line show places and he therefore wanted the best picures up. Tom strongly disagrees with that. He wants the *kids'* best pictures up. But Art teaching involves so much more than just the production of pictures, you have to do so much groundwork on basic dispositions, getting them in the right frame of mind. This is why he plays pop music in the Art room. The kids like it, it's a place they want to come to, they can feel more at home there, less threatened, less constrained. But the head objects, 'not so much to the principles of the method, as to the music. It's "infra dig". Now you can go along to the music room and there'll be strains of Bach. That's OK, it's socially acceptable, it doesn't matter that nobody's listening'.

Despite his frustrations then, Tom is able to derive some satisfaction from his teaching, both from a subject-based and personal point of view, without sacrifice of principles. This delicate balance between gains and losses extends to his views on changes and forthcoming changes in school organization. They enable him to keep the principles in sight, while their full realization is likely to be obstructed. Thus the 'block' system of time tabling was devised on principles embodied in the Newsom Report (CACE, 1963) and not just administrative convenience. 'That would be OK' Tom argued 'if we had the resources to make use of it'. For example, he could hire scaffolding at £1 a day to decorate the walls, make new gates at the front and rear of the school – they needed this vocational orientation. Then he had mates at the Art school and the Technical College who would have the pupils for a day, and that would be one less day at school, they needn't wear uniforms, they'd be with adults, they'd be human beings, and if some of them did well it could be extended to 1½ – 2 days.'

Tom was for comprehensive education, though against 11–18 all through schools. He favoured 6th form colleges where students could be more adult, and he also preferred smaller 11 – 16 schools which allowed for teachers 'knowing the kids and where you all grow up together'. He did not approve of sacrificing humanity for a dubious equality. At the time, the school did not exceed Tom's size requirements, allowing him to know a large number of pupils in the way he thought desirable.

This leads me to the other main aspect of Tom's commitment facilitating survival, namely that to the community in which he lived. He was the only member of staff who lived in the village, fraternizing with the kids and their parents out of school. If he met any pupils in one of the local pubs, he would nod and turn his back, he wouldn't 'welsh' on them, which could have a deleterious effect on his relationship with them in school. These relationships were everything. He believed in community life – and school is part, only part of that life. Others thought him odd as he was the only one living in the village, but he thought it was 'the only way'. The kids knew he fraternized with their parents, many of whom he taught himself. At every first year parents' evening he would meet a whole horde of his previous pupils who were now parents of kids he was teaching, so it was all reinforced. And by the fifth year, these kids knew him just as well.

Generally mixing then, with the people of the village, in pub, street and church, probably in that order, was one aspect of this wider commitment. Another was his association with the Adult Education evening classes held at the school, of which he was the principal. Again, the main plank of his policy was the fostering of social relationships, because he believed that was why people came – for therapy. Therefore he liked to be in the foyer at the centre of operations, welcoming all and available to all. The head tolerated it, but regarded it as still *his* school, with much greater priority. Evening school was frequently more satisfying than day school, because he preferred dealing with adults, the relationships were more mature and complete. The environment was much better, clear of all the constraints of compulsion. But you could still have frustrations. For example, the caretaker wanted to lock up at 9 p.m. sharp and this was quite a huge problem.

Tom aspired once to go on a 60% evening and 40% day school basis. He would have loved that because he could have got out of Assemblies, staff meetings and so forth – all the things unconnected with teaching. But for that he needed a roll of 500 in his evening classes, whereas he only had 360. He could work to build it up, but it would take two years and they wouldn't guarantee him the headship.

But he oscillated. At the time he was disposed to give up evening schools because of 'a hundred and one petty administrative things like collecting money, answering letters, the caretaker and poor teachers, who often were unprepared and boring.' At other times, he felt he should abandon his day work. But this oscillation is my point. The swings and roundabouts of Tom's existence kept him going. The rewards and penalties varied from time to time in each sphere, but while there were rewards somewhere, they were banked against career-continuance.

The main feature, therefore, of Tom's commitment was not its vocational or professional orientation but its range, both in respect of his teaching within the school, where his application to the practice of teaching, the teaching of Art as a subject, and school and curriculum organization balanced the strong commitment to ideals; and in respect of his whole life which was dedicated first and foremost to the community, of which the school was only a part. His range of commitments allowed Tom to ring the changes on his options and keep them all open, as now one area gratified and another disappointed, and at another time, *vice versa*.

Dick, on the other hand, did not have the same range of commitments. He had outside interests, notably in the Society of Friends, and this association, I would argue, helped to sustain his 'ideas' commitment. He corresponded with people with similar views to his own, and he told me of their aspirations to create a new Summerhill in the south of England. This no doubt helped sustain his vision against the continuously disappointing reality of the school he was in. He certainly gave a great part of his time and energies to the school – in sporting activities, in running, swimming and football teams, in organizing the film club, in preparing lessons and projects. The simple truth is that the more one puts into an organization or activity, the greater, or the more single-minded one's commitment, the greater will be the frustration and desperation when aims and aspirations are dashed. This must be even more so when the commitment is primarily one of 'ideas'.

This greater commitment to ideas, was often at the expense of practice. I have argued that Tom, in his professional commitment, showed a capacity for situational adjustment which left his ideas intact. I observed no such capacity in Dick. My feeling is that he had the 'vocational' or 'ideas' commitment of Lacey and Nias in excess in this particular situation, to which he was unwilling or unable to adjust. It seems unkind to label somebody with Dick's tremendous energies and dedication as non- or unprofessional, but in the strictest sense he was. There were those on the staff who said 'he was his own worst enemy,' and those among the pupils who said 'he was not a proper teacher'. Grace (1978) has noted some teachers in his study of inner-city schools who resisted 'immersion' into the school since it involved 'a threat to their intellectual and social vitality' (p. 187). Dick however did 'immerse' himself, for there were few who equalled his input into the school while I was there, only to extricate himself by resigning when he felt the 'threat to his intellectual and social vitality' realized. This may have been Dick's central problem – an inability to do anything other than immerse himself wholeheartedly in any enterprise he chose to engage in, coupled with a very strong commitment to principle.

This would help to explain some curious anomalies. For example, while Dick certainly had had three schools in three years, it was not his search for a more accommodating billet that was responsible, as I shall show shortly. Curiously, too, in spite of failure at each, by his own admission, his career was from more progressive institutions to less – from Cambridgeshire Village College to West Country Comprehensive to East Midlands Secondary Modern. Moreover, jobs were still fairly plentiful at the time. He talked at length and with great enthusiasm about Summerhill, junior schools and so on, and of a plan he and some friends had of founding a real community school in the south of England. The further his own experience got from his ideals, the more adventurous those ideals seemed to become.

For a more adequate explanation, however, we must move into identity theory.

Identity

Identity theory 'begins with the notion that each of us has an interest in being or becoming somebody special, sufficiently different from his fellows to save him from anonymity, and different in ways that enable him to command some admiration, respect or affection. Our cultures provide us with a repertoire of possible selves . . . from this . . . each of us chooses or assembles a package and he gives people to understand that this is the sort of person he is . . . (These choices) constitute in effect, a set of claims we make about ourselves. Having made these claims, our public reputations and our private satisfaction with ourselves depend on our success in fulfilling these claims' (Cohen, 1976, p. 49).

This has been demonstrated many times, especially in the field of deviance, for example in the Abortion Clinic (Ball, 1972), and with various types in Rubington and Weinberg (1978) – shoplifters, nudists, check-forgers, queers and peers. All illustrate the managing of identity. 'Identity establishes *what* and *where* the person is in social terms . . . One's identity is established when others *place* him as a social object by assigning him the same words of identity that he appropriates for himself or *announces*' (Stone, 1962, p. 93). The distinction is often made between personal and social identities. Personal identity is the image one has of oneself – social identity is the image others have. These are sometimes distinguished as *self*, ego as known to ego, and *identity*, ego and his self as he appears to alter (Stone, 1962). There is continuous interplay between the two performed through symbols – language, appearance, acts – and mediated through interpretive frameworks. For interaction with others to be able to occur, there must be at least some correspondence between presented self and assigned identity, between personal and social identities (Ball, 1972).

Identities have a temporal dimension. Ball has distinguished between situated and substantial identities. The latter have a more stable and enduring quality. Situated identities are more transient, more dependent on time, place and situation, though they interact with substantial identities and may affect them. If there is a wide divergence between the two, a great deal of negotiative work may be required by both actor and audience to salvage the substantial identity.

We shall find these distinctions useful in our consideration of our two heroes. My main argument is that Dick was concerned to claim a particularly radical personal and substantial identity, and that this was one of the main factors, ultimately, behind his eventual surrender. This would help to explain the consistency of his behaviour, in fact the *escalation* of attempted innovation, despite the evident lack of success. Albert Cohen (1976) argues that 'for some of us, a key portion of our identity is our claim to be among the vanguard of some movement' (p. 51). Once certain areas have been achieved, or even perhaps simply broadcast, we need to move on to still more thoroughgoing aims:

> Disillusionment with the ineffectiveness of a less radical posture may play
> an important part and so may, paradoxically, the experience of success.

> Success, by altering one's conception of what is possible, may encourage a revision upwards of aspirations and therefore of greater extremism.
>
> (1976, p. 51)

I would argue that both factors, failure and success, albeit a 'phoney' success, paradoxically played a part in the maintenance of Dick's radical identity. He had moved to three different schools in as many years. I believe that Dick wanted to be a reformer, and that his brief excursions into these three schools *each* gave him a glimpse of that characterization before threatening to undermine it. For all institutions have a certain elasticity. The norms and rules of the prevailing cultures may be strong, but ill-defined, if only because they are so rarely challenged. When they are challenged it takes time for the upholders of the culture to marshall their defences. In that space, that area of 'give', Dick enjoyed momentary but largely phoney success with his film club, his clique of malcontents, his newspaper, house badges and School Council. Once the strength of the prevailing forces began to outweigh his apparent successes, it was time for him to move on to test the pliability of some other institution. That this overall movement showed a trend towards situations that were less and less likely to favour his aims, supports my argument that Dick was acting in the service of his own preferred identity, rather than seeking out ways of creating the conditions that might help some of his ideas become practice. Of course one could argue that trying to set up a School Council etc. was his attempt to create those conditions, and that his failure was simply a product of superior forces or his own misjudgement or inexperience. But Dick was neither a novice nor unintelligent. And there could be fewer less propitious moments and situations for such a reform.

In the terms of the model of identity with which we began, it enabled Dick to pass off the situational identity as part of his substantial one, whereas Tom played off one situational identity against another in an always precarious juggling feat. Moving fairly rapidly from place to place was Dick's way of managing his identity as a radical reformer, dedicated to certain ideals and principles, which admitted of no compromise, and which called for vigorous and persistent prosecution of method. Further, what others might have interpreted as warning signs and gathering powerful opposition, was an essential component of Dick's identity. For in the shaping and honing of these identities we need not only supportive feedback from others, but also contrastive. Thus opposition would be converted to gain in Dick's (and Tom's) perception of others. Thus when Dick and Tom criticized the hierarchy, 'craftsmen' handiworkers, time-serving nine to four teachers, as they frequently did, it was not simply a question of attacking policies and ideologies, but an 'attempt to render worthless the currency in terms of which the identities of those who dwell comfortably within those institutions are currently valued' (Cohen, 1976, p. 52). The counter-criticism was a useful mirror for Dick, or as Cooley described it, 'the looking-glass self' (Cooley, 1902).

Dick's identity was projected with his usual vigour and clarity, from his long hair with hair band and other unusual symbols of clothing to the laying bare of his spiritual self in his confessions of his innermost thoughts and feelings in his assemblies. Gregory Stone has argued for the importance of appearance, as well as discourse in the establishment, maintainance and alteration of the self (1962). The headmaster and most of his staff realized this in their preoccupation with school uniform. Of course the kind of identities the head was trying to promote among the kids was greatly at variance with that of Dick.

This clash of identities, in which appearances were paramount, is illustrated by an incident which sparked off a series of events which led to Dick's eventual resignation. It is important to realize that Dick, even though periodically he spearheaded a clique, was an individualist, even more so than Tom. He was a marginal man, who championed other marginals in his teaching – tramps, gypsies, alcoholics – with passionate ideas but lacking the roots that Tom had sunk over the years.

He was not one of the staff as a collective body, and in some respects he was anti-professional. He would not have subscribed to the 'collective ideology' of the staffroom (Hammersley, 1975). Nor would Tom in many respects, but he admitted to accepting the majority view. If decisions were made that he did not like, he would not seek ways of overturning them, but of adapting them. Dick, however, could not bear to be associated however remotely with certain decisions. The occasion in question was when the head took his revenge on the whole school, for having been worsted by two fourth form boys, laid his conformist philosophy on the line, 'denigrated them as human beings', and ordered a harsh uniform and general appearance inspection the following day, as if to signal the birth of a new order. Dick marched into the staffroom afterwards and immediately declared 'That's it! I'm leaving! I'm off! Can't stay in this school any longer'. It was not only the philosophy, but the fact that the head had declared that 'he was going to see to it that *his* teachers carried out his new totalitarian oppression policy'. Dick resented this association. He 'wasn't going to bloody do it'. Some boys said that at times it was like the SS with the head as Hitler. Between the verbal fury of the onslaught, however, and the deed itself – in this case, the uniform inspection of the following day – there was a world of difference in which both teachers and pupils could manoeuvre, as most of them did, including Tom. They knew that the head's outburst, not any new policy or regime, *was* his revenge. Thus, you could go up the line of pupils under his charge, pretending to inspect them but making amusing comments, neutralizing to a large extent the previous day's damage. This mutual 'face work' (Goffman, 1967) enabled Tom and the pupils he inspected to preserve their substantial identities while going through situational motions. By making a pretence of the inspection, Tom was projecting an image of self detached from that particular framework. And by their smiles and knowing looks, the pupils confirmed the image.

Dick could not bring himself to do this any more than he could attend speech day. It is possible that he saw this particular attack as just as much an attack on him as on the pupils, since much stress was laid on the importance of *appearance,* and what certain deviant forms of it (e.g. long hair) indicated. His reaction may, then, not have arisen solely out of strong sympathy for the pupils, and their 'denigration as human beings' (Dick's words), but because it also brought on for him a severe identity crisis. I am reminded of Lemert's analysis of the identity problems of the check forger (not to be confused with moral career, in which Dick and the check forger have nothing in common):

> In a sense the forger fails because he succeeds; he is able to fend off or evade self-degradation consequences of his actions, but in so doing he rejects forms of interaction necessary to convert his rewards in positive, status-specific self-evaluations. In time he reaches a point at which he can no longer define himself in relation to others on any basis. The self becomes amorphous, without boundaries; the identity substructure is lost.
>
> (1978, pp. 459–460)

Dick could only preserve his sense of who he was by leaving. Had he stayed, he would have been a changed man. His one real achievement – the new social studies syllabus – rather significantly perhaps, had been credited to somebody else. In other respects he had gone from experiment to experiment on an ever increasing scale of pervasiveness despite their evident failure. In the circumstances, there could be only one outcome, and it was *he* who made the decision, not the headmaster. It is my guess that leaving solved at a stroke what had become for him an intolerable identity problem.

In other ways, Dick and the headmaster aggravated their identity concerns, and we can see how lack of a certain awareness compounded both their difficulties. Dick disputed not only the head's power, but also his position as 'critical reality definer' (Riseborough, 1981, p. 37). Dick's frequent utterances that some decision or action of the head's was too grotesque to be 'true' carried almost literal significance for him. They lived in different worlds. So did Tom. But, whereas Tom appreciated how those worlds had come into existence and what their social supports were, Dick did not, except in a very hazy way. The core of the projection of those worlds seemed at times within the person, almost in a spiritual sense. At others, it was seen as purely a managerial problem. But always as individualized. I suggest this was why he was so frequently outraged at the head's behaviour, and *vice versa*. They both took it personally, the headmaster who was so traditionalist 'it wasn't true', and the 'bloody anarchist' bent on nihilistic revolution. Having affixed these labels to each other, they seemed determined to make each other live up to them. Tom could have stepped outside these labels. Dick and the headmaster seemed to revel in them. Each saw the other as a 'judgemental dope' (Garfinkel, 1967). But in their outright condemnation of each other, each was reinforcing his own identity. This preoccupation, I would suggest, blunted the edge of awareness.

The starkness of Dick's position is revealed by a consideration of the rest of the staff, Tom included, whose roles and careers hung in the balance because of the forthcoming change in the school's status to comprehensive. There would be more jobs, but who would get them? Would their present positions be guaranteed? Would they need a degree to remain head of department? Who would get the key senior positions? During Dick's solitary year at the school, the rest of the staff, all on a somewhat longer time span, were in a state of unease and uncertainty about their professional careers and identities, and most were playing it safe. 'If I play my cards right', one told me, 'I might get head of department'. It was not the time to rebel; not the time to try to overthrow a ruler when he was on the point of abdicating and a new more democratic constitution had already been agreed.

Riseborough, for example, has shown that in the school of his research, career aspirations were fixed during comprehensivization and the 'old' staff thought these aspirations would and could be realistically fulfilled. Much staffroom conversation was concerned with potential career advancement, and there was an atmosphere of career uncertainty and career expectation. One of the staff remarked, 'The school was at a watershed – and you don't drop bombs in watersheds, not unless you are jettisoning them for waste' (Riseborough, 1981, pp. 18–19). That is exactly what Dick did. He dropped a bomb in a watershed.

Conclusion

The comparison of two teachers professing similar views of teaching and in the same situation, but with different strategical orientations, has suggested further refinements to prevailing models of teacher action.

The categorization of strategies employed by our two teachers on a paradigmatic – pragmatic basis led to the argument that if we are to understand correctly the origin and nature of teacher strategies, then we must investigate their type and range of commitments and their identities. I have suggested that what helps Tom maintain an admittedly precarious teaching existence, but nonetheless ideologically intact one, is a range of commitments, both within the school and in the community at large, among which he can juggle or negotiate his general interests depending on circumstances. He has, too, what I have described as a number of 'bridging devices' which enable him to cross the divide between ideals and practice, such as 'fair procedures', his counselling role, and his subject 'art'. These bridging devices might be compared with the 'partial penetrations' noted by Willis (1977) which enabled a group of 'lads' periodically to break through their conditions of existence.

I have argued that a factor playing a large part in Dick's downfall was the preservation of his own substantial identity, which was becoming increasingly at risk with every day that he remained at the school. Resignation was the final act of self-preservation. This is not to say, of course, that there were not other contributory factors. The headmaster, for example, happened to hold fundamentally different views. If Dick had arrived at the school two or three years later he would have been caught up in the initial excitement of comprehensivization. If he had come four or five years earlier, he might have established himself within a powerful reference group, with strong mutual moral support. The circumstances were not of his making and, as they were, they aggravated his identity problems.

It is in these areas of teacher biography that the individual has most choice, choosing how to distribute commitments over a range of concerns, selecting an identity from a range of roles and testing it reflexively in a continuous process of interactions with others (Brittan, 1973). These choices have implications for strategies and for careers.

I should stress again, that I do not claim to have given anything like a full explanation of Tom's and Dick's intentions and actions. That would require much more material, not only in the areas touched on in this paper, but into a deeper socio-historical dimension, into earlier socialization, class and family background that would reveal more about the development of the self concept and the criteria they used for judging how they 'coped' with the situation (see Pollard, 1980a). Rather, I have used the material that was available to me to try to indicate the potential fruitfulness of this area for understanding teacher action, and to suggest lines of future enquiries.

Finally, I have cast the problem in terms of why Tom survived in the system, and Dick did not, and in such a comparison, Dick must appear the loser. But of course it is the educational system that is the real loser, for teachers of his talents, energies and charisma are rare. While the thrust of this paper has been to focus on his own responsibility in the matter as suggested by his identity concerns, there are questions raised about significant others who may have helped shape those concerns – headteachers, colleagues, teacher educators.

One would also need to appreciate the constraints he was faced with. Dick, in fact, had the whole force of society against him – social structure, moral standards, cultural adaptations. In typically optimistic and energetic fashion he attempted to create his own structural supports from the flotsam and jetsam of an unpopular, but dying regime. In the end, that is all it was, something left on the beach between the flow of the new unknown, forthcoming comprehensivization, and the ebb of the elitist paternalism of the old order. What this study of two teachers has shown, I hope, is not only how the constraints and pressures in this tide impinge on action, but also how they can be recognized and grappled with. The results may not be revolutionary, but where there is recognition, there are possibilities.

Acknowledgement

I am indebted to Jennifer Nias, Andrew Pollard, Colin Fletcher, Martyn Hammersley, Colin Lacey, Stephen Walker and Len Barton, for their observations on an earlier draft of this paper. My thanks above all to Tom and Dick whose inspiration as teachers led me to write this paper.

References

BALL, D. (1972) 'Self and identity in the context of deviance: The case of criminal abortion' in SCOTT, R.A. and DOUGLAS, J.D. (Eds) *Theoretical perspectives on deviance* New York, Basic Books.

BECKER, H. (1977) 'Personal change in adult life' in COSIN, B. *et al* (Eds) *School and Society* (2nd edition) London, Routledge and Kegan Paul.

BRITTAN, A. (1973) *Meanings and Situations* London, Routledge and Kegan Paul.

CENTRAL ADVISORY COUNCIL FOR EDUCATION (1963) *Half Our Future* (Newsom Report) London, HMSO.

COHEN, A. (1976) 'The elasticity of evil: Changes in the social definition of deviance' in HAMMERSLEY, M. and WOODS, P. (Eds) *The Process of Schooling* London, Routledge and Kegan Paul.

COOLEY, C.H. (1902) *Human Nature and the Social Order* New York, Charles Scribner's Sons.

DALE, I.R. (1978) 'From Endorsement to Disintegration: Progressive Education from the Golden Age to the Green Paper' Paper presented to the *Conference of the Standing Committee for Studies in Education* King's College, London (December).

DENZIN, N. (1970) *The Research Act in Sociology; a Theoretical Introduction to Sociological Methods* London, The Butterworth Group Ltd.

GARFINKEL, H. (1967) *Studies in Ethnomethodology* Englewood Cliffs, Prentice-Hall.

GLASER, B.G. and STRAUSS, A.L. (1967) *The Discovery of Grounded Theory* London, Weidenfeld and Nicolson Ltd.

GOFFMAN, E. (1967) *Interaction Ritual* New York, Doubleday Anchor.

GRACE, G. (1978) *Teachers, Ideology and Control* London, Routledge and Kegan Paul.

HAMMERSLEY, M. (1977) 'Teacher Perspectives', Unit 9 of Course E202 *Schooling and Society* Milton Keynes, Open University Press.

HARGREAVES, A. (1977) 'Progressivism and pupil autonomy' *Sociological Review* August.

HARGREAVES, A. (1978) 'Towards a theory of classroom coping strategies' in BARTON, L. and MEIGHAN, R. (Eds) *Sociological Interpretations of Schooling and Classrooms* Driffield, Nafferton Books.

HARGREAVES, A. (1979) 'Strategies, decisions and control: interaction in a middle school classroom' in EGGLESTON, T. (Ed) *Teacher Decision-Making in the Classroom* London, Routledge and Kegan Paul.

KANTER, R.M. (1974) 'Commitment and social organization' in FIELD, D. (Ed) *Social Psychology for Sociologists* London, Nelson.

KOUNIN, J.S. (1970) *Discipline and Group Management in Classrooms* New York, Holt, Rinehart and Winston.

LACEY, C. (1977) *The Socialization of Teachers* London, Methuen.

LEMERT, E. (1978) 'The check forger and his identity' in RUBINGTON, E. and WEINBERG, M.S. *op. cit.*

LINDESMITH, A.R. (1947) *Opiate Addiction* Bloomington, Ind., Principia Press.

LORTIE, D.C. (1975) *Schoolteacher* Chicago, University of Chicago Press.

MILLER, C. and PARLETT, M. (1974) *Up to the Mark* London, Society for Research into Higher Education.

NIAS, J. (1980) 'Further Notes on the Concept of Commitment' Unpublished paper, University of Cambridge Institute of Education.

NEILL, A.S. (1968) *Summerhill* Harmondsworth, Penguin.

PARLETT, M.R. and HAMILTON, D. (1972) 'Evaluation as illumination: A new approach to innovatory programmes *Occasional Paper No. 9* Centre for Research in the Educational Sciences, University of Edinburgh.

POLLARD, A. (1980a) 'Towards a Revised Model of Coping Strategies' Paper presented to Middle Schools Research Group, Woburn, April, 1980.

POLLARD, A. (1980b) 'Teacher interests and changing situations of survival threat in primary school classrooms' in WOODS, P. (Ed) *Teacher Strategies* London, Croom Helm.

RISEBOROUGH, G.F. (1981) Teacher Careers and Comprehensive Schooling: An Empirical Study' *Sociology* (in press).

RUBINGTON, E. and WEINBERG, M.S. (Eds) (1978) *Deviance: The Interactionist Perspective* New York, MacMillan.

SCHUTZ, A. (1970) *On Phenomenology and Social Relations: Selected Writings* (Ed WAGNER, H.R.) Chicago, University of Chicago Press.

STONE, G.P. (1962) 'Appearance and the self' in ROSE, A.M. (Ed) *Human Behaviour and Social Processes* London, Routledge and Kegan Paul.

WILLIS, P. (1977) *Learning to Labour* Farnborough, Saxon House.

WOODS, P. (1977) 'Teaching for survival' in WOODS, P. (Ed) *School Experience* London, Croom Helm.

WOODS, P. (1979) *The Divided School* London, Routledge and Kegan Paul.

WOODS, P. (Ed) (1980) *Teacher Strategies* London, Croom Helm.

Contrastive Rhetoric and Extremist Talk: Teachers, Hegemony and the Educationist Context

Andy Hargreaves, University of Oxford

Introduction

For those people who work in the sociology of education, 1981 is an auspicious year: the tenth anniversary of the publication of a collection of theoretically dense papers, bound in an inconspicuous cover and titled *Knowledge and Control*.[1] This book gave birth to what came to be known as the New Sociology of Education which marked the end (or temporary suspension) of interest in the problems of educational opportunity and achievement,[2] and substituted two grand explorations (whose paths have only recently crossed) which went in search of the meaning and organization of school life in one direction, and the ways in which schooling contributes to the processes of social and cultural reproduction in the other.[3]

In the one empirical paper in that volume, Nell Keddie (1971) made a now familiar distinction between two contexts in which teachers' knowledge is displayed and applied: the teacher context and the educationist context. *The teacher context* concerned the teacher's routine daily contact with pupils in the classroom, and all the practical activities such as lesson planning and marking that surrounded it. This was a highly pragmatic world; the world of *is* rather than *ought*; deeds not words; practice not theory. It was therefore a world that was fundamentally organized around the principles of habitual and pragmatically-based commonsense thought and action. *The educationist context* was very different. This was a 'context of discussion of school politics' which 'draws selectively and consciously on educational theory and research' (p. 135). This context was realized in situations like school meetings or in teachers' encounters with influential and/or inquisitive outsiders, such as HMIs and educational researchers, which entailed their explaining and justifying school policy. It was a context where fine ideals were espoused even if, as Keddie argued, they would later be shattered on the rocks of classroom reality.[4]

Now this distinction between teacher and educationist contexts is an important one, but the very emphases which Keddie made in the details of her analysis marked out the lines on which the research preoccupations of people in the discipline, including myself, were to develop over the next decade.[5] The major focus of Keddie's argument, as the title of her article *Classroom Knowledge* indicates, was on the classroom; the teacher context. Seventeen pages were devoted to this while there were less than four on the educationist context, and these contained very little data indeed. It is unfortunate that as Keddie shifted from her scant discussion of the educationist context to her more detailed analysis of the teacher context in the classroom, most sociologists of education sympathetic to ethnographic study seem to have followed suit.

Why such a large part of the sociology of education should subsequently have become so concerned with the classroom at the expense of other school contexts is a matter about which we can only speculate. One clear possibility, though, is that contrary to the injunction of Seeley (1966), reiterated in *Knowledge and Control,* that researchers should no longer *take* official problems, but *make* them,[6] it might well have been the case that sociologists of education, (most of them ex-teachers) took for granted the centrality of the classroom world to teachers and, like those teachers that Lortie (1975) studied, regarded this insulated and isolated world as the only 'real' one; the world where teachers pursued their occupational goals and encountered their major problems.[7]

To be fair, not all school ethnography has amounted to *classroom* ethnography, for in recent years, some researchers (e.g. Hammersley 1980a, 1981; Woods 1979) have, as part of their investigations, looked beyond the classroom to study the nature of staffroom cultures. What is most apparent about these staffrooms, though, is that they are quite unlike the educationist context as it is defined by Keddie. Indeed, they seem to be the very places where teachers graphically confirm their anti-intellectualism. Under this view, the staffroom is a 'back-region' (Goffman, 1959) into which teachers withdraw, where they relax the official front that is presented to pupils in the classroom (Woods, 1979). It is a place where teachers compensate for many of the uncertainties and difficulties of their job by neutralizing, often in exceedingly humorous ways, the threats presented to their sense of competence and their conception of teaching by such groups as incalcitrant pupils, irate or feckless parents and sceptical, idealist outsiders like HMIs and researchers. For the purposes of collective amusement and reassurance, senior staff are 'sent up' and pupils parodied. The staffroom, then, is a place where a 'norm of cynicism' about education and educational ideas operates (Hargreaves, D., 1972). It is certainly not a place for serious reflection or discussion about educational theories and ideas.[8]

Apart from these studies of school staffrooms, we have, over the last ten years, learnt very little about the ways in which teachers interact with one another and with senior members of the school hierarchy – in particular the head and deputy headteacher.[9] This neglect of the sociology of educationist contexts is not just one small gap among many others waiting to be plugged in a vast programme of sociological inquiry, but a vital absence, the remedy of which is of the utmost urgency for two reasons.

Educationist Contexts: Their Changing Status

First, there are signs that recent changes in patterns of curriculum innovation are bringing the educationist context into greater prominence in the life of teachers. What I am referring to here is the emergence of the school-based curriculum development (SBCD) movement which, according to Eggleston, 'has, in the early 1980s, become the dominant form of the curriculum development movement' (1980, p. ix). This movement, arising in response to the expense and failure of large-scale and nationally-based programmes of curriculum change (Stenhouse, 1973; Shipman *et al,* 1974; Holly, 1974; Gleeson, 1979) and more recently as a possible solution to problems of maintaining teacher morale and an impetus for curriculum innovation in a contracting educational system where the opportunities for teacher mobility have been severely curtailed (DES and Welsh Office 1978, Lightfoot 1978, Dennison 1979, Harlen 1977, Hunter and Heighway 1980), has thrust many teachers into a

relatively unfamiliar arena of decision-making, debate and reflection about educational activity. Though depressingly little is known about the exact quality and
nature of teachers' participation in programmes of SBCD, the *fact* of their involvement is undeniable.[10]

The educationist context therefore appears to be moving inwards from the
periphery of the teacher's world. In that case there is a special need to be cautious and
sceptical when reading the SBCD literature for little of it is research-based, and very
often amounts instead to little more than an ideology of teacher participation and
grassroots democracy. A substantial and constructive contribution to such a sceptical
approach would be varied ethnographic study of the dynamics of the decision-
making process in different educationist contexts. In policy terms alone, this task is a
matter of some urgency, for if the claims of the SBCD movement are not checked
out, the buoyant optimism of teacher participation drummed up by its supporters
may, when it meets the seemingly immovable obstacle of institutionalized power,
simply plunge teachers into a deeper morass of cynicism, despair and low morale than
the one from which the SBCD movement was explicitly designed to extricate them.

Hegemony and Teachers' Thinking: An Untested Thesis

The second reason for giving high priority to the study of educationist contexts is that
in certain important respects they provide a critical testing ground for the influential
thesis that teachers' everyday thinking is hegemonically determined. This thesis has
been a major component of that second exploratory venture in recent sociology of
education – the explanation of schooling's contribution to social and cultural
reproduction. Because it raises issues of such immense sociological, educational and,
indeed, political importance, it is therefore high time that the hegemony thesis was
put to the test.

There is not the space in a paper of this kind to provide anything like a comprehensive account of the nature of hegemony, its relation to ideology and commonsense, the historical conditions under which hegemony and counter hegemony
occur, and so on, though I have touched on these issues elsewhere.[11] All that can be
done here is to give a brief glimpse of some of its constituent features which are pertinent to the alleged nature and determinations of teachers' thinking.

Those who advance the view that the thinking of teachers is hegemonically
determined do not suggest, like Althusser (1971) that teachers subscribe to or are the
victims of any particular monolithic ideology, be it conservative, social democratic, or
whatever. Nor even do they argue, like Dale (1977) that teachers share what he calls a
basic 'cognitive style' of liberal individualism which 'sees educational problems as
deriving from individuals and the solutions to them as lying in individual treatments'
(p. 20). Rather, they stress the existence of considerable variation among teachers'
perspectives. For them, the central issue is that while teachers hold a range of views
about education and exhibit a diversity of patterns of thought in this area, *they do so
within very definite and unquestioned limits.*[12] Beyond these limits lie a set of educational and social practices which would be viewed by most people as potentially
threatening to the existing order of capitalism and the broad social and political
assumptions which help sustain it. Existing practices (what passes for normal teaching
and education under capitalism that is), therefore become not one version of reality
among many, but the only conceivable one; standing at the deepest levels of
teachers' consciousness as the only normal, natural and reasonable ways of

proceeding (Williams 1973, 1977). Through this process, dominant versions of reality (of which there are several) become deeply sedimented into people's consciousness and mark the boundaries of their commonsense, for the most part remaining beyond analysis and question. In the case of schooling, alternative educational practices and social forms are therefore not only regarded by teachers and other educators as extreme or utopian, but frequently as being simply unworthy of serious discussion. They just don't get talked about. This view is put succinctly by Apple (1979):

> The conceptual rules we employ to define our situations, that we use to design our schools and select the traditions that are to be preserved and distributed by them, show a signal neglect of . . . critical appraisals. To over-come this neglect would require a critical and coherent theory of the social order in which we live. But this is exactly the point. For not only have we failed to situate the knowledge we teach, the schools we help maintain and ourselves back into the basic structural relations of which they are a part, we have misrecognized the differential benefits of these basic structures themselves. (p. 159)

The implications of this process are serious. Lacking any overall integrating theory of the relationship between schooling and society, teachers become baffled and bemused when policy changes, such as those announced in the Great Debate, and the economic, social and political forces that underpin them, threaten to alter the organization of schooling. The reason for this confusion is that, in attempting to understand such changes, teachers draw on the range of ideas available within the dominant hegemony and combine them with notions deriving from their own practical experience (sometimes consonant, sometimes at odds with those ideas). The effect of this, as Ginsburg *et al* (1979) have argued, is to produce an overall fragmentation and incoherence in the thinking of some individual teachers and, more importantly, in the teaching body as a whole. Consequently, not only do teachers normally fail to challenge the boundaries of existing practice but, when the context of that practice undergoes fundamental shifts (as since the Great Debate), the effect of the dominant hegemony (which subsumes both ideology and commonsense) is such that they do not have the resources at hand to formulate coherent and critical understandings of their changed situation and the structural reasons for that change. Not surprisingly, lacking any such 'sociological imagination' (Mills, 1959), teachers tend to be carried along by changes rather than actively intervening in and taking control of the change process itself.

As insightful and politically appealing as this analysis is to many sociologists of education, including myself, it must be said that, to date, it has been founded more upon theoretical speculation and an almost religious conviction that the essential principles of the present social order have been grasped, than upon any kind of empirical demonstration. Furthermore, the limited evidence that has been drawn upon has been deficient in crucial respects.

Most interpetations of the hegemonic character of teachers' thinking appear to be based on the maxim that, since teachers articulate a set of conceptions about education that fall within a definite range then, *ipso facto,* they must be *un*aware of alternative practices and institutional forms that lie outside that range. Methodologically speaking, this approach obviates the possibility of either confirming or refuting the hegemony thesis as it applies to teachers. While it is true that hegemony functions by a principle of exclusion, partialling out of serious debate those conceptions of an oppositional character, Marxist writers have unwittingly added to this a *methodoligical* principle of exclusion, assuming that teachers' failure to mention alternatives in interviews and so on, demonstrates their lack of awareness of them and, thus, unmasks the hegemonically determined character of their thinking.

Consequently, it is difficult to establish whether the claimed properties of teachers' thinking are a product of the dominant hegemony, of theorists' unsupported assertions deriving from their dislike of capitalism, or whether they are simply a methodological artefact. Findings concerning the limited range of teachers' thinking are based almost entirely on interviews or informal conversations that teachers have with researchers (e.g. Sharp and Green, 1975; Grace, 1978), a methodological approach that is notoriously susceptible to the production of data that are more a product of the interview situation itself than any accurate reflection of actual teacher perspectives (Hargreaves, D., 1978; McNamara, 1980). What is therefore required is some further and more adequate empirical justification for claims about the limits of teachers' commonsense, for these limits are confirmed not only by the absence of oppositional views in teachers' thinking but also, and perhaps more crucially for the purposes of empirical demonstration, by the way in which oppositional views are treated when they are introduced into discussion in natural settings. The following rare, indeed exceptional, case study of the ways in which educational alternatives are introduced into discussion and the kinds of response those introductions elicit provides one (although by no means the only) telling empirical test of the hegemony thesis as it applies to teachers.

The Case Study

It is in the dual context of elucidating some aspects of the educationist context and formulating a test for the thesis of the hegemonic influences on teachers' thinking that I want to discuss some empirical research of curriculum decision-making in Riverdale School (an open-plan, suburban middle school) which I conducted in the mid 1970s. My overall study of middle schools as such is a large project embracing investigations of their history, ideology and practice.[13] The data here are drawn from one small part of that study; a series of weekly curriculum decision-making meetings held mainly on Wednesdays after school in the Summer term and involving the participation of the Head, his Deputy and the full staff of thirteen. These meetings were tape-recorded, transcribed and analyzed. Their purpose was to decide upon a curriculum for the following year. The programme of meetings was instigated by the Head and his Deputy who was nearing the end of secondment on a one-year diploma course at a nearby University where curriculum studies was one of the major areas of enquiry. The first meeting commenced with the Deputy Head using the overhead projector (to appropriate theatrically-orchestrated gasps of astonishment from the rest of the staff) to outline a model of curriculum planning. The remaining weeks were then taken up with discussion of educational questions in decreasing order of generality; covering in sequence such things as the purposes of education, choice and responsibility, moral education, areas of knowledge; then, following a division into working groups according to the identified areas of knowledge, a programme of aims and objectives in each case. The data discussed in this paper come from the earlier meetings.

The transcripts provide a fascinating documentation of the complexities of the curriculum decision-making process: of the strategies employed by the headteacher to secure staff agreement on curriculum policy; of the sorts of accounts which teachers routinely provided to support their arguments; of the levels of involvement of senior staff as against probationers and so on. Interesting though all these processes are, regrettably there is not the space to discuss them here. My specific task, rather, is to focus on the ways in which educational alternatives were introduced and discussed and thereby to clarify the nature of teachers' thinking and its boundaries as displayed in a natural setting, that of the educationist context, or one variant of such a context. There are few acid tests for the thesis of hegemony. But if any empirical test of an ethnographic kind can turn the theorist's litmus paper red (or blue), this is probably it.

I make no claims that the case I discuss is a typical one – that it is characteristic of most educationist contexts, that it typifies the usual ways in which teachers' thinking is hegemonically determined or that it is representative of the ways in which educational alternatives are normally introduced into discussion. Rather, it is my contention that the case is a *critical* one, an *exceptional* instance which highlights the theoretical problems and social processes under review.[14] In other words, Riverdale School is a place where one might most expect educational alternatives to be introduced seriously and discussed rigorously, where studied reflection and the discussion of school politics and educational theory would be in abundance. At Riverdale, that is, one might *most* expect the characteristics of the educationist context as outlined by Keddie to be present, and *least* expect hegemonic influences on teachers' consciousness to prevail.

What are the factors which enable Riverdale to be credited with the status of a critical case? First, its teachers were, at least initially, strongly involved in and committed to the process of discussion and debate. There were several reasons for this. The school was a new one; little more than a year old in fact. Moreover, it was not part of an immediate programme of comprehensivization and as such was not staffed by compulsorily 'reorganized' teachers who held long-standing commitments to grammar, secondary modern or primary schools and who, consequently, felt any marked antipathy towards middle schools. Being a new school, it had attracted a young staff as yet untarnished by the cynicism that often comes with a long teaching career. Because of all these things, an unquestionable vitality permeated the discussions and many of those who participated considerably enjoyed much of the decision-making experience. The comment of Miss Rogers at the end of the first meeting that 'I haven't done anything as exciting as this since college' (*not* spoken tongue-in-cheek) epitomized the general tenor of early staff responses.

Furthermore, in terms of topics selected and issues raised, the discussions were far from superficial. Particularly in the early meetings, the teachers often touched on some of the deepest and most complex social issues with which schooling is concerned – for instance, whether it fosters the development of individuals or secures social integration, whether it is a potent agent of social change or whether its influence in this respect is minimal, and so on. The meetings therefore occasioned not only critical and vigorous staff involvement, but also consideration of serious, indeed fundamental social and educational questions. These features would certainly accord with many of the characteristics of the educationist context to which Keddie alluded in her seminal article. But what was the character of discussion in that context? What kinds of alternative practices and social forms were discussed? How were they introduced? Who introduced them? And what do the identified decision-making practices reveal about teachers' and headteachers' knowledge and about the exercise of power and control in the decision-making process? I want to propose that some as yet unre-searched aspects of the educationist context – specifically the ways in which educational alternatives are introduced and discussed there – which are particularly important for the understanding and testing of the hegemony thesis, can be elucidated by the use of two concepts: *contrastive rhetoric* and *extremist talk.* I shall discuss the two processes denoted by these concepts in turn.

Contrastive Rhetoric

In a one sentence definition, *contrastive rhetoric refers to that interactional strategy whereby the boundaries of normal and acceptable practice are defined by institutionally and/or interactionally dominant individuals or groups through the introduction into discussion of alternative practices and social forms in stylized, trivialized and generally pejorative terms which connote their unacceptability.* The concept is in part derived from research on interactional practices among professional groups and from the sociology of mass media and deviance; but in the main it is a *grounded concept* (Glaser and Strauss, 1968) formulated, after detailed examination of the data and of deviant cases in particular, as the most satisfactory method I could evolve of explaining the data to hand.[15] Some indication of the detailed elements and effects of contrastive rhetoric can best be gauged from a consideration of specific examples.

One of the clearest and most lengthy instances of the use of contrastive rhetoric took the form of a discussion about Countesthorpe College, a well-known comprehensive school lying very much outside the mainstream of educational practice. The discussion was initiated by the deputy head, Mr. Pool.

Mr. Pool	Perhaps I could quote an example where they took it [pupil choice] not only on an individual, intuitive basis of what's right and wrong, but at Countesthorpe . . . I don't know if you've heard of this school in Leicestershire? (Laughter) You have. Yeah. Well, you know what happened there. They gave the kids an awful lot of choice.
Mr. Stones	I've been there.
Mr. Pool	You went, Alan?
Mr. Stones	Well, my friend lives in Countesthorpe and she's . . . um . . .
Mr. Pool	Well, can you tell us more about it? You'll know more than I do.
Mr. Stones	Well, she's one of . . . she's a twenty-five year old who goes in with the kids to do her O-levels. She's doing O-level biology and they just sort . . . well, I've not actually been round while it's working. I've been to have a look at it. But from what she says, you know, they're given free choice that the pupils . . . on what they want to do . . . you know . . . they can walk out half way through a lesson if they're bored and all this sort of thing. There are grown ups and children in together on O-levels and A-levels and it's all sort of first name terms with staff. She only knows the two that are taking her for biology as Jim and Bill. It's that sort of set up.

309

Mr. Pool	Mmm . . . And did she approve of it, or . . . or what? What kind of benefits or . . . or . . .
Mr. Stones	She doesn't . . . doesn't like it. She doesn't like it. But then she's been brought up in a formal atmosphere.
Mr. Pool	On what grounds? Just because it's . . . it's different, you know, or has she got some sort of thing that she's got against it?
Mr. Stones	Well, she doesn't like the way they can sort of just walk in and walk out and come in at any time and all this sort of thing.
Mr. Pool	Yeah, yeah.
Mr. Stones	She doesn't think that should happen. I don't know, she's got a bit of . . .
Mr. Pool	The bits . . . the bits that I read the reports about it was that the kids were appointed to a . . . a home basis and then there were a variety of choices which they could make, whether they went and did . . . uh . . . O-level science courses or whether they went and did CSE science courses, or just a general thing anyway, or whether they didn't do science in fact. This went through a whole load of things. These specialist things were provided for them and whether they chose these was a matter of counselling on the part of the staff for the kids, and the parents' pressure and their own wishes of course. But apart from that, there was no . . . no compulsion to go. In fact, stay in the home base all day and read . . . just read comics until they got so bored with it, in theory, that they wanted to do something else. And if you walked around the school, you could see kids eating crisps and sitting around, you know. But that's, that's right at the far end of what we're talking about.
Mr. Stones	A long way (muttered). (Concurring laughter)
Mrs. Home	A very long way. (More laughter) 'Cos I can see the kids that once they get bored sitting around and eating crisps and reading comics, will just go out of the school and find something more . . . more exciting.
Mr. Stones	Oh, they had the . . . the trouble with the smokers' room, didn't they, which . . . there was a great big kick up about under fourteen . . . over fourteens select smokers' room. The headmaster there was the headmaster at my school. Mr. X in Southshire. He was the headmaster for the first term that I was there and he tried to get something off the ground like that, but it . . . he couldn't. It's a bit of a stronghold.

Mr. Pool   Really, I think it's . . . it's worth looking at these things when . . . you know . . . you do hand things right over to the kids and see what happens.

As some of the better known and more unconventional features of Countesthorpe were introduced into discussion, laughter broke out. That laughter was elicited by virtue of the fact that potentially serious (and conceivably threatening) educational questions and practices were reduced to trivial, peculiar and highly visible features of Countesthorpe culture – smoking, reading comics, eating crisps, calling staff by first names etc. There is much in common here with what Cohen (1973) observes to be the usual way in which instances of deviance and dissent are portrayed in the mass media. In such coverage, Cohen argues,

> Symbolization and the presentation of 'the facts' in the most simplified and melodramatic manner possible leave little room for interpretation, the presentation of competing perspectives on the same event or information which would allow the audience to see the event in context.
>
> (Cohen, 1973, p. 76)

What Cohen means by symbolization is a process whereby,

> Communication . . . of stereotypes, depends on the symbolic power of words and images. Neutral words such as place names can be made to symbolize complex ideas and emotions: for example, Pearl Harbour, Hiroshima, Dallas and Aberfan.
>
> (p. 44)

Even though it cannot be shown that it was anyone's particular intention to introduce 'Countesthorpe' into debate for just these reasons, the effect of the mere mention of the name – the evoking of a heightened emotional response (in this case through the medium of laughter) – is undeniable. In the world of teachers, certain schools like 'Countesthorpe' or 'Tyndale' become eponymous. Their very mention triggers off a vast array of educational fears and uncertainties and symbolizes the threatened extension and incursion of extreme, unreasonable or simply meaningless educational practices. In the terse though graphic descriptions of such schools, particular words and phrases are selected out to conjure up generalized images of apparently anarchic and bizarre educational practices. These images become so strongly embedded in teacher folklore, that they need no detailed elaboration, only the merest allusion to exert ther emotive effect. Thus, after noting that his friend knows only the first names of her biology teachers, Mr. Stones adds without further explanation, 'It's that sort of set up'. As with some of his other statements, the rest of the staff are simply left to 'fill in' most of the additional and presumably obvious details of 'this sort of thing' and 'that sort of set up' themselves. The statements are taken to be and treated as if they were self-explanatory. The interchangeability of teachers' standpoints is assumed.[16]

The elements of exaggeration and stylization that permeate the discussion of Countesthorpe College add to the humour of the account and to the laughter it evokes. Like much routine staffroom humour, this serves to neutralize the threats presented by alternative practices and thus implicitly reaffirms the teachers' broadly shared existing conceptions of good versus bad teaching. Indeed, there is a sense in which Countesthorpe is depicted as being *devoid* of teaching rather than simply representative of an alternative tradition. (See Hammersley, 1980a). An important feature of contrastive rhetoric, therefore, is the sometimes humorous but always dramatic definition of normality by reference to its opposite, deviance; and thus the demarcation (albeit a hazy one) of the outer limits of existing practice (Durkheim 1964, chapter 3; Taylor, Walton and Young 1973, chapter 3).

One possible response to that observation is 'So what?' – for even if this portrayal of the way in which Countesthorpe is discussed is accurate, it does not necessarily follow that these features result from the pervasive influence of a dominant hegemony, social – democratic or otherwise, on teachers' thinking. Indeed, they may provide no clarification whatsoever about the special character of schooling or of teachers' thinking under the ideological influences of capitalism.

There are several respectable lines of sociological argument which suggest that the business of making contrasts is a widespread, if not universal, feature of social, interactional and conversational practice and therefore, by implication, not specific to discussion and decision-making practices in capitalistic social democracies.

First, for instance, is it not the case, following Durkheim, that definitions of the normal are conventionally and universally constructed by reference to the pathological – is it not this fact indeed which gives deviance its socially necessary role in society as a marker of the boundaries of morality? (Durkheim 1964, chapter 3; Hargreaves, D., 1979). As Erikson (1964) puts it:

> People who gather together into communities need to be able to describe and anticipate those areas of experience which lie outside the immediate compass of the group – the unseen dangers which in any culture and in any age seem to threaten its security. Traditional folklore depicting demons, devils, witches and evil spirits, may be one way to give form to these otherwise formless dangers, but the visible deviant is another kind of reminder. As a trespasser against the group norms, he represents those forces which lie outside the group's boundaries: he informs us, as it were, what evil looks like, what shapes the devil can assume. And in doing so, he shows us the difference between the inside of the group and the outside. It may well be that without this ongoing drama at the outer edges of group space, the community would have no inner sense of identity and cohesion, no sense of the contrasts which set it off as a special place in the larger world.
>
> (p. 15)

Secondly, isn't the business of rhetorically making contrasts one important means by which occupational identities are protected and consolidated against counter conceptions of the tasks in question? Anselm Strauss and his colleagues, for instance, observed, in their study of *Psychiatric Ideologies* (1964), that psychiatric workers subscribing to different conceptions of 'treatment', developed rhetoric which 'blazed back and forth between the treatment and chronic wards' and which opposed custody and therapy in particularly stylized and exaggerated ways, such that each group of workers was equipped with 'a ready vocabulary for explaining difficulties and conducting battles' (p. 364). Dingwall (1977) in his research on health visitors argued that atrocity stories they told about social workers with whom they had to deal and from whom they wished to distinguish themselves, performed similar functions.

Thirdly, following the findings of ethnomethodology and conversational analysis, are not contrasts either explicitly or implicitly involved in all descriptions, since all our conceptions of what things *are* are also constructed according to corollaries of what they are *not?* (Gazdar, 1977; Schegloff, 1971; Sacks, 1972).

I would not seriously contest any one of these three claims. Contrastive rhetoric *does* draw on the universal and indispensable ability of individuals to build descriptions by implicit or explicit reference to comparative cases; it *does* reinforce collective occupational identifications of pertinent tasks against those of other occupations or occupational segments, and it also functions to define and redefine the boundaries of normal practice against deviant and therefore unacceptable alternatives. The interesting thing about contrastive rhetoric, though, is that it does not consist of any one of these features, but all of them – and more besides. In this respect, there are at least two additional and important points to note about the concept.

The first concerns the power dimension: *who* is it who introduces the stylized alternatives, who opposes deviance and normality, and consolidates a particular conception of occupational identity? When the transcripts were analyzed, one of the most startling facts to emerge was that in all cases the contrasts were introduced by either the headteacher or his deputy; the instigators of the programme of curriculum change.[17] In the Countesthorpe case, for instance, it is Mr. Pool who initiates discussion and later reminds the staff of the extreme character of the cited example ('That's right at the far end of what we're talking about'). The contrasts, that is, are introduced by the more senior members of the school hierarchy, the holders of formally designated institutional power.

The second point is that over time, the users of contrastive rhetoric demarcate the boundaries of existing practice at *both* ends of the educational spectrum. In other words, by excluding extreme and unacceptable alternatives of both progressive and traditional kinds, contrastive rhetoric specifies the *range* of acceptable practice. It is by no means the case that contrasts are made solely with reference to extreme progressivism. Archaic traditionalism is just as much a *bête noire* for the head and his deputy. Thus, in the case of traditional schools, Mr. Kitchen argues that

> If we took conformity, a way to make them conform would be to blow a whistle and they'd stand still. Blow another whistle and they'd move into a line and the teacher would move them in. And I know a school that was like that. They conformed! But, my God, I wouldn't like it here!

And Mr. Pool spins out a favourite haberdashery metaphor of his:

> Many tight schools tell the kids what they have to do from thread to needle. They don't have to do any of that kind of (independent) thinking at all.

Very occasionally, the extremes at each end of the spectrum can be highlighted by their juxtaposition in a single dramatic paradox which shows them to be only different sides of the same rather grubby coin. A well known example outside education was Shirley Williams' vitriolic comment during the 1980 Labour Party leadership debate that 'there can be a Fascism of the Left as well as of the Right'. In the case of Riverdale School, this essential and awesome unity of apparent opposites was skilfully displayed by the headteacher on one occasion when he combined the worst of two twilight worlds, mixing together dark visions of pupil anarchy with salutary images of headteacher despotism.

I mean, one of my lines has always been I want people to have as much choice as possible – that is, staff to be able to use their expertise, to feel that, 'Yes, I would like to try this out. I've got reasons for doing this.'
(Mmm)
Because in many, many places . . . I've been in so many places where . . . where they go on this choice business. Uh . . . one in particular I can think of in Halford where choice is the thing running across everything in that the children choose the colours the loo doors will be painted – and, you know, there's rainbow colours of them. They choose a lot of pencils they'll have in school. They go to the County Supplies Link and choose the type of books they'll have. It goes to these lengths. And yet the head has got a most rigid grip on the staff, really and truly. They have no choice at all! He's got this choice firmly fixed in his mind and he jolly well makes sure they carry it out to give children choice. And this is my big criticism of the place, you know, the staff have no choice at all. And he . . . he boasts that he always takes probationers. Now I know, he always . . . *always* takes probationers.
(Laughter)
That's right. That's why he does it!

In this expertly constructed paradox signalled by the grammatical force of what Smith (1978) calls a contrast structure ('And yet . . .'), many of the same elements are presented as in the Countesthorpe case mentioned earlier – the laughter (the meaning of which is taken to be obvious – 'That's right') the indications that the case being discussed is an extreme one ('It goes to these lengths'), the introduction of graphic images of the trivial and outrageous (loo doors, choice of pencils, etc.). Progressivism and traditionalism are, therefore, simultaneously united and distilled into a single fearful phenomenon; extremism, which is to be avoided at all costs.[18]

This is an appropriate point to recap on the major features of contrastive rhetoric as outlined so far. I have argued that it presents stylized and trivialized images of alternative practices, characterizing them as unacceptable extremes and thereby implicitly drawing the boundaries around the permissible range of present practice. Moreover, this definition of a professional and pedagogical consensus is occasioned by the strategic intervention of those holding institutional power – the head and deputy. Contrastive rhetoric is therefore a major part of their strategic repertoire; a crucial means by which they translate institutional power into interactional power and thus exercise control over the decision-making process. But the effective use of contrastive rhetoric is not simply a matter of head and deputy head-teacher strategy, however, for just as teachers trade on their pupils' ability to interpret the messages contained in their classroom strategies (Edwards and Furlong, 1978; Hargreaves, A., 1979), so the users of contrastive rhetoric rely on the capacity of other teachers to recognize the messages connoted by the particular images and symbols they present and the trivialized and stylized mode of description in which those symbols are enshrouded. The success of contrastive rhetoric in screening out undesirable alternatives is therefore contingent on the kind of knowledge, assumptions and interpretive schemes that teachers bring to the interaction, and on the capacity of its users – the head and deputy – to trade on these components of teachers' culture.

Teachers' Cultural Resources

It must be acknowledged, though, that there are great problems in demonstrating empirically the tie-up between the interactional strategies of the head and deputy on the one hand, and teachers' knowledge and assumptions on the other. One very sizeable obstacle is presented by the fact that the most likely outcome of any shared agreement among school staff on the meaning of symbols and the descriptive mode in which they are cast – non-response – is also the very thing that most confounds precise interpretation.[19] That is to say, the outcome of shared agreement is likely to be a disinclination to elaborate on or challenge any particular account presented in the form of contrastive rhetoric – no further details are felt to be required, the meaning is treated as obvious, all the supplementary information (the *etceteras,* the bits that haven't been said) are filled in unproblematically by the teachers themselves. However, non-responses, like silences, are highly ambiguous social events. Their meaning depends very much on the context of their occurrence, and to that extent can be grasped only if we locate them within the overall pattern of responses to contrastive rhetoric, and view them as part of that pattern.

What else, then, does the researcher have to go on when discerning such a pattern? Laughter, as we have seen, is certainly one testimony to the existence of shared understandings of the symbols and descriptions in contrastive rhetoric; but, like silence, laughter is also a possible indicator of the existence of many other things – the presence of tension for example. This inescapable ambiguity will always place the researcher in some difficulty when he attempts to establish which of the many possible meanings of laughter applies in any particular instance.

Because of these fundamental ambiguities surrounding the contextualized meanings of non-verbal signs, there is good reason to examine those rarer but possibly more revealing occasions when teachers make an explicit verbal reponse to the use of contrastive rhetoric. The non-verbal indicators can then be cross-referenced with these to see if any match between the two can be established.

The most telling illustration of an articulate and, in this case, protracted response to the use of contrastive rhetoric is the contribution of Mr. Stones to the Countesthorpe debate. This is an exceptional piece of data, for at no other time did anyone respond to the use of contrastive rhetoric as he did. Furthermore, he not only reacted to contrastive rhetoric, thus indicating his ability to interpret its symbols and mode of description, but formulated a considerable part of it himself. Much of the description of Countesthorpe College, as you may already have realized, was his. If we examine this case closely, we might be able to determine what it is that makes the case an exceptional one; why, that is, Mr. Stones was able to contribute to the extent that he did. Accordingly, this might also tell us something about the normal pattern; about why other teachers made no such contribution. In short, why were most teachers receivers and not producers of contrastive rhetoric?

I want to suggest that the reason for the particular nature of Mr. Stones' contribution and the very different character of other staff responses (or, rather, non-responses) to the use of contrastive rhetoric has to do with the kinds of resources on which teachers draw when they construct and interpret accounts in the educationist context. These resources are of two major types. First, to recap, there is the professionally and socially derived stock of symbols and images, and the particular descriptive mode that envelops them, on which teachers draw when educational alternatives are discussed by them or in their presence. Secondly, there is the teachers' own experience. Experience, especially professional experience, lay at the heart of virtually all the contributions that teachers made to discussion. It supplied most of the justifications for the accounts they presented. Moreover, during interview, most teachers identified experience as being the major source of their opinions on educational matters.

Since most teachers' experience excluded even the most fleeting of encounters with educational alternatives, it is hardly surprising that they made little or no contribution of their own when the question of such alternatives was raised. Like Mrs. Home, who speculated that 'the kids . . . will just go out of the school and find something more exciting' after they have got bored with eating crisps and reading comics', the teachers could only take the sketchy images with which they were presented at a face value and react accordingly within the conceptual limits of their shared interpretative scheme. Since, in their experience, they had no previous acquaintance with the particular reality to which the image referred, they could not substantially elaborate on the image or dispute its accuracy.

Mr. Stones was no exception to the rule of experience. What distinguished him from the rest of the staff was not that he used criteria other than experiential ones to present and justify his accounts but that one fragment of the *content* of his experience – the Countesthorpe connection – was different. It was this that enabled him to talk about that particular alternative at unusual length; to produce his own formulation, that is. The *fact* that he produced a formulation was a mark of the atypical nature of his experience; but the fact that his formulation was consistent in form with the other instances of contrastive rhetoric used by the head and deputy was indicative of the sort of cultural resources on which he drew. In effect, Mr. Stones constructed his unflattering description of Countesthorpe College by drawing on a standard repertoire of symbols of outrageous progressivism that carried the appropriate pejorative connotations: 'they can walk out if they're bored', 'all sort of first name terms with the staff', 'they can sort of just walk in and walk out and come in at any time'. To these symbols of first naming of staff, walking in and out and so on are added important descriptive and indeed implicitly contrastive qualifiers. Thus, the fact that 'first name terms' are, in effect, '*all sort of* first name terms' established that the first naming of staff is but the visible tip of an enormous and dangerous iceberg of unacceptable pedagogical relationships. And the fact that pupils do not simply 'walk in and walk out' but '*just* walk in and walk out . . . *at any time*' reflects on the shared assumption that in *normal* pedagogical relationships there are appropriate and inappropriate occasions and reasons for this action. No-one *just* walks in and out. Entry into and exit from the classroom are rule-governed affairs and these rules are in large part enforced and interpreted by the teacher (Hargreaves, D. *et al,* 1975). The absence of such rules, therefore, entails the suspension of normal teacher-pupil relationships. What Mr. Stones did was to draw on those shared interpretative schemes concerning alternative practices which normally enabled staff to interpret contrastive rhetoric when it was employed by others but which, given his incidental and somewhat second-hand experience of Countesthorpe, also enabled him to produce contrastive rhetoric of his own on this one occasion. What analysis of this initially discrepant case reveals, therefore, is that the routine responses of the staff to contrastive rhetoric and Mr. Stones' own production of it are each the product of their drawing on a dual repertoire; of professional experience on the one hand, and of a shared interpretative scheme concerning educational alternatives on the other.[20]

Having examined the reasons why Mr. Stones' contribution to the discussion was in certain respects different from the usual staff responses to contrastive rhetoric, what I have yet to do is explain what distinguishes the contributions of the headteacher and his deputy from the rest of the staff. Why was it that the head and his deputy produced contrastive rhetoric when the rest of the staff, with one exception, did not? It is my contention that the reason once more has to do with the different nature of their experience, except that, in this case, those experiences are systematically and unequally distributed between ordinary and senior staff.

In the main the teachers have little continuing access to educational theory or detailed comparative knowledge of other schools and practices; the head and his deputy, on the other hand, while not necessarily possessing sophisticated knowledge of educational theory or detailed familiarity with the administration of the schooling system, do move more widely in these circles than the teachers. This differential access to the cultural resources underlying decision-making, therefore, means that the head and deputy hold not only *de jure* institutional power, but also tend to possess *de facto* interactional power. It is they who have the necessary familiarity with educational alternatives such that they can introduce them in an extreme way that resonates suitably with teachers' own conceptions of present practice and its enemies.

Institutional and interactional power are of course closely and importantly related; for it is precisely by virtue of their institutional power that heads and deputies have access to (and time to participate in) a large range of non-classroom contexts where they acquire the necessary cultural resources (knowledge of theories and other institutions and also, of course, the strategic skills of decision-making) which they can then employ to good effect in the educationist context. The balance of interactional power – in particular the relative capacity to screen out discussion of alternative practices or to set them up in such a way as to invite their wholesale dismissal – is, then, in large part contingent on the balance of institutional power between heads and deputies on the one hand and the rest of the staff on the other, and on the differential access to classroom and non-classroom contexts which this entails. The maintenance of the boundaries of permissible practice is therefore achieved as a result of an intersection between head and deputy headteacher strategy, the culural resources which teachers of all kinds bring to the interaction (these consist of professional experiences and shared interpretative schemes), and the influences of the dominant hegemony and the institutional distribution of power on the content of those resources.

While I cannot honestly say that these conclusions amount to absolute confirmation or refutation of the hegemony thesis (much more research would be needed before that degree of certainty could be approached), what I can say, with some confidence, is that no elements of the critical test I have presented constitute a *disconfirmation* of that thesis: on the contrary, there appears to be considerable, if less than definitive, support for it. Until further empirical tests of an ethnographic or historical kind are devised and carried out, therefore, it is not unreasonable to proceed, if somewhat tentatively, on the understanding of there being a linkage between teachers' thinking and the dominant social hegemony. Clearly, though, the details of that linkage need to be specified much more closely than the data here have allowed.

Extremist Talk

Before examining the policy implications that are raised by this analysis of contrastive rhetoric, one important qualification must be made. Hegemony, we should remember, is never total: it cannot be equated with unrelieved brainwashing. The hegemonic process is neither monolithic nor is it immune from forces of resistance and protest which contain the potential for the creation of counter-hegemony and for pushing out rather than drawing in the boundaries of existing practice. Close scrutiny of the data revealed the presence of such forces within the fine details of staff discussion.

As the data were analyzed a discrepancy became apparent – that educational alternatives were sometimes introduced into discussion by people other than the head and deputy. However, it was also evident that the staff couched these alternatives in a form quite unlike that of contrastive rhetoric. I shall refer to this second process by which the ordinary teaching staff introduced alternative conceptions of educational practice as one of *extremist talk*. Again, for reasons of space, it is not possible to provide as elaborate a summary of this process as I did for contrastive rhetoric. Instead, a brief illustration, sufficient to pinpoint those critical features that distinguish extremist talk from contrastive rhetoric, will have to suffice.

Among the ordinary staff, extremist talk was regularly used by two teachers. The first, Mr. Button, was a young, non-graduate teacher who had moved to Riverdale from a secondary modern school in order to take a Scale 2 post. For him, the move into middle schools where male graduates were not in abundance, was a calculated attempt to improve his promotion opportunities. He was also trying to boost his career prospects further by taking an Open University degree which, at the time of the research, entailed his studying a course in the sociology of education.[21] His espousal of a range of educational opinions in discussion seemed to owe much to this course of study. Thus, Mr. Button could be heard to expound arguments which contained elements of deschooling, or Marxism, or social phenomenology, or even a mixture of all these things. This does not mean that he succeeded in transforming staff discussion into a weighty sociological seminar, nor even that he engaged in a one-sided attempt to do so. The influence of experience as virtually the only acceptable and legitimate basis of teacher accounts in staff discussions was sufficient to prevent him from quoting educational theorists chapter and verse, or pulling out protracted threads of sociological argument. Yet the residues of his recent acquaintance, albeit a fleeting one, with some sociology of education were undoubtedly present in his terse and sometimes caustic remarks about schooling and its relationship to society. These could be seen in some of his contributions to the very first meeting, where he began with a loose exposition of the culture conflict thesis intermingled with an application of the interactionist concept, 'definition of the situation'.

Mr. Button	Don't children in many ways regard these (moral) aims really as being outside the scope of the teacher, because many children define the teaching situation as what happens in the classroom? A lot of children define the situation as being what they are taught and not such things as manners. There is enough conflict in the teaching situation as it is. The more of these we introduce, the more conflict we introduce into this job. You're gonna spend a lot of your time continually checking children in that situation.
Mr. Driver	Do you necessarily have to do it by checking children, or can you do it by somehow persuading them?
Mr. Button	Well, no matter what way you do it, there's gonna be some children who naturally resent the change.

Mrs. Fletcher	Well, don't you consider yourself *in loco parentis* when you have children in your care?
Mr. Button	Well, this is slightly different, Elizabeth, because what we're doing, we're changing them to aims which we think are desirable whether their parents think they're desirable or not. And the child's own social background may not . . . his parents may not demand this sort of behaviour from the child. So there's gonna be conflict when he comes to school with what he does at home.
Others	Yes/No (vociferously)
Mrs. Fletcher	It *is* possible. Well, perhaps many parents teach their kids 'Well, if somebody hits you, you jolly well see you hit them back' and many teachers perhaps think that it's a very negative attitude and that it's much more positive to say 'Well keep away from people you can't get on with and don't use your fists'.
Mr. Button	Well, whether the child fits into the school system, you've got to make the value judgement whether it's more important that he does not become alienated from his parents. Well, I mean it's like the working class child who goes to grammar school.

The discussion then moved on to a consideration of children's rights and the legitimacy of their perspective. This gave Mr. Button the opportunity to take up a libertarian position, though the conclusions he reached would probably evoke more sympathy from Rhodes Boyson than Ivan Illich.

Mr. Button	. . . What I'm saying is that you want to minimize the amount of conflict that you've got in the situa . . . institution by cutting out a lot of some of these aims which I would say are peripheral. A lot of these aims, although they're very desirable from our point of view, I would say they're not the main aims. I would say the main aim on the whole thing was literacy and numeracy. It's what the kids expect. It's what the parents expect.
Mr. Driver	I don't agree with you.
Mrs. Fletcher	I don't. Our job is to help to open kids' eyes. Now if they come . . . come to school and they don't see everything clearly, it's because they are a child.
Mr. Button	Yeah! They are a child and we've got to not try to put adult concepts on to things that we think are desirable. I mean, children don't consider sympathy as desirable.
Mr. Driver	(Aghast) Ooh!
Mr. Button	I mean, you have to look at some of 'em to understand that.
Mrs. Fletcher	But Alan, we might just as well say that the children themselves should set . . . should be able to set up all these objectives and really, children haven't got a clear perception of what . . .

Mr. Button	But they can't. As far as we're concerned, because they have to come to school, because the law says so, they are the lower level of this institution.
Mrs. Fletcher	But are we thinking about having to come to school, or are we thinking about education?
Mr. Button	Well, it's the same thing as far as children are concerned.
Mr. Kitchen (Head)	But not as far as we're concerned!
	(together)
Others	No! No! No!

This outburst of libertarianism was by no means an isolated occurrence. Later, for instance, he described education as 'just an assault upon a child to make him conform with set aims that you've already put down'. At other points, however, Mr. Button's critique of the educational system seemed to have more affinity with Marxist economic determinism. In a discussion of the problems of failure, for example, he argued that 'Unfortunately, one of the jobs at school is the screening process. Whether we like it or not, the purpose of education in society is to provide workers. Failure is an inevitable part of it'.

There is no evidence that Mr. Button was a consistent and hard line libertarian, Marxist, phenomenologist or whatever. What he does appear to have done is weld parts of these divergent traditions into a somewhat brittle alloy of anti-liberalism which cut through the boundaries of normal debate about education.[22] Occasionally, this object of his observations and criticisms was made crystal clear as when he retorted: 'That is the liberal dichotomy that you've said, ''Right, you can do what you like as long as I tell you what you do'' '.

Extremist talk was not always left-radical talk, though. While the seeds of counter-hegemony may well be contained in extremist talk, the varied content of that talk should serve as a reminder that, as Gramsci (1971) himself understood counter-hegemony need not take any particular form: it may for example lead to fascist outcomes just as easily as to socialist ones. In this sense, an interesting contrast to Mr. Button's extremist talk is that of Mrs. Speaker. A mature entrant to teaching with a previous background in journalism, secretarial work and as a housewife and mother, she was strongly committed to teaching English as a subject where, she felt, her greatest strengths and sources of enjoyment lay. On the surface, her standpoint did at times seem to converge with Mr. Button's, thus giving the appearance of an unholy alliance, as when she specified one of her aims of education – that children 'should be literate and numerate – to throw in two old fashioned ideas'. But beneath this unlikely correspondence with Mr. Button's radicalism on the question of 'basic skills' lay a deep seated and entrenched conservatism. In this respect, Mrs. Speaker's position held much in common with the classical functionalism of sociologists like Talcott Parsons (1959) and their view that schooling socializes children into the common value system of society. As Mrs. Speaker put it:

I think that it's part of our job to see that a child is as socially acceptable as possible. It is part of our job to see that they can be assimilated into a community.

This suggestion that education ought to integrate the young into the social order was given an additional twist when she continued: 'I think their whole development is vital too – their attitude, their ideas, their thinking, their creativity, their reasoning'.

Now it is not necessarily the case that the individual and social aspects of education are incompatible, as anyone familiar with the work of Emile Durkheim will know. While he saw discipline, for example, as playing an essential role in the securing of social integration, he also argued that it benefited the individual equally, enhancing his development, granting him autonomy and security and enabling him to participate fully as an adult in social life. 'Thus', he stated, 'the antagonism that has too often been admitted between society and individual corresponds to nothing in the facts' (Durkheim, 1956, p. 78). Mrs. Speaker was not, of course, a self-avowed Durkheimian, but she did find it possible to argue for these two facets of schooling in tandem, whereas Mr. Button, like Marxists and libertarians, regarded the individual and social aspects of schooling in the present society as totally incompatible.[23] Thus, when Miss Rogers expressed her disagreement with Mrs. Speaker over 'the social conformity thing' and stated that, 'you're not going to make them start off being all child-centred and end up with them being round pegs for round holes', Mr. Button interjected, 'Yeah, but it's just unfortunate that it happens to work out that way in most schools, doesn't it?'.

What do these examples tell us about extremist talk and its differences from contrastive rhetoric? First, whereas contrastive rhetoric is introduced by institutionally and/or interactionally dominant individuals or groups (in this case, the head and deputy), extremist talk is part of the repertoire of subordinate figures (in this case, a Scale 1 and a Scale 2 teacher). In participatory decision-making contexts, extremist talk appears to be a strategy of those beneath the highest levels of the school hierarchy, presumably because its employment by the institutionally powerful would constitute an ostensible and embarrassing breach of the formal principles of democratic decision-making.[24]

Secondly, whereas contrastive rhetoric comprises stylized and trivialized accounts of actual, through frequently anonymized, cases of alternative educational practice, extremist talk consists of alternative conceptions of existing mainstream practice – these are not trivialized but stated in a matter-of-fact way as a generalized commentary on the nature of schooling, the educational system etc. Extremist talk therefore consists of a *critique of what is,* whereas contrastive rhetoric amounts to a *defence of what is* by virtue of its unfavourable treatment of those things that threaten existing practice.

Thirdly, extremist talk involves high levels of commitment on the part of the speaker to his/her observations on, and critiques of, the workings of the educational system. Because of that commitment, extremist talk is, for any speaker, addressed to *one* end of the value spectrum only. Contrastive rhetoric, however, involves little commitment to the mentioned alternatives. Any positive commitments to the essentials of existing practice are present by implication only; they are the obverse of the speakers' cloaked damnation of educational alternatives. Since the implied virtues of the present system stand out just as well against archaic traditionalism as against extreme progressivism/radicalism, and even better against them both, contrastive rhetoric therefore refers over time to *both* ends of the educational value spectrum.

Fourthly, whereas contrastive rhetoric leads to agreement (tacit or explicit) with the views expounded and, therefore, to an implied endorsement of the educational *status quo,* extremist talk is commonly followed by emphatic *dis*agreement. (This is partly because of the nature of the values communicated, but also because extremist talk is articulated at the level of generalized speculation, assertion and theorizing – and therefore open to counter-assertion. Contrastive rhetoric, meanwhile, is articulated at the level of particular cases to which teachers have no independent access and, therefore, no independent grounds for confirmation or repudiation.) There is one crucial proviso to be made here, though: whilst disagreement with extremist talk is usual, it can never be guaranteed. The normal response may well be a chorus of 'No's' or its equivalent, but just occasionally, a cacophony of 'No's' and 'Yesses' may ensue instead.

The implication of all this is that the inherent dynamic of extremist talk is centrifugal; it is a force which exerts constant pressure to push the boundaries of existing practice and debate outwards.[25] In practice, of course, given the generalized mode of discourse in which such talk is cast, other teachers are usually able to resist that centrifugal tendency by counter-assertion and counter-argument. That is to say, the disagreement that extremist talk engenders normally acts only to confirm teachers' customary conceptions of educational practice. But it is as well to remember, nonetheless, as the data indicate, that such disagreement is never total and that important spaces remain where the boundaries of existing practice can be and occasionally are negotiated.

Contrastive rhetoric meanwhile, contains few such potentials, its internal dynamic being strongly centripetal: that is to say, it serves to draw in and consolidate the boundaries of permissible practice. Even here, however, there is always a remote possibility that resistance may occur – though this is contingent upon the not impossible, but certainly very unlikely event that particular teachers have, within their experience, come across any of the educational alternatives that are introduced into discussion, and that their experience has led them to view these in a favourable light.

Table 1   Differences Between Contrastive Rhetoric and Extremist Talk

CONTRASTIVE RHETORIC	EXTREMIST TALK
introduced by institutionally and/or interactionally dominant individuals or groups – (in this case the head and deputy)	introduced by institutionally and/or interactionally subordinate individuals or groups – (in this case members of the ordinary teaching staff)
contains trivialized conceptions of actual alternative educational practices	contains generalized alternative conceptions of existing educational practices
references made to *both* ends of the educational spectrum	references made to *one* end of the educational spectrum only
low level of commitment to mentioned alternatives	high level of commitment to alternative interpretations
leads to agreement	normally leads to disagreement, but not always
centripetal effect – drawing in the boundaries of existing practice and consolidating them	centrifugal effect – acting as a force for extending the boundaries of existing practice

In this sense, from the standpoint of control, although rhetoric is a risk, it is not a substantial one. If we wish to look for sources of change in current educational practice, extremist talk would appear to be a better bet.

A summary of the differences between contrastive rhetoric and extremist talk is provided in Table 1.

Conclusions and Implications

Curriculum decision-making at Riverdale School fell far short of being a democratic process. Analysis of the details of staff discussion revealed that teacher participation in a programme of substantial curriculum change was severely restricted by the exercise of contrastive rhetoric and by a particular distribution of cultural resources that made the successful employment of that strategy possible. If Riverdale is indeed a critical case, the inhibiting influence of hegemony and institutionalized power divisions must surely be a cause for concern for all those who would like to see teachers play a major and effective role in educational decision-making. The educationist context may well be, as Keddie claims, a context for the discussion of school politics, but in these discussions, when the most profound social and educational questions are addressed, teachers seem to draw much more extensively on commonsense categories (in part, hegemonically derived) and professional experience (especially classroom experience) than on educational theory and research.

I am not suggesting that experience should have no part to play in the making of educational decisions, nor am I even trying to play down the extent of its influence. What I am saying is that when such experience overwhelmingly takes one particular form – classroom experience – it is unlikely that it will, of itself, substantially extend or breach the boundaries of normal debate and customary practice in education. Furthermore, over-reliance on classroom experience places teachers at the mercy of those with a broader and more varied educational experience when educational matters are at issue.

For those who seek a better, more humane educational system, and a democratic route to such betterment, the broadest possible expansion of debate on educational questions and the pushing back in more than one direction of the limits of customary thinking about schooling is an urgent task. The achievement of that task would contribute significantly to what Demaine (1980) calls the creation of the conditions in which democracy can be realized. The presence of extremist talk in staff discussion indicates that the potential for such an exercise is already there. But if extremist talk is to make any great impact on the scope and depth of educational debate, it will need to draw upon a wider and more rigorous source of cultural/intellectual resources than at present, and to be more widely distributed through the teaching profession so that, in effect, its 'extremist' character diminishes over time.

The goal, in short, is a more rigorous teaching profession. But this is not simply a case for pumping teachers with heavy doses of sociology or pushing them out to do more part-time diplomas and higher degrees. At a time when teachers are already under severe pressure as a result of economic cuts and falling rolls, it is both unreasonable and unjust to ask or demand that they should give up Monday, Tuesday, Thursday and Friday evenings as well as Wednesdays to the cause of in-service education. This would produce not a rigorous teaching profession, but a ragged and exhausted one. Furthermore, it would only serve to confirm the peripheral character of in-service education activities as mere adjuncts to the 'real business' of nine-till-four classroom teaching.

It was once said, by Harold Rosen (1972) of Basil Bernstein's theory of linguistic codes that working-class people could only reasonably be expected to acquire and use elaborated speech forms if they were given access to contexts where their use was appropriate: in particular, Rosen meant access to contexts where they could exercise power which had real consequences for their lives. There are clear parallels here with the conditions under which we might reasonably expect teachers to acquire and draw upon rigorous knowledge when discussing educational matters. Specifically, if the locus of *interactional* power in the decision-making process is to be shifted from its present position, there will need to be a fundamental reorganization of the *institutional* power base of schooling such that teachers participate, not only in an intermittent process of curriculum planning, but that they also make a substantial and realistic contribution to the whole governance of education by communicating directly with members of the community, the LEA and the Inspectorate, much as headteachers do at the moment. This might be achieved by forms of power sharing between the headteacher and the rest of the staff or it could be organized sequentially by making the office of headship a much more temporary one where headteachers are placed on renewable contracts, or elected for specific terms rather than appointed for indefinite periods etc.[26] If teachers could expect to be involved in the administration and control of education (and their own school in particular) as a matter of routine, there would be some purpose in acquiring rigorous knowledge and the extremist talk to which it might lead. Furthermore, their very involvement in the process of governance would give teachers access to knowledge of how other institutions operate. Once such knowledge of alternative institutions and practices was democratized the strategy of contrastive rhetoric, would almost certainly become redundant.

The transformation of the base of institutional power is, therefore, a necessary prerequisite for the development of a rigorous teaching profession. But motivation to become rigorous is not enough – teachers also need the opportunity. Such opportunity involves making theoretorical study, and involvement in the wider compass of educational decision-making, part of the teacher's normal working day, not something to be added on to it. The creation and distribution of rigorous knowledge – that would raise as problematic, and on occasions undercut, those previously taken-for-granted conceptions contained within the dominant hegemony – would require not the *elimination* of teachers' experience as a basis for argument and explanation, but its *transformation*. In other words, teachers' involvement with educational theory, and their experience of non-classroom contexts of educational governance and control (of a range of educationist contexts, that is) would need to be credited with the same status that classroom experience has enjoyed hitherto; and the re-allocation of teachers' time among these various activities would need to reflect that fact.

These reforms will not be cheap. They will entail much higher levels of teacher employment than those which have been usual to date. At the beginning of a decade when draconian cutbacks continue to affect what are considered to be the very basics of schooling, they are unlikely to receive much sympathy among politicans. But if the brief blossoming of the teacher participation movement is not to wilt in an autumn of despair because it has been strangled at its roots by the influence of hegemony and the institutionalized division of power, such a programme of reform will have to be placed on the agenda of serious political, professional and academic struggle and debate.

Notes

1   Edited by YOUNG, M.F.D. (1971).

2   It should be noted though, that there is a resurgence of interest in such problems in the early 1980s through the published work of the Oxford Social Mobility Project. See HALSEY, A.H., HEATH, A.F. and RIDGE, J.M. (1980), GOLDTHORPE, J. (1980) and ST.JOHN-BROOKS, C. (1980).

3   Strictly speaking, *Knowledge and Control* was not so much the mother of the New Sociology of Education as a midwife who assisted in the delivery. It is as well to remember that many British sociologists of education who developed an interest in classroom and school processes drew their inspiration not only or even mainly from M.F.D. Young and his colleagues but just as much from sources such as Chicago School interactionism (particularly the work of Howard Becker), American anthropology (see DELAMONT and ATKINSON, 1980, for a review of this field), and the Manchester-based work on the sociology of communities (which was influential on the work of HARGREAVES, D. 1967, LACEY, C. 1970 and later, though less directly, HAMMERSLEY, M. 1974). My own route was different again, starting from radical and humanistic social psychology and its endeavour to get to grips with peoples' experience (ARMISTEAD, N. 1974), from an inchoate libertarianism as represented in the works of HOLT, J. (1969, 1970) and from engagement with the *verstehen* sociology of Max Weber.

4   Actually, Keddie seems to employ at least two different definitions of the educationist context. At some points, the nature of 'context' seems to refer to the kind of people involved in discussion and the object of discussion: this is the meaning of 'the actual context of school politics', for example. On other occasions, the educationist context is something borne-in-mind that can be introduced into any kind of discussion as appropriate: this is the meaning of 'the educationist context may be called into being by the presence of an outsider to whom explanations . . . must be given'. In practice, it is the former usage that predominates in Keddie's work, and that is the one I employ here.

5   In the case of my own work, see HARGREAVES, A. (1978, 1979) for examples.

6   See YOUNG, M.F.D. (1971) pp. 1–2.

7   See also JACKSON, P. (1968) and WALLER, W. (1932).

8   Of course, it is possible that other staffrooms in less harsh surroundings than the secondary modern schools studied by Woods and Hammersley approximate more closely to the characteristics of an educationist context, but research has yet to demonstrate that fact.

9   The literature on the relationship between headteachers and teachers is scant, and hardly any of this focuses on the details of headteacher-teacher encounters. For a review see ROSS, J.A. (1980). One notable exception is HUNTER'S (1980) important study of decision-making in a comprehensive school, though his analysis of the interaction between head and staff forms only one small part of his paper.

10   There is a vast and undistinguished literature on SBCD, most of it prescriptive, programmatic or anecdotal. For introductions see EGGLESTON, J. (1979) and HENDERSON, E. (1978). An unusually critical account of one case of SBCD can be found in BULLOCK, A. (1980). A broader, multi-method evaluation of schemes of SBCD is being conducted in the SITE project, interim reports on which are available in BOLAM, R. (1979), and BOLAM, R. and BAKER, K. (1979).

11   In particular, see HARGREAVES, A. (1977), for which some empirical support can be found in HARGREAVES, A. (1980).

12   This is one of the difficulties with HAMMERSLEY'S (1981) analysis of staffroom talk (in this volume). His argument that careful interpretation of such talk undercuts the utility of 'ideology' as an explanatory concept of teachers' perspectives is based on a straw man, which he constructs, of consistent, conservative staffroom ideology. This critique would bear up less well against the concept of hegemony and therefore against the probable empirical reality (which his ethnography has not tapped), of a diversity of educational and social views among teachers as a whole, rather than among the few with whom he associated and whom he observed at close quarters in one small school – what Hammersley perceived is rhetoric rather than ideology (for a discussion of the difference between rhetoric and ideology see HARGREAVES, A. 1980).

13 This is documented in HARGREAVES, A. (in process).

14 On typical cases versus critical cases in school ethnography, see HAMMERSLEY, M. (1980b). To be more precise, this study of curriculum decision-making at Riverdale is a *limiting* case, where one would *least* expect a hypothesis (in this instance concerning the influence of hegemony) to be confirmed, such that if it *is* confirmed, it can legitimately be considered to be extensible to other parts of the educational system.

15 The concept therefore arises from a dual concern with theory generation *and* theory testing.

16 On the interchangeability of standpoints see the work of SCHUTZ, A. (1973), GARFINKEL, H. (1967) and CICOUREL, A.V. (1971).

17 This is one significant point on which contrastive rhetoric diverges from forms of rhetoric that researchers have identified in other occupational settings. In these settings, rhetoric is elaborated by all participants as a way of forging a collective occupational identity against intrusions by and confusions with other occupations. As DINGWALL, R. (1977) argues in the case of atrocity stories, they

> play an important part in defining the colleague group . . . They allow for the assertion of the tellers' social theories and for mutual support in redressing the illegitimate actions of others.
>
> (p. 375)

Reviewing research in this area, Dingwall states that atrocity stories are conventionally the preserve of the powerless, though not exclusively so. However, even where he notes their use by the powerful (e.g. by doctors about patients) this is in terms of what powerful groups have to say about powerless ones. He makes no mention of the use of atrocity stories or similar strategies in interactional contexts where powerful and powerless groups meet; i.e. where they talk *to,* not *about* one another.

18 This also was the force of his concluding remark about handing things 'right over to the kids'.

19 For an account of the different meanings that can be conveyed by silence in the classroom, for example, see DUMONT, R.V. and WAX, M.L. (1969).

20 By interpretative schemes I mean something very different from what ethnomethodologists have called interpretive procedures and interpretive abilities. These latter refer to *universal* abilities which make the conduct of social interaction possible, whereas interpretative schemes refer to specific sets of coding procedures used by *particular* cultural or occupational groupings.

21 *School & Society* (E282).

22 It should be noted here that there is no necessary correspondence between the position advanced in any speaker's extremist talk and the nature of his/her classroom practice. Thus, while Mr. Button's talk was broadly radical, his classroom practice was perceived by many of the other staff as that of a conventional, traditional secondary teacher – indeed, it was reported to me that before I arrived, Mr. Button had, after an experimental period teaching in the lower half of the middle school, been resited in his usual niche with the 11–13 year olds because his approach to teaching came to be regarded by his lower-school colleagues as unacceptably traditional.

23 Thus the actual conclusions reached in any particular case of traditional or radical thinking are, for the purposes of analysis, of less importance than the conceptual means by which they have been produced.

24 However, I suspect that this element is probably the *least* essential one that distinguishes contrastive rhetoric from extremist talk. A good way to test this proposition in further research might be to investigate the decision-making process where a very radical head attempts to spearhead a programme of innovation against the wishes of an entrenched, conservative staff – will they then be the users of contrastive rhetoric and the head the exponent of extremist talk? This test might enable us to disentangle institutional constraints from hegemonic ones.

25 On centrifugal and centripetal tendencies in education, see NIAS, J. (1980).

26 Experience of the broader span of the schooling system can, of course, be achieved by other strategies too. For instance, the vertical and lateral transfers of teachers between different parts of the educational system for short, though more than nominal, periods might, *in conjunction with other strategies,* achieve these ends also. The mentioned strategies do not represent a coherent programme of reform, but are examples of the sort of action that might be contemplated.

References

ALTHUSSER, L. (1971) 'Ideology and ideological state apparatuses' in *Lenin and Philosophy and other Essays* London, New Left Books.

APPLE, M. (1979) *Ideology and Curriculum* London, Routledge and Kegan Paul.

ARMISTEAD, N. (Ed) (1974) *Reconstructing Social Psychology* Harmondsworth, Penguin.

BOLAM, R. (1979) 'Evaluating inservice education and training: A national perspective' *British Journal of Teacher Education* 5 (1)

BOLAM, R. and BAKER, K. (1979) 'The schools and in-service teacher education (SITE) project' *Research in Educational Administration* 8 (1).

BULLOCK, A. (1980) 'Teacher participation in school decision-making' *Cambridge Journal of Education* 10 (1).

CICOUREL, A.V. (1971) 'Interpretive procedures and normative rules in the negotiation of status and role' in *Cognitive Sociology* Harmondsworth, Penguin.

COHEN, S. (1973) *Folk Devils and Moral Panics* St. Albans, Paladin.

DALE, R. (1977) 'The structural context of teaching', Unit 5 *Schooling and Society* (E202) Milton Keynes, Open University Press.

DELAMONT, S. and ATKINSON, P. (1980) 'The two traditions in educational ethnography: sociology and anthropology compared' *British Journal of Sociology of Education* 1 (2).

DEMAINE, J. (1980) 'Sociology of education, politics and the Left in Britain' *British Journal of the Sociology of Education* 1 (1).

DENNISON, W.F. (1979) 'Teachers and shrinking schools' *Durham and Newcastle Research Review* IX (43) Autumn.

DEPARTMENT OF EDUCATION AND SCIENCE and WELSH OFFICE (1978) *Making INSET Work: In-service Education and Training for Teachers: A Basis for Discussion* London, HMSO.

DINGWALL, R. (1977) ' "Atrocity stories" and professional relationships' *Sociology of Work and Occupations* 4 (4).

DUMONT, R.V. and WAX, M.L. (1969) 'Cherokee school society and the intercultural classroom' *Human Organization* 28 (3) Fall.

DURKHEIM, E. (1956) *Education and Sociology* Illinois, Free Press.

DURKHEIM, E. (1964) *The Rules of Sociological Method* New York, Free Press.

EDWARDS, A. and FURLONG, V.J. (1978) *The Language of Teaching* London, Heinemann.

EGGLESTON, J. (1979) *School-Based Curriculum Development* Paris, OECD.

EGGLESTON, J. (Ed) (1980) *School-Based Curriculum Development in Britain* London, Routledge and Kegan Paul.

ERIKSON, K. (1964) 'Notes on the sociology of deviance' in BECKER, H.S. (Ed) *The Other Side* New York, Free Press.

GARFINKEL, H. (1967) *Studies in Ethnomethodology* New Jersey, Prentice-Hall.

GAZDAR, G. (1977) 'Conversational analysis and conventional sociolinguistics' *Analytic Sociology* 1.

GINSBURG, M.B., MEYENN, R.J. and MILLER, H.D. (1979) 'Teachers, the "Great Debate" and education cuts' *Westminster Studies in Education* 2.

GLASER, B. and STRAUSS, A.L. (1968) *The Discovery of Grounded Theory* London, Weidenfeld and Nicolson.

GLEESON, D. (1979) 'Curriculum development and social change: Towards a reappraisal of teacher action' in EGGLESTON, J. (Ed) *Teacher Decision-Making in the Classroom* London, Routledge and Kegan Paul.

GOFFMAN, E. (1959) *The Presentation of Self in Everyday Life* Harmondsworth, Penguin.

GOLDTHORPE, J.H. (1980) *Social Mobility and Class Structure in Modern Britain* Oxford, Clarendon Press.

GRACE, G. (1978) *Teachers, Ideology and Control* London, Routledge and Kegan Paul.

GRAMSCI, A. (1971) *Selections from the Prison Notebooks* London, Lawrence and Wishart.

HALSEY, A.H., HEATH, A.F. and RIDGE, J.M. (1980) *Origins and Destinations* Oxford, Clarendon Press.

HAMMERSLEY, M. (1974) 'The organization of pupil participation' *Sociological Review* 22 (3).

HAMMERSLEY, M. (1980a) 'A Peculiar World? – Teaching and Learning in an Inner-City School', unpublished Ph.D. thesis, University of Manchester.

HAMMERSLEY, M. (1980b) 'Classroom ethnography' *Educational Analysis* 2 (2).

HAMMERSLEY, M. (1981) 'Ideology in the staffroom', in this volume.

HARGREAVES, A. (1977) 'Ideology and the Middle School' – paper delivered to the Middle Schools Research Group at University of Liverpool, unpublished mimeo.

HARGREAVES, A. (1978) 'The significance of classroom coping strategies' in BARTON, L. and MEIGHAN, R. *Sociological Interpretations of Schooling and Classrooms: A Re-appraisal* Driffield, Nafferton Books.

HARGREAVES, A. (1979) 'Strategies, decisions and control: interaction in a middle school classroom' in EGGLESTON, J. (Ed) *Teacher Decision-Making in the Classroom* London, Routledge and Kegan Paul.

HARGREAVES, A. (1980) 'The ideology of the middle school' in HARGRAVES, A. and TICKLE, L. *Middle Schools: Origins, Ideology and Practice* London, Harper and Row.

HARGREAVES, A. (in process) *The Sociology of the Middle School* London, Routledge and Kegan Paul.

HARGREAVES, D.H. (1967) *Social Relations in the Secondary School* London, Routledge and Kegan Paul.

HARGREAVES, D.H. (1972) *Interpersonal Relations and Education* London, Routledge and Kegan Paul.

HARGREAVES, D.H. (1978) 'Whatever happened to symbolic interactionism?' in BARTON, L. and MEIGHAN, R. *Sociological Interpretations of Schooling and Classrooms: A Re-appraisal* Driffield, Nafferton Books.

HARGREAVES, D.H. (1979) 'Durkheim, deviance and education' in BARTON, L. and MEIGHAN, R. *Schools, Pupils and Deviance* Driffield, Nafferton Books.

HARGREAVES, D.H., HESTER, S.K. and MELLOR, F.J. (1975) *Deviance in Classrooms* London, Routledge and Kegan Paul.

HARLEN, W. (1977) 'A stronger teacher role in curriculum development' *Journal of Curriculum Studies* 9 (1).

HENDERSON, E. (1978) *The Evaluation of In-Service Teacher Training* London, Croom Helm.

HOLLY, D. (1974) *Beyond Curriculum* St. Albans, Paladin.

HOLT, J. (1969) *How Children Fail* Harmondsworth, Penguin.

HOLT, J. (1970) *How Children Learn* Harmondsworth, Penguin.

HUNTER, C. (1980) 'The politics of participation – with special reference to teacher-pupil relationships' in WOODS, P. (Ed) *Teacher Strategies* London, Croom Helm.

HUNTER, C. and HEIGHWAY, P. (1980) 'Morale, motivation and management in middle schools' in BUSH, T., GOODEY, J. and RICHES, C. *Approaches to School Management* London, Harper and Row.

JACKSON, P. (1968) *Life in Classrooms* New York, Holt, Rinehart and Winston.

KEDDIE, N. (1971) 'Classroom knowledge' in YOUNG, M.F.D. (Ed) *Knowledge and Control* London, Collier-Macmillan.

LACEY, C. (1970) *Hightown Grammar* Manchester, Manchester University Press.

LIGHTFOOT, M. (1978) 'The educational consequences of falling rolls' in RICHARDS, C. (Ed) *Power and the Curriculum* Driffield, Nafferton Books.

LORTIE, D. (1975) *Schoolteacher* London, University of Chicago Press.

MCNAMARA, D. (1980) 'The outsider's arrogance: The failure of participant observers to understand classroom events' *British Educational Research Journal* 6 (2).

MILLS, C.W. (1959) *The Sociological Imagination* Harmondsworth, Penguin.

NIAS, J. (1980) 'The ideal middle school: its public image' in HARGREAVES, A. and TICKLE, L. (Eds) *Middle Schools: Origins, Ideology and Practice* London, Harper and Row.

PARSONS, T. (1959) 'The school class as a social system' *Harvard Educational Review* Fall.

ROSEN, H. (1972) *Language and Class* Bristol, Falling Wall Press.

ROSS, J.A. (1980) 'The influence of the principal on the curriculum decisions of teachers' *Journal of Curriculum Studies* 12 (3).

SACKS, H. (1972) 'On the analyzability of stories by children' in GUMPERZ, J.J. and HYMES, D. (Eds) *Directions in Sociolinguistics: The Ethnography of Communication* New York, Holt, Rinehart and Winston.

ST.JOHN-BROOKS, C. (1980) 'Sociologists and education: A for effort, B for achievement' *New Society* 53 (929).

SCHEGLOFF, E. (1971) 'Notes on a conversational practice: formulating place' in SUDNOW, D. (Ed) *Studies in Social Interaction* New York, Free Press.

SCHUTZ, A. (1973) *Collected Papers Vol. I* The Hague, Martinus Nijhoff.

SEELEY, J. (1966) 'The "making" and "taking" of problems' *Social Problems* 14.

SHARP, R. and GREEN, A. (1975) *Education and Social Control* London, Routledge and Kegan Paul.

SHIPMAN, M., BOLAM, D. and JENKINS, D. (1974) *Inside a Curriculum Project* London, Methuen.

SMITH, D. (1978) ' "K is mentally ill": The anatomy of a factual account' *Sociology* 22 (3).

STENHOUSE, L. (1973) 'The humanities curriculum project' in BUTCHER, H.J. and PONT, H.B. (Eds) *Educational Research in Britain, 3* London, London University Press.

STRAUSS, A.L. *et al* (1964) *Psychiatric Ideologies and Institutions* London, Collier-Macmillan.

TAYLOR, I., WALTON, P. and YOUNG, J. (1973) *The New Criminology* London, Routledge and Kegan Paul.

WALLER, W. (1932) *The Sociology of Teaching* New York, Wiley.

WILLIAMS, R. (1973) 'Base and superstructure in Marxist cultural theory' *New Left Review* 82, December.

WILLIAMS, R. (1977) *Marxism and Literature* Oxford, Oxford University Press.

WOODS, P. (1979) *The Divided School* London, Routledge and Kegan Paul.

YOUNG, M.F.D. (Ed) (1971) *Knowledge and Control* London, Collier-Macmillan.

Ideology in the Staffroom?
A Critique of False Consciousness

Martyn Hammersley, Open University

As used today, the concept of ideology functions less as an analytical device than as an argumentative one. It does not tell us much about what ideas are like, how they are formed or why they are held but enables, instead, *ad hominem* argument against them, a means of attributing sinister and malign motives, or writing off positions on the basis of their alleged social consequences.

(Sharrock and Anderson, 1981, p. 293)

The only false consciousness recognized by the interactionists is the contemplation of an alienated mind which retires to a place of distant analytic reflection.

(Rock, 1979, p. 66)

Prologue

Sociological research always provides an opportunity to learn something about *sociology* as well as about the activities of those being studied. That such learning is only rarely evidenced reflects, perhaps, the generally unreflexive character of the discipline, despite the efforts of writers like Gouldner (1970) and Friedrichs (1970). The applicability of sociological analysis to sociological work itself, and its implications for such work, continue to be neglected – no doubt for reasons that are themselves susceptible to sociological analysis.

As a result, the sociologist in his work typically presupposes a very unsociological self-image. While others are embroiled in a world of latent functions, patterned interests, mystifications and false consciousness, he purports to view that world from the Olympian heights, apparently untrammelled. At one time such a view was conventionally and conveniently justified by an appeal to 'the scientific method'. But with the public demise of 'positivism', this has become generally unpersuasive. Notwithstanding this, many sociologists, like wise Calvinists, continue to act as if their place in heaven were assured.

However, claims that the accounting procedures underlying current sociological work are sharply distinguishable from those employed by members do not survive close scrutiny. Faced with this discovery there are at least two possible responses. One can try to substitute some alternative conception of science for that of 'positivism', by means of which the accounts of sociologists can be assigned priority over others. However, those who have employed this strategy, such as Althusserians and the ethnomethodologists, have generally run into severe problems in differentiating science from commonsense or ideology (Thomas, 1978).[1]

A much more fruitful strategy, however, is to abandon any attempt at drawing an epistemological distinction, and to accept that members' accounts may be true or false to varying degees, and in various ways, and that in this respect they are no different from sociological accounts. Indeed, sociology must be viewed as a collection of practices operative in the social world, and thus as subject to the influences and constraints characteristic of that world. To one degree or another, then, sociologists also misinterpret phenomena because of interests, preconceptions etc. Indeed, there may be misconceptions characteristic of the sociological community itself. However, at the same time, sociology's distinctive concerns must be recognized. The criteria for judging the adequacy of accounts are likely to differ from the more practical considerations employed in everyday life. Moreover, while this view requires sociologists to renounce their Olympian stance, it does not remove the obligation to eliminate, as far as possible, influences other than a concern for truth from the process of developing and testing sociological theory. Indeed, sociological analysis of sociological work should be partly concerned with clarifying the relationship between the concern for truth and the other goals and interests which underlie sociological accounts, with a view to how the effects of the latter might be minimized. At the same time, this position requires recognition that, for those being studied, a concern with the truth of accounts is not necessarily uppermost, and their accounts must not be treated simply as proto-science.

This whole issue became central for me during the course of an ethnographic study of Downtown, an inner-city boys' secondary modern school (Hammersley, 1980). The particular configuration of political and intellectual commitments with which I entered the field, and the relationship between these and the perspectives of the teachers in the school, placed me in a double-bind. Politically I was in fundamental disagreement with the teachers and, initially, I regarded their comments about the pupils as simply outrageous, and their treatment of pupils as deplorable. Yet I was also committed to interactionist sociology with its injunction to adopt an 'appreciative stance' towards the attitudes and activities of those studied (Matza, 1969). It was this role conflict which forced me to re-examine my own orientation. Once I began to do this I found that, despite our different views, there were parallels between the accounting practices employed by the teachers and those I tended to use as a sociologist; and this forced me to reconsider the proper nature of sociological analysis.

The focus in this paper is on the concept of ideology and its analytic viability, an issue thrown into sharp relief by the nature of staffroom talk at Downtown. I shall begin by giving, as background, a brief outline of the nature of this talk before turning to the concept of ideology itself.

Staffroom Talk

In the Downtown staffroom, talk was undoubtedly the major activity, ranging in focus from soccer to classical music. However, most conversation was shop-talk, concerning the school and its pupils. Some of this talk involved the trading of news about events in the school: fights among the pupils, visits from parents and so on. Typifications of pupils were also exchanged – often structured by a concern with 'whose worst' – and accounts were presented for why the pupils were the way they were.

Implicit in this staffroom talk was a particular set of views about pupils, parents, teaching and the world in general. At its centre lay the assumed superiority of 'traditional' teaching, and in particular the importance of 'discipline'.

(Staffroom)
Denison   What we ought to do is to run a school using all the old traditional methods.
Webster   It'd go like a bomb.

(Greaves, Webster and MH talking in the staffroom. Greaves tells an anecdote about the lack of discipline at a junior school which feeds Downtown).
Greaves   I had to teach there for a short time. I went into a classroom of about thirty of the little buggers, stood at the front and clapped my hands: and nothing happened. I did it again and still nothing happened. Eighteen years teaching experience and I couldn't even bring a class to order. A Jamaican student was there trying to teach them, with no success. Eventually, she brought two Jamaicans, no prejudice there, out from the back of the class but put them behind her back where she couldn't see them, so of course they were pulling faces. I decided I'd have to do something about it so I picked up a standard arithmetic book, y'know with hard backs, calmly walked up behind them and gave them a good belt round the ears, praying of course that they hadn't mastoids. It was like lifting a needle from the gramophone, everything stopped and the student taught the rest of the lesson in peace. Some of those pupils are in the first form now, they remember me although I don't remember them.

(Staffroom)
Webster   Have you noticed how few graduates are coming into teaching to teach science and maths.
MH   Of course there are fewer people doing science at universities compared to arts and social science subjects.
Walker   Yes that's because science and maths are disciplines, they don't want discipline today.

Premised on this 'traditional' conception of teaching and emphasis on 'discipline' was the belief that there had been a serious decline in the standard of pupils' 'behaviour' and 'work' at Downtown over the previous few years.

(Staffroom discussion)
Larson   You talk about educating these kids.
Webster   You can't.
Larson   You're nurse-maid to them most of the time.

(Staffroom: Walker talking to me)
Walker   It's a sad deterioration from what it was.

(Staffroom: Greaves talking to me)
Greaves   You don't realize there's only eighteen of them. In twenty years teaching I've never had so many disciplinary problems and I'm not alone. I can remember having forty-three in room five and I could mark all lesson; I couldn't even hear them breathing never mind talking.

In the view of Downtown teachers, then, there has been a fall in the quality of the pupils coming to the school. This was blamed, in part, on 'immigration', locally and nationally:

(Webster talking to me in his classroom)
Webster   Used to be nice kids, good uniform, dropped in cars, but its gone down since the coloureds came.

(Greaves talking to me after a lesson)
Greaves   They're thick. Things have changed, the comprehensive school creams entry and in the local area the better class, I know it's an old-fashioned term, have moved out and Jamaicans and Pakistanis have moved in. I looked up the IQs of our present pupils and compared them with those of a few years ago, there's been a considerable decline.

(Staffroom)
Webster   I thought (that next year) we were going to get eight hundred kids and not a coon among them but it looks as if we'll have lots of coons. Larson says it's known as an immigrant school. I hadn't realized that, I'm too involved internally to think of the external view.
Holton   Yes and the tab end of the coons as well.

(Staffroom)
Larson   The coloured boys know no restraint, no discipline, it's natural for them to shout and carry on, they're used to it I suppose. Some people say they're just happy but you can't have them acting like that in a *school,* and of course our boys see them doing things which they'd like to do but are not allowed to do and so they begin to do it as well.

The other major explanation for the decline in pupil quality voiced in the Downtown staffroom was the claim that there had been a general moral decline in society, as reflected in the attitudes of pupils, parents and many teachers.

(Denison talking to me in the staffroom)
Denison   Anarchy is creeping into the classroom.
MH   Do you think the NAS are right then?
Denison   Yes, it's part of a general trend, not just restricted to this country.

(Staffroom)
French   The staff at Windsor Street (another secondary school in the same area) don't even look like teachers, scruffy, long hair, how can you expect the pupils to dress respectably if the teachers dress like that?

Important elements, or symptoms, of this moral decline were progressivism and comprehensivism:

(Staffroom: Webster talking about comprehensivization)
Webster   The changeover's going to produce rubbish and it's no good these educational experts poo-poohing it, standards have gone down.

(Walker talking to me after a lesson)
Walker   (These pupils) can't spell, some can't copy, all they believe in at junior schools now is spontaneity, they don't teach them anything, just make sure they haven't any repressions, it's wrong.

(Staffroom discussion)
Webster   People at the top will just not accept, for political reasons I suspect, that people are *born* with different amounts of talent. There's an article in *Teacher* the slant being that the universities should be open to everyone. This idiot doesn't realize that sixty-five per cent of them are illiterate. What's the use of sending people to university who can't even read the directions to get there!

This attack was occasionally generalized beyond the realm of education, for example to 'egalitarianism' and 'the welfare state', youth culture and 'radical' students, and great stress was laid on 'law and order':

(Walker and Wright talking after a lesson)
Wright   I've noticed that 3t alone are very good but with the rest of the year they're hopeless.
Walker   I believe in streaming not non-streaming and other modern things like the Welfare State and equality. Putting them all together brings them all down to the lowest level.

(Staffroom)
Denison   The idea of equality is the cause of all the rot in our society.
Teacher   It's a myth.
Denison   Yes but a very dangerous myth. It's equated with justice as if people can be the same, there's no such thing.
Aldridge   Equality of what, opportunity, ability, emolument?
Denison   Equal to the lowest level.

(Staffroom)
Webster   Class has nothing to do with it now (the working class have no brains) it's so open it's – anyone can get anywhere – I was going to say it's a farce which I suppose it is, over-loaded [refers to Hoggart etc.: 'they made it'].

(Staffroom: Denison to me)
Denison   'Law and Order' is the most important issue today, why don't the government do something about it?

This is by no means an exhaustive account of the nature of staffroom talk at Downtown (see Hammersley, 1980), but it should give sufficient flavour of it to raise the analytic issues I want to address in this paper.

Ideology and Context

Now one obvious, and currently rather fashionable, way of approaching the analysis of this data would be to treat it as documenting an ideology. The term 'ideology' has, of course, been used in a wide variety of ways (Minar, 1961; Williams, 1976). I limit myself here to usages which define ideology as a distorted or inaccurate view of the world which serves the interests of some class or group and/or facilitates the reproduction of the existing social order (Huaco, 1971; Barth, 1976; Larrain, 1979; Naish, Hartnett and Finlayson, 1976; Apple, 1979).[2] The views expressed in the Downtown staffroom positively invite treatment in this way, even more so than those ideas more commonly subjected to this form of analysis under the headings of liberal and social democratic ideology. Here we have views which are close to Black Paper conservatism (Grace, 1978), and as such are more 'obviously' ideological than the claims of liberals and social democrats. On the other hand, of course, because these views are so 'obviously' a distortion, pointing this out has rather less news value than revealing the ideological character of liberalism or social democracy. Perhaps this explains why, relatively speaking, conservative ideology has been rather neglected, though the time is now more than ripe for a reassessment! What I want to try to show here, however, is that *even* in the case of 'conservative' views of the kind expressed by the teachers at Downtown, the ideology concept is analytically unsound.

At face value the ideology model seems to work quite well on this data. Thus, it can be shown that all the task-related staffroom talk I documented at Downtown is not only infused with an underlying traditional/conservative viewpoint but is also structured in ways which deflect blame for the poor disciplinary and academic performances of pupils away from the teachers. Furthermore, it can be cogently argued that this deflection enables the teachers to continue teaching in the same 'traditional' manner despite apparent failure, and despite perceived pressures locally and nationally for a more 'progressive' approach. Moreover, it has been argued that, under capitalism, 'traditional' teaching is functionally appropriate for pupils like those at Downtown who, in the main and at best, are destined for unskilled and semi-skilled manual work (Leacock, 1969; Bowles and Gintis, 1976).

However, while it possesses some plausibility, this line of analysis also has serious drawbacks. For one thing, and ignoring the implicit functionalism, use of the concept of ideology in this way runs into the problem of the relationship between beliefs and actions, something which also plagues attitude research (Deutscher, 1973). It is a sociological commonplace that people do not always act in accordance with their stated 'beliefs'. Thus, we cannot rely solely on these in explaining behaviour. Moreover, this problem persists even where, as in the case of Althusser, ideology is identified not as a set of ideas but rather as a collection of material practices. Such an approach still leaves no room for recognition of the way in which people's behaviour, including their expressions of belief, is shaped by or to particular contexts; it assumes that a unified and internally coherent 'competence' underlies their behaviour. Yet some analysts have made much of precisely such contextual variation in the behaviour of teachers (Keddie, 1971; Sharp and Green, 1975; Lacey, 1977). Unfortunately, much of this work has tended to treat the 'educationist' or interview context as representing 'ideas', and what teachers do in the classroom as 'practice': this implies that there are only two contexts, and it discourages analysis of the material effects of staffroom or meeting talk. There are also some severe and largely untackled methodological problems involved in the identification of 'inconsistencies' in behaviour (Hammersley, 1977 and 1979). Nevertheless, this work does reveal the importance of context, something which the concept of ideology neglects, at least in its current stage of development.

The upshot of this argument for the analysis of staffroom talk at Downtown is that the latter must be treated not as a straightforward reflection of the attitudes of individual teachers but as a perspective constructed and sustained in the particular circumstances of staff relations. Furthermore, the teachers' classroom behaviour cannot simply be read off from their staffroom views. For example, we might expect that, given their resentment over 'immigration', the teachers would discriminate against black pupils in the classroom. In fact I could detect no such tendency. Moreover, racist talk was not generally used in the presence of pupils.

Now there is a conception of ideology which does allow for contradictions in people's orientations and behaviour, and it is neatly represented by Johnson's reading of Gramsci:

> Gramsci employs three key terms of cultural/ideological analysis (where culturalism and structuralism employ only one): 'common sense' which refers, concretely, to the lived culture of a particular class or social group; 'philosophy' (or sometimes 'ideology') which refers to an organized set of conceptions with a more or less transformative relation to lived culture; and 'hegemony' which describes the state of play, as it were, between the whole complex of 'educative' institutions and ideologies on the one hand, and lived culture on the other; the extent to which common sense is made to conform both to 'the necessities of production' and to the construction of consent and a political order. (Johnson, 1979, p. 73)

Commonsense is 'the more or less spontaneous way of thinking of a class', though it is 'deeply contradictory, shot through with ideological elements' and lacks 'a knowledge of the historicity and determinate origin of elements in its own folklore'. Ideologies on the other hand are 'organized' and are to be understood in relation to 'the particular "class-related" position of the intellectuals who produce them'.

This is certainly a more promising starting point than other versions of ideology theory, not least because it draws attention to the complex ways in which ideologies are received. It also seems to accept that *both* ideologies and commonsense can facilitate social reproduction *or* constitute an obstruction or challenge to it. This is certainly necessary to accommodate analyses such as those of Keddie (1971), Sharp and Green (1975), and Lacey (1977). However, this is also a cause of some serious problems. It certainly renders any general account of the role of ideology very complex. Indeed it threatens to undermine the concept altogether, since it seems unlikely that commonsense and ideology can be clearly distinguished in this approach. In what sense is ideology 'organized' and commonsense unorganized? Moreover, intellectuals themselves presumably operate in the context of commonsense, nor are they (except by means of a very broad definition) the only ones who develop and transmit world views. The Downtown data provides a good example of people drawing on the cultural resources available to them to develop a distinctive view of their circumstances (Hammersley, 1980). What we have, at best, is a difference of degree between intellectuals and non-intellectuals, and it is not at all clear that their products differ in kind; though they may differ in transmission media and in level of influence.

Misrecognition by Whom?

The second general problem I want to discuss is, I believe, inherent in the ideology model. Even if it were accepted that I had satisfactorily shown that task-related staff-room talk at Downtown is structured in ways which serve the teachers' interests, I have not established that the teachers' views are actually mistaken. Moreover, demonstrating this is not quite so straightforward as might be imagined; though it is a problem which is ignored or treated in a cavalier fashion in many sociological analyses of ideology. Willis (1977) provides a useful example since he presents a sophisticated version of the ideology model. Instead of simply treating the views of 'the lads' as ideological, he argues that they involve both 'penetrations' – true understandings of reality – and ideological distortions. However, Willis treats the identification of penetrations and ideology as straightforward, as requiring little empirical support.[3] This is made possible by reliance on the implausible assumption that only false knowledge, or knowledge of appearances, can be functional for the reproduction of the social order. But the truth or falsity of knowledge is irrelevant to its mode of operation; though people's perceptions of it *will* play an important part.

Without this implausible assumption, the distinction between penetrations and ideology rests, at best, on a judgement of 'the lads'' views against the findings of social science. What is particularly significant is that such judgement is necessary for the very *identification* of ideology. This places an unsupportable burden on the findings of sociology. We all know that the philosophical grounding of science, and especially of social science, is far from firm, and that in any case all scientific findings are necessarily provisional. Yet the use of the concept of ideology involves the assumption that there is some clear and definitive method of deciding, once and for all, whether some account is true or false. We have no such method. The most persuasive one suggested so far – Popper's falsificationism (Popper, 1972) – still fails to solve the problem (see for example Keat and Urry, 1975, chapter 3). Without such clear and definitive arbitration, our very identification of an ideology is contingent upon the current state of knowledge in the field to which the 'ideology' relates. As a result, what is judged at one point in time to be true may later have to be reclassified as ideological, and *vice versa*. This reclassification would be required not because we have found out anything new about the mode of production or functioning of the knowledge concerned, but simply because our assessment of its validity had changed. Moreover, this argument applies whether or not ideology is seen as involving distortion *or* as mistaking phenomena for real forms.

What I am arguing is not that it is impossible or illegitimate to assess the validity of participant views, simply that this is neither necessary in order to explain these views, nor a matter often open to definitive judgements. As it happens, if we examine the views of Downtown teachers, as expressed in the staffroom, to the extent that relevant evidence is available, it seems that their factual claims are substantially correct. The social composition of the neighbourhood has certainly changed, and there is some evidence to suggest that, nationally, there has been a history of steadily increasing 'permissiveness' on the part of parents and teachers (see the discussion in Woods, 1977, pp. 32–4). And we can expect that both these trends will have affected the 'amenability' of the pupils Downtown teachers are required to teach (Becker, 1951; Hammersley, 1980). But, of course, these 'facts' are sketched and interpreted in terms of a theory; and this theory *is* open to criticism.

Some writers have argued that the conservatism of many teachers is to be found in their tendency to blame the pupils and *not* the school or the wider society for their problems (Lacey, 1977). It is clear from the Downtown case, however, that this is not an adequate basis for differentiating 'conservative' and 'radical' teacher perspectives since the two options are not empirically exclusive. Downtown teachers blame both the pupils and wider social conditions; they certainly do not take their conditions of work for granted but draw on ideas about the wider society to account for changes in the quality of their pupils. However, it *is* true that the account they provide takes their own beliefs and practices as given, as not in need of description, explanation or justification.

But it is not at all clear that what I am challenging here is simply the theoretical interpretation the teachers place on 'the facts'. It seems likely, though I do not have the evidence, that the Downtown teachers would recognize that they and their current practices are relevant in principle; but that they leave them out of account because their concern is not with explanation *per se,* but with identifying the factors which are to blame for their situation and the conditions which need to be changed. In other words, a value criterion underlies their account.

However, before we start criticizing this practice as ideological, claiming that it is not just the *content* of what Downtown teachers say in the staffroom that is ideological but also the forms in which it is produced, we should note that this practice is often employed by sociologists themselves. The difference lies, in large part, in the underlying values and, thus, in who or what gets blamed. Downtown teachers blame the pupils, their parents, 'progresssives' of all kinds, immigration policy and certain secular trends in the society. Sociologists tend, implicitly at least, to blame, for example, the bourgeoisie, bureaucratization or the capitalist mode of production. In their accounts, too, it is often the case that variables are singled out for attention in large part according to value criteria. Thus, for example, in the Political Arithmetic of the 1950s and 1960s, as is well-known, the nature of what passes for knowledge and intelligence in schools was largely ignored. This topic, unlike the issue of the effects of allocation procedures such as the 11 plus and streaming, was not taken to be a political issue. In much current sociology of education what is taken for granted, again because in the relevant circles it is a political given, is that socialist education would take a libertarian form with no hierarchy between teachers and learners. Thus, the fact that schooling under capitalism does not match libertarian ideals is assumed to be because hierarchy serves to reproduce capitalism (Sharp and Green, 1975; Bowles and Gintis, 1976).

This, of course, raises the issue of the relationship between values and science and whether we can avoid, or indeed should avoid, using value criteria in this way. What seems clear, however, is that if we adopt the position that value criteria cannot be avoided (Seeley, 1966), use of the concept of ideology *itself* becomes a form of distortion unless we can show that our values are in some objective sense superior to those of the people we are studying, and we are not in a position to even begin to do that.

Conclusion

In this paper I have tried, in the context of a study of some staffroom talk, to show that the concept of ideology is fatally flawed, under all those definitions which take distortion or inaccuracy as a key criterion. It provides little basis for that analysis of contextual variation in people's behaviour; and the very identification of an ideology is premised on the reification of current, and necessarily corrigible, findings of sociological research, and/or on the taken for granted objectivity of the sociologist's own values. What I am suggesting, then, is that the road taken by many sociologists in recent years from 'culture' to 'ideology', so clearly marked in the work of the Centre for Contemporary Cultural Studies CCCS (Hall and Jefferson, 1976; CCCS, 1977), is a *cul de sac*.

Of course, this shift from the concept of culture to that of ideology reflects deeper theoretical changes in the sociology of education in the last five or six years. It also highlights a disturbing feature of these changes. The deficiencies of the ideology concept reflect a lack of concern for the principles of understanding and context which lie at the heart of social phenomenology and symbolic interactionism.

Rather than superseding interactionism and phenomenology, then, recent neo-Marxist approaches, whether of a political economy or culturalist variety (Whitty, 1978), simply ignore lessons already learned. It is not that the arguments for the importance of understanding the perspectives of participants and analyzing their activities in context have been refuted, they have simply been forgotten; presumably to be revived again in the future by some 'new, new, new sociology of education'. Indeed, I suspect that the current preference among many sociologists for the concept of ideology derives not from the analytic strengths of that concept – indeed I have suggested that these are distinctly limited – but from a desire to present their accounts as *by definition* superior to those of other people. The appeal of the concept lies, in other words, in its capacity to disguise political value judgements under a veneer of academic objectivity.[4]

Notes

1 As Thomas (1979) points out ethnomethodologists have displayed commitments to a variety of different positions on the relationship between sociology and commonsense. He goes on to argue that 'the variety of positions it takes is an index of the fact that ethnomethodology is most at home in the view that sociology must break with commonsense (an option it does not explicitly embrace), but that certain of its constituent theses prevent it from recognising this point' (p. 66). In fact there are occasions when this commitment is made explicit, notably in Sacks (1963). While ethnomethodologists generally express a disinclination to provide

alternatives to commonsense accounts, this self-restraint is frequently, and understandably, abandoned when it comes to sociological accounts, which are condemned as merely trading in commonsense.

2   Recently attempts have been made by Marxists to distinguish between false consciousness and ideology, arguing against the idea that ideology involves distortion. Instead it is to be seen as an objective level of social formations which constitutes subjects rather than being produced by them (Althusser) or as being based on 'phenomenal forms' not real relations, (Mepham, 1972; Sayer, 1979). Hirst (1976) and others have shown that Althusser's appeal to the 'imaginary' relationship which ideology bears to the real relations of individuals to their conditions of existence is merely an elaborate restatement of the misrepresentation argument. The same point can be made about the distinction between appearance and reality. This spatial analogy is specious. What are, in fact, being contrasted are commonsense experience, portrayed as a passive reflection of existing social relations, and the penetrating understanding made possible by science. The conception of science involved is, however, rarely spelt out. For the most part authors simply *assume* that they can distinguish 'penetrations' from ideology without any indication of how this is possible (but see Sayer, 1979 for an important exception). A much more radical line has been taken by McCarney (1980) who argues that Marx's use of the concept of ideology does not involve any implication of distortion or falsity. However, in my view what he succeeds in showing, despite his efforts, is that Marx did not develop a coherent conception of ideology (for a very different account which also reveals the incoherent character of Marx's conceptualization in this area, see Abercrombie, 1980, chapter 1).

3   For example, appeal is made to 'a common educational fallacy that opportunities can be *made* by education, that upward mobility is basically a matter of individual push, that qualifications make their own openings' (p. 127), which, it is claimed, 'the lads' see through. However, little evidence is provided to show that conformist pupils are committed to this view, and that the several claims conflated here are indeed fallacies. (For an argument demonstrating that one of these claims is by no means fallacious, see Demaine (1981, p. 106)). Indeed, attribution of the 'penetration' to 'the lads' is shrouded by distinctions between individual and group understanding, and between the level of 'words' and that of 'cultural practices': 'Though it would be wrong to impute to "the lads" individually any critique or analytic motive, it is clear that their collective culture shows both a responsiveness to the uniqueness of human labour power and in its own way constitutes an attempt to defeat a certain ideological definition of it' (p. 132). Such an inevitably speculative mode of attribution is perhaps *particularly* necessary for the other 'penetrations', where elements of the labour theory of value are divined in the 'cultural practices, of 'the lads'. Here again very little reference is made to arguments or evidence regarding the validity of this theory.

4   Sometimes the veneer is very thin indeed, as in the recent case of Sharp (1980).

References

ABERCROMBIE, N. (1980) *Class, Structure and Knowledge* Oxford, Blackwell.
ALTHUSSER, L. (1975) *Reading Capital* New Left Books.
ALTHUSSER, L. (1977) *For Marx* New Left Books.
APPLE, M. (1979) *Ideology and Curriculum* London, Routledge and Kegan Paul.
BARTH, H. (1976) *Truth and Ideology* Berkeley, University of California Press.
BECKER, H.S. (1951) 'Role and Career Problems of the Chicago Public School Teacher', unpublished Ph.D. Thesis, University of Chicago.
BOWLES, S. and GINTIS, H. (1976) *Schooling in Capitalist America* London, Routledge and Kegan Paul.
CENTRE FOR CONTEMPORARY CULTURAL STUDIES (1977) *On Ideology, Working Paper No. 10* University of Birmingham.
DEMAINE, J. (1981) *Contemporary Theories in the Sociology of Education* London, Macmillan.
DEUTSCHER, I. (1973) *What We Say/What We Do* Glenview, Illinois, Scott Foresman.
FRIEDRICHS, R. (1970) *A Sociology of Sociology* New York, Free Press.

GOULDNER, A. (1970) *The Coming Crisis of Western Sociology* New York, Basic Books.

GRACE, G. (1978) *Teachers, Ideology and Control* London, Routledge and Kegan Paul.

HALL, S. and JEFFERSON, T. (1976) *Resistance Through Rituals* London, Hutchinson.

HAMMERSLEY, M. (1977) 'Teacher perspectives', Unit 7 *Schooling and Society* (E202) Milton Keynes, Open University Press.

HAMMERSLEY, M. (1979) 'Towards a model of teacher activity' in EGGLESTON, J. *Teacher Decision-Making in the Classroom* London, Routledge and Kegan Paul.

HAMMERSLEY, M. (1980) 'A Peculiar World? Teaching and Learning in an Inner City School', unpublished Ph.D Thesis, University of Manchester.

HIRST, P.Q. (1976) 'Althusser and the theory of ideology' *Economy and Society* 5 (4).

HUACO, G. (1971) 'On ideology' *Acta Sociologica* 14.

JOHNSON, R. (1979) 'Histories of culture/theories of ideology' in BARRETT, M. *et al* (Eds) *Ideology and Cultural Production* London, Croom Helm.

KEAT, R. and URRY, J. (1975) *Social Theory as Science* London, Routledge and Kegan Paul.

KEDDIE, N. (1971) 'Classroom knowledge' in YOUNG, M.F.D. (Ed) *Knowledge and Control* Collier-Macmillan.

LACEY, C. (1977) *The Socialization of Teachers* London, Methuen.

LARRAIN, J. (1979) *The Concept of Ideology* London, Hutchinson.

LEACOCK, E. (1969) *Teaching and Learning in City Schools* New York, Basic Books.

MATZA, D. (1969) *Becoming Deviant* New Jersey, Prentice Hall.

MCCARNEY, J. (1980) *The Real World of Ideology* Sussex, Harvester Press.

MEPHAM, J. (1972) 'The theory of ideology in "Capital"' *Radical Philosophy* 2.

MINAR, D. (1961) 'Ideology and political behaviour' *Midwest Journal of Political Science* 4.

NAISH, M., HARTNETT, A. and FINLAYSON, D. (1976) 'Ideological documents in education: Some suggestions towards a definition' in HARTNETT, A. and NAISH, M. *Theory and Practice in Education, Vol. 2* London, Heinemann.

POPPER, K. (1972) *The Logic of Scientific Discovery* London, Hutchinson.

ROCK, P. (1979) 'The sociology of crime, symbolic interactionism and some problematic qualities of radical criminology' in DOWNES, D. and ROCK, P. *Deviant Interpretations* London, Martin Robertson.

SACKS, H. (1963) 'Sociological description' *Berkeley Journal of Sociology* 8.

SAYER, D. (1979) *Marx's Method* Sussex, Harvester Press.

SEELEY, J. (1966) 'The "Making" and "Taking" of problems' *Social Problems* 44.

SHARP, R. (1980) *Knowledge, Ideology and the Politics of Schooling* London, Routledge and Kegan Paul.

SHARP, R. and GREEN, A. (1975) *Education and Social Control* London, Routledge and Kegan Paul.

SHARROCK, W.W. and ANDERSON, D.C. (1981) 'Language, thought and reality, again' *Sociology* 15 (2).

THOMAS, D. (1978) 'Sociology and common sense' *Inquiry* 21, pp. 1–32.

THOMAS, D. (1979) *Naturalism and Social Science* Cambridge, Cambridge University Press.

WHITTY, G. (1978) 'School examinations and the politics of school knowledge' in BARTON, L. and MEIGHAN, R. *Sociological Interpretations of Schooling and Classrooms, A Reappraisal* Driffield, Nafferton.

WILLIAMS, R. (1976) *Keywords* London, Fontana.

WILLIS, P. (1977) *Learning to Labour* Farnborough, Saxon House.

WOODS, P. (1977) 'Youth generations and social class', Units 27–8 *Schooling and Society* (E202) Milton Keynes, Open University Press.

Contributors

Stephen Ball	Education Area, Education Development Building, University of Sussex, Brighton, England, BN1 9RG.
Len Barton	Education Department, Westhill College, Selly Oak, Birmingham, England, B29 6LL.
Patricia Broadfoot	Education Department, Westhill College, Selly Oak, Birmingham, England, B29 6LL.
Peter Corbishley	Centre for Science Education, Chelsea College, University of London, Bridges Place, London SW6, England.
Brian Davies	Centre for Science Education, Chelsea College, University of London, Bridges Place, London SW6, England.
John Evans	Centre for Science Education, Chelsea College, University of London, Bridges Place, London SW6, England.
Colin Fletcher	Sutton Centre Research Project, University of Nottingham, High Pavement, Sutton-in-Ashfield, Nottinghamshire, England.
Andy Hargreaves	Department of Educational Studies, University of Oxford, 15 Norham Gardens, Oxford, OX2 6PY, England.
David Hargreaves	Department of Educational Studies, University of Oxford, 15 Norham Gardens, Oxford, OX2 6PY, England.
Martyn Hammersley	Faculty of Educational Studies, Walton Hall, Open University, Milton Keynes, Bucks., MK7 6AA, England.
Colin Hunter	School of Education, Leeds Polytechnic, Beckett Park, Leeds, LS6 3QS, England.
Catherine Kenrick	Centre for Science Education, Chelsea College, University of London, Bridges Place, London SW6, England.
Martin Lawn	Education Department, Westhill College, Selly Oak, Birmingham, B29 6LL, England.
Paul Olson	Ontario Institute for Studies in Education, 252 Bloor Street West, Toronto, Ontario, Canada, M5S 1V6.
Jenny Ozga	Faculty of Educational Studies, Walton Hall, Open University, Milton Keynes, Bucks., MK7 6AA, England.
June Purvis	Faculty of Educational Studies, Walton Hall, Open University, Milton Keynes, Bucks., MK7 6AA, England.
David Reynolds	Department of Social Administration, University College, Cardiff, CF1 1XL, Wales.
Robert Stebbins	Department of Sociology, The University of Calgary, 2500 University Drive N.W., Calgary, Alberta, Canada T2N 1N4.
Michael Sullivan	Tutorial Fellow, Department of Social Administration, University College, Cardiff, CF1 1XL, Wales.

Stephen Walker   Education Department, Newman College, Bartley Green, Birmingham, B32 3NT, England.

Geoff Whitty   Faculty of Education, King's College, University of London, Strand, London WC2R 2LS, England.

Bill Williamson   Department of Sociology and Social Administration, University of Durham, Elvet Riverside, New Elvet, Durham, England.

Peter Woods   Faculty of Educational Studies, Walton Hall, Open University, Milton Keynes, Bucks., MK7 6AA, England.

Author Index

Subject Index

academic perspectives of mixed-ability teaching 161-9
accountability 68, 210-1, 214
administration see management
adults in community school 146-51, 155
age, school leaving 124
aims see goals
alienation 127
anomie 13, 131
APU see Assessment of Performance Unit
art teacher 284-301
assessment, sociology of 15, 197-218
    see also CSE
           examinations
           GCE
           testing
Assessment of Performance Unit 71, 207, 216
attendance, school 82-4, 89-91, 111, 129, 155
Australia 39-40, 225
autonomy
    school 131-4, 227
    teacher 19, 62, 199, 209
avoidance strategy 249

behaviour, classification by 246-7
    see also delinquency
           deviance
bilingual classes 232-3
biographies, teacher 169-71, 191-4, 284-301
birthrates, declining 67
Black Paper (1975) 126
black pupils see ethnic minorities
Block Grant system 68, 71
board schools 111
bourgeoisie see middle class
British and Foreign School Society 103-10
bureaucracy 69, 127, 210, 216
Burnham scales 52, 69-70, 73-4

CAL see computer-assisted learning
Canada 223, 231-4, 249
Capital Expenditure control system 68

capitalism 37, 65, 133, 203-5, 214-5, 305
careers, teacher
    and collegial esteem 169-71
    continuance 291-6
    and politics 65-75
    in secondary modern schools 124
    structure 69-70, 73-4
    and subject-centredness 161
cenralized education 209-11
Certificate of Vocational Education 215
character moulding as goal 125-7, 129
charity schools 103-4
child-centredness 163
civil servant, teacher as 212
class
    in Canada 232-3
    and capitalism 205
    conflict 231
    and curriculum 37-40, 135
    and delinquency 230-1
    in 19th century 77-116 passim
    of parents 125-9
    perception of 246, 252
    and politics 210
    and schooling 131-2, 224, 229-30
    and speech 220, 227-8
    and teachers 45, 48-51, 61-2
classical mode 204
classification, pupil and teacher 246-7
classroom see ethnography
cleaning staff 147
closure, school 68
codes, linguistic 220, 227-8, 324
coercive individualism 128-9, 172
coercive schools 19-20, 228
cognitive strategy 257
collectivity
    in delinquency 17-8, 129-30, 230
    lack of 128-9, 135
commitment, teacher 291-6
community
    contact with 294
    school 139-58

intelligence testing 202
interaction
  conversational 265-82
  symbolic 245-56
investment, education as 123
isolation solution 270

knowledge 121, 128
  types of 34, 102, 125, 138, 180, 221-2
  see also curriculum
known and understood 219-38

labelling 180, 232, 299
and delinquency 14, 17, 21-2
labour process 54-61
language teachers and mixed ability
  teaching 161-8
left policy and practice 27-44
libertarianism 319-20
linear subjects 167-8
linguistic codes 220, 227-8, 324
literacy, adult 147
looking glass, social 247
low delinquency schools 20-1

management, school 56, 62, 207, 210
  and politics 65-75
  see also control
Manpower Services Commission 72
Marxism 121, 222, 224, 229
  see also neo-Marxism
mathematics and science teachers and mixed
  ability teaching 164-8, 170, 177-96
Mathematics in Education and Industry 190
meals, schools 68, 72
media studies 30
MEI *see* Mathematics in Education etc
meritocracy 202
microprocessors *see* computers
middle class
  control of 19th century education 77-116
  curriculum 121, 125
  parents and comprehensive education
    125-9
  and standards in schools 14
  teachers 45, 48, 62
  see also class
misrecognition 338-40
mixed ability teaching 69, 74, 124, 141-2,
  152, 159-95
Mode 3 *see* CSE
monitorial teaching 109
moonlighting 70
motherhood, education for 102
motivation, pupil 172, 190, 233

National Children's Bureau 134
National Society schools 103-9
necrolatry stance 269
needlework 108-10
negativity in delinquency 130
negotiation strategy 248, 251, 253-4, 292
neo-Marxism
  on class 48, 50
  on control 16, 23
  on curriculum 128, 134-5
  and inaction 27, 29, 32
  on role of schools 219
  on social reproduction 40, 49
neutrality of schools 226
new sociology of education 28-35 *passim*
Newcastle Commission on Popular
  Education (1981) 110
Newsom Report (1963) 123
nineteenth century education
  in Northumberland 77-96
  working class girls 97-116
noise strategy 250
non-alienating school *see* Sutton Centre
non-cumulative nature of theory and
  research 10
normality concepts 13, 206-7, 312
Northumberland, 19th century education
  77-96
Nottinghamshire, community school in
  139-58
nursery education 124

occupational therapy strategy 249
Open University 31, 57
organizational frames 257

packages, curriculum 36, 56-60, 178-96
parents
  charter 70-1
  and community school 144-51, 155
  and comprehensive schools 124-6
  and examination success 124-5
  and mixed ability teaching 165
  organizational control over 105
  see also home
patriarchy 113-4
payment by results 110
  see also wages
penetrations 300, 302, 338
perception of others 246-7
personality approach 251-2
pessimism 37
phenomenology 134, 159, 221
Plowden Report (1967) 128
policing *see* control

DATE DUE			

358